On Uneven Ground

On Uneven Ground

MIYAZAWA KENJI AND
THE MAKING OF PLACE
IN MODERN JAPAN

Hoyt Long

STANFORD UNIVERSITY PRESS
STANFORD, CALIFORNIA

Stanford University Press
Stanford, California

Printed in the United States of America on acid-free, archival-quality paper

Library of Congress Cataloging-in-Publication Data

Long, Hoyt J. author.
  On uneven ground : Miyazawa Kenji and the making of place in modern Japan / Hoyt
Long.
    pages cm
  Includes bibliographical references and index.
  ISBN 978-0-8047-7686-8 (cloth : alk. paper)
    1. Miyazawa, Kenji, 1896–1933—Criticism and interpretation. 2. Japanese literature—
20th century—History and criticism. 3. Literature and society—Japan—History—20th
century. I. Title.
  PL833.195Z735 2012
  895.6'144—dc22

                                  2011012229

Typeset by Bruce Lundquist in 11/14 Adobe Garamond

Contents

Acknowledgments

There are many who helped to see this book to completion, in ways both professional and personal. I am indebted to them for making the long journey both possible and rewarding.

Portions of the manuscript have benefited from criticism and comments by the following people: Allison Alexy, Gabriela Carrión, Robert Culp, Lianne Habinek, Elizabeth Holt, Ken Ito, John Knott, Lydia Liu, Leslie Pincus, Jordan Sand, Benjamin Stevens, and Jonathan Zwicker. I have done my best to incorporate their invaluable feedback. I am also grateful for the meticulous and thoughtful advice given by my two anonymous readers at the initial review stage.

While researching the project in Japan, I worked closely with Andō Kyōko and Sugiura Shizuka at Ōtsuma Women's University. Their expertise and guidance helped me to discover aspects of Miyazawa's life and work that I would never have found on my own. Thanks must also go to Yutaka Suga for sponsoring me at Tokyo University and to Kitahara Kanako for her support with archival work in Hirosaki. The staff at the Iihatov Center, the Iwate Prefectural Library, and the Iwate University Library graciously handled my often difficult requests.

In both the research and writing phases of the project, collaboration and conversations with the following individuals were instrumental in clarifying and complicating my thoughts: Alex Bates, Stephanie DeBoer, Mark Driscoll, David Henry, Jason Herlands, Reggie Jackson, Edward Mack, Markus Nornes, Emer O'Dwyer, Tim VanCompernolle, Kristina Vassil, Roderick Wilson, and Julian Worrall. To those in Japan who went out of their way to talk with me about Miyazawa, put me up in their homes, and introduce me to some of Iwate's best-kept secrets, I owe an extra debt of gratitude. I am especially grateful to Miyazawa Takeshi, Mochizuki Tatsuya, Saiki Kenji, Sakurai Noriaki, and the Tomizawa family.

Research for this book was made possible by the support of the University of Michigan, the Center for Japanese Studies at Michigan, the IIE Fulbright Program, and the Japan Society for the Promotion of Science. Funds from the Humanities Division at the University of Chicago also helped to defray certain publishing costs. I must also thank Stacy Wagner at Stanford University Press for her steadfast support of the project as well as the various editors, including Carolyn Brown and Richard Gunde, who helped to bring the book to its final form.

Ken Ito and Jonathan Zwicker have been and continue to be invaluable mentors. I could not have gotten this far without their critical eye and passion for historical detail.

An alternate version of Chapter Six appears as "Performing the Village Square in Interwar Japan: Toward a Hidden History of Public Space" in the *Journal of Asian Studies* 70, no. 3 (August 2011).

Finally, I am thankful to my parents, family, and friends for their enduring patience and moral support. It is strangely ironic that a book about place has kept me from staying in any one place for very long. For putting up with all the moving and uncertainty, my deepest thanks goes to Mea and Kai, to whom this book is dedicated.

A Note on Naming

Japanese names mentioned in this book are given with the family name first. When writing the names of authors, I follow the Japanese convention of using pennames where both first and last names are not used. I refer to Natsume Sōseki, for instance, by his penname "Sōseki" and not by his surname. It should be noted that while it is standard practice in Japan for scholars to refer to Miyazawa Kenji only by his first name, "Kenji," this was never a penname nor was it the name used by his earliest critics. I have thus chosen to use his family name instead.

On Uneven Ground

Prologue
Making Place for the Author

> How strange that the greatest literary glories of our
> time should be born of entirely posthumous works:
> Kafka, Simone Weil, Hopkins; or of works partially
> posthumous, as is the case with Hölderlin, Rimbaud,
> Lautréament, Trakl, Musil, and in an even crueler sense,
> Nietzsche. One would like to recommend to writers:
> leave nothing behind, destroy everything you wish to
> see disappear; do not be weak, have confidence in no
> one, for you will necessarily be betrayed one day.
>
> MAURICE BLANCHOT, *The Infinite Conversation*

In September 1933 Miyazawa Kenji (1896–1933), laying prostrate at his family home in the northern town of Hanamaki, finally succumbed to the lung ailment that had plagued him for much of his adult life. After nearly a decade and a half of literary output, he left for the opposite shore as a mostly obscure provincial poet and author of children's fiction, having published just a single volume in each genre. A smattering of material had found its way into a few small coterie magazines (*dōjin zasshi*), enough to earn him recognition amongst a handful of local and metropolitan poets, but there was little at the time of his death to indicate that any of it would escape burial in the dustbin of literary history. Miyazawa himself was unsure about the present and future value of his work, recognizing the divergent routes it might take once handed over, as Borges put it, to "that other man" whose name appears "in some biographical dictionary" and whose pages are soon to belong to "language itself, or to tradition."[1] Speaking to his father, who had never taken his son's artistic ambitions seriously, Miyazawa explained that his manuscripts were merely the traces of his disillusionment and should be disposed of accordingly. To his mother, who had been more accepting of her son's life choices, he declared them the resolute transcription of the blessed Buddha's teachings and believed that they would one day be joyfully read by all. And to his younger brother Seiroku, arguably his longest and most devoted fan, he gave these simple instructions: "If some bookstore comes wanting to publish them, I don't care how tiny it might be, then let them. If not, don't bother."[2] In giving such varied directives to each family member, Miyazawa seems to have been prefiguring at the moment before death the multiplicity of appropriations to which all writers and works are subject in the author's absence.

When I first came across these last requests by Miyazawa, I was uncertain what significance they might have, if any, for the present book. They felt a bit too personal and tangential for a project meant as a broad historical investigation into the intersection of geographical unevenness, place-based identity, and cultural production in Japan's interwar period. A project seeking to investigate, that is, how writers and intellectuals at this time identified with various expressions of locality (e.g., the native place, the region, the province) and how their choices did or did not reflect the increasing centralization, and increasing spatial inequality, of the literary marketplace. Miyazawa from the start had been the key organizing frame for this investigation, but I did not want to make him the subject of an author-study in that somewhat disdainful sense that critics in the academy typically regard literary biography.[3] By which I mean, I did not want to be held captive by a life imagined as a transcendent totality, or feel pressure to make every element of the author's oeuvre and biography sound in complete harmony, as if part of the same finely calibrated music box. After all, "what difference [did] it make who [was] speaking" when the author's own indecisiveness at death suggested an already fragmented subject and a proliferation of both writerly intention and readerly interpretation?[4] As I delved further into the local conditions under which his texts were produced, however, and recovered the experience of what it was to write from the geographical margins of a centralized literary field, I realized that the individual particularity of his life and afterlife, no matter how fragmented, was precisely what would allow me to map out the intricate network of connections—between literary expression, systems of textual production, and spatially situated subjects—that I sought to capture.

This became most apparent when I began tracing the history of Miyazawa's posthumous resurrection, or more accurately *vivification*, on the literary stage. Within just a few years after his death, as we will see, his final requests were drowned out by "the inordinate interest we bring to works that come into our possession not by life, but by the death of their author."[5] Today, he has been read by every school-age child since his inclusion in primary language textbooks in 1946, has been the subject of countless volumes of scholarship, has had his works adapted into hundreds of picture books and dozens of live-action and animated films, and has had his name affixed to everything from a museum and research center to a tropically themed water park. This remarkable gap between Miyazawa's lack of access to cultural capital while alive (largely due to his decision to remain in the provinces) and his later canonization and commercialization as national literary icon and symbol of local pride is what initially drew me to the earliest events in his posthumous rise. I wanted to unravel the paradox of a writer whose strategies for capturing local difference were ignored in his day and yet whose image now facilitates some of the most popular forms of place making and local branding. But to do so I first needed to understand why Miyazawa and his texts had survived at all. As Bruno Latour reminds us, "even an idea of genius, even an idea that is to save millions of people, never moves of its own accord. It requires a force to fetch it, seize upon it for its own motives, move it, and transform it."[6] Taking his death as my starting point, I began to search for the actors and material agents responsible for generating and sustaining the idea of Miyazawa as an author worth reading, but also for insuring that his texts were available to be read.

What I initially found was that in the first several months after his funeral, the most visible actors were local poets and friends writing for the regional newspaper. Wielding an intimate language of personal encounter and familial loss, they wrote about Miyazawa as if they were addressing a circle of acquaintances who knew implicitly the significance of this man and his position in local literary culture. Some tried to exaggerate his stature by praising him as a "magnificent artist" with a "unique, glittering presence in Japan's poetry establishment," or as a creator of "world-class art" whose "enigmatic genius"—on par, they proclaimed, with Rimbaud and Mallarmé—should be a point of pride in the history of Japanese poetry. Others framed his death in more local terms, placing him alongside other accomplished poets from his native Iwate Prefecture (the renowned Ishikawa Takuboku, for instance, and the now forgotten Hahaki Hikaru), or else associating his passing with other recent deaths in the field of local letters (namely the folklorist Sasaki Kizen).[7] For those closest to him, Miyazawa's death was without question tragic and noteworthy, but the ripples it stirred up were initially confined to a small pond. Of the few voices that trickled in from elsewhere, many expressed regret at never having had a chance to meet the man or even to have read much of his work. In fact one metropolitan poet, Yoshida Issui (1898–1973), when asked by Hahaki Hikaru to write a few words for the local paper, proceeded to give a cursory critique of Miyazawa's poetic style after admitting to having read just two of his poems. There was, or so he claimed, simply nothing else available.[8]

How then to explain the appearance in January 1934 of a slim volume of essays with the title *Miyazawa Kenji tsuitō* (In Memory of Miyazawa Kenji)? It not only bore a Tokyo address, but contained roughly thirty contributions from local friends, family, and, most astonishingly, established poets in the urban avant-garde like Yoshida, Kusano Shinpei (1903–1988), Takamura Kōtarō (1883–1956), Tsuji Jun (1884–1944), and Hagiwara Kyōjirō (1899–1938). In preceding decades, memorial volumes had typically been produced as special issues of literary journals for authors who, unlike Miyazawa, had a much wider following at their time of death. Dependent as the genre was on the most literal executions of "man-and-his-work" criticism, wherein life and art were made to speak in unison, it was important that there be plenty of literary associates and disciples who could vouch for *both* man *and* work. For instance, when the popular novelist Ozaki Kōyō (1867–1903) passed away, fellow founding members of the influential Ken'yūsha (Friends of the Inkstone) coterie contributed essays that were printed together with sketches of some of Kōyō's possessions: his brush and ink stone, his bookshelves and calling card, even his front gate. The memorial volume for literary giant Natsume Sōseki (1867–1916) boasted a wealth of commentary from leading writers and intellectuals of the day, and significantly opened with an essay by the doctor who had performed his autopsy. That readers were expected to take seriously the link he drew between Sōseki's literary genius and the weight of his brain (not to mention the terminally poor condition of his intestinal tract) is indicative of how accepted was the practice of using a writer's life to evaluate his or her work.[9] By the time of Miyazawa's death two decades later, authorial criticism was still heavily invested in the idea that how a writer had lived—now encapsulated in the notion of lifestyle (*seikatsu*) or way of living (*ikikata*)—was inseparable from an understanding of his or her art.[10]

We know this in part because of the ways contributors wrote of Miyazawa in his memorial volume, despite there being no obvious life, nor life's work, for them to fetishize and pass judgment on. Nearly half stated that they had never once met Miyazawa, or that they knew of his work only vicariously, through the editor Kusano Shinpei.[11] If they did know his work, it was typically only his poetry volume, *Spring and Asura* (1924), that they had read, and they invariably expressed a desire to go back and read it again or have it reprinted with all the other posthumously uncovered manuscripts they were anxious to see. This lack of familiarity did not inhibit them, however, from elevating the "unknown provincial author" to a figure larger than life—a figure who transcended locale, the present-day artistic milieu, and at times even history itself. One contributor declared him to be one of the greatest poets since the time of the ancient Manyōshū poetry anthology (eighth century), arguing that his writing was the product of sensory experiences transferred directly, and without conceptualization, onto paper. It thus lacked the odor of deliberateness and desk-work pervasive in contemporary poetry. Other contributors similarly fixated on the biographical Miyazawa as someone whose subjective mentality and aesthetic methods remained defiantly pure. They upheld his lifestyle and way of living as models for a beleaguered age and variously set them in contrast to the maelstrom of contemporary life and the chaos of urban intellectualism. In some cases, this sentiment carried over into praise for Miyazawa's intimate knowledge of his native place and grounding in the realities of agrarian life.[12]

What is so curious about these claims of rootedness and purity is that they were made by some of the same people who denied having any real firsthand knowledge of the biographical Miyazawa. Even supposing they had read the reminiscences of the mere half-dozen contributors who knew him personally (e.g., memories of his devotion to the farming community, his jaunts through the forests and fields with notebook in hand, or his life-long abstinence from sex), these hardly warranted such exaggerated statements as, "the value of his poems is only a fraction, nay tenths of a fraction, of his value as a human being," or, "the 'cosmos' that he possessed within allowed him to transcend his singularly provincial existence."[13] Why this compulsion to inflate the very thing—the life of Miyazawa—that was for most of them the furthest out of reach? In the months to follow, as Kusano and others worked to drum up support for the publication of a first *zenshū* (collected works), this tendency only persisted and the memorial volume became a promissory note on the potential future returns of Miyazawa's published writing.[14] All those involved seemed to assume that a life so authentically lived could not but produce desirable art.

When a third-rate publishing outfit in Tokyo finally agreed to produce a three-volume *zenshū* in October 1934, Miyazawa's life was once again held up as substitute for the as yet unconfirmed value of his work (and again by people who knew him only in death, and at a remove).[15] Popular modernist writer Yokomitsu Riichi (1898–1947), for instance, in a review written for the *Yomiuri shinbun*, admitted to knowing nothing about him as a person even while praising his noble lifestyle and the fact of its rootedness in the study of the natural sciences. He felt that his poetry, as a product of this lifestyle, was "filled with a sense of life (*seimeikan*) that goes one step deeper than anything in previous ages."[16] A few months on, philosopher Tanikawa Tetsuzō (1895–1989), writing for the *Tōkyō Asahi shinbun*, commented on how "practical" and "realistic" was his lifestyle, and on the degree to which this down-to-earth quality permeated his writing. Taking note of Miyazawa's engagement with the local farming community, he remarked how refreshing it was to imagine him "quietly cultivating the fields and composing poetry in the far recesses of Tōhoku, unbeknownst to the wider world" and free from the stench of the literary establishment.[17] The eagerness with which these posthumous promoters conjured up a life from so little, overcompensating with hyperbole for a lack of firsthand evidence, once again suggests how entrenched was the belief in life and art as mutually constitutive. So much so that some sublimated the former over all else, transferring to the absent figure of Miyazawa their own desires about what it was to live a socially engaged and truly selfless existence.

While Miyazawa's curious afterlife has much to say about the state of authorial criticism in 1930s Japan, it has even greater implications for how we deal with the contested place of the author, as both real individual and discursive construct, in the writing of literary history. Given a pile of incomplete manuscripts by a writer with very little public recognition and even fractured intentions at death, we would seem to have the ideal situation for distancing literary analysis from the impositions of the biographical signified. Instead, we find the author's life is present everywhere, and overwhelmingly so. And not, as Foucault would have it, as a purely negative principle "to limit, exclude, and choose; in short, by which to impede the free circulation, the free manipulation, the free composition, decomposition, and recomposition of fiction."[18] But rather as a positive and necessary force that allowed a body of texts to circulate precisely by liberating them from the deadening weight of anonymity. It did so by giving the agents of literary production—editors, publishers, critics, and fans—a means to position Miyazawa in the existing cultural field as a particular kind of author writing from a particular kind of place. That is, to situate him vis-à-vis the many concrete forms and positionalities that the labor of writing had come to assume by this time (e.g., establishment figure, popular genre writer, avant-garde intellectual, children's author), as well as those imagined to be possible (e.g., the isolated provincial poet). Surely we can reject the conclusions drawn by these agents in their efforts to give "life" to Miyazawa's work, relying as they did on a romantic image of a sovereign author whose "biography commands [the work's] writing with transparent immediacy."[19] But we cannot ignore the material effects engendered by their ideas of authorship and the structuring force of these ideas in working to produce texts as objects worthy of circulation. Here is confirmation of Roger Chartier's assertion that "the author-function, inscribed in the books themselves, ordering all attempts to establish textual classifications commanding the rules for the publication of texts, is henceforth at the center of all questions linking the study of the production, forms, and readers of texts."[20] Or in this case, at the center of all questions linking the study of production, geography, and narrative strategies of place-based identification.

If we understand the author-function to be a set of ideas that both delineate and define the parameters of authorship within a specific cultural moment, then its centrality is justified to the extent it serves, as Seán Burke has described it, as a *principle of specificity in the world of texts.* That is, as a means to retrace connections between authors and works, between authorial positions and contexts of production, in ways that work back to a sense of "historical, cultural, political," and I would add *spatial,* "embeddedness" on the part of speaking subjects.[21] Where the difficulty lies is in finding ways to "work back" that avoid romantic notions of a unitary transcendental subject or sovereign authorial will—as these tend only to obscure the social and material points of intersection between text and context—while also counterbalancing the anti-authorial bias present in many current modes of critical discourse. It is a bias present, as Burke notes, in "postmodern emphases on locality, on little narratives, on singularity . . . [and in] postcolonial specifications of the subaltern, of national and historical contexts," all which "pass from the text to its histories without properly acknowledging that an authorial life and its work allow such a passage to be made."[22] Yet this bias also resides implicitly in the specific forms that scholarly monographs have taken in recent decades, at least in Anglo-American studies of Japanese literature. Here the trend has been toward ever wider scales of analysis (e.g., historical genres, bodies of discourse, new theoretical paradigms) in which individual authors and works are reduced or compartmentalized in ways resonant with an overarching analytical or narrative frame. While these kinds of studies can be effective in what they set out to accomplish, they also represent a mode of literary history that inevitably pushes the question of the author-function to the margins. Driven by different principles of specificity, such studies actually risk squeezing authors and works into discrete niches that, like conventional biography, close off competing avenues of interpretation and thereby elide the indeterminacy and multiplicity of the author as situated subject.[23]

A mode of literary history that appears even less suited to foregrounding the author-function is that proposed by Franco Moretti. He asks the historian to stand at a distance from the literary archive in order to ask questions that go beyond the level of the individual author or work and instead direct themselves toward "the large mass of facts" (i.e., data) that literature, as a collective system, has left behind in the form of bibliographic records. In pursuit of a "more rational literary history," Moretti builds on Fernand Braudel's assertion that "history is indeed 'a poor little conjectural science' when it selects individuals as objects . . . but much more rational in its procedures and results, when it examines groups and repetitions."[24] It certainly *is* much more rational, but this has everything to do with the move to define the "individual" as a single, static data point within a much larger array. Viewed from this distance, as if looking out over a crowd, the individual cannot help but look analytically useless until plotted against the other individuals with whom it stands in relation. This strikes me as fundamentally a problem of *scale*, however, not a statement on the inherent worth of that individual node as a frame for investigation. For one can imagine zooming in on this individual to treat *it* as the system under analysis, constituted by its own set of discrete data points.

Moretti's call for a rational literary history thus offers a clue as to how we might reorient our perspective of the individualized author to make him or her the center of our analysis, but not its ultimate end-point. Imagine defining our scale in such a way that the name of the author becomes the larger organizing system for constellations of data points that are in some way connected to the individual in question, whether as biographical figure or as posthumous literary icon. These points might consist of any discursive or material object bearing an association, strong or weak, with that author—a literary text, a piece of critical commentary, a letter from a friend, a newspaper account of some public deed, a building once occupied, a landscape once traversed. A rational approach to these data would then entail identifying patterns of association or coherence amongst the data points as functions of more general sociohistorical properties and relations. Thus, for instance, we might look at the evolution of an author's literary style as a function of his or her degree of social connectedness. We might plot the history of that author's critical appraisal against the quantity and quality of texts available over time. Or instead, as is my interest here, we might look for patterns within the data that correspond in some way to real geographical relations. The image of the author to emerge from these approaches would thus rely not on a treatment of the individual as a self-contained and internally motivated entity, nor as a transcendent will, but as constituted by multiple overlaying patterns of social, historical, political, and spatial relations observable in the "mass of facts" that coalesce—across both space and time—around that individual as situated subject.

One pattern that emerged while researching *On Uneven Ground* is defined by a string of moments in Miyazawa's life and afterlife where a correlation can be observed between the geographical locus of a statement or action—whether made by Miyazawa himself or merely in his name—and the ideational content of that statement or action. In other words, where the *what* of the data seems motivated by the *where* of its appearance. The first of these moments comes in 1921, at the age of 25. As the eldest son of a merchant family with deep and flourishing roots in Hanamaki, Miyazawa was destined from a young age to inherit the family business, and was given all the moral and educational training he would need to do so.[25] Yet like many of his generation who similarly benefited from the desire of wealthy rural households to be upwardly mobile, the opportunity for higher education also introduced him to the pleasures of intellectual freedom and the possibility of shedding familial obligations (and financial privilege) in pursuit of loftier social goals. Upon graduating from Iwate's most prestigious middle school in 1914, he pleaded with his father to be allowed to continue his studies in Tokyo, but was denied this wish. His father did allow him, however, to attend the Morioka Higher School of Agriculture and Forestry, just twenty miles north of Hanamaki at the far end of the Kitakami River valley. At the school, one of only two of its kind in the country, Miyazawa studied chemistry, pedology, geology, and mineralogy, establishing his scientific credentials as well as a lifelong interest in agricultural science. He also spent his free time trekking, often for days on end, through the hilly and mountainous terrain that rises quickly from the valley floor up to highland plateaus and dense pockets of mixed deciduous and evergreen forests. The intimate knowledge

of the local landscape he gained from these hikes, which was already providing him with poetic inspiration, was put to good use as a post-graduate
research student assigned to conduct geological surveys in his native Hienuki
county and in other parts of the prefecture. He soon realized, however, that
the tedious work of quantitative analysis was not for him; nor could he accept the alternative of staying home indefinitely to manage the family pawnshop. Having reached an impasse, he made a break for Tokyo in early 1921
and there began toying seriously with the idea of literature as a profession.

Late that same year is when the moments of correlation between *what*
and *where* begin, most specifically in the children's fiction (*dōwa*) he began
writing upon returning home—after just eight months—to take a teaching position at the local Hienuki (later Hanamaki) School of Agriculture.[26]
In this case, the correlation was motivated by Miyazawa's own awareness
that he was writing as a geographical outsider for a literary market that had
largely become centered *on* and *in* Tokyo. The city's cultural dominance was
so fixed by capital accumulation, in fact, and so naturalized in the cognitive maps of Tokyo writers and critics, that most could not imagine any
literature thriving independently outside its borders. A few did, however,
particularly after the Great Kantō Earthquake of 1923 temporarily crippled
the city's publishing industry. As I discuss in Chapter Two, their proposals
for how to decentralize the machinery of literary production, and for how
to correct the urban bias latent in its products, are key to understanding
just how much of a role geography played at this time in discussions of
literary form and aesthetic strategy. They also help to frame Miyazawa's own
position as a writer who, having been turned away several times by popular
dōwa magazines in Tokyo, knew well the limitations of a highly centralized
field. His response was to develop representational strategies that linked the
narrative locus and actual site of writing in Iwate (the where) with attempts
to critically reimagine this locus in ways that countered or contradicted the
expectations of those at the center (the what).

It is these strategies that I examine in the book's middle chapters. The
first, found in some of Miyazawa's earliest children's stories, relativized certain spatial and temporal biases prevalent in prominent *dōwa* publications
of the day, including magazines like *Akai tori* (Red Bird) and *Kin no hoshi*
(Golden Star). In Chapter Three, I demonstrate that editors and contributors to these magazines appropriated folk or regional material in ways that
positioned the provinces allochronically, or as spaces outside of historical
time. Miyazawa, in contrast, restored to them a sense of contemporaneity

by resituating the same folk material within nonmetropolitan spaces more fully in dialogue with the modern moment. In the years ahead, he would localize these spaces through an imagined literary region he called "Iihatov," which acted as a critical filter for perceiving anew the real landscapes of his native Iwate and for reimagining their historical potential. Chapter Four explores the historical context and theoretical implications of this filter, which Miyazawa deployed in assembling and marketing his first and only published *dōwa* collection, *The Restaurant of Many Orders* (1924). By situating this particular strategy against other attempts in local media and the regional press to reimagine the future of Iwate and the larger Tōhoku, or northeast, region, I call attention to the broader struggle by provincial elites at this time to speak for the value of specific localities within discursive networks that were unevenly distributed in space and increasingly a part of national or global systems of knowledge and material exchange.[27] Significantly, Miyazawa attempted to narrativize this struggle in several of his Iihatov stories, two of which are taken up in Chapter Five. I argue that these stories, one about a globe-trotting wind imp and the other about an alpine flower, reveal the capacity of his narrative strategies to expose critical sites of epistemological conflict between locality and the nation-state in education, language, and scientific discourse. As such, they constitute a record of the perceived impact of culturally homogenizing processes (i.e., national education, linguistic standardization) on local systems of knowledge.

Miyazawa's strategies were not limited to narrative, however, and in my final two chapters I turn to moments of correlation in which the *what* is manifest more through praxis and public action than through literary experimentation. That is, moments when ideas about what does, and what should, constitute local cultural production were translated into practical steps toward the realization of those ideas. In Chapter Six, I consider his interest in amateur theater and look at a play, *Poran's Square*, that he conceived while teaching and which later became for him a vehicle for rethinking the borders of village public space. Through this play, we see how theater was for Miyazawa a means not only to challenge assumptions about who had the right to speak out in agrarian communities, but also to imagine what forms an ideal village public might take given the social and political structures by which public space had historically been bound. Of special interest to this study are his attempts to realize this ideal through the performance of the play by area students and young farmers, and also the choices he made to hide certain aspects of his vision from the public eye. Miyazawa's conviction in theater as a means for social change belonged to a broader intellectual movement to decentralize and/or democratize cultural production by putting it squarely in the hands of a rising generation of rural laborers. It was in pursuit of an art created both for and by the farmer that he resigned from teaching in 1926 to develop his own philosophy of farmers' art (*nōmin geijutsu*). This found him lecturing to local youth about his ideas for invigorating agricultural work, giving advice on planting and fertilizing techniques to area tenant farmers, and even establishing a new village cooperative for cultural, economic, and technical exchange. Chapter Seven considers what these activities, when set against parallel efforts by Tokyo-based intellectuals and the backdrop of a rapidly transitioning rural society, have to tell us about the institutional pathways (cooperatives, schools, political groups, artist coteries) and many discursive channels (public lectures, regional newspapers, foreign translations, mimeographed pamphlets) available in the interwar period for reinventing rural locality in real time. I am interested in how Miyazawa used these to translate thought into action and to make the local feel socially and culturally relevant, but also in how these same pathways and channels circumscribed what it was possible for him to achieve.

Each "moment of correlation" taken up in *On Uneven Ground* reveals something of the intricate network of connections that inhered in interwar Japan between cultural expression, material acts and texts, and spatially situated subjects. Together, they form a pattern by which it is possible to restore a sense—obscured by the natural leveling effect of the archive—of what it meant for Miyazawa to write and work on the margins of an uneven cultural field while trying to speak for and alter that marginal site. What it meant, in other words, to be submerged under the sign of the local (which typically carried more pejorative connotations like provincial, backward, unknown) while trying to redefine the terms of its representation. In the seventy years since his death, of course, these terms have undergone a dramatic reversal as the "local" has come to be valued both politically and economically in Japan, as elsewhere, for the kinds of difference that it can signify. Curiously, this reversal has only increased the potential of Miyazawa and his work to inform acts of place making in Iwate. The situation has evolved from one in which his various critical strategies had little or no bearing on the identity and physical character of Iwate to one in which it is difficult to imagine the landscape without him. His posthumous rise to the status of a national literary icon has coincided, as I explore in Chapter One and again in the Epilogue, with further "moments of correlation" in which he and his narratives are entwined with the local as a positive sign of things like regional identity, environmental protection, heritage preservation, and cultural tourism. Paradoxically, the less that spatial unevenness has been a determining factor in the circulation of Miyazawa's image and texts, the more valuable they have become as signifiers for, and generators of, a sense of place.

A central conceit of this book is that this paradox illuminates something essential about the history of how locality has been written, produced, and consumed in Japan since the turn of the last century. For not only does it underscore the radical multiplicity of "the local" as a site of identification, suggesting that this multiplicity is partly generated by the uneven ways that discourse about a place, and the actions taken there, enter wider networks of cultural production, it also raises important questions about how this unevenness impacts the potential of things said and done locally to work back upon the physical and cultural character of a place. This paradox would have remained invisible, suffice to say, had Miyazawa not been used as a consistent and stable frame for organizing the "mass of facts" that makes up this study. His "pluralized private-public figure," though changeable and open to endless interpretation, has for me been a way to connect "individual discourse with the social text" and to constitute "a specific sociohistorical locus for the archival intertext."[28] Though my focus on certain facts has led, recalling Blanchot, to a necessary betrayal of other aspects of Miyazawa's life and writing, this is precisely because the questions I am asking call for a particular kind of author-centered study. I can neither treat the author-figure as a hermetically sealed universe of texts and actions intelligible only to itself, nor do I want to minimize its relevance by replacing it, like Foucault, with a decentered system of language, or by subsuming it, like Moretti, under a higher order scale of analysis. Instead, I have found it most productive to focus on the interstitial space that defines the relation of the individual author-figure to the larger encompassing systems by which the figure is sustained and through which it evolves. To the extent that *On Uneven Ground* is successful in bringing this interstitial space to the analytic foreground, it is my own statement on the theoretical usefulness, and sometimes necessity, of seeing the literary forest through the single tree.

PART ONE

Thinking the Local

CHAPTER ONE

Finding Value in Locality

Capitalizing on Place

In the late 1990s, Tokyo's Ginza district welcomed a new member to its collection of high-end department stores, brand-name outlets, and trendy boutiques. Under the banner of "Iwate Ginga Puraza" (Iwate Milky Way Plaza), this new addition, situated across from the famous Kabuki-za Theater, was a retail outlet designed to offer a number of distinct services to the Tokyo consumer curious about Japan's northern prefecture of Iwate. Travel advice and business consultation were among some of the primary services on hand, but the biggest draw was to be the ready availability of traditional souvenirs and local foodstuffs shipped direct from "chilly Iwate."[1] Here was a chance to consume the region, or at least a small piece of it, without actually having to be there. If the flavors of Iwate failed to suit you, however, you could always sample from one of the many other "antenna shops" (so-called because they help to feel out consumer response) to appear in Tokyo's trendiest neighborhoods at this time. It was a concept that proved so successful that by 2009, 35 of the country's 47 prefectures were represented by one or more of these shops, each seeking to enhance the brand recognition of their respective locales against a wash of other designer names and labels.[2]

If the Iwate Ginga Plaza set itself apart from the competition in any way, it was with its name. *Ginga* (Milky Way) is a deliberate reference to *Night of the Milky Way Railroad* (*Ginga tetsudō no yoru*), the famous novella by native son Miyazawa Kenji. This fantastic tale depicting the spiritual journey of two young boys who hurdle through space on a galactic train is arguably one of his most recognized works.[3] Because of this, the word *ginga* has come to assume a metonymic role by which it infuses objects from Iwate— whether beer (Ginga Alpine Beer), a rail line (Iwate Ginga Railway), or an assisted living home (Ginga Village)—with any positive connotations that the term, and by extension the figure of Miyazawa, can be made to conjure up. Thus its adoption by the Plaza. *Ginga*, however, only scratches the surface of the work that Miyazawa and his texts have been made to perform in the service of acts of place making.

This work began almost immediately after his death and initially followed a conventional trajectory. Friends, fellow poets, and fans would, in the interest of commemorating his passing, collect funds for large poetry stones to be placed near landmarks and topographical features alluded to in his verse. Seventy of these impressive stones are now scattered throughout Iwate, and if plotted on a map would serve as a cartographic record of his extensive wanderings.[4] By the 1980s, this traditional form of intersection between text, author, and locality gradually came to be superseded by more capital intensive projects. In 1982, for instance, fans of his work raised funds for a Miyazawa Kenji museum to be erected near his hometown. Built on a forested hilltop (Koshiō-zan) that appears in several of his poems as a sacred site, it soon attracted visitors from all across the country and by the late 1990s was one of the most popular literary museums of its kind.[5] The realization that Miyazawa had such popular appeal opened the door to more commercial ventures, including a water park called "Kenji World" built in 1995; a small-scale amusement park built in 1996 to bring his fictional world to life via diorama and high-tech display; and an assortment of tours and guidebooks meant to introduce visitors to sites associated with him or his writings.[6] Today, his connection with the Iwate landscape is so entrenched that the mere fact of his association with a particular built structure or natural site can determine how that site is developed or otherwise utilized by the community. In 2005, to cite but a recent example, a famous geodetic observatory built in 1920 was spared demolition when fans, who claimed it as a key inspiration for *Night of the Milky Way Railroad*, successfully lobbied for its preservation.[7]

Part of the reason I began *On Uneven Ground* was to understand why Miyazawa and his artistic legacy have proved so successful in contemporary practices of place construction and local branding, and so infinitely more adaptable to these practices than some of the more staid faces of the literary canon. What have made his narratives and biography so good for thinking and constructing a version of locality that others find valuable? And why, for instance, has the Iwate Ginga Plaza been so willing to invest in him as a symbol of Iwate, going so far as to have once renamed the boulevard in front of the store "Kenji Street" as part of a two-day exhibition of regional foods, crafts, and folk performance?[8] As I proceeded to wrestle with these questions, the problem became for me both a historical and a theoretical one. Historical because the success of Miyazawa in this regard has, as we will see, much to do with the conditions under which his fiction was produced and the ways he and his work were rescued from obscurity. Theoretical because the history of his relation to a particular locality and to acts of place making cannot be told without inquiring first into the nature of locality as an object of social and cultural value. How and under what conditions is this value produced? How and why is it sustained? Are there transhistorical processes underpinning its production? How should we situate this value in a system of competing values? And most critically, how do values assigned to a locale intersect with the physical locality itself? It soon became apparent that to try to understand why Miyazawa holds such significance for contemporary practices of place making was to ask after the longer history of how locality has been made and made relevant in modern Japan, but also how it is we can measure that relevance at all.

The simplest answer to the question of how the value of a place or locality is produced is to say that it is through the notion of "difference." A local product, for instance, comes to have value for both seller and consumer because it is perceived to be only *here* or *there* and nowhere else. As soon as this monopoly is lost, whether because it is diluted by overselling (i.e., it becomes available everywhere) or usurped by some other locale, then so too is the difference that guarantees its value. Recent efforts in Japan to both manage "local brands" (*chiiki burando*) and extend trademark law to regionally branded products are indicative of how significant this monopoly has become.[9] Spatial difference by itself, however, does not explain why that difference is seen as desirable and thus valued. As Terry Eagleton has observed, the relation between difference and identity (i.e., the perceived value of that difference) must be mediated by some kind of structure, for "there can be no specificity without some general notion to contrast it with."[10] Only in the context of a larger structure of value attribution, that is, does local difference come to be worth anything.

In Japan, this larger structure has been defined by a matrix of binaries that have shaped practices of place making, each to varying degrees, for much of the modern period: present and past, modern and traditional, change and stasis, foreign and native, artificial and natural. Like the antenna shops that now represent them in Tokyo, provincial localities have been especially keen to seek out the coordinates on this matrix that will produce for them an image of place appealing to both outsiders and native residents. The search has grown only more intense in recent decades as these localities suffer from declining and aging populations, the exodus of youth, a loss of industry to cheaper labor markets overseas, and the shuttering of once vibrant town and village centers due to shifting patterns of consumption and changing lifestyles. The sense of crisis is such that municipal governments, business leaders, and local community organizations have since the 1980s sought to literally *make* place anew, whether under the guise of "native-place making" (*furusato-zukuri*), "town making" (*machi-zukuri*), or "locality making" (*chiiki-zukuri*).[11] Because while industry and people can move readily with the flow of capital, places cannot. The discursive and material ties that bind a particular social formation to a discrete space, hardened by time and memory, are not easily amenable to relocation. What can be done, however, and what has been happening more frequently with the transition to a post-Fordist economy and with "diminishing spatial barriers to exchange, movement, and communication," is to try to make places attractive to the flexible accumulation of global capitalism.[12] That is, to reconstruct them at the levels of symbolic representation *and* material infrastructure to generate newly valuable locales that can be marketed as desirable places to live, travel to, invest in, or even, as with the antenna shops, consume from afar.[13]

Some localities, particularly those dependent on fixed natural resources, have had to work at this more than others, as their economic and social marginalization—owing to their inherent immobility—has made them all the more vulnerable to the "intense phases of spatial reorganization" by which capitalism operates. For other locales, the very processes of uneven development that have produced them as marginalized spaces have fortunately spared them from the leveling effects of urbanization and industrialization.

They are thus more easily fashioned into symbols of what modern metropolitan life is perceived to lack: an urban retreat, natural sanctuary, close-knit community, a refuge for traditional values, and even an embodiment of "place" itself (i.e., a symbol of rootedness and connection). In an age where global capitalism is often demonized for paving over cultural differences by substituting mass-produced products and practices for local ones—what some call "Coca-colonization"—these localities have sought to restore value to local difference by reframing *lack* as the presence of that which has elsewhere disappeared.[14] If localities face different choices about how to make themselves valuable again, there is no question that place making has become an integral part of all expressions of local and regional identity in Japan, as is true in East Asia generally, where "local color has proven to be a lucrative marketing tool . . . [such] that symbols of local distinctiveness are coming to function much like corporate logos."[15] These expressions take the shape of everything from theme-park construction and urban renewal projects to heritage-site preservation, wilderness conservation, promotion of tourism, and the sponsorship of traditional celebrations (e.g., community and religious festivals) and newly fashioned cultural events (e.g., international art shows).[16]

Contemporary efforts to produce and sustain an image of locality as desirable commodity belong to a longer global history of exploring "new meanings for space and place" that began in the modern era when, as David Harvey describes it, there was a knee-jerk response to the experience of increasing spatial and temporal compression under capitalism. As geographically disparate communities were brought closer together by homogenizing modes of production and universalist discourses, the result was "a heightened sense of awareness of what makes a place special."[17] This in turn led politicians, writers, intellectuals, and other local elites to attempt to articulate, defend, valorize, or otherwise celebrate the value of place in more vociferous and coordinated ways than their forebears, as is well documented for late-nineteenth and early-twentieth-century Western Europe and America.[18] Japan was no exception in witnessing such a heightened awareness, as will become evident in later chapters. In fact, in looking back to the years when Miyazawa was starting to explore new ways of conveying Iwate's uniqueness to readers both inside and outside the region, one stumbles upon an act of place making that feels uncannily familiar.

In September 1921 the resplendent upper floors of the Mitsukoshi department store, located on the glittering streets of Tokyo's Nihonbashi district, became for two weeks the site of the Tōhoku Bussan Chinretsukai (Tōhoku Goods Exhibition). The event opened with a full slate of Tōhoku dignitaries in attendance, including then prime minister, and Iwate native, Hara Kei. Standing as these men were at the leading edge of the nation's commodity culture—and just a few blocks north from where the Iwate Ginga Plaza now stands—they were thrilled to have an opportunity to introduce fellow countrymen to some of the products unique to the area's six prefectures (Akita, Aomori, Fukushima, Iwate, Miyagi, and Yamagata) and thus to potentially spark economic growth in a region generally seen to have been left behind. A reporter from Iwate described the scene for readers back home, remarking on the intense atmosphere of inter-regional competition that permeated the two floors of exhibition space. Items on display included Masaoka bean candies and *umoregi* (buried tree) handicrafts from Miyagi, Nanbu ironware and hand-dyed purple cloth from Iwate, pickled butterbur and traditional copperware from Akita, textiles and sour-plum sweets from Yamagata. The strange mix of simple foodstuffs and manufactured goods prompted him to wonder if some exhibitors had not confused "local souvenirs" (what he referred to derisively as *meibutsu*) for "local products" (*meisan*), though he did notice that the former, being easily consumable and reasonably priced, attracted the largest crowds. As for the latter, further research and refinement were clearly needed. Some of the textiles "reeked too much of the provinces" and were of a quality unworthy of the heart of Tokyo; some of the metalware might just as well have been displayed in a student showcase at a "school for apprentice craftsmen." Equally undeniable, at least in the reporter's eyes, was that many of the products from the different prefectures were beginning to look much the same, their "regional particularity" (*kokuyūsei*) thinned out by the influence of shared markets and distribution routes.[19]

Despite this critical appraisal, the exhibition, of which this was the third to be held, had made significant progress since its inception in 1917. When it started, even the director of the sponsoring organization, the Tōhoku Shinkō Kai (Society for the Promotion of Tōhoku), had expressed doubts. For one, many of the products had never before been sold or marketed beyond their local area, and thus lacked adequate methods of shipping and display. In fact, some of the most basic conditions had yet to be met: durable and spill-proof containers, sufficient labeling, and attractive packaging.[20] But if this presented a major obstacle, it was also part of the reason why the exhibition had been devised in the first place. The Shinkō Kai, formally established in 1913 by a group of Seiyūkai bureaucrats and Kantō-area industrialists, saw the original 1917 exhibition not as an opportunity to show off Tōhoku goods, as if their authenticity and value had already been confirmed, but as a chance to improve their quality and marketability. Procurers at Mitsukoshi were asked to evaluate the products and suggest ways they might be fashioned into more profitable commodities: objects capable of capturing consumer attention in Tokyo, first and foremost, but also at Mitsukoshi branches in Osaka, Seoul, and Dalian.[21] This in turn, or so Shinkō Kai members asserted, would help revitalize the struggling economy of Tōhoku. By the time of the second exhibition, minimal improvements in product quality had been made, but it was obvious that the goal of boosting economic productivity would be much longer in coming. The Shinkō Kai nevertheless sponsored the exhibition four more times before dissolving in 1926, its members ever convinced that by securing shelf space at the center of commodity culture they would secure a more prominent place for Tōhoku in the nation's future.

One thing this exhibition makes vivid is that locality has not always been ready for sale. There have been times when its particularity was still too messy for long-distance travel and its signifying marks still in need of proper labeling. That Iwate Ginga Plaza was so easily able to assemble a store full of local goods speaks not only to how far the mechanisms of place making have evolved since Miyazawa's time, but also to how much larger the market for these goods has become. Moreover, the lack of infrastructural support at so many different levels reminds us of the physical and creative labor required for making the local available for purchase outside its immediate place of origin. In the case of the exhibition, this labor had to begin with a top-down style of civic boosterism, a reliance on outside arbiters of taste like Mitsukoshi, and an emphasis on external reform rather than an appeal to the inherent value of the local as a positive sign of difference. Yet while the exhibition reveals how much things have changed, it also shows that a general matrix of value attribution—defined along similar axes of urban-rural and center-periphery—was already available to assess how much local difference was worth. And so too a market in which this difference, at least in the form of consumable products like handicrafts and foodstuffs, was actually worth something.

Evidence of a historical continuum between the Plaza and the exhibition returns us to the reality of their shared origins in periods of increased spatial and temporal compression. While it is important not to downplay their differences in conception and execution, both can be construed as indirect effects of globalization's gradual "lifting out" of social relations from local contexts of interaction and its restructuring of them across "indefinite spans of time-space" (what Anthony Giddens refers to as *disembedding*).[22] That is to say, as local contexts become linked up with social systems and market mechanisms that are national and global in scope, the bonds that once held preexisting local cultural formations together are more easily pulled apart, becoming bound up with nonlocal concerns. This potentially renders the formations less competitive, less necessary, or even obsolete. In response to this thinning out of local relations, communities find ways to preserve, reassert, or reinvent the value of local difference so as to tighten internal bonds between culture and place, even if that means marketing this difference in cosmopolitan settings where such bonds have become an object of longing and desire.[23] There are instances, of course, when this response goes beyond a simple interest in profit or speculative gain, lending itself, as Harvey reminds us, "to an interpretation and a politics that is both exclusionary and parochialist, communitarian if not intensely nationalist."[24] Indeed, valorizations of local difference that assert a cohesive collective identity are often prone to the reactionary tactics of a zealous nationalism, especially when "conflated with race, ethnic, gender, religious, [or] class differentiation."[25] At their most extreme, they lend themselves to "a regressive politics of global delinkage, bounded particularity, and claims of ontological pastness, where locality becomes some backward-gazing fetish of purity to disguise how global, hybrid, compromised, and unprotected everyday identity already is."[26]

Some scholars have rightfully pointed out that to the extent this fetish is manifest by localities everywhere—each using invented traditions and commercialized heritage culture to produce themselves as marketable "museum items" or as essentially *other*—the result is "a kind of serial replication of homogeneity" that reinforces the very same global processes of spatial abstraction and disembedding they are attempting, whether for political or economic gain, to counteract.[27] Considered thus, global economic imperatives appear not only to be the primary motivator for expressions of local difference, but also to provide the underlying relational matrix necessary for these expressions to be meaningful at all. This is an important point to recognize, but it should not lead us to conclude that these expressions therefore do not matter. To borrow from Doreen Massey, if there is "a recrudescence of some problematical senses of place, from reactionary nationalisms to competitive localisms, to sanitized, introverted obsessions with 'heritage,'" then we should not refuse to deal with this, but instead "recognize it and to try to understand what it represents. . . . The question is how to hold on to that notion of spatial difference, of uniqueness, even of rootedness if people want that, without it being reactionary."[28] And, I would add, without it being reduced to a mere effect of global capitalism denuded of real political or critical value. For as long as locality and place remain vital and viable categories of identification, even if it is in the interest of profit, we have to leave ourselves room to theorize "the local" as a site of indeterminacy and undecidability within much larger systems of social and cultural meaning—a site capable of dialectically engaging with these universalizing systems and their normative injunctions about what a place should or should not be.

Henri Lefebvre, in analyzing the increased abstraction and domination of "social space" under global capital and mass urbanization, also argued for the theoretical value of the local. He wrote that, in selecting social space as an object of analysis,

> We are confronted not by one social space but by many—indeed, by an unlimited multiplicity or uncountable set of social spaces which we refer to generically as 'social space'. No space disappears in the course of growth and development: the *worldwide does not abolish the local*. This is not a consequence of the law of uneven development, but a law in its own right.[29]

For Lefebvre, the irreducibility of the local was ultimately what made a critique of abstract space possible, for he found there the spaces of fragmentation and contradiction that, though every bit a product of the dominant capitalist order, at once represented the potential for its destabilization. Foucault also privileged the local as a sign of irreducible otherness, though for him it served as a spatial metaphor for a specific subdivision of a field of knowledge.

> I also believe that it is through . . . a particular, local, regional knowledge, a differential knowledge incapable of unanimity and which owes its force only to the harshness with which it is opposed by everything surrounding it—that it is through the re-appearance of this knowledge, of these local popular knowledges, these disqualified knowledges, that criticism performs its work.[30]

These local, disqualified knowledges were a means to counter "the claims of a unitary body of theory which would filter hierarchies and order them in the name of some true knowledge and some arbitrary idea of what constitutes a science and its object."[31] They were a means, in other words, to undermine and expose the constitution of hegemonic discourses and ways of knowing by taking up a position external to them and wholly invisible to their categories of description. More recently, Vicente Rafael has captured this sense of critical externality on a geographical register by writing of "the practice of spacing" that is implied by regional or local partitions and that complicates "the claims of powerful centers."

> The indefiniteness of its ontology, the porousness of its borders, and the mobility of its geographical location have made the regional ineluctably unstable and arguably destabilizing. Thus has it also furnished sites for surprising insurrections and recalcitrant alterities. For whatever else the local might seem in various discourses of regionalism, it acts to designate some other place, indeed the very place (and displaceability) of otherness itself.[32]

Like Rafael, scholars in postcolonial studies and human geography have tried to retain the idea of locality as a theoretically productive unit of analysis without reifying the essentialist claims seen in more extreme expressions of local difference, or without subsuming it completely within global forces. One way they do this is by treating locality as the specific articulation of a *process*, rather than as some static, a priori essence. Rob Wilson and Wimal Dissanayake, for example, see the local as a particularized site forever mediated by global forces and technologies in a "global/local assemblage." Rejecting "the modernist binary of the universal (global) sublating the particular (local)," which they argue is too often explained by "a colonizing master-narrative of undifferentiated homogenizing forces meeting endlessly specific and hyper-detailed adaptations," they insist that an "attention to local conjunctures needs to be linked, at all points, to global processes."[33] For them, the process of producing local difference must be seen as the utilization of "the nonsynchronized" and "temporarily autonomous" terrain of the local so as to "achieve renewed social agency" or "articulate place-bound identity."[34] Massey is also helpful in providing an image of locality as process:

> The uniqueness of a place, or a locality, [is] constructed out of particular interactions and mutual articulations of social relations, social processes, experiences and understandings, in a situation of co-presence, but where a large proportion of those relations, experiences and understandings are actually constructed on a far larger scale than what we happen to define for that moment as the place itself, whether that be street, a region or even a continent.

Instead, then, of thinking of places as areas with boundaries around, they can be imagined as articulated moments in networks of social relations and understandings.[35]

In short, Massey suggests that we construe place as a node whose unique-ness is defined by its singular position in a system of universal forces. Just as every point of intersection in a spiderweb is constituted by a unique configuration and combination of the same essential thread, every locality is constituted by a unique combination of the same underlying social forces (e.g., relations, processes, experiences). Here is a vision of local difference existing as a function and byproduct of a networked structure. For me, it has proved a useful jumping off point for thinking about why certain sym-bolic values have been attributed to certain localities at certain times, how and why they are sustained within a field of competing values, and why they have mattered even when they overinflate actual difference.

Toward a Networked Model of Local Difference

To draw out Massey's vision a bit further, let us assume that each node in the network, no matter on what scale it is conceived (village, town, city, na-tion), has its own particular existential reality, always in process and forever being woven anew. This reality is not to be conflated with the node (or locality) as it is manifested in discourse or acts of place making; the "Iwate" that is up for sale at Iwate Ginga Plaza is only an abstraction and condensa-tion of Iwate as "articulated moment" in socio-material space. The difficulty, of course, is that such abstractions are the only means we really have of representing the particularity of a locale. Even if we were to limit our object of analysis to a city street or a tiny hamlet, we could never hope to capture the reality of that node except through partial abstractions and filters—in economic terms, for instance, or in any of the other disciplinary languages available to us: politics, sociology, ecology, and artistic expression, just to name a few. Some may argue that certain filters bring us closer to the truth of a place or locality than others, assuming that not all of the threads that go to constitute a node are of the same thickness or structural importance. I am here less interested in arguing the merits of any one particular filter, however, than in interrogating how one of these filters—that relating to narrative discourse—tries to speak for local difference. I want to know how this filter succeeds at abstracting and condensing the complex network of forces that go to produce a place; how it articulates the uniqueness of the node it speaks for so as to add value to it; and how it potentially works back to alter and recombine the threads from which that node is spun.

A great deal of scholarly attention has been given in recent decades to the powerful role that narrative plays in the processes by which places are not only conceptualized, remembered, and (mis)recognized, but also appropriated and experienced in the most material and physical of ways. Stories have been deemed the "coat hangers" upon which assorted memories of a place are hung, the cognitive "maps" by which are delineated the complex relationships of humans to a place, the "invisible" signposts that transform nowhere into a somewhere for those capable of reading them.[36] Or in their novelistic form, as a means for representing and associating oneself with the geographical totality of the nation-state.[37] To assert the centrality of narrative in place-formation, however, does not get us closer to understanding how the dialogue between the two is carried out. To do that, we need to complicate Massey's networked model of localities by considering how discourse about these localities emerges from and circulates within the network as a whole.

Imagine that the simplest form of dialogue takes place when someone who identifies with a particular locality, either as home or place of residence, offers up a statement about that locality. As for instance when Miyazawa, writing from his native town of Hanamaki, laid out his vision for an imaginary literary region (Iihatov) that was to be a symbolic reconfiguration of the actual place of Iwate. Naturally, his statement had to be articulated within a field of existing statements about Iwate, a field to which he could have responded in any number of ways. He could have, for example, aligned his statement with public opinion so that it might circulate more widely in local media channels; he could have brought to life residual kinds of statements that had fallen out of use; or he could, as was the case, express an entirely new kind of statement through a medium (a book advertisement) to which few paid much attention. Every statement made about a place must inevitably begin within a contested field of discourse defined similarly by a variety of media that do not reach everyone in the same way or with the same degree of success.

This field does not exist at just one node, however, but at (and across) every node in a given network of localities. This is where the dialogue between discourse and place becomes infinitely more complex. For if the nodes are part of the same network, they are also open to influence by statements made elsewhere, and "Iwate" must then be thought of as composed not only of statements by self-declared insiders like Miyazawa, but of statements made from other subject positions and cognitive mappings: Iwate as a former home, perhaps, or as a part of the wider Tōhoku region, or as belonging to that undifferentiated space known by Tokyoites as the provinces (*chihō*). Moreover, since power—whether of the political, economic, or cultural sort—is always distributed unevenly across these nodes, we must consider the possibility that discourse issuing from the most powerful of them will travel farther (and with a greater magnitude) than discourse emanating from elsewhere, potentially interfering with or even canceling out voices too weak to extend much beyond their place of origin. Just imagine throwing countless pebbles, all of varying sizes, into a tranquil pond and you have an idea of what I am proposing here: an intricate and overlapping mesh of ripples expanding out from multiple sources and with varying strengths. The image needs further concretization, but the key principle is that the ripples expand *unevenly*, both in magnitude and distance, from their points of origin.

Any attempt to conceptualize and historicize the dialogue between discourse and place-formation requires attention to the uneven quality of these ripples, as it helps to foreground the hierarchies of force and positionality that structure all fields of discursive production. Statements made about a particular locality may speak of the same socio-material node, but they never do so on equal ground. And yet this uneven quality is something easily lost sight of under the flattening power of the archive, which in its ideal form provides equal and ready access to all materials regardless of how much time or space might have separated them in their contexts of production. The archive certainly does not hide their original spatio-temporal coordinates, but the burden falls to users to restore these coordinates to meaningful presence. It also falls upon users to carefully reconstruct the cultural force and positionality of texts that, while appearing to sit side-by-side in the archive, had a very specific relation to other texts at their moment of dissemination, and then again later on as the uneven ground beneath them inevitably shifted. In the case of Miyazawa, consider that Iihatov and the narratives associated with it began as the smallest of ripples on a surface already stirred up by more powerful and far-reaching statements about Iwate and northeastern Japan. This meant that at their time of conception, they had almost no affect on how these regions were being talked about. Since Miyazawa's death, however, they have come to underwrite the value of locality in Iwate with increasing frequency and, as noted earlier, are appropriated for a wide variety of place-making efforts and expressions of local identity. Thus in trying to describe the ongoing dialogue between these narratives and attempts at constructing local difference, we are confronted with a situation in which their discursive content has remained constant (e.g., texts that helped Miyazawa revalue the local *then* are used to revalue the local *now*) even as their influence on the value of place has changed radically (e.g., Iihatov was largely ignored in the 1920s whereas today it readily stands in as a signifier of Iwate). While much of the focus in the following chapters will be on the conditions under which Miyazawa tried but failed to inject his locality with new meaning, it behooves us to consider how conditions changed such that his ideas and narratives have been able to set down firmer roots in the real spaces of Iwate. How is it that texts that still speak about Iwate in the same way now do so with a magnitude and frequency that stir up a quite different pattern of ripples? As will be made apparent, what ultimately allows us to chart the evolving nature of these patterns—and to restore something of their complexity prior to being submerged within the dimensionless space of the archive—is exactly the idea of a networked model of local difference structured at all times by the principle of unevenness.

Telling the Local Time

Unevenness, however, is important not just as a means of historicizing the relation of discourse to place. It must also be recognized as a category of historical experience that captures a very real effect of both economic growth and the vicissitudes of capital investment. An effect, moreover, that underwrote expressions of local difference in Miyazawa's day as much as ours, and one that many felt had to be overcome if a locality was going to remain viable at all. In fact, as different as the idea of Iihatov was from the rhetoric and rationale behind the Tōhoku Goods Exhibition, both were sustained by the conviction that Iwate and Tōhoku were of a qualitatively different cast than other subnational spaces—a part of the greater empire and yet socially and economically unequal in their relation to it. The conviction was a widespread one at a time when processes of disembedding were forcing Iwate and Tōhoku into newly competitive relations with other subnational regions and with foreign markets. This enhanced competition led to a heightened sense of disparity between localities all across Japan and to the creation of symbolic hierarchies of development by which places like Tōhoku came to be seen as "left behind" or "out-of-step" with the singular historical time of capitalism. Organizations like the Shinkō Kai responded by trying to reinvent Tōhoku as a region ready to satisfy the desires of the nation's consumers and prepared to awake from its economic slumber. Miyazawa, for his part, dealt with the sense of disparity by writing against the dominant symbolic hierarchies by which Iwate and Tōhoku had come to be construed as "backward" at all, imagining the former as a site for an alternative agrarian future. What we see in both instances, as well as in other expressions of local identity to be examined later, is a proclivity for representing unevenness in temporal terms as much as spatial ones. Thus in this final section I consider how *time* might be incorporated into our model of local difference.

There are at least two ways in which it is important to think about time in a local context. The first relates to the common practice by which localities are marked in political discourse and the popular imaginary as being either in or out of sync with an imagined singular present and a predefined timeline of historical progress. In interwar Japan, this timeline was organized around the ideal of an urban-industrial and capitalist present—typically marked as Western—to which all of society was meant to orient itself. The result was that colonial peripheries and subnational regions like Tōhoku were forever being classified vis-à-vis this end point as advanced or backward, developed or developing, modern or traditional, civilized or barbaric. To be marked as "behind" or "backward" was never a positive thing in economic terms, but it could be in cultural terms. One finds many instances of ethnographers and intellectuals who, having flipped this temporal hierarchy on its head, mapped older times onto the space of the rural margins and called for their preservation as a way to defend against a destabilizing and culturally inauthentic capitalist "Now." Yanagita Kunio (1875–1962), for instance, imagined that earlier and essential layers of national life were still available in traces and vestiges beyond the cities and towns, and that their luster could still be perceived through the most recent, modern overlays.[38] Similarly, prominent fellow ethnologist Orikuchi Shinobu (1887–1953) practiced a kind of mythologizing archaeology by which he aimed to show how archaic, agricultural modes of life "had generated archetypal literary forms . . . and how traces of [this] inaugural moment were still available in folk practices and words in the Japanese countryside."[39] Whether intended as a negative or positive appellation, that representational labels such as "advanced" or "backward" became an integral part of how colonial and provincial localities were talked about should remind us of Neil Larsen's ob-

servation that when spaces are given these labels they tend to enter into social relations of absolute exteriority "despite having emerged from the same
crucible of historical contingency, the identical world-historical ground."[40]
Hence we too must take them seriously as influential determinants of how
local difference was configured in interwar acts of place making.

Yet while the realities of economic, social, and cultural unevenness inevitably facilitate the mapping of temporal hierarchies onto localities—and
while the effects of this mapping will always inform the dialogue between
discourse and place—it is important that we not take these mappings at face
value. We must instead recognize them, following Latour, as "interpretations of the passage of time." When this passage is conceived as an irrevers-
ible arrow, as capitalization, or as progress, it is "nothing but a particular
form of historicity . . . [a particular] means of connecting entities and filing
them away. If we change the classification principle, we get a different temporality on the basis of the same events. . . . *It is the sorting that makes the
times, not the times that make the sorting*."[41] Hence the "local time" of Iwate,
or of the provinces, looks to be "behind" only to the extent that we take as
truth the principle of sorting that places it there. If we resist this tempta-
tion, we can then hold the door open to alternate ways of *sorting* the local
time that might have been dreamed up in the interwar period. Ways of sorting, for instance, that sought to demarcate a temporality different from the
one by which those at the most central and powerful nodes in the network
set their clocks. Theorizing locality so that other possible sortings become
visible is the second way we need to think about time in local contexts.

Suggestions for how to do this have been offered by a number of historians over the past decade. Jennifer Jenkins, for instance, uses the concept of
"provincial modernity" as a way to highlight how politicians and educators
in fin-de-siècle Hamburg negotiated the lived reality of modernization even
as it transformed their local environment. For her, the concept captures a
layer of social history wherein the larger, more abstract paradigms of knowledge (e.g., class and nation) were criticized in order "to focus on particular
forms and local expressions of subjectivity and identity."[42] Vicente Rafael
has proposed that we shift our focus from a concern with the modernization of local difference to an investigation of specific strategies adopted for
localizing modernity. He sees modernity "less as the future condition toward
which everyone is headed than as a set of events whose coming to pass takes
place in contingent, infinitely variable ways."[43] Celia Applegate is likewise
compelled by the promise of a local historiography, which in giving atten-

tion to the specificity of regions and places can itself be a critique of the top-down narratives of modernization theory and the "axiomatic assumptions" of nation-based histories.[44] Postcolonial scholar Dipesh Chakrabarty has perhaps been the most influential in thinking about a "local time" that exists in contradistinction to, and in conflict with, a higher temporal order. As he explains it, this order is defined by a "global historical time" that narrates both modernity and capitalism as historical processes that originate in Europe and have since spread across the globe. By relativizing (or "provincializing") the universal claims of this narrative, however, we come to see the modern as "inevitably contested" and can thus begin "to write over it other narratives of human connections that draw sustenance from dreamed-up pasts and futures where collectivities are defined neither by the rituals of [national] citizenship nor by the nightmare of 'tradition' that 'modernity' creates."[45] For Chakrabarty, a focus on local, alternative ways of sorting time brings to light subaltern pasts (the diverse ways of "being-in-the-world") otherwise subordinated to the hegemonic meta-narratives and teleologies of global historical time.

Some scholars rightfully warn that to envision alternative modernities residing in spaces distinct from those coded as modern or developed (e.g., the "West," "Europe") is to recuperate "the very binarism [of modernization theory] that has imperially reduced the rest of the world to the status of a second term."[46] In other words, by making the primacy of space a fixed guarantor of difference and by exceptionalizing locations as alternatives to some prior, original model, the result is a reassertion of essentialized cultures and identities that are supposedly undisturbed by, or in need of protection from, a capitalist modernity emanating from elsewhere. The prospect of multiple times existing under a unitary, homogenous time has also been criticized by Antonio Negri as a "postmodern conception" that fails to truly resolve the problem of time under capitalism. "The dialectical content may increase, but the schema remains functional, formal and unifying."[47] These warnings highlight the need for a comparative framework that can adequately account for local difference—both spatial and temporal—without "reducing one to the other or displacing one by the other."[48] What is needed is a methodology that does not try to tell the local time by setting it apart and below a universal time, but which instead views it as coexisting with other times in a differentiated present. A methodology of coevalness, in other words, that sees opposition and conflict as relations that unfold, as Johannes Fabian puts it, not between "the same societies at different stages of development, but [between] different societies facing each other at the same Time."[49] If we substitute "societies" here with the nodes of locality discussed earlier, we have an image of "local time" as differentiated from, and simultaneously relatable to, other times within a shared historical context. It is this image that I will attempt to enhance and concretize as I proceed to elucidate not only the *where* of Miyazawa's strategies for reimagining local difference, but also the *when*.

While this chapter has sketched only the most basic contours of a theoretical approach to the problem of local difference, what should be evident is how difficult is the task of measuring its value. The matrix of competing discourses and social processes that go to define any place or locality is impossible to capture in its totality, and has always to be considered from multiple vantage points and through multiple lenses. To be aware of this complexity, however, is a first step toward understanding how the dialogue between discourse and place making operates, and the ways in which it both underwrites and sustains the value of local difference while leaving room for its critical re-valuation. For if we wish to delineate with more precision when this value is subversive and when it is merely reactionary, when socially progressive and when politically authoritarian, when essential to survival and when a consumer ploy, then we have to do a better job of explaining how and why discourse and narratives about a place do, or do not, inform the actual production of social space. Miyazawa is an effective starting point for such an endeavor in that he provides a set of common coordinates (e.g., his texts, his biography) with which to examine both this dialogue over time and in disparate historical contexts. Utilizing these coordinates, we can begin to tell the story of how locality emerged as a vigorous site of contest and compromise in the interwar period, but also of how it continues to mediate in fundamental ways the relation of people to the social spaces and natural environments they inhabit.

CHAPTER TWO

Decentering the Uneven Geography of Cultural Production

In the Absence of a Center

On September 14, 1923, the *Iwate nippō* (Iwate Daily Report) carried an article on the state of the Morioka book trade. Here, in the prefecture's principal urban center, owners of the city's half-dozen major bookstores were in a panic over their fast disappearing merchandise. Not only were books and popular magazines flying off the shelves, research volumes and reference items were being snapped up too, and at a pace that was certain to see stocks depleted by the end of the month. The representatives of book merchants in Tokyo were also visiting with increased frequency, seeming more eager than usual to balance their ledgers. The book business in Morioka, it would appear, was booming.[1] More ominous forces, however, were at work. Just two weeks before, a catastrophic earthquake had struck the Kantō Plain, reducing large swaths of Yokohama and Tokyo to ash and rubble. The damage to the latter was particularly severe as the quake crippled instantly many of the city's industries and institutions. The publishing industry was especially hard hit. Of the eighteen large daily newspapers based in the city, all but three were reduced to technological infancy. Magazines, of which there were nearly six hundred titles circulating before the quake, went on virtual hiatus in September. Even had they wanted to publish, it would have been difficult as many of Tokyo's printers, binders, distributors, and booksellers remained out of commission for weeks, in some cases months. The sector that suffered the most was book publication. It went from producing, on average, three hundred hardcover books per month to not a single volume in the month after the quake.[2]

Given the widespread collapse of the publishing industry's core, it is little surprise that the effects were felt so quickly on its outer edges. Provincial book and magazine dealers, operating on slim profit margins and limited inventories, naturally grew concerned about how and when their disappearing stock might be replenished. On top of local consumer demand, they also had to contend with agents from Tokyo sent to scour the country's shelves in hopes of replacing the six to eight million volumes lost in Tokyo bookstore stock alone. Booksellers in Morioka were thus justified in fearing that the flow of cultural goods might soon dry up. That this was even considered a possibility says a great deal about the marketplace in which they were operating, one where a single center served as source of all cultural material deemed valuable and worthy of sale. A marketplace, that is, where centrality as a conceptual form—an emptiness that attracts and concentrates all things at once—had manifest itself as a physical location and was made to seem all the more permanent for it.[3] At least, that is, until the ground beneath it was abruptly torn asunder, revealing to many how uneven was the geography of interwar cultural production and thus how deleterious to the representation of nonmetropolitan places and times. As we will see, it was in the absence of a center, first real and then imagined, that there emerged some of the clearest statements on the ultimate consequences of spatial hegemony for artistic and literary expression.

While the earthquake caused anxiety amongst provincial booksellers, it was for other segments of the print culture industry a rare business opportunity. Several regional newspaper companies, filled with a new sense of urgency and importance, shipped out thousands of extra copies to help feed the news-hungry public. Sapporo's *Hokkai taimusu*, for instance, sent 10,000 copies to Tokyo just a week after the quake.[4] Two of Osaka's major newspapers, the *Ōsaka Mainichi shinbun* and the *Ōsaka Asahi shinbun*, having already established large subsidiaries in Tokyo, seized the chance to increase their market share. Within days they had sent not only newspapers, but also capital and machinery, to aid in the quick recovery of their partner firms.[5]

Amidst such maneuverings, some grew prophetic about the fate of the in-dustry as a whole. On September 8, a professor from the University of Tokyo told the *Tōkyō Nichinichi shinbun* that the general publishing world, at least for the foreseeable future, would probably be moving to Osaka, even if many from the "writing class" (*shippitsusha*) decided to stay behind. The article ran as a headline story and was picked up by provincial newspapers as far south as Fukuoka and as far north as Sapporo.[6] And though this Tokyo observer would soon recant his predictions, the idea that Osaka, a once powerful center of print culture, might reclaim its former glory was a common and persistent one in the months following the quake.[7] For many, it seemed the most logical choice given the city's second-tier but still formidable print-ing capacity. But such aspirations faded fast. By November, the majority of Tokyo's newspaper and magazine publishers were well on the road to recov-ery, if not fully operational. The book industry too would regain its former strength, though it would take a few months more.[8]

That the publishing industry recovered so quickly was both a matter of chance, as certain key infrastructural elements were spared destruction, and a testament to Tokyo's prior dominance. It also helped that many leaders in the business survived the quake unscathed. With their social networks and capital base largely intact, they had every reason to ensure that production resumed as quickly as possible, and in the same place as before. The field of production, even when it lacked its material center, continued to func-tion as if that center were still in place. Yet this did not prevent some from advocating a spatial reconfiguration of the field. Indeed, the void left by the quake, or at least the perception of a void, survived much longer in the mental geographies of writers and critics than it did in the minds of indus-try professionals. For the former, the event was an opportunity not only to "think" the very structure of the literary establishment, but to rethink that structure along spatial lines.[9]

In doing so, they were attempting to counteract nearly a century of structural changes that had helped to guarantee Tokyo's dominance over other major publishing centers. By the end of the eighteenth century, in fact, Edo had already surpassed Kyoto and Osaka in terms of number of publications, and its higher concentrations of book-lenders in the Bunka-Bunsei period (1804–1830), which led to higher demand, insured that Edo publishers wielded the greatest influence over the shape of the market as a whole.[10] After the Meiji Restoration (1868), increasing centralization and ra-tionalization of the market was encouraged by a rise in new forms of media (e.g., newspapers, magazines), advances in printing technologies designed for mass production, and Tokyo's evolution into a new center for learning. This last factor was especially crucial in that it generated an expanding market for textbooks and instructional materials that could meet the growing demands of the country's compulsory education system. Many of the major bookseller-publishers that opened shop in Tokyo in the 1870s and 1880s, while originally similar to their Edo predecessors in terms of what they sold and how they sold it, moved quickly to capture a share of this market. The publisher Kinkōdō, founded in 1875, was by far the most successful, and at one point accounted for nearly sixty percent of all textbooks produced. It is no accident, then, that it also published what is considered Japan's "first modern novel," Futabatei Shimei's *Ukigumo* (Floating Clouds, 1887–1889). The capital base that Kinkōdō acquired through textbook sales, and the network of sales agents and bookstores it established in the process, were necessary stepping stones for its entry into the riskier business of selling literary texts on a large scale.[11]

Another Tokyo company that helped lay the foundations of the post-Tokugawa field of literary production was Hakubunkan, founded in 1887. It took advantage of the growing network of provincial booksellers that the textbook boom had spawned and aggressively negotiated contracts with sellers willing to turn their shops into display cases for the publisher's expansive catalog of popular magazines and books. At a time when reading material had to be purchased by special order through a local bookstore or through direct contact with the publisher, Hakubunkan sought to have its products on the shelves at all times.[12] Market monopolization of this sort by a single Tokyo company did not bode well for the rest of the nation's publishers. Nor the fact that the owner, Ōhashi Sahei, presided over both a major printing company and a corporation with a large stake in the manufacture of Ōji paper.[13] Hakubunkan's success inspired another revolutionary change in the publishing industry: the corporatization of distribution under the *toritsugi* (intermediary agent) system. This system, which allowed distribution companies to create partnerships with publishers and bookstores to form a vertical monopoly, stood in marked contrast to the *hongae* (book exchange) system of late Tokugawa and early Meiji. Under the earlier model, bookseller-publishers from different regions exchanged an equal value of books and settled accounts at the end of the year, promoting a degree of mutual support between the different regional publishers and insuring a more balanced exchange of cultural capital. The *toritsugi* system, in contrast, tended to fix the flow of published goods from Tokyo outward to the provinces. As the number of publishers in Tokyo grew through the 1890s, and as Hakubunkan increased production of its best-selling magazines (e.g., *Taiyō*, *Shōnen sekai*, and *Bungei kurabu*), this new model of distribution grew to be quite profitable.[14] It also came to be monopolized by a few Tokyo companies that used the expanding railway infrastructure and standardized shipping costs to help expand their distribution networks.[15] While most of their business remained focused on newspapers and magazines until the 1920s, a fact attributable to the great number of book publishers in operation and their low volume of production, the structural changes they gave rise to accelerated the general trend toward industry centralization.

All of these changes hit provincial book publishers hard. Between 1889 and 1897, the number of books shipped by post from areas outside of Tokyo fell from eighty-four percent to just forty-nine percent of the total. By 1907 the number had risen back to fifty-four percent, but individual percentages for most prefectures stayed low, hovering around one percent.[16] And though the overall number of publications increased, nowhere was the increase as fast as in Tokyo. Only Osaka, which was responsible for ten percent of the total books shipped, managed to retain a substantial share of the pie; publishers there held on by cornering the market on historical fiction (*kōdan shōsetsu*), popular picture books (*akabon*), and how-to literature (*jitsuyōsho*). By 1922, market centralization had so intensified that the percentage of books published in Tokyo compared with the rest of the country reached nearly seventy percent, up from around forty percent just a decade earlier.[17] Were statistics available for literary works alone, the percentage would almost surely be higher. As Nagamine Shigetoshi has demonstrated in a survey of nineteen popular writers and their Meiji-period publications, the literary market was by 1900 already dominated by Tokyo publishers. Of the 1,095 books he surveys, eighty-six percent list Tokyo as the place of publication. Twelve percent list Osaka. A mere seventeen were published outside these two cities.[18] The unevenness of Japan's post-Restoration growth at the economic, social, and political levels was thus being mirrored at the level of cultural production. As the capital and infrastructure fueling this production increasingly concentrated itself in Tokyo, so too did the market for literary recognition and the expanding networks of writers who sustained it.

The reasons why so many aspiring writers ended up in Tokyo were naturally varied and complex, having as much to do with previous educational and employment opportunities as with naïve hopes about how the city might advance their artistic careers. Yet given the established practice by which up-and-coming writers acquired legitimacy through affiliation with mature writers or recognized coteries, it made sense to be where everyone else was. By the teens and twenties, as major publishing houses (many still dominant today) started operations in Tokyo, the uneven concentration of literati in the nation's capital intensified only further.[19] Now, whether the goal was to become a best-selling author or simply a recognized name in one of the elite literary journals, it seemed both natural and inevitable that one would have to pass through Tokyo. All too common was the sentiment expressed in the semi-autobiographical *Mumei sakka no nikki* (The Diary of the Unknown Author, 1918) by Kikuchi Kan (1888–1948), that to be a provincial student was a great disadvantage for making it in the *bundan* (literary establishment).[20] Geography, in the form of where a writer practiced his or her art, had wedged itself into the matrix of literary positions and position-takings that go toward shaping any field of cultural production.

Bleak though the situation was in the eyes of someone like Kikuchi's narrator, the notion that being in the provinces was akin to cultural banishment should not lead us to believe that everywhere outside of Tokyo was bereft of literary activity. Osaka, for one, had the resources and infrastructure to support ample networks of writers, especially as its newspaper industry remained competitive with Tokyo's until the mid-1930s. This was a critical venue for those still inclined to write for a medium increasingly less popular with high-brow artists.[21] The Kyoto publishing industry declined considerably after 1890, but preserved its own niche with the publication of religious material. (It also boasted one of the highest rates of bookstores per capita.) Even in areas far removed from these dominant nodes of Japanese print culture—whether the smaller towns and villages of the domestic sphere or the colonial and diasporic communities of the greater empire—writers and poets established thriving local networks of literary creation and appreciation.[22] Iwate too had by the 1910s and '20s seen the rise and fall of numerous literary outlets for the work of aspiring writers and members of poetry circles.[23] Some of these were organized purely for local interest; others, such as those in which influential poet and Iwate native Ishikawa Takuboku (1886–1912) was involved, served as pipelines to literary activity in Tokyo.

What sustained nonmetropolitan literary communities domestically, and facilitated their expansion overseas, was the increasing availability of, and access to, less costly forms of print media. Whereas the percentage of books published outside Tokyo decreased steadily throughout the Meiji

(1868–1912) and Taishō (1912–1926) periods, the percentage of non-Tokyo newspapers and magazines rose in nearly inverse proportion, jumping from sixty-five percent of total domestic output in 1912 to nearly eighty percent by 1923.[24] Though we cannot know how many of these served as outlets for literary material, some portion certainly helped meet the needs of local literati. One outlet that did cater to the needs of provincial poets and writers was the coterie magazine (*dōjin zasshi*), which gained in stature and legitimacy in the 1920s. In Hokkaidō, for instance, there was an explosion in the number of such magazines after 1918, from a paltry two or three in the years prior to a total of 19 in 1920, 34 in 1921, and 48 in 1926.[25] Looking at a roster of 195 *dōjin zasshi* assembled in April and May 1926 by the journal *Bungei shijō* (Literary Market), we find that over sixty percent bore non-Tokyo addresses.[26] Though often short-lived and produced in limited numbers, such a cheap and accessible form of media was essential to maintaining the kinds of literary networks that persisted in Izumo, Iwate, and other provincial regions. The success of these networks, particularly among poets of classical genres, can well be construed as the continuation of trends begun in the early Tokugawa period, when provincial elites grew increasingly involved in *waka*, *haiku*, and *kanshi* groups. In fact, Richard Torrance has shown that the early twentieth-century successors to such groups in Izumo, though influenced by a broader range of participants and styles, went about their business unaware of, or if aware then largely unconcerned with, new literary developments in Tokyo.[27] He argues that this was likely true for other regions as well, and thus paints an image of "modern Japanese literature" as formed from "a number of autonomous or semi-autonomous literary traditions based on culturally defined regions."[28]

While this formulation is important for helping to rethink the diversity of modern Japanese literary production, the loss of subtlety with regard to generic difference is problematic. For all the activity taking place in the provinces and overseas in the early part of the twentieth century, writers who sought recognition in contemporary genres (e.g., the novel, short fiction, modern poetry, and juvenile literature) had little choice but to engage with Tokyo in one form or another: whether by making personal connections to its literary scene, responding to its evolving trends, or placing one's work in the paths of distribution centered there.[29] It was fine to ignore literary happenings in the great metropolis, but not if one hoped to establish oneself as a professional writer. An expanding infrastructure for distribution, the increasing reach of Tokyo newspapers and magazines, a rise in the number of bookstores (3,000 in 1912, 6,000 in 1919, and roughly 10,000 by 1927)—all contributed to a growing sense that readers of Japanese, wherever they may be located, had increasing access to the body of "national" literature that emanated from Tokyo.[30] Yet these same factors made it so if someone wanted to contribute to this body, there was but one place to be. To remain in the provinces was to be limited to self-publishing, literary submission contests, the pages of the regional press, or a minor venue like the coterie magazine. These were a good place to start, but could only take one so far. No one was going to become nationally recognized as an Izumo writer living in Izumo.[31]

The Argument for Decentralization

This acute unevenness at the level of literary production was little affected by the earthquake, and would in fact grow more extreme in the years to follow. The temporary absence of a center did, nonetheless, prompt some writers and critics to contemplate alternative geographies of literary production. While their colleagues used the disaster to initiate debates over the social relevance of art, weigh the benefits of serious literature against popular entertainment, or embark on radically new modernist projects, these individuals channeled their angst into a desire for spatial reorganization. Their statements typically fell into two categories, arguing either for a transformation at the level of material infrastructure or for one at the level of literary content and subject matter. Both categories are useful for understanding contemporary perspectives on cultural unevenness and the way critics perceived the link between what Franco Moretti has described as "space *in* literature" (spaces as they exist in literary representation) and "literature *in* space" (the geography of where literary texts are written, read, and distributed).[32]

The first category of statements emerged in parallel with a line of argument that was especially pronounced in the regional press and that argued for the decentralization of key elements of the national infrastructure, including government, industry, and even education. For some individuals, the earthquake proved the folly of placing all one's institutional eggs in one basket, and it was felt that future catastrophe could be averted by building up the provinces (*chihō*) in tandem with the reconstruction of Tokyo. The same reasoning was applied to the cultural sphere. In early October, for instance, just one month after the quake, a commentator for Osaka's *Sunday*

Mainichi wrote on the literary establishment and the reasons why its base (*dan*) had come to be fixed in Tokyo. It naturally had to do with the city's status as cultural center of the nation. Now, however, this arrangement no longer seemed sensible.

> What we've come to understand with this earthquake is how disadvantageous it is to have the whole of the nation's culture centered in Tokyo while other provinces (*chihō*) remain, as per their name, "provincial." The quake has made clear that as we revive Tokyo, we must also invigorate the "provinces." The time to do it is now and we must begin from here in the Kyoto-Osaka (Keihan) region.[33]

He went on to propose the immediate formation of a literary base unique to the Kyoto-Osaka area, a project he saw both as the responsibility of local writers and as ultimately beneficial to Japanese literature as a whole.

A month later, the veteran critic and playwright Tsubouchi Shōyō (1859–1935), also writing for the *Sunday Mainichi*, offered his own suggestion for how to spatially reconfigure the literary field. For him, the way forward lay not in a mere shift of artistic activity to Osaka, a city that, being too business-oriented and matter-of-fact, was in any case unsuited to such a noble charge. A much broader geographical dispersion was necessary.

> At the very least, writers and artists should not now swarm, like all seem wont to do, just to larger cities like Osaka and Kyoto. They should take this opportunity to split off toward Tōhoku or Shinetsu, Kyūshū or even Nagoya, carrying with them both the ambition and insistence to dismantle cultural centralization (*bunkateki chūō shūken*) as it once existed. That is to say, they should disperse to [regional] posts and compete with one another, establishing new centers of culture at locales far and wide. When they do, then surely they will be capable of making the kinds of influential contributions (*kōken*) offered by the great domainal and clan leaders in the days of the Shogunate.[34]

Implicitly linking the diversity and richness of political expression in the Tokugawa era with decentralized rule, Tsubouchi suggests that a field of cultural production similarly decentralized would foster a spirit of inter-regional competition and exchange no less dynamic. It was only a few weeks earlier that the proletarian writer and future chronicler of the proletarian literary movement, Yamada Seizaburō (1896–1987), had proposed an analogous decentering in the pages of the *Fukuoka Nichinichi shinbun* (Fukuoka Daily Newspaper). Fearing what would have happened to the literary world had more members of the *bundan* been lost in the fire and rubble, he encouraged the creation of additional literary centers in cities like Kyoto, Nagoya, Fukuoka, and Sapporo. This, he argued, would promote not only the wider diffusion of literature, but would also allow for a truly native art (*kyōdo geijutsu*) to flower in each location.[35]

In early 1924, by which time Tokyo's reinstatement as the nation's literary center was no longer a matter for debate, some writers and critics still imagined that a shift in spatial structure, or at least a more optimal balance of power, might yet be achieved. The Tokyo-based critic Kojima Tokuya, for instance, called in January for a native-place literature (*kyōdo bungei*) that could stand against the literature of the capital. Its creation was to be facilitated by local literary groups (*jichitai-teki bungei shūdan*) that, independent of the central *bundan*, would offer an outlet for provincial writers whose passion and zeal had heretofore been snubbed by the "indifference" shown them by the Tokyo literary establishment. The article, which ran in the literary arts section of the *Iwate nippō*, concluded with prayers for a day when provincial artists would eventually overwhelm the literature of the current age.[36] One week later, the *Nippō* published another essay calling for a post-quake provincialization (*chihōka*) of the *bundan*, this time by writer and accomplished member of that *bundan*, Kanō Sakujirō (1885–1941). Arguing that an art with real roots could only emerge from those who fully observed and understood the lifestyle of their respective regions, he himself would return to write about his native Ishikawa Prefecture in the year after the quake.[37]

Absent from these later essays was any sense that the geographical position of the *bundan* was still in flux. No longer a question of how to eliminate or pluralize the center, the concern now lay with how to promote literary activity outside a place whose dominance was once again unassailable. This shift in emphasis marks a transition to the second category of statements that are of interest here, namely those focused on literary form and content as opposed to the geographical structure of the market. That there were some who thought to transform this structure at all, however, is remarkable given the state of affairs at the time: a field of production in which the material infrastructure for producing texts was coterminous with the physical location of most of its producers. A field where those who wanted to join had little choice, as both Kojima and Kanō note, but to congregate in Tokyo with all the other writers, publishers, printers, and distributors; where success was determined not only by the amounts of symbolic and social capital that one had, but by "spatial capital" as well. In fact, if the latter is understood as the measure of a writer's social or physical proximity to the primary nodes of production—a variable correlating relative status in the *bundan* to geographical location—then it was arguably this form of capital that writers in the 1920s had to acquire before all others. As a "free pass" granted to any with the will and means to move to Tokyo, it was best utilized early, and often, than not at all.

With the center in ruins, however, and this pass rendered temporarily void, a new space was opened for writers and critics to both "think" the geographical structure of the field and imagine, as an alternative, a field where spatial capital might be distributed more evenly; where it might be diversified in ways that made it equally valuable, and thus equally insignificant, whether one was a writer in Kantō, Kansai, Kyūshū, or Tōhoku. The quake provided, in other words, an opportunity to argue for a more even development of literary production and for a definition of "Japanese literature" that refused to substitute the center for the totality. Such arguments soon lost momentum due to Tokyo's quick recovery, but even as they waned they gave way to a second kind of proposal for how spatial unevenness might be overcome. If a geographical restructuring of the field was impossible, some reasoned, then why not redistribute spatial capital by transforming the aims and scope of literature itself.

Their proposals, which generally took the form of critical essays, appeared in both Tokyo and regional media for nearly a year after the quake. And while their ideological and rhetorical approaches differed, all sought to define a mode of literary production whose center lay outside the urban core. This geographical bias inscribed itself in the very names of the modes proposed: *kyōdo geijutsu* (native place art), *kyōdo bungei* (native place literature), *chihōshugi* (regionalism), *tochishugi* (land-ism), *tsuchi no geijutsu* (art of the soil) and *nōmin geijutsu* (farmers' art). Shifting the aesthetic gaze away from Tokyo, of course, hardly constituted a radical move. Since the late 1880s, the village and provincial home had served for writers as objects of nostalgic lament and pastoral sentiment, and as a means to critique urban life.[38] After the quake, however, the very idea of a nonurban mode of cultural production came to harbor a radical new sense of relevance and urgency. Critics drew a parallel between the structure of socio-material space (the field of production) on the one hand and the structure of representational space (literary texts) on the other, and the hope was that by redrawing the contours of the latter, it might be possible to smooth out the spatial inequities inherent in the former. This was a chance to reapportion the representation of space across the axis that divided urban from rural, capital from province, and abstract universal space from particular locale.

Some set out to redraw these contours through a critique of "city art" (*toshi no geijutsu*) and "city literature" (*tokai bungei*), invoking some of the hackneyed antiurban refrains that gained strength in the months after the quake. These refrains, which had always depicted the metropolis as a breeding ground for depravity and frivolity, seemed now to have the will of heaven on their side. Poet Shirotori Seigo (1890–1973), while not convinced that the earthquake embodied divine punishment, nevertheless felt that an attachment to material goods and a lack of "artistic objectivity" had contributed to the needless loss of life in the chaotic days following the initial tremors.[39] The inhumane, and in some cases violent, attitudes shown by Tokyoites were proof to Shirotori that the artistic spirit (*geijutsuteki seishin*) of city residents had to be raised to a higher plane. And this meant that they would have to be nourished on something other than the debased urban literature of old.

> The ease with which literature has been talked about after the quake as either powerless or in decline proves how fundamental city literature has been in shaping the central currents of present-day [literature]. "City Literature" is a literature that affirms urban civilization and urban bourgeois life, taking hedonism (*kyōraku*), decadence (*haitai*), and vulgarity (*tsūzoku*) as its primary elements. . . . The destruction of the nation's core city of Tokyo is a tragedy that announces the collapse, or at least cessation, of such literature, its object of reference lost. But we are anyway better off without it as it has existed until now.[40]

In its place, Shirotori proposed a literature born of a unity between nature and civilization, a fresh new kind of city literature that would incorporate the simple and colorful qualities of rural life. If the literature of Tokyo had to this point defined the field as a whole, it was now time for it to be transformed by what the city itself had relegated to the margins.

A month before Shirotori's essay appeared, a critic writing for the *Shinano Mainichi shinbun* (Shinano Daily Newspaper) also lashed out at the materialism of city life and all art forged from urban environs. But whereas Shirotori's reformist spirit remained confined to city limits, this critic took up a position on the outside and drew a line between the deadlocked artistic movements of Tokyo and a newly revived art born wholly of the rural village.

> What the countryside (*den'en*) needs is a movement for village art (*nōson geijutsu*) centered on the farm village (*nōson*). Village art is strange and rather

plain compared with city art, but this quality is none other than the root of the pure heart of human nature—indeed, the root of all art. . . . To those who would say that modern life and its anxieties should be thought of universally, irrespective of categories like country and city, I ask: if true art is not born of where one lives or of one's self, then how is a supreme art to be born of some obscure world object?[41]

Expressed here is the notion that an art not born of its surroundings ends up missing something essential, that it fails to fully represent those for whom it speaks. How could a city art blindly imitated by rural inhabitants ever hope to capture their own particular experiences? Moreover, the critic declares, is not village art the truest means for expressing authentic humanhood? The logical reversal enacted here, by which particularism comes to stand in for a new universal ideal, is one that would appear frequently in post-quake discourse of this kind.

Other writers and critics, adopting a less hoary style of argument, looked to the country's rural laborers and sought to grant them representational equality in the field of literary production. Kanō Sakujirō, for example, in the previously cited essay from February 1924, lamented that centralization had forced a great many aspiring writers to move to the unfamiliar streets of Tokyo. The consequence for literary content was that these newcomers, who could hardly be expected to understand the "true Tokyo life," inevitably focused too narrowly on matters of the self. When they tried then to write of the provincial locales with which they were most familiar, the results tended to be equally solipsistic, verging toward the overtly nostalgic or the purely imaginative. Tokyo's centrality had, in effect, created a disjuncture between subjective knowledge and the place of writing, leaving both center and margins destitute of authentic modes of representation. Kanō suggested in response that writers return to their native environs and learn to observe them with greater accuracy, and that they address such topics as the lives of tenant farmers (kosakunin). Such a strategy, he added, would likely do more to further the goals of the proletarian movement than a focus on the urban worker.[42] A week after Kanō's piece ran in the Iwate nippō, an essay by a local Iwate critic, Watanabe Minji, expressed a similar desire to cultivate a "native-place art." It too would seek inspiration in the actual lives of Japan's farmers and was positioned against the recent trend in the literary arts to focus incessantly on the self. Watanabe felt that this new art should depict the power and suffering of farmers as a means to interrogate the very form (*keishiki*) of humanity itself, and he urged local writers and poets not to follow slavishly upon the heels of Tokyo's established artists.[43]

In March of the same year, Tokyo-based writer and critic Nakazawa Shizuo commented on the phenomenon of *kyōdo geijutsu* for the *Tokyo Asahi*, praising it as a crucial counterweight to the work of "bourgeois writers" who had come to embody the materialistic and imitative tendencies of the "urbanite form" (*tokaijin-gata*). Although this form was thought by Nakazawa to have been smashed to bits by the earthquake, he had since watched it revive to become the driving force behind these bourgeois writers and their material. That this material now served to represent Japan's literary world as a whole filled him with indignation, and it frightened him to think of how such a literature—lacking truth (*shinjitsu*), righteousness (*seigi*), and hope—might possibly influence the muddled and directionless mentality of the people (*minshū*). What was needed was a *kyōdo geijutsu* both attuned to the consciousness of the rural proletariat and capable of piercing the very flesh and blood of the "new farmer's" (*atarashii nōmin*) way of life. Not an art that merely dressed up an urban mentality in peasant clothes, as with the so-called "peasant novels" (*nōmin shōsetsu*) of recent years. No, this was to be an art that, by shining light on the lives of tradition-bound farmers, would help to bring about their own social liberation and encourage a "spiritual homecoming" of the people.[44]

Locating new forms of literary authenticity in the marginalized spaces of the rural, and then arguing for their equal and accurate representation in the field, reached perhaps its most intense expression in the writings of Fukushi Kōjirō (1889–1946). After nearly two decades in Tokyo as a poet and literary critic, Fukushi was prompted by the earthquake to return to his native Aomori Prefecture, where in January he began waving the banner of a new "regionalism" (*chihōshugi*). Supported by funds from a prominent local banker, he set up a Regional Culture Society (Chihō Bunka Sha) and issued a manifesto on the importance of "promoting the unique qualities of each locality in each of Japan's regions, so that we might witness the flourishing of domestic culture."[45] The manifesto, reportedly mailed to thousands across the country, also promised a series of monthly pamphlets for the next 100 months, a monthly lecture series, a research group on folk customs and poetry, and a monthly journal. Little of this came to pass though and only two pamphlets were ever printed. Yet Fukushi did manage to get his message into the pages of the regional and national press, where he would broadcast it repeatedly over the next two years. One of his most important essays on "native-place literature" was serialized in Tokyo's *Miyako shinbun* in February 1924, and opened in his characteristically strident tone.

> The supreme essence of native-place literature (*kyōdo bungaku*) can be captured by the single "ism" of "regionalism" (*chihōshugi*), a word I employ here for what is likely the first time in the history of our nation's thought. In the realm of literature, regionalism signals a declaration to thoroughly repel the power and reign of the center with provincial taste (*shumi*), emotion (*kanjō*), and spirit (*seishin*)—a declaration to stand utterly and defiantly against [the center] from a position of provincial independence.[46]

His geographical allegiances thus defined, Fukushi proceeded to argue for the ontological unity of knowledge and place and declared that the ideas and literature born of a particular environment can truly be appreciated only by those who share close ties with that environment. "No literary masterpiece," he remarked, "is universal. Its absolute value is limited to a particular kind of person. Is that not why we turn away from the great literature of the world to read the wretched Japanese works (*dasaku*) of the present day? And is that not why, disgusted by the literature of the central *bundan*, we turn to support the no-name literary magazines that share an environment the same [as our own]?"[47]

Convinced that environment and expression were irrefutably linked, Fukushi directed his anger toward centralization (*chūō shūken*) and what he saw as its degrading effects on Japanese literature as a whole. In his view, it was the concentration of literary activity in Tokyo that had caused the "illogical presence" of regional particularity—elsewhere defined as "the essence deep within literature that is explainable only by regionalism"—to go undernourished and ignored. Or when not ignored, then expressed in artistic forms (e.g., "local color" and "peasant novels") intended for audiences in the center.[48] The result was that the literature of a single region had come to assume, to the detriment of all other regions, the status of a universal. This high degree of centralization was, Fukushi insisted, not in any way natural or inherent to literary production, as should be apparent to anyone who looked at other parts of the world.

> The literature of Ireland has no relation to the capital of Great Britain. As for Germany, the low-lying provinces are distinctly separate from the highland areas. In Russia, Moscow and the prerevolutionary capital of St. Petersburg make superb rivals. America has nothing that can even be called a literary

center. And Paris! What claim to sovereignty does Paris have!? Does it not have the most extensive market for regional literature anywhere, including [literature] from within France, of course, but also from the entire world?[49]

Disregarding their veracity, these observations do illustrate how convinced Fukushi was that the present geography of the literary field in Japan was abnormally skewed as compared with the rest of the world. He argued that in order to overcome this distortion, regions would have to develop both for themselves and from the respective grounds that defined them so as to acquire a new self-awareness of their unique qualities. Thus awakened, they could then begin to explore and cultivate literatures of their own. "Rise Osaka and Nagoya! Stand up Kanazawa and Sapporo, Gunma and Ibaragi. You too Hakata, Kōchi, Sendai, and Nagano. In the past I have advocated sentimentalism (*kanjōshugi*) and traditionalism (*dentōshugi*); here I bring to light a part of regionalism, intimately related to these first two movements, and hope for some public response."[50]

As it turned out, the response he got was far from enthusiastic. Few in the *bundan* paid Fukushi much attention, in fact, except to criticize him as anachronistic and traditionalist, a reputation he had earned for himself even before the earthquake.[51] In his native Aomori, where he struggled to get his movement off the ground, he was taken to task in the pages of the local press for his "petit-bourgeois and counterrevolutionary" attitude by left-leaning thinkers busy enacting their own regionalist culture experiments.[52] Despite the negative reception, Fukushi's ideas are emblematic of the logic that drove much post-quake regionalist discourse, capturing as they do the impulse in this discourse to see the centralized geography of socio-material space (i.e., literature *in* space) as somehow responsible for distorting representational space (i.e., space *in* literature) and rendering it hopelessly out of balance. The impulse, that is, to see centralization of the market as responsible for creating a body of literature in which certain forms, styles, and narrative perspectives were held up as universal norms merely by virtue of their being the dominant practices of the center. For many critics, as we have seen, the most obvious way to resolve this disparity was to posit various kinds of essential difference in the spaces outside the core and argue for their equal representation while also insisting that this equalization take place at the hands of writers physically and psychologically connected to those spaces.

In some respects, especially in Fukushi's case, the solutions that these critics devised prefigure the discourse of romantic nationalism in the 1930s and the "overcoming modernity" debates of 1942, except here the focus was strictly on subnational spaces instead of Japan as a whole. We could also say that they have the scent of the "neorealist aesthetics" and "national language" that Pascale Casanova identifies as the "preeminent form of the literary heteronomy experienced by writers in literary spaces under political domination."[53] Significant as these parallels are, it is important not to conflate these distinct strategies for producing literary and cultural difference and thereby lose sight of the specific historical intervention that Fukushi and others believed they were making. In arguing for the significance of *where* in Japan a writer practiced his or her art, they were suggesting that even a marginal node in the nation's centrally dominated array could be strategically and productively occupied. If writers who lacked spatial capital had heretofore responded by chasing after that capital in Tokyo or by emulating one of the various literary trends that competed for attention in the central marketplace, now was the time for an alternative approach. It was time to say something other than what was being said in Tokyo—to incorporate, as Moretti puts it, local material and local narrative voice into forms whose stylistic and spatial boundaries were marked or patrolled elsewhere—by rethinking a lack of spatial capital as a negotiable position from which to confront, appropriate, or reorient literary forms and practices of the center.[54] Critics had difficulty articulating how this negotiation would play out and what exactly it might produce, an issue discussed in more detail in Chapter Seven, but that they even believed such negotiation to be possible points to a coming to consciousness of nonmetropolitan literary production as harboring a radically new value.

Merely to talk of this possibility was also, of course, not the same as addressing questions about literary infrastructure that would have to be answered if any leveling of the playing field was to occur. Where would the small provincial networks of publishers and authors gain the strength and financial support they needed to sustain a "native place art"? Would they be able to capture the attention of readers who had their eyes focused on what came out of the metropolis? When young upstart novelist Kawabata Yasunari (1899–1972) entered the debate in August 1924, he observed that a provincial literature was simply unsustainable given how media distribution was then structured. Literary material moved from Tokyo outward, not the other direction, and until the triumvirate of "creator, consumer, and benefactor" came together in a particular region, that region would have no real "native-place art" of which to speak. In the meantime, the only viable option was to nurture those venues—the *dōjin zasshi*, the *kairan zasshi* (circulation magazines), the *tanka* and *haiku* associations, the "little magazines"—capable of supporting an independent regional literature. A literature in which provincial writers "represented their lives through their own eyes" to provide a "refreshing tonic" to the disaffected urbanite and "a challenge to the assumed universality of metropolitan culture."[55] Such are the opinions, of course, of a writer who was already benefiting from the opportunities for literary advancement afforded by being in the center. Did he believe that those in the provinces would patiently bear the cross of their second-tier status until their moment had arrived? Who would be the one to decide that this moment had come? And most critically, to borrow from Raymond Williams, what was to be the specific "social language," or "the particular form of socio-cultural organization," that would render their literary stance distinct from others?[56] If Kawabata was skeptical about the chances for success, and largely silent as to how it might be achieved, there were some provincials who, just as he had hoped, identified with their localities and sought out concrete ways to generate a *different discourse*—a different literary product—from their perceived positions of subnational marginality. Miyazawa Kenji, who published his first collection of *dōwa* not long after Kawabata's essay, was one such individual.

PART TWO

The Marginal Case
and the Texture of Locality

CHAPTER THREE

Toward a Provincializing Literary Production

Exploring the Marginal Case

As he stepped into his favorite bookshop one cold December day, ducking under the icicle-laden eaves and sliding back the glass-paneled wooden door, Mori Sōichi (1907–1999) found himself in warm and familiar surroundings. The hustle and bustle of Morioka's main commercial district, the to and fro of its shopkeepers, tradesmen, and bankers, receded slowly into the winter chill as this young middle school student greeted the owner and scanned the shelves for something of interest. It was then that his eyes lit upon the unexpected.

> The first time I saw it was at the Hokuryūkan bookstore, which was managed by the newspaper dealer Tōhokudō on Nakanohashi street in Morioka. . . . On entering Hokuryūkan there was a shelf on the left containing all the newly published books; on the right were two large bookcases with glass doors, inside of which non-sellers like dictionaries and old compendiums of law as well as some surplus items had been stacked tightly. In front of these cases was a table with picture books, and placed in the walkway between were some boxes and a bicycle. The glass cases looked as if they were being used for storage.

Perhaps the manager predicted from the start that the book wouldn't sell, or perhaps the number of volumes he'd been asked to sell were too many, but nearly twenty to thirty copies of *The Restaurant of Many Orders* were crammed into one of these cases.

Each time I went to look I couldn't help noticing that the number of copies wasn't decreasing at all. It started to get to me and I began to wonder why people weren't buying this beautifully designed book written by an Iwate native. At the time, most books put out by Iwate authors were rather haggard and unsightly. Having said this, however, I too didn't buy it. I read all of it while standing in front of that dark glass case.[1]

The year was 1924 and the book that so caught Mori's eye belonged to none other than Miyazawa Kenji. It was a handsome, Western-style volume that had been released earlier in the month by Toryō Shuppanbu (soon renamed Kōgensha), a tiny publisher of agricultural textbooks based just across town and a short walk from Morioka's central train terminal. Bound in cotton paper, the book's dark indigo cover was artfully decorated with an illustration of a snowy rural landscape; into its cardboard skin had been carved the title in striking gold letters: *Iihatov dōwa: Chūmon no ōi ryōriten* (Tales from Iihatov: The Restaurant of Many Orders).

Mori's recollection, though written three decades after the fact, offers a rare glimpse of literary consumption in a place where it typically goes unnoticed. Here, at a small booksellers in a mid-sized provincial capital (the population of Morioka at the time was roughly 45,000), a local resident landed upon what, in retrospect, he would compare to a diamond in the rough. But on that cold December day, it served only to confound expectations. Noting a marked contrast with the imperfect and shoddily assembled books that he had grown accustomed to seeing from area publishers, Mori was equally surprised to find that so many copies of this attractive volume had been left to gather dust in the case for low-turnover items. Fairly routine observations, to be sure, but had the book not disrupted the familiar space of the Hokuryūkan bookstore in this way, Mori might never have noticed it at all. Not only were local publications not supposed to look as this one, new items were not expected to move to the marginal bookcase so quickly and in such great numbers. Something in the structure of the literary marketplace made it so that this scenario could only appear to him as an anomaly.

By all accounts, sales of the book were abysmal. Of the 1,000 copies in the initial print run, Miyazawa was obliged to take 100 as royalty and to purchase another 200 with money borrowed from his father. Much of the remaining stock had to be given away. Some went as gifts to friends and fellow poets, some gathered dust in the home of the publisher, still others took a more circuitous route: they were sent in sets of ten to prefectural elementary schools, together with a request that interested buyers send in payment of their own accord.[2] Although attempts were made to market the book through standard channels of advertising, this too failed to attract interest from the reading public. Originally promoted as just the first in a twelve-volume series, *The Restaurant of Many Orders* ultimately became Miyazawa's first, and last, collection of *dōwa*. For the rest of his short life, the work, while recognized by a handful of friends and local literati, remained both unknown and unread.

As such, it initially fell into a peculiar segment of what Margaret Cohen calls the "great unread"—the extensive body of "forgotten texts" whose popularity has succumbed to the shifting tides of literary history, along with the particular "aesthetics" that made them coherent to readers.[3] Peculiar because the text has followed a reverse trajectory: forgotten before it was even read, it has since gone on to become universally known and appreciated, avoiding the fate of that "99.5% of literature" that vanishes with time.[4] In trying to recover its original moment of reception, then, we must do the opposite of what Cohen does for the sentimental novel in France, which is to search for the genre's lost aesthetic. We must instead historicize the temporary fact of the text's *not mattering*. This means, to borrow Bourdieu's terminology, trying to understand why Miyazawa's literary position-taking (i.e., the style, form, and content of the text) failed to spark a response and what role, if any, his literary position (i.e., his degree of social and economic capital) played in that failure.[5] It is only by treating the text as a "failure" first that we can account for the historical conditions that initially kept it in—and then later drew it out from—obscurity.

Yet if Bourdieu helps to plot the points by which Miyazawa's failure can be graphed, his theoretical model of social change neglects the variable of most interest to this study: geography. It does so by tending to reduce physical space to an abstract plane where social processes unfold and upon which social relations are then mapped. Though the resulting contour lines provide a detailed, if somewhat schematic, representation of the social sphere, they fail to account for the impact of geography itself and the real distances separating actors and objects. A central aim of this book is to explore what Bourdieu's method of analyzing positions and position-takings, for all its reliance on spatial metaphors, can gain from being tied down to the physical ground it so often elides. This is accomplished in part through the notion of "spatial capital," which was introduced in the preceding chapter.[6] Given a field of production that consists of a chain of people and institutions (coteries, publishers, distributors, paper manufacturers) distributed unevenly, and hierarchically, in physical space, spatial capital is a variable we can use to first acknowledge the geographical distance of a work or author from the chain's most central and powerful nodes, and then account for the real effects of this distance for literary form and acts of cultural production. As we saw in Chapter Two, the continued concentration of literary production in Tokyo in the early twentieth century meant that one's physical distance from the metropolis had a significant impact on one's potential to enter the ranks of the literary establishment. Not only did it cause one to be forever late to the table of mass media production upon which rapid changes in literary style and form unfolded (one was lucky to see even a fraction of what was laid out), distance also made it difficult to offer up a dish of one's own.[7] Judging by the numbers alone, provincial literary publication was itself an anomaly, at least as far as book publication was concerned. In the case of children's fiction (dōwa), consider that between 1921 and 1925, at the height of the so-called "dōwa boom," 45 (or just nine percent) of 495 volumes published with the word dōwa in the title originated outside Tokyo. Of these, thirty-two hailed from Osaka, seven from Kyoto, two from Nagoya, and just one each from Morioka, Tottori, Kumamoto, and Seoul.[8]

The story of how *The Restaurant of Many Orders* came to be is itself revealing of what provincial publishers were up against in trying to compete in such an uneven market. When Toryō Shuppanbu decided to take on the collection, it had been in operation only a few months, and had no experience publishing literary material. Owners Oikawa Shirō and Chikamori Yoshikatsu, both graduates of the Morioka Higher School of Agriculture and Forestry, dreamed up the tiny publishing outfit after a chance reunion in 1923. They began by selling a simple pamphlet on pest control alongside an insecticide engineered by Chikamori, but quickly expanded their catalog of practical agricultural guides.[9] Making use of contacts with former classmates and alumni who were now teaching at agricultural schools around the country, they also built up a reliable sales network. In fact, it was after a sales visit to the nearby Hanamaki School of Agriculture in December 1923 that they came to know Miyazawa and first heard of the dōwa manuscripts he had been compiling over the past few years. It was perhaps out of deference to him as a senior alumnus, or perhaps out of sheer entrepreneurial spirit, that they immediately agreed to publish the stories, leveraging the capital

PROVINCIALIZING LITERARY PRODUCTION 59

from their previous successes to finance their entry into the far riskier trade in literary texts.

Having agreed to the project, Oikawa and Chikamori were faced with the task of turning Miyazawa's manuscripts into a marketable commodity. The first obstacle was the author's own particular ideas about the appearance of the final product: the quality of the printing, the style of the paper, the look and feel of the front cover. Miyazawa desired the kind of text that would not immediately betray its provincial origins. His requests were by no means excessive, but they were certainly difficult and costly to honor in Morioka, where printing technologies lagged far behind the capital. The second obstacle was marketing. The sales network that Toryō Shuppanbu had established was hardly suited to the promotion of children's fiction, nor could it depend on sales in Morioka to generate interest elsewhere. The structure of the marketplace, as we have seen, meant that non-Tokyo publications, especially literary ones, found it a challenge to navigate their way upstream. The only truly viable option was to start out from the source.[10]

Fortunately, Oikawa had an acquaintance in Tokyo, Yoshida Shunzō, who was both a fellow Iwate native and someone with experience in the publishing business. He agreed to become the book's printer and distributor, using the opportunity as an excuse to quit his job at a large textbook publisher and start his own small company, Tōkyō Kōgensha.[11] Once a contract was signed, various personal and financial complications delayed the process for several months, but by the end of 1924 the *dōwa* collection was ready for sale. Here, however, another obstacle presented itself. Tōkyō Kōgensha was not yet a member of the Tokyo Book-Trade Union (Tōkyō shosekishō kumiai) and would not become one until April 1926.[12] Since 1919 the union—whose members consisted of booksellers, publishers, and small-scale distributors—had written into their constitution an article stating that members were not allowed to carry out transactions with nonmember companies.[13] As failure to comply did not bode well for one's standing in the organization, and could potentially cut one off from other suppliers, booksellers may have been dissuaded from doing business with Tōkyō Kōgensha at the time of the volume's release. *The Restaurant of Many Orders* also never appeared in the union's monthly listing of new publications.

More will be said about the production history of Miyazawa's text in the next chapter, but what should already be apparent is that the uneven spatial organization of the late-Taishō literary infrastructure played no small part in the book's failed reception. A lack of spatial capital may not have been the only reason for its failure, but distance from the center went a long way to limiting its access to the marketplace and to the social machinery of value attribution. It is not difficult to imagine how it, along with so many other provincial publications, slid so easily into the vast ocean of the "great un-read." The more important question raised by all this, however, especially if we follow Casanova's assertion that "the hierarchy of the literary world . . . gives literature its very form,"[14] is what impact these conditions of spatial inequality had on the particular literary position-takings adopted by Miya-zawa. Or on any writer who chose to write from a position of geographic marginality. How, in other words, was the lack of spatial capital reflected at the level of form, content, or even the paratextual posturing common to modern print capitalism (e.g., prefaces, advertisements, epilogues)?

The question is posed not in the interest of a spatial determinism that views the physical site of authorship as a primary influence on content and form. There is no reason why it should matter any more than genre, class, ethnicity, or gender. But there is also no reason why spatial location—the triangulation of a writer's position in the field of production, in physical space, and in the symbolic places of the social imaginary (e.g., city, country, region, nation, empire)—should matter any less. In recent decades, when space or geography have been taken up by critics of Japanese literature, discussion has often centered on representation (i.e., space *in* literature).[15] More recent scholarship has expanded on this work by showing how par-ticular kinds of spaces (the metropolis, the native-place, the suburb, the co-lonial city) influenced literary style and content even as they became nodes for entire bodies of literary discourse. As valuable as these studies have been, they rarely give attention to the geography of the field of production itself. Tokyo so dominates this field as its singular publishing center that its cen-trality is left unmarked or unacknowledged, and the literature produced there allowed to fill in for all that is modern, avant-garde, or representative of the national canon.

To eclipse the specificity of Tokyo literary production with labels like "modern" or "Japanese" is to engage in a deception that equates that pro-duction with a space seen to be coterminous with the nation (i.e., it equates a single locus of production with the entire space in which the texts are assumed to circulate). This in turn places that locus at the leading tempo-ral edge of all Japanese language literature production, making literature produced elsewhere appear as derivative, provincial, traditional, or sec-ondary. As capable, in other words, only of repeating or reproducing what has already happened in Tokyo. It is thus condemned to the fate of being stuck forever in what Meaghan Morris calls "the project of positive unoriginality."[16] Or conversely, it is construed as far enough from the center of production to warrant a category all its own (i.e., regional literature)—an isolated particular set outside and against an implied universal. Here I propose a third way of viewing things. Rather than subsume all writers, provincial or otherwise, beneath the same national umbrella, or cordon them off into distinct regional pockets, why not foreground their spatial location in a way that "provincializes" the domestic field as a whole?[17] This means, on the one hand, de-naturalizing and decentering Tokyo so that it appears as but one node among many, as but the most powerful and dominant point in a larger array. On the other, it means thinking about "modernity" not as the sole possession of the metropolis, but as a temporal moment experienced, even if unevenly, by all who occupy the same socially unified space. To provincialize the field is, in essence, to bring geographically disparate elements into relation with each other on the same spatio-temporal plain.

One benefit of this provincializing perspective is that it allows us to think of spatial location as engendering certain strategic possibilities, and thus as a possible site of dialogue between Tokyo and non-Tokyo literary production. The latter is no longer to be confined to the merely imitative or secondary, but can be seen as potentially engaged in conversation with Tokyo even if writers and publishers there were not inclined to talk back, or even lend an ear. Tokyo too is relativized as a particular site, albeit an internally fragmented and spatially diverse one, where narratives unique to its position as an urban metropole and national center were produced.[18] A second benefit is that literary production outside of Tokyo can be construed as synchronous with developments in the capital (i.e., fully part of the modern moment), even while retaining a degree of difference owing to the particularities of geographic, social, and economic location. A provincializing mode of analysis will, of course, have more relevance for some acts of literary production than others; spatial location can be ignored just as easily as it can be capitalized upon.[19] But what we find in the glass case at the Hokuryūkan bookstore is a work whose conditions of production intersect with content and form in ways that demand such a mode. And to the extent that this mode makes visible the spatial inequities inherent to any marketplace, it reminds us that the physical distances that originally obtained between literary texts, authors, and publishers—and that tend to be flattened out by the organizing power of the archive—once had real historical consequences.

Venturing into Dōwa *Literature*

To understand what those consequences were for Miyazawa, we must now inquire into the spatial organization of the literary arena he was stepping into. His decision to label his stories as *dōwa* signaled his intent to compete in what was a newly emergent subgenre in the field of juvenile literature (*jidō bungaku*).[20] Its official start is generally considered to be the publication in July 1918 of *Akai tori* (Red Bird), a magazine for young children founded by author and critic Suzuki Miekichi (1882–1936). He saw himself as a pioneer in the movement to purge children's reading material of the secular (*sezokuteki*) and the vulgar (*gebita*) and to create stories that protected and nurtured the child's purity (*junsei*). His genius lay less in this call for purity, however, than in the decision he made to take advantage of a recent trend toward authorship of "original" children's stories by established writers. In 1910, writer Ogawa Mimei (1882–1961) had published *Akai fune: otogibanashi-shū* (Red Boat: A Collection of *Otogibanashi*), a volume of lyrical tales that took the inner life of the "modern" child as their subject and infused it with a romantic sensibility. The stories, rooted as they were in the world of fantasy, marked a significant departure from the highly moralistic and educational narratives that had previously been composed under the label *otogibanashi*.[21] In 1913, publisher Jitsugyō no Nihonsha continued the trend when it contracted five well-known authors (Shimazaki Tōson, Tokuda Shūsei, Yosano Akiko, Tayama Katai, and Nogami Yaeko) to produce novel-length children's stories written in a naturalist style. The venture was ultimately unsuccessful, but the fact that the publisher of a very successful magazine for young boys, *Nihon shōnen* (Japanese Boys), had invested in such a project surely made it easier for accomplished writers to reconsider the potential of juvenile fiction as a worthy endeavor and even a legitimate art form.[22] When *Akai tori* appeared a few years later, a space was opened up to explore this potential even further. Not only did Suzuki vow to recruit such literary giants as Tōson, Tokuda, Izumi Kyōka, and Akutagawa Ryūnosuke, he was also careful to redefine *dōwa* as a genre that included not just adapted folk or fairy tales (*saiwa*), but also truly original works (*sōsaku dōwa*). With the magazine's rise to prominence as the "dragon's gate" of *dōwa* literature, this emphasis on originality became the genre's new hallmark.[23]

The notion that *dōwa* literature was a pursuit worthy of all writers, especially aspiring ones, was present from the first issue of *Akai tori*, in which

Suzuki placed a call for both *dōwa* and *dōyō* (children's songs, nursery rhymes) submissions. Readers were told that winning entries for each category would be selected by Suzuki and respected poet Kitahara Hakushū (1885–1942). Outstanding contributions were to receive honorable mention in each month's issue, and the very best were to be published alongside the work of some of the most influential writers and poets of the day. The magazine also promised that anyone whose work was praised by the editors more than ten times would be treated thereafter as a "reputable author" (*rippa na sakka*).[24] Though it is unclear what such a promise, if granted, actually entailed, young writers who wished to see their words in print must have seen in it an attractive opportunity. Within half a year, Suzuki found himself selecting from roughly fifty submissions every month; by June of 1919, that number had climbed to nearly two hundred, sent from both domestic locales and the wider colonial sphere.[25] While Miyazawa's name does not appear to be among them, it is significant that in August 1918, only a month after *Akai tori*'s inception, his younger brother Seiroku remembers listening to him read aloud, and with great enthusiasm, two of his own original *dōwa*.[26]

The success of *Akai tori* soon generated a market for magazines similarly devoted to the *dōwa* genre and to the practice of soliciting reader submissions of original work.[27] *Otogi no sekai* (World of Children's Tales) was the first to follow suit in April 1919, enlisting Ogawa Mimei as its primary reviewer. He soon became a strong advocate of *dōwa* as a form of "literature" directed to "all humans who had not lost the heart of the child."[28] In November of the same year, *Kin no fune* (Golden Boat) released its inaugural issue under the direction of Saitō Sajirō, who succeeded in recruiting Shimazaki Tōson and Arishima Ikuma (1882–1974) to help judge submissions. Their fame was surely meant to raise the profile of the magazine and to lend support to Saitō's own attempts at redirecting the course of *dōwa* literature.[29] In April 1920, the magazine *Dōwa* appeared under the editorial direction of Chiba Shōzō (1892–1975), who was himself an author of *dōwa*. Similar in form and content, it began calling for submissions from adult writers in 1922 and offered a small payment to those whose stories were selected.

These titles represent but a small subset of the growing market for youth-oriented magazines. There were others that tried with less success to profit from the *dōwa* boom and still others that, geared toward a slightly older readership, were more popular and ultimately more concerned with promoting moral strengthening and worldly success.[30] The aforementioned *Nihon shōnen*, for example, a general interest magazine containing adolescent novels, poetry, and a popular section for readers' letters, had a circulation of about 200,000 by the late teens. *Akai tori*, even at its peak in the early 1920s, had print runs of just over 30,000. *Kin no fune*, its main competitor, operated on roughly the same scale. Such statistics, however, belie the social influence of the *dōwa* magazines. For one, they were embraced by a new generation of elementary school teachers who increasingly set themselves against the conservative and mechanistic style of learning promoted by the Ministry of Education. Uniting under the banner of the Free Education movement (*jiyū kyōiku undō*), these educators saw the *dōwa* magazines as a vehicle for developing a new style of learning that would both respect and nurture individual expression and creativity. They encouraged their students, primarily in the form of "art education" (*geijutsu kyōiku*), to express themselves openly through essays, songs, and drawings, all of which could be submitted to the *dōwa* magazines for comment and possible publication.[31] As a result, the popularity of the magazines as educational tools soared during the early 1920s, affording them a cultural presence that far outweighed their modest print runs.

This presence was bolstered by shifting attitudes toward childhood among the urban, upper middle class, who made up the core readership of the *dōwa* magazines and who were drawn to the ways that figures like Suzuki and Ogawa idealized a free and pure children's spirit (*dōshin*).[32] The demand for *dōwa* that could speak to such romantic images soon generated a cottage industry for children's book publication and led to the creation of additional outlets for children's literature in national and regional newspapers, popular women's and general interest magazines, and even serious literary journals like *Waseda bungaku*. With this increased demand, of course, came increased need for *dōwa* authors. By soliciting submissions and awarding recognition to winning entries, the *dōwa* magazines were both responding to this need while shrewdly insuring the formation of a core of repeat readers, both young and old. The result was a space in which writers of all ages, and from around the empire, could, at least in theory, participate in the creation of a new cultural product.

Many did take part, with some even going on to become recognized authors in the genre.[33] Yet the nature of their participation, with submissions moving as they did from peripheral locations to a central core, was wholly bound up in the geographically uneven structure of literary production.

Even as the efficiency of the postal system made it easy for texts to travel to Tokyo in place of the authors' physical bodies, thus facilitating what would seem an equal degree of participatory access, it was still only by way of the center that one could gain assured entrance to the machinery of *dōwa* production and evaluation. If the editors and established literati who served as gatekeepers tended to downplay their own origins in similar processes of artistic "discovery," it was painfully clear to amateurs that the path to recognition required a Tokyo address.[34] The magazines told them plainly that those who would grant legitimacy to their work sat in Tokyo ready to apply their standards of judgment.

These standards, while not always consistent, tended to emphasize an everyday, unornamented, and non-adult language that spoke directly to children and their individual emotions—an infantilized complement to the styles that naturalist writers had invested in through the 1910s. In the back pages of the magazines, editors often commented on why nominated submissions did or did not make for suitable *dōwa*, giving a sense of how these standards were deployed by the genre's self-appointed gatekeepers. Suzuki, for his part, remarked in an early issue of *Akai tori* that many of the entries he had received were written in an affected style, full of needlessly thick and decorative language. "How about writing the story in just a standard (*futsū*), obvious (*atarimae*) vernacular? . . . Even if what you're writing about is only a superficial event, try doing so in a lively way that directly touches our emotions (*kanjō*) and those of the children."[35] One can find similar advice in the pages of *Kin no fune*, where contestants were encouraged to use "pure" words capable of "melting into the feelings (*kibun*) of children."[36] Despite such efforts to demarcate the proper stylistic boundaries of the *dōwa*, plenty of ambiguity remained. Many of the *dōwa* appearing in the magazines continued to rely on formulaic retellings of Western tales or native folklore.[37] But the point to be made here is that editors like Suzuki considered themselves the arbiters of taste for written submissions flowing *into* Tokyo from elsewhere, creating a situation in which symbolic and spatial capital were concentrated in the hands of a select few residing in the metropolis. Thus even as the diffusion of *dōwa* magazines like *Akai tori* led to a heightened sense of a shared national community from the perspective of consumers, the mechanisms of production remained yoked to the same spatial hierarchy that defined the centralized literary marketplace as a whole.

This hierarchy, which was largely submerged beneath the illusion of, as Casanova puts it, "a world of free and equal access in which literary recognition is available to all writers," did occasionally make its way to the surface in the form of references to Japan's provincial regions.[38] There was, for instance, the largely positive attitude shown towards "local color" (*chihōshoku*), a term made popular by naturalist writers early in the century and which by the late teens referred to the explicit foregrounding of a locale's distinct and exceptional qualities, whether in the form of place names, dialect, or landscape. Owing to its early promotion by writers like Tōson, Katai, and Kunikida Doppo as a corrective to decorative stereotypes of nature employed merely as background to social reality, "local color" was generally associated with the "natural" and provincial settings to which these authors were attracted, and which they had recently left behind.[39] These associations persisted in the pages of the *dōwa* magazines, with editors praising stories for their attention to local detail, or else urging contributors to work harder to capture the atmosphere of their native places.[40] Ironically, the representation of provincial localities by those who actually lived in and identified with them was subject to evaluation by metropolitan editors who had very specific ideas as to what constituted "local color" and as to the kinds of "color" that would appeal to their predominantly urban audiences.[41]

These ideas, which manifested themselves in certain editorial decisions, reveal distinct forms of spatial and temporal bias. Take, for instance, the decision to publish and promote material, much of it by established authors, that outwardly associated provincial locales with quaint rusticity, childhood innocence, and a vanishing past. The creators of this material, eager to represent the world through a child's eyes, typically harkened back to their own childhood experiences in Japan's rural hinterlands, inadvertently *dis-locating* such spaces from the narrating present and from the implicit *now* of the metropolis. In a piece by Tayama Katai called "Aki no tabi" (Fall Journey, 1920), readers were offered an account of a solitary trip taken on foot to northern Tōhoku during his student days. Appearing to follow much the same path as Matsuo Bashō in *Oku no hosomichi* (Narrow Road to the Deep North, 1694), Katai combines references to famous poetic sites with landscape description steeped in the sentiment of *sabishii* (lonely, forlorn, desolate). He uses the adjective nearly a dozen times in the four-page piece. He also emphasizes that the journey was taken before the introduction of the railroad and, as if to accentuate the sense of spatial isolation and temporal distance, claims it to be an experience unavailable to today's travelers.[42] A similar lament for a lost time appears in Shimazaki Tōson's *Furusato* (Native Place), a collection of vignettes published in 1920 and extensively promoted in *Akai tori* as a work that would finally give readers access to "tales of old and tales from the mountains in every direction."[43] In one of the opening chapters, as the narrator begins to tell his children stories of the mountains and forests in which he played as a child, he reminisces:

> When your father was young, they didn't have anything like the boys' magazines (*shōnen zasshi*) you have today. And unlike you, I wasn't able to read books of interesting folk tales (*otogibanashi*) or magazines filled with cute drawings. Even had I wanted to, there just wasn't anything of the sort. On top of that, I was born in the countryside (*inaka*), deep in the mountains. But this simply meant that for young Papa, everything I saw and heard was just like an *otogibanashi*.[44]

Here we see the provinces *dis-located* to a space and time prior to the print commodities through which their allochronic image now circulates. It is the very absence of such commodities that turns the rural margins into a primal site for storytelling, where all manner of experience is retroactively recognized as the stuff of folk and children's tales. Just as with "Aki no tabi," the provinces become a source of suitable narrative by virtue of their distance from an urbanized present and their proximity to long displaced, but still supposedly intact, childhood memories.[45]

Another way in which "local color" was celebrated in the *dōwa* magazines was through editorial commentary encouraging the use of regional dialect, both in the stories submitted by aspiring authors and in the compositions (*tsuzurikata*) from elementary-school-age readers. Dialect in the latter was of special concern to Suzuki, who on numerous occasions advocated its use on artistic grounds. In his mind, it not only helped children convey the special "atmosphere of the provinces" (*chihōteki jōchō*), it also afforded them an opportunity to express themselves in the language most natural to them. Why they would choose to do otherwise can be explained by nearly two decades of educational policy that compelled teachers to "correct" (and even punish) dialect use in favor of a standard vernacular (*hyōjungo*). Already by the late teens, as will be discussed in Chapter Five, the ideal of a standard speech was so socially entrenched as to generate a static image of nonstandard dialects (*hōgen*) existing in negative temporal relation to *hyōjungo*. They came to be situated along a developmental continuum in which the latter represented an end point and mark of civilizational achievement. Suzuki was certainly not trying to redraw or do away with the established ideological map of Japan's many different speech styles. His primary concern was that if children were forced to write about their lives in *hyōjungo* before they had mastered it, their prose would somehow lose its vitality and power to communicate, the same as if they were made to "think and speak in a foreign language." Thus he sought to provide a provisional space in which those in the lowest grades were freed from the burden of translating their thoughts into *hyōjungo* and allowed to sketch their lives as truthfully as possible.[46] If this seems a step toward granting a measure of autonomy in expressing local difference, remember that Suzuki was still the one setting limits on how much, and until what age, dialect use was appropriate. Moreover, what little freedom he did grant came with the implicit understanding that children would eventually graduate from their "natural" tongue into one more befitting their status as national citizens.

A desire for authentic and internally generated expressions of "local color" is likewise seen in the calls for submissions put out by the magazines. *Akai tori* began in its fourth month to solicit material with explicitly provincial origins, asking readers to distinguish it from "original" stories and songs with the labels *chihō densetsu* (regional legend) or *chihō dōyō* (regional song).[47] In making such a distinction, editors wanted an easy way to separate new artistic pieces from more obviously historical works. Yet in juxtaposing the categories on the call-for-submissions page, and by insisting that *chihō* be affixed to the latter, we see again their tendency to map historical difference over time onto geographical distance across space. Whereas "original" material was not marked spatially and potentially came from anywhere, "traditional" material was fixed to provincial localities situated outside an implied modern core, thus leaving little room to imagine *dōwa* or *dōyō* that might fall somewhere in between.[48] Editors did replace "*chihō densetsu*" with "*chihō dōwa*" for a few months in 1919, but judging by the stories printed under this new heading, editors' assumptions about the kind of material appropriate to this category were unchanged.[49] All were retellings of local legends or folklore rooted in the indeterminacy of the distant past.

Interest in this material continued through the early 1920s, both in *Akai tori* and in other of the most popular children's magazines. In 1921, *Dōwa* asked its young readers to submit *densetsu* told to them by their grandparents.[50] In 1923, *Kin no hoshi* called upon readers to record *densetsu* native to their area, especially those in which young children figured as protagonists; upwards of five hundred submissions were received.[51] That the *dōwa* magazines would solicit such material even as they sought to articulate a new brand of children's literature distinct from more "vulgar" antecedents is hardly surprising. Most of the editors still relied heavily on the practice begun by Iwaya Sazanami in the 1890s of adapting traditional folktales and legends to the ideological needs and readerly expectations of contemporary audiences. While those needs and expectations changed, the potential for older narratives to be refashioned and updated did not, especially to the extent that they could be presented as part of an enduring cultural heritage.[52] Even Suzuki, for instance, was busy in 1920 editing a six-volume set of "classic" *dōwa* and *densetsu* to replace "the mistaken variants and superfluous stylings of previous ages" with more easily accessible standard versions of which the Japanese could be proud.[53]

Concomitant with continuing efforts to adapt folklore to ever newer literary and stylistic idioms, the calls for regional material also extended the range of what counted as adaptable. These calls suggested that it was not just widely circulated tales like "Momotarō" (The Peach Boy) or "Kachi-kachi yama" (Crackling Mountain) that made for viable children's reading material, but potentially any tale handed down from the past, no matter its provenance. It was an implication eagerly capitalized upon by *dōwa* authors of the day like Okino Iwasaburō (1876–1956), a major contributor to *Kin no fune*. His stories embodied the trend toward adapting local, less-recognized folklore to the language of the *dōwa* aesthetic. As a native of the Kumano region, he drew on tales passed down by his grandfather and on his early experiences as a logger, relying on that now familiar temporal frame that put the past at a clear distance from the narrating present.[54] His work exemplifies the seeming natural affinity created within the *dōwa* magazines between images of a reinvigorated folk and the displaced ideals of a true, naïve, and childlike sensibility. In the words of Michel de Certeau, children had effectively become "the repository of a culture that perpetuated itself on the fringes of adult culture, of which it represented an altered form."[55]

The formation of such a repository by *dōwa* editors and authors is of less interest, however, than the way this repository was configured spatially and temporally by the submission process and the uneven structure of the market. As the above examples demonstrate, there was an overwhelming tendency amongst the gatekeepers of the *dōwa* movement to reinforce a hierarchical division of center and province that was ubiquitous in contemporary cognitive mappings of Japan's political, economic, and cultural spheres. But also a tendency to follow in the path of that generation of writers, ethnographers, and urban intellectuals who by late Taishō were themselves perpetuating regimes of spatial representation that cast the nation's outlying and rural regions as an "anachronistic" and static repository of tradition.[56] At a time when increasing integration into global markets raised the threat of social and economic unevenness in ever more immediate and tangible ways, they believed that social stability and cultural autonomy could be better maintained by recovering the beliefs and practices that survived in this repository.

To the extent that individuals at the center of *dōwa* production adhered to these kinds of temporally skewed regimes, we have to consider what the consequences might have been for a writer like Miyazawa. What stylistic and aesthetic choices were available to a writer who, lacking in spatial capital, identified with the less "timely" side of these regimes? Or to recall Moretti's question from the preceding chapter, what compromises were made and unmade by authors who wished to incorporate their own local material into a form whose boundaries were marked and patrolled elsewhere?[57] In the same way we have learned to ask these questions of the colonial writer who looks to the metropole, or the non-Western novelist who looks to the global market, we must also learn to ask them of the provincial writer who looked to Tokyo. In Miyazawa we find a writer who incorporated local material in ways that relativized the centrist geography at the heart of *dōwa* production, awarding to the provinces an alternative to the fate of mere anachronism.

Restoring Historicity to the Periphery

In December 1921, soon after his return to Iwate from an eight month sojourn in Tokyo, Miyazawa published the first and only *dōwa* manuscript for which he was ever paid. "Yuki watari" (Snow Crossing), serialized in two parts in *Aikoku fujin*, is the story of two young siblings, Shirō and Kanko, whose geographic identity is only as specific as the frozen and bitterly cold landscape through which they tread in the opening scene.[58] Not even the chill is immediately identifiable, softened as it is by a lily-scented sunlight and frost-covered trees that look as if they are coated in crystal sugar. As the children move through this aestheticized space, they make their way to the edge of a large wood while singing a short refrain: "*Katayuki kanko, shimiyuki shinko.*"[59] Repeated three times in the first page alone, it is like the opening riff of a jazz tune, one that will be repeated and improvised upon in a series of lyrical exchanges between the children and a group of young foxes. It is also the one element that links the tale to a specific geographic locale. In a 1909 compilation of children's songs (*dōyō*) edited by the Association for the Study of *Dōyō*, the same refrain appears in a "Snow Crossing Song" said to hail from Kunohe, a district at the far northern edge of Iwate Prefecture.[60] We can only guess how Miyazawa obtained this fragment of regional oral history, but its presence certainly implicates "Yuki watari" in the contemporary inclination to try to enrich the new *dōwa* aesthetic with ever more authentic shades of local color.

Yet while we might label the story a participant in this trend, its participation was for several reasons unconventional. The first of these becomes apparent after Shirō and Kanko, having reached the woods, turn to the trees and shout, "*Katayuki kanko, shimiyuki shinko*. The young fox wants a bride, wants a bride" (101). To their surprise, the call is answered by a white fox who emerges from the trees and sings an altered version of the original refrain: "*Shimiyuki shinshin, katayuki kankan*" (102). In this instant, the story moves from a logic of straight repetition to one improvisational in tone, leading to a burst of verbal exchanges that play out like an impromptu round of *kaeuta* (altered or parodic verse), each iteration adding yet one more variation to the string of calls and responses.[61] The effect of this for the reader is that the opening refrain can no longer be construed as merely a lyrical specimen to be pinned down alongside countless others of its kind. Instead, by virtue of being subject to spontaneous variation in the present time of the story, it becomes something much more malleable and thus much less typical, as will be shown, of how *dōyō* were treated as aesthetic objects.

After the fox makes clear to the children that he is not in need of a bride, he proceeds to make an offer of his own: "Shirō is shinko, Kanko is kanko, how 'bout I give you some millet dumplings?" To which Kanko replies: "Kitsune [fox] konkon, kitsune no ko [young fox], the fox's dumplings are just rabbit poop!" Her words bring the exchange to an abrupt halt and prompt the fox, whose name is given as Konsaburō, to respond in a highly refined tone of voice.

> "Oh no, that is not true at all. Would two fine young people like yourselves eat the brown dumplings of the rabbit? Up until now we foxes have been made to bear such wholly false accusations of trickery."
> Shirō was a bit taken aback. "Gee, is it really just a lie then that foxes trick people?"
> Konsaburō replied in earnest. "It most certainly is. And the most awful of lies at that. Those folks who say they've been tricked are usually drunk and staggering around in circles like cowards. It's really interesting sometimes. Just the other night, when the moon was out, Jinbei sat in front of our house all evening singing *shamisen* ballads. . . ."

". . . In any case, please do have some dumplings. The ones I'm offering are made of millet that I planted and cultivated in my own field, weeding it just as one is supposed to. Then I ground the millet into flour, kneaded and steamed the dumplings, and added some sugar. How about it? Would you like a plate full?" (102–3)

Shirō politely declines by telling the fox that they have just eaten. Old suspicions clearly die hard. But the fox is not discouraged and invites the two to attend a lantern show when the moon is next out and the snow once again frozen solid. He wants to show them some images of drunk villagers eating things in the wild they should not (e.g., field dumplings and field noodles) and images of foxes who have gotten into trouble with humans. The children accept and begin another round of singing, each composing a verse that alludes to the images the fox has just described. Shirō, for his part, sings about the fox that once stuck its paw in a hunter's trap.

This intricate interweaving of *dōwa* and *dōyō* (story and verse) into a single narrative text is a second way in which "Yuki watari" strayed from expectation, since popular children's magazines of the day tended to enforce a clear separation of the two genres through a strict division of editorial labor.[62] All of the top tier magazines, in fact, hired prominent poets to preside over the compilation and critique of *dōyō* submissions. Kitahara Hakushū was brought on at *Akai tori*, folksong poet Noguchi Ujō (1882–1945) at *Kin no fune*, and symbolist Saijō Yaso (1892–1970) at *Dōwa*. The three of them together used their editorial authority, along with published essays and the national lecture circuit, to redirect the Japanese nursery rhyme toward individual and authentically childlike forms of expression, thus legitimating *dōyō* as a poetic genre.[63] Given the intellectual energy they were investing in demarcating and shoring up the foundations of this new genre, they and others were surely not inclined to begin destabilizing it with hybrid forms. Even in those rare instances when *dōyō* and *dōwa* were placed together, the boundaries between them remained nearly impermeable. Consider, for instance, Noguchi's "Kodomo ni baketa kitsune" (The Foxes Who Turned into Children), published in the magazine *Shōgaku dansei* (Elementary School Boys) in August 1922. Relying on the archetypal narrative of a peasant who is led by a shape-shifting fox into a frightening alternate universe and then thrust back into reality as if it were all a strange dream, Noguchi adds his own lyrical touch by incorporating the singing voices of children. These children (or could they be foxes?) tease the peasant in verse during the course of his nightmarish journey. But to say that he incorporates these voices into the tale is to put it too strongly, for each verse is introduced by the narrator as a stand-alone *dōyō*. Consequently, the implicit message to readers becomes that these verses are freely extractable from the story itself.

The contrast with "Yuki watari" could not be starker. Here the verses are presented as the product of dialogic interaction, emerging from moments of spontaneous orality that have been woven firmly into the fabric of the unfolding narrative present. It is a point deftly driven home during the lantern show when Konsaburō displays an image titled "Take traps seriously" and the other young foxes begin to sing the verse earlier composed by Shirō. The boy promptly turns to his sister and says, "That's the song that *I made*, isn't it" (112, emphasis added). The very act of lyric creation is thus deliberately foregrounded as part and parcel of the advancing story line, contributing to a dialogic structure that outwardly resists the tendency, hinted at earlier, toward representing regional verse as the static "survival" of an imagined provincial folk. That is, by embedding the "Snow Crossing Song" within the diachronic progression that narrative inevitably provides, and by subjecting it to multiple acts of improvisation along the way, Miyazawa's story avoids casting the refrain as the fossilized product of immutable tradition, or as a mere sampling of local color. Instead, it appears as something organically rooted in a localized, still evolving site of production.

Such a framing was a less obvious choice for prominent figures like Kitahara and Noguchi, who were busy constructing, as well as patrolling, the divide between their new brand of *dōyō* and an expansive catalog of older, folk-based verse. For them, the boundary served not as a means to reject this older material—in fact, they promoted its collection and dissemination as a counterweight to the de-localized *shōgaku shōka* (elementary school songs) that had dominated the educational landscape since the 1880s.[64] Rather, the boundary helped clarify the spatio-temporal relationship between this material—variously conceived as static archive and still living fount of inspiration—and their own poetic stylings. Noguchi, for instance, while a proponent of regionally inflected children's songs, tended to burden them with the heavy sentiment of nostalgic longing and with his own unwritten rules about the appropriate use of dialectical variation.[65] Thus even as he defined *kyōdo dōyō* (native-place songs) as a locally generated style of verse that could accommodate the dialects and accents of every region, both urban and rural, he insisted that only those "words with an artistic ring to them" should be used.[66] That is, nothing that might cloud the assumed transparency of the standard vernacular. Much like the stance that Suzuki took as editor of *Akai tori*, this was an open invitation to use local color as long as one stayed within the limits set by an implied center.

Kitahara, for his part, opened the gate between newer and older verse much wider. On the one hand, he argued that Japan's traditional children's songs (*warabe-uta*) should form the very root of contemporary *dōyō*, and to that effect turned the pages of *Akai tori* into a display case for local songs (*chihō dōyō*) either collected on his own or solicited from readers. At the same time, insisted that *dōyō* reflect the experiences of children in the immediate present. "My *dōyō* yearn for the familiarity and freshness of the still muddied hands of the child. . . . I want them to capture the very scent and color of that pure life of the child set completely free within nature."[67] Kitahara's desire to combine the spirit of a lingering folk tradition with the lives of children in an idealized present seems, if one takes a narrow view, to be exactly the wish that "Yuki watari" too tries to satisfy. To assume thus, however, is to fail to ask after the specific folk, and also children, for whom Kitahara claims to speak. Implicit in his demands is the idea that all local difference, whether of oral tradition or of bodily experience, can be effortlessly subsumed under the umbrella of an imagined national folk and a universalizing notion of childhood.

Not surprisingly, there were some in the *dōyō* community who challenged Kitahara's totalizing hubris. A group of poets based in the northern city of Sendai, for instance, who created their own *dōyō* magazine in 1921, declared from the very first issue that "true children's song" should be crafted in the language specific to its place of origin and that no poet should feel compelled to use the Tokyo dialect. A few months later, the head editor Suzuki Eikichi roundly criticized Kitahara and others for wanting to meddle with regional verse in order to construct some "grand, nationally unified whole." He argued instead that "those lullabies sung by children on the shores of Awa must harbor the vitality of that locale (*tochi no seimei*)—the coldly lit homes situated upon the sand mixed in with the forlorn crashing of waves."[68] If Suzuki shares Kitahara's insistence on capturing the immediacy of the child's experience, he implies here that such immediacy was more meaningful, and thus more authentic, the tighter one's geographical focus. How, he wants to ask, can Kitahara's *dōyō* possibly speak for *all* children when he dilutes, in the name of the nation, the specific language and landscape known to each?

While "Yuki watari" gives only indirect voice to this kind of strident localist critique, there are reasons to believe that by the time Miyazawa wrote the story in late 1921, he was at least capable of adopting a similar strategic position vis-à-vis the literary marketplace. After all, during his brief stint in Tokyo, he sent a series of letters to a friend back home that reveal a clear sense of himself as a writer who wanted no part of the urban literary establishment and the success-hungry fray.[69] A letter from July reads,

> I'm making an attempt to sell some of the things I've written. Please don't try to tell me that this is irresponsible, sincere, or whatever. . . . When I go to the library, there are about a hundred people who try everyday to check out *How to Write a Novel* or *The Road to Literary Creation*. I suppose that makes sense. If one just wants to write, then there's nothing more random and unordered than a novel. And if you succeed, you'll make a name for yourself as a genius and earn 70,000 yen in no time, just like Shimada Seijirō. What do you think? Can you imagine the face I'm making as I write my manuscripts in the middle of all this? None at all. From hereafter religion will be art, and art will be religion.[70]

In another letter sent just before his return, he told his friend to "keep writing excellent things. Transcend the beriberi-like literary establishment and give expression to the Buddha with utmost seriousness."[71] Although couched in the language of religious awakening, the conditions of enunciation for both of these remarks (i.e., letters between an Iwate native in Tokyo and his aspiring poet friend back home) suggest the early integration of spatial location into Miyazawa's artistic identity. Consider as well that during his time in Tokyo he became involved in the founding of the Takuboku Society, a networking organization set up by displaced Iwate youth for the ostensible purpose of honoring poet Ishikawa Takuboku, a famous native son whom they could claim as one of their own.[72] When Miyazawa finally did return home, the move only strengthened his capacity to identify as geographical outsider, and also as a spokesperson for those local inhabitants, both human and non, whose voices were all too easily whitewashed by urban writers and their purported expertise in local color.

Becoming such a spokesperson meant, of course, being in a position to interfere with the clean brushstrokes of the center in yet other ways. Thus in "Yuki watari" we find Miyazawa also confronting the tendency of popular *dōwa* writers to adhere to folkloric convention. He does this by calling into question the long-standing stereotype of foxes as lying and deceptive tricksters. Such stereotypes continued to be relied on, as in the story by Noguchi, despite the calls for a new *dōwa* aesthetic. Even in the hands of a more innovative writer like Ogawa Mimei, the fox strayed little from its culturally ordained path. In his "Ōkina kani" (The Large Crab, 1922), a young boy from the Hokuriku region fears for his grandfather's safety when he fails to return home one evening. Waking up in the middle of the night, the boy peers into the darkness and looks out to the star-lit field that stretches in front of his house. Off in the distance, he spots what appears to be an odd cluster of glowing candles and quickly concludes that a fox wedding is taking place and that the foxes have tricked his grandfather into being part of the festivities. When his grandfather returns home safely that night with a mundane account of his travails, the boy remains convinced that his arrival was delayed by the mischievous work of foxes. And the coy narrator declines to say otherwise, suggesting that the boy's assumptions about foxes are better left unquestioned.[73]

Compare this with the more fully anthropomorphized, yet still innately fox-like Konsaburō, who wields the subjectivity proffered by his name to relativize and contest those negative associations for so long affixed to him and his kind. His desire to disrupt convention is evident in both his initial encounter with the children ("For so long now we foxes have been made to bear such wholly false accusations"), and again towards the end of the story when he brings the lantern show to a close. Having finally convinced Shirō and Kanko that his dumplings are the genuine article, he turns and addresses the other young foxes.

> "This evening's lantern show is thus concluded. Tonight, there is one thing you all must keep firmly within your heart. It is the knowledge that two smart and very sober human children have kindly eaten something prepared by foxes. From now on, as we grow into adults, I believe that we foxes (*watakushidomo kitsune*) can rid ourselves of the awful reputation we've had just as long as we don't lie to humans or show them envy." (112)

By telling the foxes that they themselves have the power to overcome the stereotypes perpetuated by humans, Konsaburō grants them a historical agency denied in popular human accounts. He himself embodies the possibility of transcending such stereotypes, as emphasized by his fancy tuxedo and his skillful deployment of visual technology. These various modern accoutrements, along with his words and actions, stand as an implicit rejection of any mode of representation that would cast him and his fellow foxes as essentially static and unchanging in their ways. Instead, by virtue of being situated in a continuously unfolding (and improvised) present, the figure of Konsaburō confirms Certeau's assertion that "time is precisely the impossibility of an identity fixed by place."[74] The assertion, in other words, that time (and by extension the act of creation) is only imaginable when identities and objects are seen to move freely across and within space, rather than as locked up in a state of "non-coincidence" by allochronic discourse or a "denial of coevalness."[75] While the subaltern fox may not move far from his provincial wood, he is at least free to choose the terms by which his identity will hereafter be created and defined.[76]

Or is he? On the one hand, these terms (to neither "lie" or "show envy") seem to be based in a human moral order imposed from above. You can be less like a fox, in other words, by being more like a human. That said, Konsaburō has already declared that the notion of foxes as tricksters is a complete fabrication, perpetuated by those who are "usually drunk and staggering around in circles like cowards." The foxes, according to this logic, have done nothing wrong and have only to inform humans that their prejudices are woefully inaccurate and misguided. Such ambiguity over who is ultimately to blame hints at the culpability of both sides, but also suggests that any improvement in the relationship will require self-examination of one's assumptions about the other and a mutual openness to what each has to say about himself. For Shirō and Kanko, the message is thus twofold: that their own preconceptions of the fox are the product of a skewed and prejudicial history, and that whatever they may think the fox to be, they should not pass judgment until they grant him the right to speak for himself on his own turf. One can imagine a similar message being directed at the young dōwa reader who was accustomed to more conventional appropriations of local folklore. Namely, that one should not assume that the picture of provincial life presented in these stories is always the most accurate or authentic. Far better to wait and hear about it from the proverbial horse's (or fox's) mouth.

Whether this was the message actually received by the middle- and upper-class readers of Aikoku fujin is impossible to know. Although its audience was far more geographically diffuse than even the most prominent dōwa magazines, nonmetropolitan readers were just as likely to deem Miyazawa's use of folk song and animal imagery as appropriately provincial. "Yuki watari," after all, had its own way of filtering out the complex realities of the rural landscape with layers of romantic sensibility and rich metaphorical description. Yet when read against the dōwa field as a whole, it is clear that its simplifying of the landscape and its reducing of it to a set of abstract ideals operated according to a different spatio-temporal logic—a logic that rejected some of the more obvious narrative strategies that were available to a writer like Miyazawa. He could just as easily have capitalized on his marginal position by appealing to the center's dominant expectations and upholding the image of the periphery as locus of staid tradition or as an object of nostalgic longing. Or he might have ignored his position entirely so as to imitate position-takings considered more "modern" and "up-to-date." Instead, he deployed it in a way that relativized the representational authority and temporal biases of those who held the greatest share of spatial capital.

In the years that followed, Miyazawa would continue to experiment with narrative strategies that were similarly provincializing in their intent. Several of these would come to be incorporated into *The Restaurant of Many Orders*, including the story for which the book was named. Though this story does not explicitly draw on folk elements, it is his most violent example of a silenced entity attempting to speak back to those who would pretend to know and speak for it. Here, the voice belongs to a clever wildcat who turns a pair of inept Tokyo hunters from consumers of nature into the very nearly consumed by preying upon their urbanite desires and leading them through a series of doors that end at his wide open mouth. Another story from the same volume, "Shika odori no hajimari" (The First Deer Dance), narrates the origins of a folk dance "still performed in the hills and valleys of the Kitakami," a region in central Iwate. The narratorial voice that frames the story, however, derives from neither the disembodied gaze of the ethnographer nor the displaced gaze of the metropolitan. Instead, it is situated at a specific point in the natural and human history of the local landscape and appears to emanate from the land itself, or at least from the memory of the land as preserved in the rustling breeze and made available to any passerby with patience enough to listen. By representing the rural margin as capable of speaking for itself, and of speaking back to those who would claim to know it, these and other stories are evidence that Miyazawa's initial exchange with the *dōwa* movement was in fact the beginning of a far more serious and urgent conversation. This conversation would, as we see in the next chapter, eventually lead him to the curious strategy of renaming his native Iwate with the toponym that graces the front cover of his *dōwa* collection: Iihatov.

Making Space for a New Literary Region

The Road to Iihatov

The three years separating "Yuki watari" from the publication of *The Restaurant of Many Orders* in 1924 must have seemed an eternity for Miyazawa. Having returned from Tokyo with a trunk full of manuscripts and a wealth of creative energy, he likely felt that "Yuki watari" would be just the first of his stories to win a national audience, not the last. But fate proved unkind. When he returned to the capital in January 1923 and presented several *dōwa* to the publisher Tōkyōsha, all were rejected as unsuitable to their line of publications.[1] Around the same time, rumor had it that he also visited the offices of *Akai tori* to talk with head editor Suzuki Miekichi. But again he was met with a cold reception and was allegedly told that his stories were interesting but not appropriate for young children.[2] Not only was he writing from the wrong place, then, he had also miscalculated the "proper" boundaries of his chosen genre.

After failing to gain entry into Tokyo media channels, Miyazawa began to explore some of the options available closer to home, including the regional newspaper. In April and May of 1923, he published three *dōwa* in the *Iwate*

Mainichi shinbun, a Morioka paper that competed with the *Iwate nippō* for the largest share of readers in the prefecture. Two of these stories adopted narrative strategies that notably foregrounded an imagined region with much clearer semiotic ties to Iwate, at least as compared with his earlier work. "Hyōga nezumi no kegawa" (Fur of the Glacial Mouse), serialized in April, was in fact the first of his prose works to deploy the toponym "Iihatov."[3] Rather than referring to a literary region, however, as it would a bit later, the term referred to a snowy provincial town that was the departure point for a chilling tale in which an overnight express train bound for the far north is hijacked by a group of pistol-wielding polar bears. "Shigunaru to shigunaresu" (Signal and Signalless), which ran in May, turned the unrequited love of two railroad signal poles—one alongside the Tōhoku Main Line (completed in 1891) and the other, marked as feminine, along the Iwate Light-Railway Line (completed in 1915)—into a parable about the hierarchical power relations embedded in the nation's transport and communications infrastructure. A regional act of subversion, or rather romantic diversion, initiated by the female pole is quickly quashed by a central authority that demands constant attention and discipline from its constituent parts. Both stories exhibit a turn toward regional specificity that coincides with Miyazawa's pursuit of local publishing options, suggesting that the awareness of a limited audience might have strengthened his resolve to speak in more direct terms about his native place. This regional turn also appeared in other manuscripts from the time, to be taken up in the next chapter. All of these stories show how the provincializing strategy eventually embodied in Iihatov evolved from a playful renaming to a far more ambitious re-imagining of the local region.

The scope of this ambition became clear with the publication of *The Restaurant of Many Orders*, a project Miyazawa had been pondering at least as early as December 1923. The preface to the work, dated December 20, was likely conceived just a few days after a visit from former classmate Chikamori.[4] A few months later, Toryō Shuppanbu put an ad out for the April release of a *dōwa* collection under the title *Yama otoko no shigatsu* (The Mountain Man of April), but publication was delayed after Chikamori became embroiled in family matters back home.[5] His partner Oikawa decided to see the book through to completion anyway and contacted Yoshida Shunzō, an acquaintance and newly independent publisher in Tokyo. In August, a second ad for the volume declared its forthcoming release under the present-day title, minus the word Iihatov.[6] This too turned out to be premature. Beset by a lack of funds, publication was this time stalled until

November, when another set of advertisements promised the book's release within the month.[7] Markedly different in both technical quality and level of detail, these ads were the first in which Iihatov appeared in the volume's title.[8] One of them, measuring over half a foot wide and two and a half feet in length, was folded into a pamphlet of which Yoshida's company was asked to print 1,000.[9] The text of the advertisement, which most scholars attribute to Miyazawa, begins as follows:

> Iihatov is the name of a place. If you must seek this place, think of it as part of the same world as the fields tilled by Big Claus and Little Claus, or the Wonderland that little Alice traveled through; think of it as a place to the distant northeast of the Tepântar desert, or to the far east of King Ivan's realm. In truth, this place is Japan's Iwate Prefecture existing as a dreamland (*doriimurando*), brought into being by scenes from the author's own mental images (*shinshō*).
>
> There, everything is possible. At one moment a person can leap over icy clouds, traveling northward to follow the winds raised by the global circulation of air; at another moment one can talk to an ant crawling at the bottom of a crimson flower-cup. Even sins and sadness shine with beautiful purity. Thick forests of beech, wind and shadows, evening primrose, mysterious cities, a line of electric poles that stretches to Bering City; it is truly a strange and exciting land (*kokudo*).[10]

Steeped in allusions barely recognizable today, except the nod to Lewis Carroll, the passage offers less clarification on Iihatov than one might initially hope. It exists as a place largely defined by intertextual reference. Immediately following this passage we are told that the stories in the collection are "mental-image sketches" that, aimed at boys and girls just entering adolescence, embody four special qualities:

1. These stories hold the seeds of truth and its beautiful sprouts. They have not been dressed up in the tarnished mask of tired religions or the dregs of established morals so as to deceive those with pure hearts.

2. These stories have been presented so that they might become materials for forming a new, better world. Not an ashen-colored utopia (*yūtopia*) kneaded together in a deformed manner, but a miraculous development (*hatten*) of the world itself that is yet unknown to this author.

3. These stories are not lies, make-believe (*kakū*), or stolen. Even if there has been repeated self-reflection and analysis since, it is certain that at the time, they appeared as mental images in just this way. Thus no matter how ridiculous or incomprehensible they may seem, they are shared

within the deep recesses of the heart by tens of thousands of people. It is only mean-spirited adults that find them incomprehensible.

4. These stories are the fresh product (*sanbutsu*) of the countryside (*den'en*). We offer these mental sketches to society (*seken*) together with the glistening fruits and green vegetables grown from the wind and sunlight of the country (*den'en*).[11]

Whether the few individuals who read *The Restaurant of Many Orders* were aware of these qualities, or even privy to this curious pamphlet, is difficult to ascertain. We simply do not know if the two texts circulated together. Readers who searched the book itself for references to Iihatov would have looked in vain. The word appears neither in the preface nor in any of the stories in the collection, a reminder that Miyazawa was assembling these stories, and thus searching for a logic by which they might cohere, well after the moment of original authorship. This temporal gap is actually highlighted in the table of contents, which attaches specific dates to each story that range from August 25, 1921, to April 7, 1922.[12] August, of course, coincides with his return from Tokyo and the start of a frenetic period of writing.[13] Still harboring hopes for publication in the capital during these months, Miyazawa may have conceived of his potential audience as more broadly based than he did in 1924, by which time such hopes were rerouted to Morioka. Or if not more broadly based, then at the very least not interested in regional specificity. Only three of the nine stories in the volume cite recognizable Iwate landmarks (Koiwai Farm, the Kitakami Range, Mt. Iwate), and no mention is made of the prefecture or any other domestic geopolitical locale except for a single allusion to Tokyo in the titular story. The pamphlet thus marks a striking divergence in its push to particularize center-periphery and urban-rural dichotomies by explicit mention of Iwate as site and source of Iihatov. In three years' time, Miyazawa had devised a rather different approach to spatial representation and a new paratextual frame through which to resituate the import and creative thrust of his earlier work. The task now is to consider the historical context for, and theoretical implications of, this shift in strategy.

A Place by Any Other Name

Every birth is memorialized by an act of naming. In the case of Iihatov, it is an act we know only after the fact ("Iihatov is the name of a place"), and one that outwardly refuses a search for etymological origins. Jacques Derrida once inquired into the nature of this act, asking, "What occurs when one gives a name? What does one give then? One does not offer a thing, one delivers nothing, and still something comes to be, which comes down to giving that which one does not have."[14] Miyazawa too delivered nothing tangible, but his act was ultimately to secure in the social imaginary—and even in the real landscapes of Iwate—a place for Iihatov that long survived him. How is it that a certain something came to be from nothing? Or more to the point, what was the "something" he created? Answers lay not in the word itself. To look there would be to revive "the most archaic language theory of all . . . that of the indissoluble link between words and things, which is to say the apprehension of language as names and naming."[15] Instead, we must look to historical context and to naming as a performative act; to the many discursive accretions that hold tight upon a name; to the social processes by which names insert themselves into existing structures of knowledge and by which they reinforce or alter the physical realities with which those structures converse. Only then will we come close to finding that something, or someplace, which seemingly issues forth from nowhere.

In trying to find the place that Miyazawa wished to bring forth with the name Iihatov, it is the advertisement pamphlet that offers the best provisional guide. It will later be necessary to venture beyond this guide's narrow constraints, but I want to begin by examining its points of intersection with, and divergence from, other contemporary practices of spatial identification and naming. One passage worth looking at in this regard is the fourth item in the list of special qualities, which declares the *dōwa* of Iihatov to be "products" (*sanbutsu*) nurtured by the wind and light of the countryside (*den'en*). Equating them with the same fruits and vegetables that a farmer might take to the local market or ship off for sale in a distant town, the advertisement dresses the work of literary creation in the clothes of a natural growth metaphor and situates the site of production outside an assumed urban core. The term that Miyazawa invokes here, *den'en*, stood in its early-twentieth-century incarnation as a dichotomous other to the city (*tokai, toshi*): the positive pole of the nonurban as represented by those who did not live there; a pastoral setting that in its ideal form was shaped solely by the hands of the rural laborer and by the forces of nature.[16] Locked in a dialectical relationship similar to that described by Raymond Williams in his analysis of the "country" and "city" in English society, *den'en* and *toshi* formed a pair around which urbanites typically praised the authenticity and simplicity of rural living over and against the ills of city life.[17] Tempting as it may be to read the *den'en* of Miyazawa's text as similarly privileging a rural site of purity and organic wholeness set in contrast to an implicitly impure urban space, one must keep in mind that the intended recipient of these products is society in general (*seken*) and *not* the disaffected urbanite in particular. *Den'en* here stands as the *productive* origin of creative material made in the here-and-now for the benefit of all members of society, not just those looking to escape from it.

What must also be taken into account is that Miyazawa's *den'en* is a very specific kind of countryside, one already localized as "Japan's Iwate Prefecture existing as a dreamland [and] brought into being by scenes from the author's own mental images." It is a space existing at the nexus of two overlapping geographies, one imagined and intertextual, the other mundane and political. In dealing with the former, it is helpful to know something of the fictional worlds to which the opening lines make reference. The Wonderland of Alice, which first appeared in 1865, needs little introduction, but the others are less familiar. The world of Big Claus and Little Claus alludes to an 1835 Hans Christian Andersen (1805–1875) tale about two farmers, the smaller of whom takes revenge upon a wealthier and stronger opponent after having been duped by him one too many times. Tepântar Desert is the mythical place-name employed by Bengali poet Rabindranath Tagore (1861–1941) in a collection of poems from 1913 called *The Crescent Moon*. Finally, the realm of King Ivan refers to the utopian socialist kingdom founded by Ivan the Fool in Leo Tolstoy's 1886 story of the same name. Access to each of these worlds would have been possible through translation by 1915 and each of their creators enjoyed considerable popularity throughout the Taishō period.[18]

Having tied these diverse fictional worlds together into a single borderless and timeless space, the text of the advertisement proceeds to insert Iihatov into this space as a metonymic equivalent. By way of comparison with an internationally recognized and preexisting body of imaginary landscapes, the text implies that Iihatov is a fictional space of equal form and stature. This comparison, however, is not confined to the symbolic or intertextual levels. For the text also triangulates Iihatov's position using a spatial logic based on actually existing geopolitical regions and their observed relation to one another in the material world. That is, it employs directional markers that situate Iihatov to the *east* of King Ivan's realm and to the *northeast* of Tepântar Desert while also localizing Iihatov in "Japan's Iwate Prefecture." This logic is only meaningful once we equate the fictional worlds in question to their original language of expression, whereby it makes sense to say that Iihatov—or rather the geopolitical space of Iwate to which it is linked—lies to the east of King Ivan's realm (i.e., Russia) and to the northeast of Tepântar Desert (i.e., Bengal). And thus Miyazawa's "dreamland" transcends the physical world as a unique mental and literary representation even as it remains caught up in a very real web of geopolitical relations. It presents itself, in short, as a partly imagined, partly real space.[19]

Miyazawa's decision to situate Iihatov in this indefinite state of in-between-ness raises the question of what he hoped to gain with a representational strategy that sat perched between pure fantasy on the one hand and something more realist in orientation. And was a critical part of this balancing act his choice of a toponym with no known referent and no ascertainable linguistic home?[20] One reason for choosing Iihatov may have been for its peculiar exotifying effect and the sense of difference it surely generated from the real space of Iwate and any preconceived notions readers might have had of the place. In this regard, it looks as though Miyazawa was mimicking the practice, made popular from the late Meiji period onward, of translating geographical landmarks and native locales into a toponymic hierarchy centered on Western Europe as the supreme arbiter of value. That is to say, the practice by which the Shinano highlands of central Honshū were rechristened the "Japanese Alps," by which the river Kiso took on the label "Rhine of Japan," and by which the industrial city of Osaka came to be popularly referred to as the "Manchester of the East."[21] An analogous exotification is certainly taking place in Miyazawa's decision to exchange Iwate for a decidedly foreign name, but the critical difference is that Iihatov, unlike the Swiss Alps or the German Rhine, cannot be located on any map or in any dictionary. What this indeterminacy allows Miyazawa to do is bypass Eurocentric hierarchies that would reduce Iwate to a mere copy or second-tier version of some authentic original. Instead, through the figure of Iihatov, it stands as a place uniquely its own. And though it could be said that as a literary trope Iihatov resembles the Wessex of Thomas Hardy (1840–1928), the Yoknapatawpa County of William Faulkner (1897–1962), or the West Hunan of Shen Congwen (1902–1988), here too the word's linguistic distance from available languages of expression renders it a less than comfortable fit for such a lineage.

Is Iihatov then an historical anomaly? Some scholars have treated it as such, yoking their interpretations to an image of the author as isolated genius trapped within the confines of his own oeuvre. But there is much to be gained by reading it instead in relation to the general dispersion of things spoken and written at the time. That is, by reading Miyazawa's definition of Iihatov as a statement whose presence—indeed whose very possibility of presence—was structured by a field of statements it derived support from and against which it distinguished itself. Moreover, as part of a network of statements in which, to cite Foucault, it had a role, however minor, to play.[22] To elucidate Iihatov's relation to this enunciative field, this "realm of the possible," we have then to ask after the kinds of statements by which this field was constituted, innumerable as those might be. Here the field is narrowed by a focus on statements that, like the pamphlet, invoke locality or region from the position of an insider who not only identifies these sites as qualitatively distinct, but who also identifies *with* them vis-à-vis a particular subject position.[23] By situating Iihatov against other such "statements of regional identification," as I refer to them, we can understand how it emerged dialectically to say something different about place. How it participated, that is, in "the interplay of word and object" (or of statement and place) that Mikhail Bakhtin describes thus:

> Any concrete discourse (utterance) finds the object at which it was directed already as it were overlain with qualifications, open to dispute, charged with value, already enveloped in an obscuring mist—or, on the contrary, by the "light" of alien words that have already been spoken about it. . . . The word, directed toward its object, enters a dialogically agitated and tension-filled environment of alien words, value judgments and accents, weaves in and out of complex interrelationships, merges with some, recoils from others. . . . The living utterance, having taken meaning and shape at a particular historical moment in a socially specific environment, cannot fail to brush up against thousands of living dialogic threads, woven by socio-ideological consciousness around the given object of an utterance.[24]

Viewed as part of this interplay, Iihatov becomes less an anomaly than a productive entry point for historicizing discursive strategies of spatial identification in local and regional media of the Taishō period.

Overcoming Place: The "Region" in Local Media

The strategy displayed in Miyazawa's advertising pamphlet consists of three discursive elements that, taken together, find a homology in Partha Chatterjee's formulation of the social ideology upon which nationalist thought relies. The first element is the existential claim made on a geographical space (in this case Iihatov) and its historical potential. This type of claim is what Chatterjee refers to as the *problematic*. The second element is the attempt to legitimate this claim by way of inter-regional hierarchies of moral comparison, or the *thematic*.[25] We see this in the use of already existing and recognized spaces (Alice's Wonderland, King Ivan's realm) as a way to both validate and make comprehensible Iihatov's own existence. The last element involves the combined use of the problematic and thematic registers to "produce a *different* discourse" and thus to imagine an alternate future for the space in question.[26] This is reflected in the declaration that these stories are ultimately to be used as "materials for forming a new, better world." Yet if this brings us closer to deciphering the ideology behind the pamphlet, it still leaves us to wonder why Miyazawa felt the need to claim the existence of a new space and set forth the possibility of a different discourse. Why not use "Iwate" by itself? Or why not "Tōhoku" (Northeast), the regional toponym under which Iwate was routinely subsumed?

When one considers the longer history of these spatial signifiers, it becomes clear that Miyazawa had good reason to be unsatisfied with them, and also good reason to want to relativize their claims to symbolic authority. In truth, they were not really all that old. "Iwate" came to refer to its current physical referent (the area of land defined by the Pacific Ocean to the east, the Ōu Mountain Range to the west, and the political boundaries with Aomori and Miyagi prefectures to the north and south) only in 1872.[27] "Tōhoku" took even longer to assume a fixed place in the spatial imaginary. Adopted in the late 1870s as a substitute for Ōu, which included the former provinces of Mutsu and Dewa, it was not until the turn of the century that it finally superseded its predecessor and came to be recognized as the umbrella term for the northern prefectures of Aomori, Akita, Iwate, Yamagata, Miyagi, and Fukushima.[28] Both toponyms were thus recent products of the radical restructuring of domainal boundaries that took place after the Restoration.

As to why the names might have been unsatisfying to Miyazawa's literary project, we need only consider some of the historical factors that, in the preceding fifty years, had led them to acquire harshly negative associations. One factor was the Boshin War of 1868, in which several domainal lords from northeastern Honshū allied with the Aizu clan (based in the western part of what is now Fukushima Prefecture) to resist Restoration forces. The alliance was quickly crushed, but it lasted long enough that the victors felt inclined to condemn the whole of Tōhoku as a potential enemy whose unenlightened inhabitants were lacking in respect for the emperor. Tokyo newspaper reports from the 1870s often portrayed residents as backward, dirty, indolent, or lascivious.[29] The political scars did not run so deep, however, as to eliminate all hope for the region as a potential engine of economic growth. In the push to colonize and develop Hokkaidō, a number of high-ranking officials believed the northeast was a key stepping stone in this process and a critical source of labor and natural resources.[30] As Meiji wore on, politicians and industrialists who identified with the region extended this line of argument and claimed even more vociferously that Tōhoku was ideally situated—in terms of both rail and shipping transport—to capitalize on the expanding global market.[31] Some even went so far as to call for a second Restoration.[32] Despite such sentiments, the region's subordination to the nation-state was rarely questioned; it was secondary *to*, not a replacement *for*, the national body. Political and economic centralization were thus already circumscribing patterns of regional identification, even as the region remained a focal point for imagining alternate national histories, both past and future.[33]

Despite these efforts to imagine a positive economic future for Tōhoku, the region inevitably fell behind, producing a unified economic space (or at least the appearance of one) that could be readily cast as "underdeveloped" when compared with other parts of the empire. Investments in rail and communications infrastructure, for instance, as well as in industry, shifted to the south after the Sino-Japanese War (1895–1896), or else north to Hokkaidō; natural disaster struck in the form of a massive *tsunami* in 1896, which left at least 25,000 dead and financial losses of nearly two million yen in Iwate alone,[34] but also in the form of unseasonably cool summers (*reika*), including one in 1904 that led to the rice harvest being thirty-five percent of the annual average;[35] population growth also lagged behind so that by 1908 just one of Japan's thirty largest cities was located in the region, despite the fact that Tōhoku makes up seventeen percent of the archipelago's land mass.[36] While the effects of these economic and environmental factors were not felt uniformly across the region, the patterns of failed growth and underinvestment cohered enough to generate and then solidify an image of "Tōhoku" as economically backward.

This was not the only image that came to circulate by the early 1920s, but it was certainly the dominant one, both locally and in the metropole. That the disparate localities of the region had come to reside together under the single banner of economic backwardness at all, however, is a testament to how powerful the toponym of Tōhoku had become as a node for regional identification. Much of that power came from local media itself, especially newspapers, which allowed for the articulation of a consistent regional stance that could then be diffused and shared by a geographically distinct community. The nation was by no means the first, or only, community with which Japanese identified when they picked up their morning paper(s).[37] In Iwate, the paper of choice was the *Iwate nippō*, and a survey of its pages in the years 1912, 1915, 1918, and 1920–1924 makes clear the extent to which the provincial press was fertile ground for statements of regional identification. Whether in the form of local boosterism (e.g., extolling the virtues of local products and landmarks),[38] paeans to native heroes (e.g., lament for Prime Minister Hara Kei upon his assassination in 1921),[39] or suggested blueprints for stimulating the regional economy (e.g., a proposal to attract travelers on their way to the Hokkaidō Exposition in 1918),[40] such statements operated on the assumption that the whole of Tōhoku, or in some cases the whole of Iwate, shared certain essential qualities. Similar to the statement of Iihatov, they demarcated spaces of subnational difference and imagined within those spaces a social unity and historical potential. Further examination of these statements can thus be useful for reconstructing the enunciative field and realm of the possible in which Iihatov was immersed.[41]

First, however, it is worth noting that hardly three decades had passed since the Japanese provincial press was at a point where it could sustain any sort of imagined community. And this despite the fact that regional newspapers had been around almost as long as metropolitan ones.[42] They first became commercially viable in the decade between the Sino-Japanese (1894–1895) and Russo-Japanese (1904–1905) wars, transitioning from political mouthpieces into forums for up-to-date political and social commentary as well as literary entertainment.[43] The *Iwate nippō* got its start in these same years, in 1897, and began with a modest circulation of one thousand copies.[44] Print runs increased, however, along with overall journalistic quality, when the Russo-Japanese War sparked an unprecedented demand for coverage.[45] After the war, the *Nippō* continued to expand its base of reporters, placing correspondents in major towns across the prefecture and establishing branch offices in Aomori and Sendai. In the mid-teens, an injection of capital from area industrialists, who came together to manage the company, allowed for upgrades of printing equipment, including the purchase of a rotary press in 1917. By 1920 the *Nippō* had attained daily print runs of nearly 10,000 and by late 1923 was the first Tōhoku paper to have an evening edition, giving it a clear edge over its regional competitors.[46] The edge was important not only for attaining dominance over the local market, but also for holding back the expanding tide of newspapers from Tokyo and Osaka. For during the same years that the regional press was establishing itself as a viable enterprise, the Tokyo and Osaka dailies were increasing their circulation and attempting to command an ever larger share of the national market. They made inroads into the provinces by establishing branch offices, printing regional editions (*chihōban*), and linking up with regional newspaper companies to offer dual delivery. By the end of the nineteenth century, three of every ten papers taken in regional areas were published in Tokyo; by 1905, the *Ōsaka Asahi shinbun* was selling a third (49,608) of its daily copies outside the Osaka-Kyoto-Kobe area.[47] Peripheral regions like Tōhoku obviously did not feel the effects of these changes as quickly, but it would only be a matter of time. Regional papers able to hold their ground soon found themselves, like the *Nippō*, having to champion the one thing that metropolitan papers could never hope to deliver: coverage of regional and local issues.[48]

As newspapers and other regional media outlets capitalized on this advantage, the kinds of statements of regional identification they generated were just as likely to make existential claims (the *problematic*) and moral comparisons (the *thematic*) of a negative and disparaging sort as they were to offer up exaggerated praise. Indeed, it was typically in the eyes of those with a vested interest in Tōhoku where its reputation suffered the most and where the truth of its unity as a region seemed all the more unassailable. To give but a small taste of these statements, consider what Iwate native Nitobe Inazō (1862–1933) had to say in 1914 in a lecture given in Iwate. He declared that "within our Japan, the Tōhoku area is a feminine region. I cannot think of it as masculine." The reason, he argued, was that in order for Tōhoku to be productive, a masculine region was needed to step in and make it so.[49] In 1915, another Iwate native and active promoter of Tōhoku development, Asano Gengo, published *Tōhoku oyobi Tōhokujin* (Tōhoku and Its People) and devoted a whole section to criticizing Tōhoku inhabitants for their lack of a unifying spirit, lack of effort, lack of sensitivity to social stimulus, and for their tendency toward laziness during the long winter months.[50] Such statements of self-critique were prevalent in the *Nippō* as well. In 1912, the founder of a religious university in Sendai stated that Tōhoku's slow pace of development could be attributed to a lack of diligence; compared with those in the Kantō and Kansai regions, Tōhoku folk (farmers are his main target here) lacked the desire to work hard for future gains.[51] Another common critique was the inability of Iwate and Tōhoku natives to unite (*danketsu*) under the banner of a single cause, creating another obstacle to development.[52] When blame was not being placed on the people, it was often directed to the climate and environment. Many felt that Tōhoku was unblessed by heaven's favor (*tenkei ni usui*), for not only did it suffer harsh winters, it was cursed by cool summers that wreaked havoc on the annual rice crop.[53] Taken together, such statements are representative of a consistent thread of self-deprecation that ran through local media of the time, unifying both people and environment under a shared set of negative qualities. Even near the end of the period surveyed, a *Nippō* editorialist lamented at length that "Tōhoku people are an obstinate and stubborn group. They are a breed who give in to nature and have no desire to conquer it or to pioneer any projects. In winter they hole up in their homes and do nothing; they make no attempt to break with tradition. . . . They make no effort to advance."[54] The kinds of criticism that in early Meiji had primarily come from external observers had by now been sufficiently internalized, allowing local ideologues to more easily, if less accurately, pinpoint the cause of the region's economic problems and offer heavy-handed solutions unconcerned with internal lines of difference.

Implicit in this discourse of self-critique were hierarchies of regional comparison that positioned Tōhoku and its inhabitants on a lower moral rung than other parts of the country. These hierarchies naturally extended to comparisons along other dimensions as well, including levels of economic and civilizational development. In the first instance, "Tōhoku" was portrayed as a region burdened by historical and economic factors that had delayed its movement along the singular path of progress. Commentators actually treated Tōhoku's regional particularity as an a priori condition for its perpetually slow growth. In 1904, Tamari Kizō (1856–1931), the first director of the Morioka Higher School of Agriculture and Forestry, characterized the region as burdened by too much uncultivated land, substandard agricultural growth, and a near total lack of an industrial or commercial sector. Was it not obvious, he wrote, why Tōhoku was unable to advance and develop like other regions?[55] Two years later, Hangai Seijū labeled it as unadvanced (*fushinpo*) and undeveloped (*fuhattatsu*), a stagnant region whose development was nevertheless still critical to the national economy.[56] The situation did not look nearly as bleak to Asano Gengo in 1920 owing to the gains made during the boom years of World War I, but he conceded regardless that Tōhoku was but a lumbering cow plodding behind the race horse economies of Tokyo, Osaka, and Nagoya.[57] The Iwate born Satō Shōsuke (1856–1939), who was head of the Sapporo School of Agriculture from 1894 to 1930, agreed: "Compared to other regions, Tōhoku is always behind. Whether it be in agriculture, industry, or commerce, its level of cultural advancement seems always to lag."[58] Such statements appeared in the pages of the *Nippō* too, where attention was occasionally given to Iwate alone and the causes of uneven development attributed to everything from a lack of rail lines to passive styles of thinking and the failure of government to adequately support communications infrastructure.[59]

Tōhoku was certainly not alone in being characterized as a region at the wrong end of an imagined developmental hierarchy.[60] Provincial newspapers in every part of Japan were filled with just such statements of regional identification. And from the perspective of the center, the whole of the provinces were easily construed as being at an economic and social disadvantage, their perennially "backward" farming villages (*nōson*) forever in need of revitalization.[61] Tōhoku stands out, however, in the degree to which its economic failures became the object of national policy initiatives. The Tōhoku Shinkō Kai (Society for the Promotion of Tōhoku), introduced in Chapter One, is exemplary of the political energy exerted in the hopes of setting the region on the right track. Founded in 1913 by then Minister of the Interior Hara Kei, it initially attracted an impressive list of Seiyūkai bureaucrats and Kantō industrialists who were led, at least on paper, by the great business mogul Shibusawa Eiichi (1840–1931). For all this political and economic muscle, however, a lack of real connection to elites in the region made the group little more than a glorified relief agency. Though it provided an important forum for debate on Tōhoku development, tangible achievements were limited to the series of regional goods exhibitions held in Tokyo.[62] Indirectly, however, the group did help popularize the phrase "Tōhoku shinkō," which was ubiquitous in the *Nippō* in the early 1920s as a banner under which to float a diverse range of economic and social policy initiatives.

The image of Tōhoku as woefully underdeveloped also fed into statements that constructed the region as an internal colony at once subservient to, but also neglected by, the policies of the state—a region lower on the ladder of civilization than the rest of the Japanese empire.[63] Some, like Tamari Kizō, expressed anger at the rationale promoting colonization of Siberia and emigration to Manchuria, areas far colder and less hospitable, before the successful development of Tōhoku itself.[64] It was Hokkaidō, however, that loomed largest as both an object of comparison and envy. Many struggled to understand why this colder island to the north was advancing so much more rapidly than mainland Tōhoku. In 1912, a railroad engineer working in the region remarked in the *Nippō* that the disparity between the two places could only be explained by a lack of effort on the part of Tōhoku residents.[65] In 1915, Satō Shōsuke wrote that "despite the fact that our country's culture has progressed from the southwest to the northeast since the state was founded 2,500 years ago, it still feels like the Tōhoku region is an internal colony (*naikokuteki shokuminchi*). . . . In the forty years since we've arrived in Hokkaidō, the work of colonization has continued to advance rapidly while Tōhoku apparently wishes to remain in its long night's slumber."[66] Satō went on to argue, and he was not alone, that the region's problems might be solved by a large-scale migration from other parts of Japan.[67] Hearing here the echo of later calls for overseas migration to Manchuria reinforces the uncanny overlap between colonialist discourse and the place of Tōhoku in the cultural imaginary at this time.[68] Even the Aomori native and prominent playwright Akita Ujaku (1883–1962) was of the opinion that culturally, the residents of Tōhoku were furthest behind in their development. He found no reason to disagree with the observation of a friend that, "When I talk to someone from Tōhoku, I don't feel as if I'm speaking to another Japanese."[69]

In all of the statements of regional identification thus far highlighted, the *problematic* and *thematic* both stand out as defining elements. But what about the third element in Chatterjee's model: the combination of the *problematic* and *thematic* in the hope of producing a "different discourse"? This too can be found in certain statements of regional identification from the time. While the difference produced is not of the same quality as that produced within the context of colonial-era nationalism, the statements similarly relied on positing the ontological uniqueness of a region (here a subnational one) and narrating from there an alternate future.[70] In the materials surveyed, these futures appear in several different guises. Some commentators resisted the image of Tōhoku as solely an agricultural and rice-producing region and imagined it instead as a new kind of industrial powerhouse. Arguing that the area's climate was simply not suited to rice agriculture as it was then being practiced—a fact attested to by a history of failed harvests—they believed that Tōhoku should model itself on the cold industrialized countries of northern Europe.[71] Various suggestions for facilitating such a transition were made, with some arguing that total industrialization was the key and some arguing for a more balanced approach that would combine industrial development with a shift toward cultivating crops better suited to the climate. Satō Yoshinaga (1867–1937), who presided over the Morioka Higher School of Agriculture during Miyazawa's student days, offered a wide array of creative proposals in his 1909 treatise, including such peculiar sounding industries as goat herding and sowing oats.[72]

In the opposite camp were ideologues, scientists, and officials who had difficulty imagining a "rice-less" Tōhoku. They were inclined to search for solutions in the region's already established historical trajectory. Many of those whom Miyazawa studied under, in fact, including the nationally recognized soil scientist Seki Toyotarō, were members of this camp. From the turn of the century onward, they were active in holding up Tōhoku as a scientific object united by various geological and climatic factors (e.g., soil composition, ocean currents, and weather patterns). For them, an alternative future lay in a Tōhoku set free from the whims of nature and made bountiful by fertilizer enhancement, development of new rice strains, more accurate methods of predicting poor harvests, and advancements in farming technique and technology.[73] Beyond the industry-versus-agriculture debates, there were other visions for the future that centered on themes like tourism, transportation, and education. An essay from 1922, for example, emphasized the need to reimagine Tōhoku as a place of natural beauty, historical sites, and hot springs, much as it is marketed today in the seasonal advertising campaigns of the Japan Railway Company.[74] With regard to transportation, copious amounts of ink were spilled by the *Nippō* for promoting and praising the construction of new train lines. Each new section of track seemed yet another reason to believe that the region was becoming an integrated and prosperous unit of the national economy.[75] In education, it was suggested that if all the residents of Iwate devoted the winter months to reading in the library, they might help to start a cultural movement that the prefecture could call its own.[76]

As impractical or implausible as some of these imagined futures seem, the desire to chart an alternate course for Tōhoku went hand in hand with the tendency to see the region as held together by the shared factors of lagging industrial development, agricultural stagnation, and an unforgiving natural environment. The image of a collective economic fate, encountered over and over again in the local media, generated a concomitant need to imagine a "Tōhoku" in which that fate might be overcome. This compulsion to juxtapose an image of what a place was perceived to be with an image of what it might become is neither particularly radical nor unique to the time. It speaks to a process endemic to the specific geography of capitalism through which regional social formations are brought into being by the inherent unevenness of development and consequently enter into a "socio-spatial dialectic," to borrow Edward Soja's term, wherein social relations and the organization of space mutually constitute and inform one another.[77] At the level of discourse, the result is that a subset of features are abstracted from all the elements that go to shape the social space (i.e., the social-material world in all its degrees of human modification) of a particular regional formation, creating condensed and comparable images of that space. Thus as certain social and economic conditions came to prevail in northeastern Honshū and in the area designated politically as Iwate Prefecture, specific elements were abstracted from these social spaces to form unified images of "Tōhoku" and "Iwate" that could then circulate as normative statements on what these places were. At the same time, the more that these images appeared to merge with their referents, the more inclined individuals were to try to manipulate them in the hope of working back upon space itself and ushering in a new reality. Thus they imagined a "Tōhoku" wherein thrived a new strain of rice better adapted to the region's cooler climate, and then used the image to support investment in the institutions and personnel necessary to make this happen. Or they imagined an "Iwate" whose isolated towns and hamlets were linked by a network of new rail lines, and then sought out the capital and political support needed to bring that vision into being.

This desire to work back upon reality, to tell a different story about a place in the hopes of provoking a reorganization of spatial relations, is the driving force behind the third element in Chatterjee's model. As Henri Lefebvre has written, "any 'social existence' aspiring or claiming to be 'real,' but failing to produce its own space, would be a strange entity, a very peculiar kind of abstraction unable to escape from the ideological or even the 'cultural' realm. It would fall to the level of folklore and sooner or later disappear altogether, thereby immediately losing its identity, its denomination and its feeble degree of reality."[78] Taking "social existence" to mean a social body *and* the discursive statements by which it recognizes and projects itself as image, Lefebvre seems to be saying that should this body fail to produce the actual spaces where its image can be realized, then it condemns itself to the fate of mere image and thus of historical irrelevancy. Difficult as it may be to trace the processes that facilitate the conversion of an image into the (re)production of actual spaces, the idea that a dialectical relation

must exist between the two is critical for how we read the intentional-
ity and impact of the visions set forth in statements of regional identification. It compels us to take these visions seriously as urgent attempts to
both change the conversation about a place and redirect its present course.
Though Miyazawa's vision was articulated differently than in other local
media, its immersion in the same enunciative field is reason to take just as
seriously its intent to impact social space.

Grounding Iihatov

Turning back now to the statement of Iihatov, it should be clear that despite
taking the form of a book advertisement, its triadic rhetorical structure puts
it in conversation with a wider field of statements of regional identification
from the period. Not only does it claim the existence of a unique region and
support this claim by comparing it with similar kinds of spaces (e.g., Alice's
Wonderland, the realm of King Ivan) and by delineating certain essential
characteristics (e.g., talking ants, beech forests), it also imagines a future for
this Iihatov, and by association "Iwate," different from the one that history
seemed determined to thrust upon it. "These stories have been presented so
that they might become materials for forming a new, better world. Not an
ashen-colored utopia kneaded together in a deformed way, but a miraculous
development (*hatten*) of the world itself that is yet unknown to this author."
Although the meaning of "miraculous development" is left open to interpretation, the commitment to reality is undeniable, and so too the desire to
promote real-world change. The statement outwardly assumes that by altering the image of a place—"Japan's Iwate Prefecture as dreamland"—one can
potentially alter the space itself and push it toward alternate futures.

   Yet if the advertisement functions within the same "realm of the possible," it also utilizes its literary stance to extend the boundaries of that realm,
even at the risk of isolating itself from more conventional statements. Consider, for example, the passage regarding the intended purpose of the stories
in the collection. Whereas most statements sought betterment primarily for
the region, and beyond that the nation, the project of Iihatov was aimed at
"the world itself." Iwate was merely the first priority in a far broader strategy, a fact reinforced by Miyazawa's offering of his stories to society (*seken*)
at large and not to any one group of spatially bound individuals. So while
the statement used the provincial region of Iwate as a conscious base for its
message, it aimed to transmit that message more widely. Looking past the

region or even the nation-state, it looked to the world. Speaking not just to urbanites or rural inhabitants alone, it directed itself to all of society.

Another point of difference is the substitution of Iwate for a toponym lacking a known spatial referent and an identifiable linguistic home. To revisit a question raised earlier, what did Miyazawa expect to gain by forgoing the use of Tōhoku or Iwate as spatial identifiers?[79] One can imagine how the sheer foreignness of Iihatov, as both word and concept, dissociated it from Iwate and from the various niches that had by this time been marked out for Iwate in the social imaginary: Iwate as a rural backwater, for instance, or as part of Japan's underdeveloped Tōhoku region. Or even as subsumed under the general term for periphery (*chihō*). The name was, in other words, a means to generate a space of both linguistic and conceptual difference. But in the statement's refusal to sever all links with the sociopolitical entity of Iwate, there is an attempt to continue to speak for the particularity of the locale while circumventing representations bound to either metropolitan culture or internalized hierarchies of social and economic difference. Iihatov is acting as a filter that de-privileges, or at least relativizes, other filters, particularly those that stake a claim on "truth" by way of association with hegemonic or dominant discursive strains. If this filter looks to be more fanciful or out of touch with reality, keep in mind that the dominant images of Tōhoku and Iwate circulating at the time were also distorting in their own way. That is, they similarly functioned to filter out the complexities inherent to any place in order to project an image of a unified social space. Iihatov was a means to perform this function differently and toward alternative ends.

Miyazawa had been experimenting with such a filtering technique in the months before the advertisement came out. In several poetic sketches from 1924, later edited and compiled into the second volume of his *Spring and Asura*, he adapted the classic *mitate* literary device as a metaphorical brush by which to paint over everyday landscapes and people in strange, unfamiliar colors.[80] A train passenger is described, for instance, as clothed in a red piece of *nassen* style flannel worn in an Egyptian manner. Another poem depicts two young girls in a grassy field gazing into the distance as if standing upon the Asian steppes in spring. A third sketch presents a pair of peasant girls as Ukrainian dancers heading into town for the morning market. In another we find night descending in the same way it would in the Gandhara region of Pakistan.[81] By recasting the mundane scenes of rural Iwate in the aura of distant, almost mythical locales, these sketches encourage readers to step outside their ingrained ways of parsing and categorizing the world around them. And to do so, significantly, without relying on a Euro-centric framework.

The most interesting use of this filtering technique appears in an official school report from the same year. Written in late May, it was ostensibly meant as an account of the school's annual trip to Hokkaidō to observe factories and agricultural research farms, for which Miyazawa had served as chaperone.[82] Knowing that the document was likely written so as to impress upon school administrators the pedagogical value of the trip, the degree to which it channels the streams of discourse discussed above is uncanny. During a visit to Sapporo Imperial University, for instance, the students were welcomed by Dean Satō Shōsuke, a native of Hanamaki and a key contributor to public discourse on Tōhoku. He lectured to them about the difficulty of farming established agricultural areas like Iwate, as compared with the newly opened lands of Hokkaidō, and warned them that the former task would require extra resolve and effort to improve upon outdated methods and to absorb the culture of progress (*nisshin no bunmei*).[83] Later, the students visited the Hall of Development (Takushokukan) in Nakajima Park. Built in 1918 for the fiftieth anniversary celebration of Hokkaidō's "official" opening, it contained a diorama charting the island's evolution as a colonial space: from forests and fields of a wild and wretched sort to a land neatly divided into 5-hectare units; from barren fields of nothing to a fertile and pleasant countryside (*den'en*) with schools and railroads. "Who," Miyazawa wrote, "could see this and not shed tears? I dare say that the influence of this diorama on our students' futures will be extremely great. My only wish is that several such dioramas, displaying the ideal living conditions of farmers, might exist in our own prefecture. For it would give our future farmers a goal toward which to build a pleasant and bright country setting (*den'en*) of their own."[84]

Near the end of the report, on the train ride south from Sapporo, Miyazawa offered a similarly curious proposal for visualizing anew the space of Iwate.

> From the train window we saw the Ishikari River before entering stands of larch and German spruce. The students praised the scenery to no end. How true it is that one's emotions become vivid and fresh when traveling, separated from reality as they are, thus making it that much easier to judge beauty. If students return home while retaining the mindset of Western tourists, will not the mountains and rivers look like one of those old-fashioned

Hiroshige or Hokusai paintings? Indeed, if not trained to see things in this way, the wind and light of the pastoral setting will fade with the hardship of dull and oppressive labor; they will look down upon farming as nothing more than a sacred act one carries out alone, a torturous type of *skimmed milk*. Furthermore, in contrast to Hokkaidō's landscape, whose simple harmony can be grasped quite readily, how difficult it is to comprehend the scenes of long-settled Michinoku in all their complexity. Rows and forests of dark, crimson pine; numerous ancient cedars sacred to the tree gods; groves of Chinese and red willow; large roofs of straw and fences of cypress: the composition of these elements is too dark and entangled. All that is required to remedy this would be a couple of white birch at each residence, an upright German spruce, or perhaps a grove of glittering box-willow and red poppy. Truly, nothing surpasses trees in bringing peaceful harmony to the countryside (*den'en*).[85]

The filtering technique used by Miyazawa in his poetic sketches undergoes here a shift in spatial orientation—the idea is not to look at one's native place as if it were a foreign land, but to assume the role of a foreign tourist so as to see it in an exotic and unfamiliar light. The guiding principle, however, is roughly the same. By reenvisioning one's native landscape as a foreign locale, as a kind of *other* place, the possibility is opened up of attaching to that landscape a different set of values—values that otherwise might be ignored or obscured by the numbing effects of daily routine and the oppressive hardship of agricultural labor. It is a naïve assertion, to be sure, and one intelligible only to a privileged elite who knew little of what it meant to live by the soil alone. But it does reconfirm Miyazawa's belief in the power of a reconfigured spatial imagination to transform real-world conditions. We also get the sense that if imagination proved not enough, Miyazawa was willing, at least judging from his proposal to uproot and replant the embedded and entangled spaces of old Iwate, to try to alter the arrangement of reality itself.

Despite the outward desire expressed here and in the advertising pamphlet to impact the organization of space, we are left to consider what could actually come of such a desire in the historical context in which it was expressed. As a representational strategy, Iihatov was indeed capable of critically remapping the spaces of Iwate in the narrative and cultural imaginaries, as I show in the next chapter. What is harder to demonstrate, however, is whether Iihatov could have informed the socio-spatial dialectic in the same way as more conventional statements of regional identification that pushed for things like railway expansion and agricultural innovation.

Exactly how would such a discursive formation have been translated into the socio-material processes by which space is differentiated and organized? Spatial theorists like Lefebvre, Soja, David Harvey, and Doreen Massey have come a long way toward convincing us of the reality of a socio-spatial dialectic mediated not only by our physical bodies and movements in space, but *also* by language and representation.[86] And they have argued convincingly that discursive elements, particularly those with an explicit ideological function, are informed by space even as they influence, with varying degrees of success, its actual production.[87] But do these theoretical assumptions carry through to discursive elements like the imagined literary region, fictional narrative, or poetic verse? Can such elements function not just as passive records of spatial representation, but as active agents of spatial production?

One can think of instances where literary material has participated in the socio-spatial dialectic once disseminated amongst a social elite or a broad enough swathe of the populace. Consider the role that Japanese classical poetry played for centuries in isolating features in the landscape and canonizing them as lyrically important sites, or the influence of "the sublime" on late-nineteenth- and early-twentieth-century preservation movements in Europe and America.[88] A more relevant example would be the fact that Thomas Hardy's partly fictional Wessex became a recognized place-name during his own lifetime.[89] Iihatov would eventually come to wield this sort of influence over the real space of Iwate, but not at the outset. Its failure in this regard can be attributed to its lack of exposure, which kept it from entering those social and political channels through which decisions about the region's future were being made. Even had it reached these channels, however, one suspects that it would have fallen upon deaf ears given its distance from other statements in the enunciative field. Miyazawa may have had some inkling of this because it was not long, as will be discussed in Chapters Six and Seven, before he set aside the strategy of Iihatov in search of less obviously literary ways to reorganize social space.

For a brief instant, nevertheless, it clearly seemed reasonable to Miyazawa to think that an idea like Iihatov could bring about some sort of social transformation. Here was a provincial writer who held no illusions about where he stood in relation to Tokyo's literary establishment—a writer who had resigned himself to working outside dominant media channels for a mostly local audience. Limiting as this position was, it also provided him an autonomous space within which to experiment with strategies of spatial representation unfettered by conventional approaches. He was in a position to contest or relativize such approaches precisely because he felt no pressure to adhere to or abide by them. On the literary front, this translated into an ability to imagine a literary region that confounded horizons of expectation. Iihatov was not a purely fictional space lacking connection to the environmental and geographical reality of Iwate, nor a space bound to reality in such a way that it might easily be subsumed under the labels of "traditional" and "provincial." Not a space of pure fantasy, then, but also not an anachronistic space standing forever behind and outside the present moment. On the social front, Miyazawa was able to use the idea of Iihatov to present an alternative to prominent strains of regional discourse, dominated as they were by talk of economic and political backwardness, and to thus expand the borders of what could and could not be said about the region. Rather than privilege space by locating and fixing a stable identity, which Harvey characterizes as a typically modern response to the growing homogenization of society under time-space compression, he sought to produce difference in ways that pushed the region forward and beyond its present condition.[90] Born of Miyazawa's own movement between center and periphery, Iihatov rejected a strategy of isolated resistance in favor of one that leveled received spatial hierarchies and placed the periphery at the forefront of progressive social change.

For all its interest in renegotiating spatial hierarchies, Iihatov was, in the end, unable to overcome a lack of spatial capital and it thus failed to gain entry into the necessary circuits of distribution and institutions of value distinction. Perhaps this was for the best. Had it secured a place in the cultural imaginary, its critical potential might have been absorbed and diffused by dominant discursive formations. Just consider the one chance it did have for wider dissemination. A month after the publication of *The Restaurant of Many Orders*, the illustrator for the volume, Kikuchi Takeo, managed to place an advertisement in the pages of *Akai tori*. Because some of the phrases in this ad match those on the outer edges of the advertisement pamphlet, it is likely that he referred to the latter when he designed the ad, and it may even have been available to the copy editors at *Akai tori*.[91] Two key differences, however, stand out. One is a passage in bold that dominates the center of the advertisement: "[This book] is a fabulous yacht that races across Tōhoku's vast fields of snow." The other is a short phrase contained in a list of people who might be interested in the work. Not just for literature lovers, educators, and cute children, the book was also ideal for those who "truly want to savor Tōhoku."[92] Iihatov had gone missing, replaced by a toponym from which the statement of Iihatov had distanced itself.[93] Not merely re-placed, but replaced in such a way as to render all of northeastern Japan exotic. In effect, the *Akai tori* ad reversed the trajectory of Miyazawa's strat-egy, turning its thrust from the region outward into a commodifying look back from the outside. Iihatov's original impulse—to generate difference at the level of representation and material space—went entirely unrecognized at the center of literary production even as the language by which readers might recover that impulse was erased.

CHAPTER FIVE

Conversations with Nature

In describing the "strange and exciting land" of Iihatov, the place where anything is possible, the advertisement for *The Restaurant of Many Orders* provides merely a glimpse into a fictional world where one can "leap over icy clouds" to follow the global winds or "talk to an ant crawling at the bottom of a crimson flower-cup." Should one go searching for this world in the volume itself, however, one would be disappointed. It contains no stories of racing winds nor of talking ants. In fact, the two stories alluded to here were written in the period between the publication of the volume in 1924 and the months when the tales in the volume were originally conceived (that is, after Miyazawa's return from Tokyo in 1921). This was a time, as noted in the preceding chapter, when Miyazawa began to experiment with narrative strategies more directly in dialogue with his local landscape and with his idea of Iihatov. Thus while the two stories never made it into the Iihatov collection, they prove to be, as the advertisement itself implies, a far better guide to the narrative contours of his imagined literary region. Both can be used to show, as I do in this chapter, how the conceit of Iihatov—as a representational strategy for decentering dominant mappings of social space—gave Miyazawa room to confront the changing character of local experience under universalizing regimes of knowledge. The first tale did so by addressing the leveling effects of scientific description and educational instruction on the construction of local and regional identity. The second by considering the impact of linguistic standardization and universal classificatory schema on subjective perception of the local object-world.

Each of these confrontations is framed, significantly, through conversations between human and nonhuman actors. It is *conversation* in the basic sense of discursive interchange, but also in the broader sense of "consorting or having dealings with others," a sustained "occupation or engagement with things."[1] As readers of Miyazawa's fiction well know, he was fond of anthropomorphization as a literary device and used it liberally in his work. But while it would be easy to consign his use of the device to his chosen genre, *dōwa* being a place where talking animals and animate things still thrived in the world of modern letters, his staged conversations—between child and wind, ant and flower, mosquito and volcanic rock—generally performed more critical conceptual work than typical *dōwa* fare. Rather than displace human thought and action onto improbable stand-ins, or offer a gratuitous simulation of human society using nonhuman performers, Miyazawa aimed in his conversations to retain the specific otherness of the objects or creatures involved. In some instances, his texts explicitly restructured and refashioned human thought and action to capture the uniqueness, even if expressed in human terms, of an alien perspective. The rhetorical effect of such conversations, as will become clear, amounted to a decentering, or relativization, of accepted discursive and epistemological practices not unlike that performed by Iihatov in the arena of spatial representation. For Miyazawa, Iihatov was ultimately both a narrative strategy *and* the strategic setting for provincializing conversations seldom heard in more realist genres of the day.

In his case, of course, genre was not the only factor limiting the audible range of these conversations; both of the stories taken up here went unpublished during his lifetime. If this limits what we can say about their social and political impact, it does not preclude us from situating them within a specific enunciative and historical context. Miyazawa was still a no-name provincial author at the time, and so to say that his stories went "unpublished" means something different than if we were to say the same for an established professional writer. The fact of not publishing was less a willful decision to keep the text from public view than a matter of having few publishing options to choose from. Moreover, the pedagogical tone of his stories is a strong indication that Miyazawa wrote them with a socially and historically specific audience in mind: his students. It is by giving attention to this immediate local context that we can meaningfully situate the stories as texts trying to speak to a particular moment and then use this as a jumping-off point for making more speculative claims about what they might have achieved had they been afforded a wider audience.

Conversations outside the National Classroom

The first conversation takes places between the children of a small village and a mischievous wind imp named Kazeno Matasaburō. It comes from a story of the same name composed in early 1924 and likely read aloud by Miyazawa to his students.[2] He would return to the manuscript years later to create a second, revised version known today as "Kaze no Matasaburō" (Matasaburō of the Wind), which proved to be the more popular and recognized of the two owing to its inclusion in several posthumous collections of Miyazawa's fiction and its adaptation to film in 1940.[3] But as an Iihatov narrative, and within the context of this chapter's theoretical concerns, it is the former that offers the most provocative material for analysis. Structured like a veritable textbook on the wind, and written when Miyazawa himself was teaching a variety of scientific subjects, including meteorology, "Kazeno Matasaburō" offers a window onto the practice and politics of elementary science instruction in the waning years of the Taishō period. At a time when this instruction, at least as articulated by policy makers and higher-level administrators, depended heavily on discourses both centrist and universalizing, the implementation of science education in the classroom raised crucial questions about the value and significance of local knowledge against the imperatives of national learning. "Kazeno Matasaburō" was Miyazawa's attempt at an answer.

Divided into ten sections, each marking a different day, the story is in essence an account of Matasaburō's ten-day sojourn in an anonymous Iwate hamlet. In the opening scene, the third-person narrator introduces us to a tiny, nondescript schoolhouse nestled at the base of a narrow river valley. It is a sunny September morning, a light breeze is in the air, and the twenty children who attend the school are just returning from summer break. Two of the first-year students, eager to arrive ahead of the others, rush through the schoolhouse gates and up to the classroom window to peer in. To their surprise, an unfamiliar someone has beaten them in the chase. As the other students arrive, they too rush up to catch a glimpse of the red-headed boy who sits perfectly still, returning their stares in silence. Ichirō, the lone sixth-grader, steps in to take charge.

> "Who do you think you are getting to class ahead of time?" Ichiro had crawled up onto the windowsill and was sticking his head in.
> "The teacher is going to scold you good!" shouted Kōsuke from below.
> "Don't look at me if you get in trouble," chimed Kasuke.
> "Hurry up and get out of there, just get out of there," urged Ichiro.
> . . . Everything about the boy, beginning with his appearance, just seemed odd. He had on a bizarre gray cape and his shoes (were they crystal or glass?) were beautifully transparent. His face looked just like a ripe apple and he had perfectly round, pitch black eyes. Ichiro and the rest were befuddled as to why not a single word seemed to be getting through to the boy.
> "He's a foreigner!" "No, he's our new classmate!" Everyone was shouting noisily.[4]

Finally bringing the commotion to an end is the teacher's whistle. The students, without missing a beat, line up in their assigned rows and march inside at his orders. But to their dismay, the stranger from before is nowhere to be found. The teacher, who remains oblivious to all that has gone on that morning, then proceeds to reintegrate them into the disciplined space of learning.[5]

> "I bet you all had an interesting vacation, right. From morning on you were able to go swimming, or play in the forest shouting and screaming louder than a hawk, or you may have even gone to cut weeds with your older brother. That's all very fine and good. But vacation has come to an end. It's autumn now, and many have long said that autumn is the best time to study. So starting today, let's all study hard." (8)

Notably, the teacher's speech is represented using the standard dialect (*hyōjungo*), a fact that serves to augment his authority because of its sharp contrast with the locally inflected speech of the children. On this particular morning, however, no amount of authoritative voice does him any good. The still distracted students want to know more about the boy.

> "*Sensei*," shouted the fourth grader Setsuji, raising his hand.
> "Yes."
> "*Sensei*, who's that person from before?"
> The teacher paused a while, looking perplexed. "The person from before . . ."

"He was here a little bit ago, the kid with red hair." The children began to shout all at once. "*Sensei*, his hair was bright red and he looked really strange." "He was wearing a cape!" "He came in here before you blew the whistle!"

The teacher was at a loss. "Speak one at a time, please. Are you saying there was someone in here with red hair?"

"That's right, *sensei*." (8)

The boy's visit has rendered almost farcical the teacher's efforts to establish order: the students have no interest in studying, they refuse to speak in turn, and they all seem to be suffering from collective delusion. And when they cannot keep themselves from looking out to the grassy hill that rises just beyond the schoolhouse window, presumably because the boy stands there taunting them, the teacher concedes to their insatiable curiosity and ends class early.[6] They race "like the wind" to the top of the hill only to find that the boy has once again gone missing; in his place, just as the teacher said there would be, are stands of plume poppy simply rustling in the breeze. But when the two older boys, Ichirō and Kōichi, return the next afternoon to put their doubts to rest, they find who it is they have been after; Matasaburō sits there waiting in the grass, eager to begin a conversation that will last until his departure on the tenth day. During this time he will tell the boys, and later the other children, of his adventures both locally and around the globe, all the while weaving into his tales a series of lessons on the wind, the nature of its movement, and its environmental effects. This stranger from the skies, taking advantage of his invisibility in the eyes of educational authority, has led them away from the conventional site of pedagogy to establish a new space of learning uniquely determined by the subject of study itself. Situated safely outside the compulsory classroom and its nationally standardized rhetoric, Matasaburō will introduce the children to a different way of knowing the world.

Before they hear him out, however, the boys demand to know who it is they have been chasing after.

"Who are you? What are you?" shouted Ichirō, still trying to catch his breath. The boy answered in a calm and resolute manner, just as if he were an adult.

"Kazeno Matasaburō."

"Where are you from? Are you Russian?" At this the boy looked up and let out a hearty laugh. His voice was like that of a deer whistle. He finally became serious again, replying bluntly,

"It's Matasaburō!"
"Oh, Matasaburō of the Wind!" shouted Ichirō and Kōichi instantly,
their faces turning to one another.
"That's what I said, isn't it!?" (10)

This may well be what Matasaburō said, voiced in the unmistakable dialect
of the center, but it is not what the boys heard; the text makes this clear
by using two different lexical representations for phrases that would sound
identical in speech. Thus while they initially hear the surname Kazeno followed by the given name Matasaburō, what they recognize, and what they
quickly recall with prompting from Matasaburō himself, is that which
translates literally as "Matasaburō of the Wind." The text does not indicate
why they are familiar with the latter name, but we know that in areas of
Niigata and Tōhoku, "Saburō of the Wind" was a popular appellation for a
local wind spirit venerated in festival, folklore, and regional children's songs.
Miyazawa may have been counting on his listeners to recognize the name
just as the two boys did, even as he altered it to his own purposes.[7]

Having confirmed his identity, the boys ask Matasaburō why he ran away
the day before.

"I didn't run away. Yesterday was the 210th Day, you see. Normally I
would have headed off with my older brothers to the far, far north."
"So why didn't you?"
"Well, my brother didn't come calling."
"What's his name, your older brother?"
"Kazeno Matasaburō. What did you think it'd be?" Matasaburō was upset
again.
"Oh, I get it. Your brother's name is Kazeno Matasaburō too, and so is
your father's, and so is your grandfather's, right," said Kōichi.
"Yeah, yeah, that's right. I travel all over the place, you know."
"Have you been to China?"
"Yep."
"What about Mt. Iwate?"
"I just came from that direction, didn't I? I actually spent last night up
there in the mountain valley."
"Wow, that's so neat. I wanna be like the wind too!" (11)[8]

At this point the well-traveled Matasaburō, whom we now know to be the
youngest in a strictly "male" lineage of wind spirits all bearing the same
name, begins to tell the boys of his myriad adventures. And he starts, significantly, in their very own backyard.

His first tale relates his evening stay on Mt. Iwate and his predawn flight up its rocky slopes. An active volcano in the central Ōu mountain range of northern Honshū, it is the highest peak in Iwate Prefecture and stands tall over the city of Morioka and its environs. Matasaburō explains to the boys how he followed a torch-lit procession of worshippers climbing to pray at a tutelary shrine on the summit, himself forced to pause with each leap so as to wait for a pocket of empty space to open up ahead of him. Described in great detail are not only the dress and movement of the worshippers, but also the view from the top, where Matasaburō gazed out to the surrounding hills and down to the crater lakes of Onawashiro and Okama glowing green amidst the stands of white birch. The whole scene was apparently lit by an amber sky full of giant, lizard shaped clouds. We also learn at this point that the imp has been to the area before.

> "It wasn't quite light out yet and I could see a deep red flame moving along the valley ridge, flickering as it went. With the flame shining through the branches of the oak and birch trees, it looked just like a gourd lantern."
>
> "Really. I made a gourd lantern last year. But when I hung it up over the veranda, the wind came and blew it down," said Kōichi.
>
> Matasaburō could hardly contain himself. "I saw your gourd lantern, you know. That thing was so pretty that I smashed straight into it and knocked it down."
>
> "Whaaa . . . ," is all that Kōichi could muster, a perturbed look on his face. Matasaburō, though, found the whole thing so amusing that he laughed with all his might, his throat rippling like the waves as he looked skyward. He was finally able to suppress his laughter and, wiping his tears away, said to Kōichi,
>
> "That wasn't nice of me. How 'bout I bring you something good in return. Next time I'll carry five beautiful aspen trees to your place. Sound good?" (12–13)

The gesture is enough to assuage Kōichi's anger, and the boys are so fascinated by Matasaburō's tales that they return the next day, day three, with ten of their classmates in tow. This time they call out to Matasaburō with several verses of a local children's song and he promptly sweeps down to greet them in his signature cape and crystalline shoes.[9] Catching his breath, he begins to tell them of his grandfather, who travels at the greatest of heights, his nearly frozen mantle leaving a trail of tiny, shattered ice crystals in its wake. He speaks of his trip up the Japanese archipelago the preceding year, and of how he leapt from southern Kyūshū all the way to Tokyo in a single bound, arriving the next night in Iwate to push a tuft of clouds against the black, serpentine rocks of Mt. Takabora. The next day he speaks of various types of whirlwinds—including the tiny dust-whirls known as *kama'itachi*, cyclones, tornadoes, and typhoons—explaining how they take shape when the sun beats down on a particular spot or when wind imps hurriedly rush past each other in opposing directions.[10] Though never involved with one of the great typhoons that occasionally blow up from the southern seas, Matasaburō does recall a time before "what all of you call the Meiji Restoration" when he took part in a small tornado, or *tatsumaki* (lit., dragon coil), over the nearby town of Hizume. The event proved especially memorable because as he and his friends gained speed, they drew in water from an outlying marsh and turned their flittering funnel, at least as seen in the bright rays of the sun, into the shimmering tail of a dragon. Confirming the verity of the illusion were the frightened cries of the townspeople, which soon turned to shouts of heavenly gratitude as the water, replete with floundering fish, dropped smack upon their rooftops.

On day five Matasaburō boasts of setting record wind speeds at the Great China Weather Observatory in Shanghai. There, much like at Japan's Central Weather Observatory in Tokyo, wind imps hurry past in order to impress the scientists busily attending to their measuring devices. During a recent visit, Matasaburō found himself moving back and forth between land and sea, resting over the water at night before returning inland the next day. As his speed increased with each pass of the observatory, he listened excitedly to a Chinese meteorologist and eager young assistant as they tried to assess his formidable strength on the official Beaufort Wind Scale.[11]

By the sixth day, the children show signs of losing interest in Matasaburō and his endless stories. He who seemed such a mysterious stranger upon arrival was now more like a friendly transfer student just up from Tokyo. Not one to be ignored, Matasaburō tries to win back their attention by teasing the fifth-grader Kōichi, flipping his umbrella inside out. Outraged, the boy marches up the grassy hill the very next day to tell the obnoxious wind imp why the world would be better off without him. Matasaburō challenges him, as might any good teacher, to come up with a list of reasons. And so Kōichi counts, one by one, all the ways the wind causes trouble. For starters, he declares, it ruins umbrellas. It snaps limbs from trees and overturns their roots, knocks over rice stalks, upturns houses and telegraph poles and towers, and blows sand. It even, he declares after a long, searching pause, smashes up windmills. Matasaburō breaks into wild laughter at this last suggestion and, after apologizing to Kōichi, counters with a list of his own:

> I certainly cause mischief on occasion, but the good things I do are so much more. Just count them. I transport the flowers of pine trees and willow, the feathery seed of the cotton plant, and things like that, right? Then there's the rice pollen of course. We carry that too. And whenever I blow past the grasses and trees they all become stronger for it. I also carry away the bad air and bring in the good. I'll take the air of Tokyo's Asakusa, for instance, looking like muddied gelatin, and whisk it off to the Pacific Ocean. Then I'll replace it with the clean air of the Japan Alps. If I weren't around, do you know how much more illness and musty air there'd be? (35–36)

Days eight and nine bring Matasaburō's most far-reaching tale—an exhilarating account of his trip from the equatorial doldrums to the North Pole and back. It also serves as introduction to the basic thermal mechanisms driving the general atmospheric circulation of air (*daijunkan*). This process, first described by George Hadley in 1735, is set into motion when moist, heated air expands and rises from low pressure areas at the equator. The air moves poleward through the higher, cooler levels of the atmosphere before again sinking down to the planet's surface at 30° north or south latitude. The resulting loop, which helps to generate the trade winds at the lower latitudes, is known as the Hadley cell and is balanced by a similar convection cycle at the upper latitudes, known as the Polar cell. Here the air rises at the 60th parallel and then drops rapidly at the poles, spinning off to the east in a giant circular motion.[12] Although Matasaburō does not mention these cells by name, the path of his journey is clearly meant to invoke them and the larger system they represent. He tells the children, for instance, how he started off his "great loop" near the Gilbert Islands—a string of tiny atolls straddling the equator—and from there ascended quickly into the sky with his fellow wind imps. Racing across the broad expanses of the Pacific at high altitude, and watching many of his companions fall to the wayside as he went, he found himself days later in the chilly air of the Arctic Circle with all those who had persevered. Here, he too began his inevitable descent, traversing the vast glaciers of northern Greenland in an easterly sweep around the North Pole, finally touching down on a drifting iceberg for a sorely needed rest. The slow drift back begins a week later, Matasaburō moving now leisurely over land and sea—through the foggy waters of the Tsugaru Straits, through the serene and melancholy skies above Korea—and eventually winding up again out over the Pacific Ocean.

If this summary of Matasaburō's adventures seems overly detailed, it is only to demonstrate how closely his carefully crafted lessons align—at least in their scientific content—with the history of education on the wind in Japan. While unique in their style of narration and manner of conveyance, they cover many of the same natural phenomena that were included in textbooks and elementary science readers from the turn of the century onward. Matasaburō, it turns out, was highly attuned to the other voices with which he had to compete for the children's attention. His response was to draw from the standard playbook even as he rewrote the rules of the game.

Casting the Textbook Approach to the Wind

This playbook did not exist as a single canonical text, but was rather a core set of topics around which instruction on the wind had come to be codified by the early 1920s. Many of the lessons learned in "Kazeno Matasaburō," in fact, were just as easily found in textbooks and science readers printed two decades earlier. At that time, publishers were already beginning to develop a market for general science primers even though science education at the primary level was still restricted to the fifth and sixth grades and mandated to be taught a mere two hours each week. One such primer, released in 1900 by the textbook publisher Fukyūsha, contained simple introductory chapters to a wide variety of topics, the wind included.

> Wind is what we call the movement of air. Air, though it cannot be seen by the eye, is a gas covering the entire globe with a thickness of nearly 20 *ri* [80 km].
> When air is heated it expands, and when it expands it becomes lighter. Once it becomes lighter it rises, and soon after air comes from elsewhere to fill its place. It is on the path of incoming air that wind is born.
> The direction the wind blows depends on things such as topography and climate. In our country (*wagakuni*), there is generally a southerly wind in the summer and a northerly wind in the winter. As for the wind near the seashore, it moves toward land during the day and toward the ocean at night. . . .
> Sometimes there are even whirlwinds. On land they sweep up rocks and tiles into the air, and at sea they suck up the ocean water. Whirlwinds at sea are called *tatsumaki*. The scariest of all winds are the stormy winds of the 210th Day.
> When people see violent winds and whirlwinds that damage fields, topple houses, or submerge ships, they think that the wind can only do harm. But

calm winds offer important benefits. They cleanse the air, balance out humidity and heat, carry pollen to plants, and even transport seeds. There is not room to list them all.[13]

The points of correspondence with Matasaburō's own pedagogical discourse should be obvious: the origin of wind in changing temperatures, the damage done by whirlwinds, the fears aroused by the 210th Day, the wind's beneficial qualities. It is these same basic points, significantly, that are reiterated, and even expanded upon, in other science primers of the time. While the elementary science textbook became nationally standardized only in 1911, privately produced texts were already required at this time to receive government certification. This naturally encouraged publishers to address the same kinds of material as their competitors, if not more thoroughly.

The more advanced textbook used by Miyazawa's students at the Hanamaki School of Agriculture also covered the same fundamental points, though at a higher level of complexity. Originally published in 1903 by the large Tokyo firm Kōbunsha, the text was written for agricultural school students as an introduction to meteorology. It began by emphasizing how important time and place were in determining climate, and then proceeded to explain the origin of the wind in heat-induced air pressure changes, the use of the Beaufort scale to assess wind speed, the processes giving rise to the equatorial trade winds, the cyclical movement of air between land and sea, the formation of whirlwinds, and the significance in Japan of the 210th Day. As its final lesson, it even weighed the wind's positive effects against the negative, declaring the wind to be essential for plant growth because of its ability to moderate temperature, cleanse the air, promote evaporation, and carry both seed and pollen.[14]

Alongside the expanding market for science primers and intermediate-level textbooks, many educators were busy pioneering a slightly less formal approach to elementary science education: the science reader (*kagaku* or *rika yomimono*). This was a genre that rendered the explanation of natural phenomena and scientific principle into a distinctly narrative mode, its loosely bound stories structured by an omniscient, authorial voice that assumed a reader both childishly inquisitive and eager to learn the ways of rational scientific thought. Fukuzawa Yukichi provided an early model for this kind of text with his 1868 *Kyūri-zukai* (An Illustrated Investigation of Scientific Principles), but it was not until the appearance of a twelve-volume series by Ishii Kendō in 1901 that the genre truly came into its own.[15] Published as *Rika jūnikagetsu* (Twelve Months of Science) by Hakubunkan, the individual volumes were dedicated to such commonplace topics as flowers, insects, snow, the seashore, and climbing Mt. Fuji. All proved popular enough to undergo multiple printings in the decades to follow.

The month of September was given over to wind and rain, Ishii weaving together sixteen lessons on the two topics with a series of patently staged dialogues and events.[16] In the first, a young boy named Natsuki tells an elderly foster parent about the "real" meaning of the 210th Day, correcting the old man's misguided belief that this day alone, rather than the time of year in general, is the only occasion to worry about strong winds damaging the rice crops. In the third lesson, Natsuki and his erudite young friends demonstrate the connection between air movement and temperature difference by performing a simple experiment at home.[17] In lesson five we are introduced to Akiyama-san, a boy who has been cut on the leg by a *kama'itachi*. The event is a chance to learn that his injury has nothing to do with a vindictive weasel, as the ideographs for the term imply. And as the boy recovers in lessons six and seven, he hears of yet other kinds of whirlwinds from his aged aunt and a fifty-year-old hospital orderly, both of whom he listens to with a mix of curiosity and skepticism. The former tells of an instance in the third year of Ansei (1856)—that time, as Matasaburō refers to it, before "what all of you call the Meiji Restoration"—when she caught sight of a tornado so powerful that it lifted the roof right off a house. The latter reminisces about his days as a sailor when he saw the frightful tail of a dragon (or what Akiyama knows in truth to be a *tatsumaki*) drop down from an ominously black ocean sky. As in the earlier lessons, superstition rationally discerned serves as the path to genuine scientific knowledge.

Over the next twenty years, the science reader would emerge as a permanent feature of the nation's growing market for supplementary educational material. By late Taishō, amidst a relentless wave of books, magazines, and study guides that promised academic success to "superior students" (*yūtōsei*) and their ever-mindful middle-class parents, there were also to be found "Stories of Nature," "Science Fairy Tales," and "Interesting Stories of Science That Children Want to Hear."[18] The first of these, a popular nine-volume series published in 1923, sought to impart the truth and principles of science in a way both "easy to understand" and inspiring to readers eager to feel "the immense powers that rule over the natural world." Volume four in the series, bearing the modest title *Kumo, ame, kaze* (Clouds, Rain, and Wind), provided a comprehensive and detailed look at that "utterly mysterious" entity the wind, addressing all the topics considered at this time to be standard. Entire sections were devoted to the principal cause of wind, the utility of the Beaufort scale, the 210th Day, how to measure wind speed, the destructive power of typhoons and tornadoes, and the nature of wind movement between land and sea, mountain and valley. Significantly, it also contained sections listing the wind's benefits for daily life (principal among them being the cleansing of urban air, the spinning of wind mills, and the moderation of warm temperatures) and a section, markedly absent from any of the earlier texts, which explained the processes driving the general atmospheric circulation of air (*daiki no junkan*). This latter section even included a diagram charting the direction of wind flow at the three primary latitudinal stages (equatorial, mid-latitude, and polar).[19]

If these lessons on the wind seem to coincide with the lessons taught in "Kazeno Matasaburō," or at least constitute the palette from which Miyazawa arranged his own pedagogical content, they also exhibit fundamental differences in rhetorical structure and manner of presentation. In all of the texts surveyed, for instance, information emerges as part of an organized and straightforward procession of facts linked only by the serial logic of increasing complexity. When there is an attempt at narration, as in Ishii's volume, the techniques employed are generally feeble and unconvincing, plot being forever made secondary to content. True, the science readers do frequently use dialogue to propel discussion along, particularly in the form of rudimentary questions (e.g., What is wind? Where does it come from? Where does it go?). But never is this dialogue allowed to stray beyond the unassailable authority of the narrating voice, every question coming always already complete with a definitive and unambiguous answer. And perhaps we should expect nothing more from texts intended first and foremost to be instructional.

Another critical difference concerns the geographical unit to which these lessons on the wind are invariably tethered: that of the nation. Recall the passage from the Fukyūsha primer of 1900, where "our country" (*wagakuni*) provides the central, and in this case the only, spatial locus for knowledge. The same is largely true for Ishii's text, which opens with the statement, "Just as elementary school students worry about tests, so do the farmers of *our country* worry about the stormy winds of the 210th Day."[20] Here, as in the pages that follow, "our country" is a means to incorporate the wind, as well as any related phenomena and folklore, under a national umbrella— one conveniently stretched, at least when talk turns to typhoons, to include Taiwan and the Ryūkyū islands.[21] In Ishii's pedagogical discourse, the wind abides by universal principles but is experienced uniquely within national borders, the uniqueness reinforced by shared beliefs (even if irrational) and a shared network of weather stations that, as he notes, daily send their data back to Tokyo. This division between universal principles and national particularity is far starker in the advanced textbook from Kōbunsha, which outlines the former before devoting a separate section to the latter. When it finally does discuss wind and weather patterns in Japan, however, it too subsumes description under the abstract unit of nation, nodding in only a few instances to the presence of subnational difference.[22] Of all the texts, *Kumo, ame, kaze* is the most explicit in acknowledging regional variation. It notes differences in wind speed across the country and even stops at one point to list the major "fall winds" (*oroshi*) of Japan and the mountains where they occur.[23] Its starting point, however, is still very much the nation. In fact, all the texts tend to situate natural phenomena and objects within a highly abstract and homogenized space. One finds minimal attention to regional specificity, a reliance on indistinct spatial markers (e.g., the city, the farm, the mountains), and a holistic image of Japan's geographical and cultural borders. Again, it would be naïve to expect much else from material published in Tokyo for an education system national in scope.

And yet teachers *did* complain about how abstract and disconnected from local conditions this material was, especially when it came to the standardized textbooks mandated for primary-school use after 1911. Equally restricted in their geographical outlook, these texts assembled short descriptive passages on various natural phenomena, most of which were unique to Tokyo and its immediate environs, and framed the entire assemblage as a "national" science reader.[24] This might have remained a nonissue except for the fact that science education at the primary level had since the mid-1880s been organized around the principle of direct observation (*kansatsu*). Teachers were encouraged to take children outside the classroom and into the local environment where they could observe firsthand the plants, animals, and other natural features native to the area. Such lessons, it was believed, would not only "foster the students' capacity to observe what is in front of their eyes," but would also awaken their "thirst for learning." By the time the first edition of the standard textbook was released in 1911, "direct observation" was thus already an integral part of the school syllabus and was consistently advocated by science educators at the local level.[25] It is not surprising, then, that this first edition sparked criticism from teachers and practitioners, many of whom complained about the absence of local material and the complete ineffectiveness of the textbook as a guide to local observation. Some of these complaints were compiled into an opinion report by the Ministry of Education in 1912, and the following comment from a teacher at the Tokyo Higher Normal School illustrates well the principal causes for concern.

> True, the textbook clearly states that teachers who use it in regions different [from Tokyo] should edit and alter the material accordingly. But when one looks at how science is actually being taught at most primary schools these days, one finds that teachers are adhering strictly to the lessons in the textbook and that very few know how to go about supplementing material appropriate to their own regions. We believe that the carelessness of teachers trying to implement this text on an individual basis, let alone the attempt to have the same textbook used nationwide, will only prove detrimental over time. Therefore, we ask that you quickly assemble several different varieties of the textbook so that all elementary schools will be able to carry out instruction that is suited to their respective areas.[26]

Clearly, it was not easy for teachers to turn a blind eye to textbooks whose use had been mandated by the state; and those who did found the task of creating new lessons on local topics to be difficult given that many of them were sojourners in the regions where they were teaching. Debate over how best to localize science pedagogy would remain contentious through much of the Taishō period, and one can find in Iwate a steady stream of concern over the shortcomings of the national primer and the need for more suitable local materials.[27] Yet for all the criticism of the first edition, few changes were made when the second edition was issued in 1918. Teachers were again simply asked to adjust for geographical bias by adapting the material to local conditions. As one member of the editorial board put it, "[this textbook] is similar to canned food in that everyone finds it palatable. But if you feed it to children just as it is, they're sure to find it unsatisfying."[28] Some became so frustrated with this line of argument that there were calls to abolish the textbook entirely in 1920 at the annual conference of the Society for Research on Science Education (Rika Kyōiku Kenkyūkai), but this came to nothing. The wind, incidentally, was given but a few lines in all three of the standard textbooks issued between 1911 and 1921.[29]

It was not long after this period of debate that Miyazawa began teaching science in Hanamaki to his seventh- and eighth-year students. By their own accounts, he rarely followed the textbook and preferred to take them outside to hold field practicums and to discuss issues of local concern.[30] Viewed in this light, "Kazeno Matasaburō" looks in many ways to be a response to the predicament educators had been grappling with for over a decade. Rather than settle for the material available through textbooks published in Tokyo, Miyazawa produced a textbook of his own in which learning about the wind was correlated with the very place of study. He took the basic knowledge on the wind that educators of the day deemed worth knowing (i.e., the canned food) and flavored it with such things as local place names, accounts of local events, and detailed descriptions of the experiences of local residents. Here was an introduction to scientific principles that students could really sink their teeth into.

Miyazawa offered them more, however, than just a localized pedagogy. Just as he used the label of Iihatov to filter out received patterns of spatial representation, he uses the children's conversations with Matasaburō to filter the local landscape and make visible relations and experiences impossible to see in other textbooks. What he makes visible, that is, are both the subtle texture of natural phenomena experienced at the levels of the body and local geography as well as how these phenomena are embedded in universal processes. On the one hand, Miyazawa portrays the wind as an entity that knows intimately the contours of the local landscape and even takes on the name by which it is best known there. Yet this wind spirit also refuses to be assigned a nationality or other place-based identity, appears to know multiple languages, and transcends both temporal and spatial boundaries (e.g., it refuses to measure time by any single national history). Limits to its universality do exist, of course, for it is gendered male and speaks only the standard Japanese dialect.[31] But the larger point is that Matasaburō's dual nature allows for local reality to be represented on its own terms *and* from the perspective of a global phenomenon that responds to unique environmental conditions everywhere the same way. This is locality as both a specific place and as one place among many.

Significantly, when locality *is* subsumed under universals, it is not done in such a way that the local space of Iwate can only appear as standing in marginal relation to an implied national center. Just consider what happens when one of the boys does invoke the Tokyo-countryside dichotomy. Matasaburō is getting ready to describe his fantastic trip to the North Pole and tells the children of how bitterly cold it is there. Kōichi, still upset from the day before and no longer in the mood for Matasaburō's boisterousness, has his doubts. "Hmm, it's really all that cold, huh?" Matasaburō will have none of it. "What was that? Are you trying to make a fool out of me? I won't be made a fool of by the likes of all you. And if you're going to bad mouth someone, you ought to do it with a bit more skill. 'Is it really all that cold?' That's such a hick thing to say (*inaka kusai*)." To which Kōichi retorts in his thick local accent, "Oh yeah, well you're from Tokyo, right? You spend all year wandering 'bout aimlessly and causing trouble." At this point, and the narrator notes how strange it is, Matasaburō breaks into a smile. "I don't have anything to do with Tokyo—you should know that. I travel all year, you see, and that's far superior to Tokyo. And that doesn't mean I wander aimlessly, either. I blow when it's time to blow. I've even done the great loop from the equator to the North Pole. I can't tell you how much better that is than Tokyo or wherever."[32]

The exchange is a kind of challenge to the children, and to the implied reader, to think beyond conventional spatial binaries. The text as a whole, in fact, seems to push in that direction. Iwate appears as not just another non-descript rural area marginalized by a transcendent center, nor a place wait-ing to catch up to a modern moment coded as the end point of progress. Rather, it appears as a unique locality caught up in global forces, a place that need not look to Tokyo first to get its bearings or set its developmental clock. David Harvey writes that "modernism, seen as a whole, explored the dialectic of place versus space, of present versus past, in a variety of ways. While celebrating universality and the collapse of spatial barriers, it also explored new meanings for space and place in ways that tacitly reinforced local identity."[33] By this definition, "Kazeno Matasaburō" stands as a fully modernist text. Yet whereas many urban-based writers and ethnographers of the time tended, as we have seen, to explore meanings that rewrote the na-tion's margins as bounded locales outside of time, Miyazawa was attempting with this Iihatov narrative to offer something very different. The children who interact with Matasaburō do not do so as inhabitants of a prior modal-ity that has no relation to the present. Nor are they forced to trade in their local ways of knowing and engaging with the phenomenal world for ways deemed more modern and rational. Instead, they occupy a position some-where between these two extremes. What Miyazawa offered was a vision of provincial locality that did not privilege Tokyo-centered narratives of prog-ress nor turn them on their head in a search for fossilized remainders to be reified as objects of nostalgia. On the contrary, locality appears as something far more fluid and open-ended—an evolving and dynamic process within a transnational network of flows. Here too, then, he was straying far from the standard textbook approach.

Speaking of Flowers

The second conversation, or rather series of conversations, that I take up in this chapter comes from a story that, much like "Kazeno Matasaburō," displays an interest in the problem of local difference within universalizing regimes of knowledge. More specifically, it is interested in how the value of that difference (i.e., a sense of particularity) can be compromised under such regimes, but also in how it might be retained. The story, which Miya-zawa began work on in June 1923, is titled "Okinagusa" and opens with a curious ode to a tiny alpine flower.

> Have you heard of *uzu no shuge*? *Uzu no shuge* is what in botany they call *okinagusa*, though somehow I feel that this name doesn't quite capture the flower's gentle youth.
> Yet if you ask me what is this *uzu no shuge*, I feel like I both know it and I don't.
> It's the exact same feeling I get when, for instance, I hear the word *bemubero*. That's what we around here call the buds of the *nekoyanagi* (pussy willow). Just the sound of the word *bemubero* reminds you of the buds' silvery velvet feel and the way they look in the soft light of early spring. Likewise, when one hears the name *uzu no shuge*, it's the black lacquer petals of the *okinagusa*, member of the buttercup family—with its green leaves crossed by lines of silver velvet and its glossy feathered crown of June—that appear clearly before one's eyes.
> There is no one who dislikes this *uzu no shuge*, elder cousin to the scarlet windflower (*anemone*) and friend of both the lily-of-the-valley (*kimikagesō*) and the dog-tooth-violet (*katakuri*).[34]

The *okinagusa* is one of about thirty species of what in English is known as the pasque flower. Botanists might recognize the flower by its Latin name, *pulsatilla cernua*. To try to designate a familiar equivalent for non-Japanese speakers, however, is really beside the point. For what the story's opening lines call into question is the very relation between the name of an object and one's knowledge of it. The narrator is not interested in whether readers have seen the *okinagusa* or the pussy willow before, but whether they know (and perceive) them in terms other than those designated by botanists as standard nomenclature. Or, equally important, whether they know them in the way that "we around here" do.

The reason a reader might not have known the flowers in the same way has to do with the simple fact of dialectical difference. In the case of *okinagusa*, for instance, nearly three hundred distinct names for the flower have been recorded in Japan, and almost eighty of these are known to originate in Iwate.[35] Although it is impossible to know how many of these terms were in circulation in the 1920s, or even the extent of their geographical range, the inclusion of just one (*uzu no shuge*) is enough to constitute an instance of deliberate *hybridization*, or what Bakhtin has defined as "an encounter, within the arena of an utterance, between two different linguistic consciousnesses, separated from one another by an epoch, by social differentiation or by some other factor."[36] The underlying factor of differentiation in this utterance is spatial, but it is also deeply sociological in that linguistic difference across space was at the time a means of marking cultural and epistemic difference across the national body. To speak of this tiny flower in names other than the one considered standard by botanists and by those at the center of cultural production and learning (*okinagusa* happens to have been the name common to the Tokyo area), was not only to speak from a different place, but also to know the flower in ways that many deemed less civilized, less modern, or less rational. "Okinagusa" was Miyazawa's way of suggesting otherwise.

In arguing for *uzu no shuge* as an equally valid way of recognizing the *okinagusa* flower, "Okinagusa" counteracted, and also frustrated, the linguistic standardization that was occurring on several fronts at the time, including education, literature, and scientific classification. Education was the front to which Miyazawa and his students were most intensely exposed, as the late-Meiji and Taishō classroom became instrumental in the introduction of a standardized national language (*hyōjungo*). The movement to institute standard forms of writing and speech under which all citizens could socially and spiritually unite had begun in earnest in the 1890s. A key figure in the movement was linguist Ueda Kazutoshi (1867–1937), whose writings and lectures prompted efforts to survey dialect use across Japan—especially the speech of educated Tokyoites—in order to systematize and then disseminate a new national standard.[37] By the turn of the century, the successful implementation in colonial Taiwan of a "national language" (*kokugo*) curriculum encouraged Ueda and others to utilize the domestic classroom more aggressively for the instruction of *hyōjungo* and the forced "correction" (or what in some cases amounted to eradication) of dialectical variation.[38] One result was the formation in 1902 of the Kokugo Chōsa Iin Kai (National Language Survey Advisory Council), which was set up to discuss how best to define a standard dialect, how to render it phonetically, and how to diffuse it most effectively. Members failed to reach consensus on many of these points, but they all agreed that the foundation for any standard had to be a polished version of masculine, upper-class Tokyo speech. Significantly, when the first state-mandated elementary primers were published in 1903, the language employed reflected this majority opinion.

The salient point here is not so much that a standard was engineered and diffused in ways that seem wholly inorganic and authoritarian; such a strategy was common (and arguably necessary) to the project of modern state-formation in Western Europe and America too. What needs to be emphasized, rather, is the choice of the Tokyo dialect as the basis for a national language and the subsequent codification of this local speech style as the most "normal" and "up-to-date" way for all citizens of the empire to communicate. In just a few decades, the term "dialect" (*hōgen*), once a neutral designator for the variants of spoken Japanese that circulated within the country's highly fragmented linguistic landscape, became synonymous for provincial speech styles understood as a distorted and inaccurate variation on the standard tongue.[39] This was especially true in outlying regions like Tōhoku and Okinawa where dialectical difference was particularly pronounced, and so too the perceived burden of not being able to speak "properly." Indeed, it was educators in these areas who most assiduously worked to "correct" (*kyōsei*) dialect use in the classroom by publishing collections of local lexical and grammatical forms that were meant to be eliminated from students' everyday speech.[40] Ueda himself had hardly been so strident in his views on the need for dialect correction, believing that dialects should be allowed to flourish in their own native environments.[41] As these more conservative efforts at language reform progressed, they gave rise to a powerful ideological concept that mapped dialectical difference onto social and spatial hierarchies and left speakers of nonstandard dialects caught between an "enlightened" national language not their own and a native tongue that marked them, at least in official, public realms, as uneducated at best and, at worst, as being both out of time and place with the modern moment. This state of linguistic in-betweeness—of being at once both internal and other, of being a speaker of Japanese and a speaker of not-quite-Japanese—is what "Okinagusa" gestures toward in its opening lines. Although *uzu no shuge* and *bemubero* could pass as "Japanese," and though the narrator himself writes in what was already naturalized as the standard form of represented speech, his knowledge of these dialectical variants is enough to mark him as somehow different from readers otherwise beholden to the flowers' all too common names.

There were some circles, of course, in which such difference was prized, whether for its literary value as a sign of the exotic and/or "the real," or for its historical value as a means of accessing Japan's linguistic past. Meiji-era novelists, in fact, had a large hand in the construction of literary images of regional dialect and in the coding of its symbolic significance. This was due to the fact that they were simultaneously working to create a written vernacular and a dialogic model of *hyōjungo* based on a reified image of the Tokyo dialect.[42] Tokutomi Roka, for instance, in his best-selling *Hototogisu* (The Cuckoo, 1898), associated Tokyo speech with the language of the modern, successful male (i.e., the protagonist Kawashima Takeo) while recasting the dialects of other areas (e.g., Kansai and Satsuma) as the language of temporally and spatially displaced people unable to escape their regional affiliations (i.e., Kawashima's parents).[43] Others, like the naturalist writers Shimazaki Tōson, Tayama Katai, and Nagatsuka Takashi, used dialect as a means of adding "local color" and an aura of authenticity to their works in a literary market that had come to be dominated by a single dialectical standard. Its domination, however, led them to use other dialects sparingly and with considerable condensation of detail for fear that readers might be alienated by unintelligible dialogue. When they did use it, the effect was often one of relegating characters who spoke in nonstandard dialect to positions of quaint rusticity and social immobility, as in Tōson's *Hakai* (The Broken Commandment, 1906) and Katai's *Inaka kyōshi* (The Country Teacher, 1909).[44]

"Okinagusa" in no way challenged how regional dialects had come to be hierarchically configured in the literary language of the time, nor was it especially interested in the problem of dialect writing.[45] Miyazawa had, to be sure, experimented with the representation of dialect in other of his stories. Some took the form of naturalist-style sketches that depicted, for example, the daily routines and conversations of an intergenerational farm family in "Jūgatsu no sue" (End of October, 1921), or the attempts by a poor rural couple to make bootleg wine in "Budōmizu" (Grape Wine, 1923). Others, such as "Taneyamagahara" (Taneyama Plain, 1921) and "Hikari no suashi" (The Shining Feet, n.d.) pushed the boundaries of dialect writing even further by presenting characters who speak in dialect but think in "standard" speech. Or, as in the latter story, shift effortlessly into *hyōjungo* upon entering a dream-like space that straddles the worlds of the living and the dead. In both these stories, Miyazawa gestures toward a bilingual model of linguistic representation through which provincial inhabitants might be able to speak their own tongue and yet still be heard as social equals. It is, in other words, an image of dialect as its own unique system for knowing the world but not one that is marked as derivative or one that automatically excludes its users from contemporary discourses and concerns. This is the image that "Okinagusa" gestures toward as well, though it does so far more subtly and at the level of lexical, as opposed to grammatical, meaning. It is interested in how to present dialect not as an aberration or remainder of a centrally unified speech, as was proposed by some linguists of the day, but as a living and breathing access point to alternative versions of reality.[46]

The front of linguistic standardization that provides deepest insight into how *okinagusa* came to have the prominence it did pertains to the scientific classification of plants. By the time Miyazawa began writing his story, the study and collection of plants in Japan had enjoyed not only several decades of prosperity as an academic discipline, it had also flourished for centuries as a popular pursuit of scholars, herbalists, and amateur enthusiasts. The late-Edo period was a particularly rich time for such studies as practitioners in the emerging field of *hakubutsu-gaku* (often translated as "natural history"), combining recently imported European methods of identification and classification with their own forms of local knowledge, produced an array of illustrated plant guides. It was these guides that transformed *okinagusa* from a local dialectical variation into a universally recognized standard. An early example is the 1836 edition of *Sōmoku kajitsu shashin zufu* (An Illustrated Guide to Grasses and Trees), created by the painter Kawahara Keiga (1786–?). Best known for the intricate and colorful depictions of flora and fauna he carried out in the service of Dutch physician Phillip Franz von Siebold (1796–1866), Kawahara displays this refined technique in the guide's entry for *okinagusa*, which shows the flower in early bloom. To the top left of the illustration is the plant's Linnaean name, spelled incorrectly as *anemony cernuta*; to the right side sits the formal Chinese name, *hakutōō*, whose characters literally mean "white-headed old man."[47] Surrounding the flower are boxed inserts describing when and where it blooms, the ailments it is known to treat, its reddish-purple color, and the drooping, hair-like seedlings that apparently warrant its Chinese moniker. Most noteworthy, however, is the list of colloquial variants given below *hakutōō*, which includes names from across the archipelago: *chigo-kusa*, *u'naiko*, *neko-kusa*, and *kawara-ichigo*.[48] The first two carry connotations of young child or infant while the third and fourth translate literally as "cat-grass" and "river-berry." *Okinagusa*, which consists of the characters for "old man" and "grass," appears in the table of contents as a subheading under the Chinese name, but is marked specifically as the Edo variant. Directly adjacent to it is the Osaka variant, *himebana* (princess flower).[49] What Kawahara's guide provides, then, is an image of different dialectical variations situated comfortably alongside one another—an image that, befitting of the time, hints at the perceived parallels between the act of collecting and comparing plants and that of gathering and comparing lexical specimens of dialect.[50]

Compare this with the *Sōmoku zusetsu* (An Illustrated Guide to Grasses and Trees), a plant guide compiled by Iinuma Yokusai (1783–1865) in 1856. This was the first compendium of plants by a native Japanese to be based entirely on Linnaean models of classification and description.[51] Of primary interest here was his decision to index entries by Japanese, rather than by Chinese or Latin, name. Though Iinuma surely intended for this organizational schema to facilitate easy look-up of plants by their popular designations, it also forced him to choose just one of several possible variants as the primary heading. In the case of the flower in question, that choice was *okinagusa*. Underneath this heading he offered just one alternate name, *shaguma-saiko* (lit., red-bear medicinal-root), and the Chinese name. Iinuma also gave a plain description that, adhering to the Linnaean emphasis on classifying plants according to their visibly distinct parts, concentrated on the pistil and stamen structure of the flower, before briefly listing the plant's medicinal uses.

As fate would have it, Iinuma's guide became a canonical source in the emerging field of botany, its influence lasting well into the Meiji period because of its reprinting in 1874 as *Shintei sōmoku zusetsu* and because it served as the basis for an important revised edition in 1907 titled *Zōtei sōmoku zusetsu*. This heavily updated and amended version belonged to Makino Tomitarō (1862–1957), who at the time was well on his way to becoming Japan's premier twentieth-century botanical authority. Employed as a researcher at Tokyo Imperial University, he had already collaborated on several seminal guides to Japanese flora, had helped to found a leading botanical journal, and had traveled extensively in the domestic and colonial periphery for the purpose of classifying and collecting specimens.[52] Drawing from this extensive knowledge and experience, he appended his own notes to Iinuma's original descriptions while choosing to preserve the overall indexing and naming scheme. On the one hand, this choice is understandable given the need to codify and reinforce standard names so that, as the disciplinary field became increasingly interconnected and authoritative, any botanist in Japan could easily understand which plant any other botanist might be referring to. What this meant in practice, however, is that dialectical variants came to have less and less significance in plant guide descriptions. Makino's entry for *okinagusa*, for instance, retains the same list of names used in Iinuma's text. Furthermore, his supplementary comments, while carefully dissecting the plant into its constituent parts, repeatedly emphasize the tiny white hairs that cover the stem, leaves, and petals of the flower. They are mentioned no less than five times, almost as if to insure that the plant's assigned name would not be called into question. Significantly, this came to be a rhetorical feature common to descriptions of the *okinagusa* in subsequent plant guides.

In a particularly notable guide produced for amateur botanists in 1908 and reprinted in 1917, the entry for *okinagusa* includes this name only and offers no indication of any dialectical variants. It also goes one step further than Makino's text in explicitly linking the choice of name to the plant's anatomy, noting that, "once the flower fades, [the seed head's] many shiny white pistils look just like the ruffled silver hair of an old man."[53] This explanation, which was to be a near permanent fixture in plant guides that followed, including Makino's own *Nihon shokubutsu zukan* (Illustrated Japanese Botanical Specimens, 1925), operates by abstracting a single aspect of the plant and, through metaphor, establishing a direct equivalence between it and its assigned signifier.[54] To borrow from the work of Lydia Liu on the political economy of the sign, metaphor here replicates the very way that exchange-value (i.e., monetary worth) makes equivalents out of nonequivalent material goods "through a process of abstraction or translation."[55] And once this particular metaphor became the standard currency in botanical guides, the effect was to lower the value of other possible names in the wider market of linguistic exchange. What need was there to continue to keep these names in circulation when the *okinagusa* seemed so intent on mimicking its given nomenclature?

It is the apparent naturalness of this equivalence, of course, that Miyazawa's "Okinagusa" problematizes in its opening lines. The narrator accomplishes this by first asserting a reciprocity of meaning-value between the plant's standard name and the one he knows it by ("*Uzu no shuge* is what in botany they call *okinagusa*") and then by casting doubt on the relative value of the latter, at least from where he stands ("though somehow I feel that the name *okinagusa* doesn't quite capture the flower's gentle youth"). He performs a similar rhetorical gesture for the buds of the pussy willow, making clear that "we around here" call it by another name, and that we do so because the very sound of this name captures more accurately our phenomenological experience of the buds themselves. In such a way, the narrator renders unstable those signifiers with which, at the expense of local knowledge, the national language and the science of botany laid claim to these flowers. Subverting a discourse that encased the *okinagusa* under a single metaphor tied to a single physical trait, the narrator turns our attention to an alternate set of qualities with which to validate the name that he, but also his ears, knows most intimately.

One could argue that the narrator has merely substituted *okinagusa* for another transcendental signified—another abstraction by which to press the multiplicity of the flower's being into the rigid pages of a different book. *Uzu no shuge*, while opening the flower up to a new set of youthful connotations, certainly reduces its complexity in ways similar to *okinagusa*. But this ignores two key aspects of *uzu no shuge* that make it categorically distinct from its rival. First, the name exists within a larger field of hegemonic discourses that do not become irrelevant the moment it is introduced. On the contrary, the authoritative presence of these discourses continues to haunt the text both in the title of the work and in the "standard speech" used by the narrator. *Uzu no shuge* is not just another name, but a name that remains structurally marginal and whose very position allows it to quietly challenge claims on total representation. Second, *uzu no shuge* is distinct because there is no attempt to translate the term into a standard Japanese equivalent. Even the narrator, the one person whom we would expect to be capable of performing this task, expresses uncertainty about its meaning: "Yet if you ask me what is this *uzu no shuge*, I feel like I both know it and I don't." Unlike *okinagusa*, whose denotation is readily discernable, *uzu no shuge* has been left untethered to the concretizing effects of lexical meaning. Instead, it floats freely in the hazy ambiguity of orality and sound, capable of being joined with the flower through any manner of metaphorical association the narrator deems fit. That Miyazawa likely sought out an intentionally obscure variant only reconfirms the extent to which he wanted to leave room for alternative ways of knowing this, and presumably other, plants.[56]

Flowers, as Derrida argues, "seem to occupy . . . degree zero in the chain of signification. Involved as they are in the process of dissemination, [they] appear only to disappear, are present only as they metamorphose themselves endlessly into other things."[57] An attenuated and variable life cycle invests them with a multiplicity of meaning, a "disseminative agency" that can "open a gap in the system of signification as [flowers] refuse to be reduced to any mimetic representation relying on an equivalence between the word and the thing."[58] The variable and variegated nature of the *uzu no shuge* helps Miyazawa's narrator to open up a similar gap, revealing the dominant system of signification to be biased toward a singular interpretation of its biological features. In disrupting this system, a space is created in which to disseminate the seeds of new meanings and equivalencies, allowing local experience and local knowledge to slip in between the cracks of totalizing or ostensibly more rational ways of schematizing the world that end up reducing "things themselves," in the words of Maurice Merleau-Ponty, to "an abstract and derivative sign-language."[59] The rest of "Okinagusa" is in fact preoccupied with offering its readers radically particular perspectives on the *uzu no shuge*, first from a passing ant, then from a mountain man, and finally from the flowers themselves. The ant, for instance, is quick to tell the narrator that,

> "The *uzu no shuge* is my absolute favorite. There's no one who dislikes that person (*ano hito*)."
> "But the flower is pitch black!"
> "No, it just looks that way at times. Sometimes it bursts into a flaming red."
> "Oh, I see. That's the way all of you see it."
> "No, I think it'd look red to anyone who saw it when the sun was shining."
> "Right, right. I understand now. It's because you're always looking at the flower as light passes through it." (180)

After this encounter with the ant, the narrator proceeds to show us that even the ravenous heart of the mountain man can be tamed by the sight of the *uzu no shuge* (180) before he describes his own early spring encounter with two of the flowers in a sunny meadow just south of Koiwai Farm.[60] He turns a careful ear to these flowers, which speak in voices "quieter than a dream," and transcribes their hushed conversation concerning the clouds that move overhead. He also records their short exchange with a circling lark, to whom they express the desire to fly up into the wind. "Just wait two months," says the lark, and sure enough, when the narrator returns two months later, the flowers have transformed into dandelion-like puffs and are getting ready to send their silver seedlings off into the breeze. In the final scene, he gazes intently at the flowers which, after giving a final goodbye to the lark, are blown apart by the wind, their seeds sent flying northwards and on up into the heavens (183).

When set against the history of plant guides in Japan, "Okinagusa" looks to be a revisionist and highly localized interpretation—both in terms of geography and perception—of what passed for standard botanical description. Having been trained as a soil scientist and geologist, Miyazawa was certainly not one to reject scientific classificatory schemes and their ability to facilitate the global transfer of knowledge by entering, as Foucault puts it, "the great proliferation of beings occupying the surface of the globe . . . both into the sequence of a descriptive language and into the field of a mathesis."[61] After all, he depends on these schemes in the story's opening passage. What he *was* reluctant to do, however, was allow them to supplant or render meaningless alternative methods of capturing and categorizing the phenomenal world. To do so was not only to devalue alternate subjectivities (i.e., those who call the flower by other names), but also, as is suggested by the incorporation of multiple perspectives on the *uzu no shuge*, to eclipse the infinity of possible ways that objects are experienced. If these ways seem trivial or politically insignificant, it is important to consider that Miyazawa was, both in this story and in "Kazeno Matasaburō," condensing complex ideological conflicts on the margins of the Japanese empire into the readily digestible idioms of parable and allegory. The kinds of conversations with nature that ensued, reductionist as they inevitably had to be, made it possible for even the child to see that knowledge of the object-world was at its core constituted from multiple lines of sight (e.g., the gaze from here, from over there, from the level of the nation-state or the globe, even from the perspective of nonhuman entities). But just as critical to the message embodied in the strategy of Iihatov was that no single line of sight had the right to claim absolute legitimacy over any other.

PART THREE

The New Roles of Local Engagement

CHAPTER SIX

Performing the Village Square

In January 1927 the *Iwate nippō* reported that Miyazawa Kenji, son of Hanamaki town councilman Miyazawa Seijirō, was leading nearly thirty village youth to form the Rasu Farmers Association (Rasu Chijin Kyōkai), a new-style cooperative to be run out of a repurposed family cottage on the outskirts of town. The small, two-story wooden house sat atop a small rise abutting a wide flood plain, from which one could look east to patchy fields and stands of mulberry trees, the banks of the broadly flowing Kitakami River, and onward to the low-lying hills of the Kitakami Range.[1] According to the article, the space was going to be used for exchanging ideas on agriculture and art, but also for putting those ideas into practice through physical labor, a barter system, musical concerts, and amateur theater. Here members would "initiate a grand revitalization movement for the farmer (*nōmin*)" capable of creating (*sōzō*) "a village culture" strong enough to resist its "evil" urban counterpart.[2] In fact, as the article noted, preparations were underway for an original six-act play titled *Poran's Square* (*Poran no hiroba*), to be performed that fall. The fascinating story of this play—as a piece of amateur theater, as an evolving series of unpublished manuscripts, and as a meditation on the structure of rural public space—serves in this chapter as an introduction to Miyazawa's strategies for reimagining place through more than just words. What emerges is a history of local praxis far more messy and complicated, though no less ambitious, than the confident image first presented to *Nippō* readers.

After spending the early 1920s pursuing a critical local stance through literary discourse, Miyazawa began to refocus his energies toward those who worked the real fields of his imagined dreamland. In just four years of teaching at the Hanamaki School of Agriculture, he had covered a great deal of new ground in rethinking "the local" across fields as diverse as literature, language, and science pedagogy. But in three separate letters from 1925, he expressed a desire to live as a "true peasant" (*hontō no hyakushō*) and leave behind a profession he increasingly felt to be "tepid" and socially ineffective. In a letter to a longtime friend he explained that water was no longer the "cold, transparent essence" he had considered it in his youth, but a "warm, muddy substance found in rice paddies and beds of grasses, filled with microscopic organisms flowing joyfully along."[3] Looking down to the soil at his feet, Miyazawa was now seeking ways to extricate himself from the position of a disengaged intellectual and to discover at the confluence of art and agrarian labor a more relevant form of local imagining. In a sense, he was looking to translate the discursive strategy of Iihatov into a concrete method for assembling actions and objects in ways that had real socio-material effect. This search eventually led him to projects like the Rasu Association, free fertilizer consultation for area farmers, and a series of public lectures on "farmers' art" (*nōmin geijutsu*), which will be taken up in the following chapter. Prior to any of this, however, he was drawn to theater, which he came to see as a crucial intermediary step in establishing a truly transformative praxis. Indeed, when two agricultural students studying in Morioka visited him in 1927 to ask about how to revitalize their own villages, he said to them, "First, be like the tenant farmer. Second, do farmers' theater."[4]

Although Miyazawa was one of the earliest interwar intellectuals to so explicitly connect theater with an interest in rural reform, he was far from alone in seeking ways to improve the life of farmers by reorienting cultural production around their perceived interests and needs. In Chapter Two, we saw how the desire for a decentralized literary marketplace slid into calls for a newly autonomous art produced *for* and *by* those who lived and worked in the provinces. These calls gained in urgency through the 1920s as economic conditions in the countryside worsened and as it became apparent to many urban and rural intellectuals that the very fabric of village society was being torn asunder. Rice prices steadily declined over the decade even as the cost of fertilizers and other agricultural inputs went up, creating a scissors effect that forced many tenant and middling (i.e., those who both rented and owned land) farmers to either give up what little land they had or spiral ever further into debt.[5] Adding to the sense of crisis was the increasing outflow of people, especially young men, to the rapidly industrializing cities.[6] Villages were losing one of their most valuable resources, or so it seemed, to an "urban fever" that made the lights of the city look far brighter than any at home.[7] Consequently, it became the self-appointed mission of numerous politicians, ideologues, agrarianists, village leaders, and artists of the period to give these young men a reason to see things differently. Some in the last group felt this could be done by artistically empowering rural youth and giving them greater access to the pathways of cultural production. Some, like Miyazawa, felt it necessary to go further and enact—through communalist experiments and cooperative ventures—the alternative rural futures they envisioned for their own localities, or for the ethnic nation as a whole. The Rasu Association was but one of many attempts by anarchists and reformers in the late 1920s to reimagine the village cooperative as a means of cultural edification, socioeconomic restructuring, and even radical political intervention.

These reformers, as will become clear, were driven by diverse personal histories and ideological rationales in their struggle to convince rural youth of the value of staying put. At the most fundamental level, however, they were each essentially trying to reinvent the farm village as place (i.e., as social space). That is, if we understand *place* as a product of everyday practices and social processes repeated over time within a specific geographic locus, these were attempts to modify culturally, but also economically and politically, the patterns of repetition that made modern village life such a struggle.[8] Some had more success than others, at least in the degree to which they inserted their ideas into the existing social order and offered residents a reason, beyond mere lack of other opportunities, to stay committed to the land. Some aimed too high, overshooting the realm of the possible in pursuit of utopias too abstract and too lofty to be of practical relevance to anyone but the visionaries themselves. Yet the fact of "failure" alone should not prevent us from interpreting any of these efforts, untenable as they may have been, as historically meaningful in their own right. Surely we can learn something of the existing social structures of a place and time through those structures that are denied a presence and kept at the edges, much as we can ascertain the shape of a metal object by the edges of the mold from which it is cast. To the extent that Miyazawa and his contemporaries tried to extend their own ideas about rural reform into existing structures and failed, we gain as much insight into the character of interwar village life by looking at when and why they succeeded as by looking at when and why they did *not*.

To make this point clearer, it is useful to borrow from sociologist Bruno Latour his notion that "ideas never escape from the networks that make them."[9] By this he means that ideas gain a grounding in reality only to the extent that they are supported by a chain of *connections* between various *mediators* (which might include human and nonhuman actors, words, concepts, social organizations, built structures, and environments) that hold together as a *network* of active agents.[10] As long as these connections continue to be activated and traversed, or even extended and strengthened through the incorporation of new entities, then an idea remains durable and takes on the aura of truth for those who take part in, or in some way benefit from, this *network*. Latour has used the idea of "vaccination" to illustrate this point, arguing that it came to seem like scientific fact (and social necessity) only because of the real *work* carried out by Louis Pasteur and his allies to create and maintain a *net* of links between newer experimental methods, published theories on infection, members of the medical profession, and the modern institution of the laboratory. All of this work was needed in order to "discover" microbes as a phenomenon treatable through specific measures. Deactivate or disassemble any one of these connections and the microbe itself would have looked quite different, or might even have vanished to be replaced by some other idea.[11] When applied to the activities of rural reformers like Miyazawa, such a *network*-based approach forces the historian to avoid the use of abstract social notions (e.g., modernity, tradition, culture, ideology) as explanatory causes. These tend only to stuff into a black box the truly innovative and historically specific ways that reformers reassembled actors and objects so as to make their ideas both more durable and real. Instead, we are compelled to ask about who and what they recruited in their efforts, and the extent to which they responded to or ignored existing *networks*. How did a provincial intellectual like Miyazawa, whose ties to the rural community were more proximate and robust than any of his urban counterparts, relate to these existing networks differently? And most importantly, what is it that kept him and others from extending their newer networks any further than they did? Reframing our inquiry in these terms, we obtain a more nuanced picture of how ideas drawn from global circuits of intellectual exchange were instantiated at the level of local praxis and what the limited success of these ideas says about the strength and durability of the *networks* (and thus ideas) that were already in place. In this chapter the focus will be on Miyazawa's engagement with ideas of public space and performance, and in the next with ideas of art and agrarian labor.

Poran's Square, *Act One*

Of all the forms of praxis Miyazawa experimented with in the 1920s, theater has received the least attention. This is in part because he wrote only four plays, all of them during his time as an educator.[12] *Poran's Square* was among them, and was first staged as a one-act vignette in August 1924 for an audience of about three hundred friends, family, and alumni from the surrounding community.[13] As described in the original script, his seventh- and eighth-year students were to be dressed as so many country gentlemen, village maidens, shepherds, and grape farmers. When the play opens, they are gathered in a field far from any human settlement at a *hiroba* (square, open space) defined on stage by linen-covered tables, a small conductor's podium, and two alder trees decorated in lanterns and tinsel. Behind them is a wide backdrop depicting a vast field of blooming clover and a night sky through which the Milky Way traces a luminous arc.[14]

Into this space stumble the characters Kyuste and Fazero. The former is an intellectual type and a low-ranking civil servant from the Department of Museums, the latter an impoverished elementary school student. They arrive to find a lively summer festival where revelers are dancing joyfully to the sounds of an orchestra as wine flows freely into their cups. One reveler, however, a belligerent hunter by the name of Dr. Wildcat, sits despondently off to stage right and berates a waiter for failing to notice his empty glass. He has come to believe that the space is his to lord over as he pleases, and he soon makes himself the center of attention by commanding the orchestra to play a song of his choosing and by insulting the two newcomers in verse, claiming that they have ruined the atmosphere of the place by requesting grape juice rather than wine. The young Fazero retorts with an insulting verse of his own, angering Wildcat enough to challenge the boy to a duel. The older Kyuste tries to intercede, but to no avail. "Fine. A child is the perfect match for a cowardly brute who can say nothing without a sip of liquor first" (347). A comical fight with steak knives ensues and the bully is sent fleeing from what he disparages to be "a return to the Poran's Square of old." The festival-goers are elated, and one grape farmer is led to proclaim,

"For the rest of the night, let us not think of such trifling things as our daily lives and the question of who is better than who. Oh, on this evening let us sing happily as we are bathed in the light of the clover and the faint glimmer of the Milky Way. Let us sing until the brave constellation of Orion rises from the east" (348). Fazero has restored to the community, at least for a night, a space to call its own.

At first glance, *Poran's Square* looks like children's theater as Walter Benjamin once envisioned it: "a great creative pause in the process of upbringing . . . [representing] in the realm of children what the carnival was in the old cults. Everything . . . turned upside down [as] children stand on the stage and instruct and teach the attentive educators."[15] The lesson learned is that public space can be socially transformative when one performs roles different from those prescribed by society. This message has a suggestive homology in the structure of the event itself: an intellectual who is helping students to stand before their community and enact the ousting of a tyrant. The overlap hints at Miyazawa's own conviction that the nexus of stage and public space could serve as a conduit for influencing lived social relations and, ultimately, the character of rural civil society.[16] And significantly, he was putting his students on stage at a time when a rising interest in school theater saw, just three months earlier, a national conference on arts education attract some 230 educators to help create guidelines for integrating theater into the elementary-school curriculum.[17] Closer to home, a fellow Iwate educator claimed that even in the country's most remote mountainous areas, no school assembly, alumni reunion, or commemorative event occurred without at least one or two children's plays.[18] There was, in other words, an expanding *network* of actors and venues with which Miyazawa could have potentially associated himself as he tried to link performance to his own ideas about public space as a transformative site.

For all this apparent potential, however, what we find is that his attempts to extend these ideas locally did not get very far. *Poran's Square*, which was based on a longer prose version, was performed only once, and for a limited audience. Aside from a few references in local media, it left few traces on the public record. Miyazawa did return to the story in 1927 to expand on his vision of rural community, as will be discussed later, but neither this nor the earliest prose version were ever published in his lifetime.[19] It surely did not help, at least in terms of activating already existing conceptual networks, that the narrative itself incorporated non-Japanese names, a distinctly foreign rural economy, and an image of public space that, with each subsequent version, strayed from the "horizons of meaning" associated with the *hiroba*, and public sites like it, in the interwar period.[20] It was an image neither obviously homegrown, nor one borrowed from an idealized notion of the European town square, as an announcement for the play in the *Iwate nippō* seemed to suggest.[21] Given its inscription on the conceptual and archival fringe, the fate of *Poran's Square* raises again the question of how it is we evaluate the "failure" of ideas to set down permanent roots. Where do we include in a history of local praxis those ideas less visible as material form or event—ideas inscribed as unpublished personal memory or creative vision—and yet which clearly address themselves to the possibility of public action? As we trace the story of *Poran's Square* across its many versions, what we find is that the historical significance of these hidden ideas may lie in their very inability or refusal to obtain a public presence. The story, it turns out, is a valuable record of transformative public space *in potentia*, but also, in the form of a negative imprint, of those entrenched patterns of association and social order that kept it from being anything more.

Mapping the Temporal Horizons of Interwar Public Space

Poran's Square initially distinguishes itself in its representation of public space by refusing more familiar spaces of interwar encounter: city streets and entertainment districts, theaters and cafes, temple and shrine grounds. It also refuses to give the titular *hiroba* a formal shape, though the word had since the 1880s served as an equivalent to the architectural form known variously as square, platz, piazza, and place.[22] By late Meiji, in fact, writers were using it to describe the squares and plazas they encountered abroad, as when Nagai Kafū visited the monumental, though temporary, St. Louis Plaza that lay at the heart of the 1904 World's Fair.[23] Owing to this refusal, one is inclined to think that Miyazawa was relying on the word's other connotation at the time as "a wide or spacious place."[24] Since the early 1600s, *hiroba* had been used to designate a wide, open space, often an official or public (*ōyake*) one, where people typically congregated.[25] It later became associated with the Edo period *hirokōji*—planned open spaces intended as firebreaks—but rarely served as a proper noun (i.e., such-and-such *hiroba*) and remained into Meiji a general signifier for intersections of people and place or for empty, void-like spaces in general, both urban and rural.[26] And yet while it lacks a concrete form and seems to exist in the middle of nowhere, the *hiroba* in *Poran's Square* does have a name and, according to the script, a specific spatio-temporal location in the 1920s and in Miyazawa's imagined region of Iihatov. It straddles the divide between *hiroba* as translated concept and as lingering linguistic trace.

The lack of concreteness may simply reflect the dearth of planned *hiroba* in Japan at the time Miyazawa was writing. Although by late Meiji they had materialized as a central feature of large metropolitan parks and as a spatial unit attached to train station buildings (*teishaba hiroba*), it was not until the City Planning Law of 1919 that planners began to think seriously about integrating them into the urban landscape.[27] Prior to the 1920s, in fact, one was more apt to find *hiroba*—in the form of station fronts and traffic circles—in the rising new cities of Manchuria.[28] In Tokyo, as in other domestic cities, a traditional reliance on local shrines and temples as public open space slowed the adoption of policies that would promote the construction of alternative open areas in tandem with urban growth, and it remained common practice to develop large tracts of urban land with little or no public space.[29] The formal *hiroba* thus remained, at least until the mid-1920s, a mere figment of planners' imaginations, existing mainly as a unit to be integrated into public parks or as a kind of "small park" (*shōkōen*) in and of itself.

Its absence was even more pronounced in provincial towns like Hanamaki, whose population was nearing 15,000 by 1925. Naturally, there were plenty of other public sites that could serve a similar purpose, including the streets of the town's commercial center, a park below the old castle grounds, and the open area in front of the local Asahi Theater. During the annual three-day autumn festival, townspeople and area farmers alike flocked to the latter to witness sideshows and circuses, to partake from food stalls, and to crowd into a large tent to watch the latest moving-picture shows from the city.[30] Outside of the town proper, many sites might well have qualified as *hiroba* in the sense of "open area," including shrine and temple grounds, the village crossroads, spaces in front of prominent buildings or homes, and the fallow fields between dispersed residences.[31] It is significant, however, that Miyazawa took inspiration from none of these sites, perhaps deeming them insufficient to the vision of rural public space he sought.

If we turn attention away from formal architectural properties towards representations of the *hiroba* as a particular social space (i.e., public space as ideological construct), then the points of correspondence with the historical record become much more apparent. One way of looking at the contest between Dr. Wildcat and Fazero, in fact, is to see it as a conflict between competing conceptions of public space: one sees it as a *personal* space designed for his individual benefit, the other as a *shared* space that rightfully belongs to any and all members of the community who find their way there. There is evidence of a similar split in contemporary discourse on public parks by city planners, journalists, and authors. For instance, while visitors to modern parks may not have been as brash as Wildcat, they did at times treat them much like private property. Thus within two months of opening in 1903, Tokyo's Hibiya Park had to put an end to late-night hours because too many people were coming in to steal the flowers and trees.[32] This "personalizing" urge was evident amongst intellectuals too, even as there emerged a greater awareness of parks as disciplined, shared spaces. For these individuals, public space entailed an equal right to what Richard Sennett described as "an invisible shield, a right to be left alone."[33] Ishikawa Takuboku, reminiscing about a visit to his hometown of Morioka, expressed the idle thought that he might close the gates of Morioka Park and build a grand private residence of marble where he would immerse himself in reading and astronomy.[34] In 1917, the poet Hagiwara Sakutarō rendered the park as a space for holding a quiet, intimate conversation cut off from all familial and social ties and interrupted only by the sound of a fountain in the distance.[35] Several years later, essayist Terada Torahiko expressed great frustration that he could not use Hibiya Park as a space of his own. In search of a place to sketch, he wandered into a "*hiroba* of grass and flowers" only to find it already occupied by "someone cleaning his mouth with a toothpick, someone walking a dog, someone with a camera running to-and-fro in affected anguish, and someone who found pleasure in observing them all."[36]

Taishō city planners, who lobbied for the construction of parks on the grounds of personal health and welfare, certainly contributed to their popular identification as sites of leisure and self-enjoyment.[37] But there were also planners who argued for their inherently public and populist character, and who promoted parks and *hiroba* as places for the gathering and integration of all members of society, both lady and laborer alike.[38] This notion of parks as a shared communal space was most apparent in their appropriation for the purposes of public celebration and protest, a tendency that emerged at Hibiya Park as soon as the gates opened. "Tokyoites of all sorts felt *entitled* to claim [it] as theirs" in the name of both state-sponsored events (e.g., wartime victory celebrations) and demonstrations of state opposition (e.g., the riots against the Russo-Japanese War treaty negotiations).[39] By the late teens and early twenties, while urban parks in Tokyo and elsewhere still functioned as sites of state-sponsored ceremony, they also increasingly served as loci for a range of political gatherings, including the rice riots of 1918, the May Day celebrations of worker solidarity inaugurated in 1920, and demonstrations in support of establishing universal manhood suffrage.[40] Articles from the *Yomiuri shinbun* show that throughout the Taishō period, *hiroba* too were appropriated in similar ways and served as sites for athletic field days, military reviews, victory celebrations, demonstrations against rising streetcar fares, sendoff and welcome ceremonies, and even a student brawl.

More pertinent than these admittedly superficial correspondences between notions of personal and shared space, however, are those that come to light when we consider how the *hiroba* in *Poran's Square* functions symbolically to facilitate Fazero's victory and the sense of group solidarity achieved as a result. At this point, it is instructive to look at the first prose version of the story, which contains several layers of narrative detail absent on stage. It begins with Fazero visiting Kyuste's home to talk about his nightly wanderings in search of Poran's Square, a place he knew as a child for having sweets, an orchestra, fireworks, and "just about anything in any amount."[41] The boy explains how, in the evenings, he has gone to look at the clover fields that come aglow at dusk—each individual flower shining like a whitish-blue moth and revealing a number in the light it gives off—convinced that if he carefully counts them higher and higher into the thousands he will find his way to the magical spot. Kyuste, who doubles as narrator, is intrigued, though he soon learns that this idyllic place is presently lorded over by Dr. Wildcat. Much less aloof than his stage persona, here he twiddles his moustache as he moves about in his long frock coat, shaking hands with the other gentlemen and feigning interest in such things as Japanese foreign investments in China.[42] Adding to the caricature is the fact that he has never allowed his carriage driver in for a drink. By the time Kyuste and Fazero arrive, then, one is inclined to think of Dr. Wildcat as an arrogant capitalist who treats public space as his own while denying the rights of others to enter. Fazero's victory is consequently imbued with a greater sense of social justice, as he appears to be expunging the corrosive effects of moneyed private interest on the greater public good.

When considered as a function of the space itself, there are at least two ways we can read his decision to act out: as the intrinsic by-product of the festive atmosphere and the temporary sense of liberation to which it gives rise, or as the product of extrinsic social anxieties (e.g., class friction) finally allowed a voice due to the site's ostensible openness to all. The first reading suggests that the *hiroba* is a temporary retreat from the work of existence and the flow of everyday life—a space ordered by *cyclical* progression and recurrent ritual where community members assemble, celebrate their shared escape from routine, and then disperse in anticipation of next summer's event. To visit such a *hiroba* is, borrowing from Chakrabarty's work on the *adda* of Calcutta, "to enjoy a sense of time and space that is not subject to the gravitational pull of any explicit purpose,"[43] much in the way that the dancing Kyuste momentarily loses himself (as he explains in the first prose version) to the mystical sights, sounds, and smells of the *hiroba* and its increasingly fuzzy borders.[44] The second reading reframes Fazero's victory as a singularly important event that advances the space, and the public gathered there, towards something other than what it was before. The *hiroba*, in other words, comes to appear as a *monumental* site where "one's private world becomes a world-view, personal passion is transmuted into public conflict, and one has not only to make small talk, but to make history."[45] Both of these ideological formulations find critical resonance with contemporary discourses.

In the case of the first, it has already been hinted how city planners and advocates of park construction contributed to an idealized image of parks as sites for escaping the everyday and for engendering social unity. It would have been difficult for them to do otherwise given their professional training and a bureaucratic audience with little interest in creating sites that might facilitate unregulated assembly or popular protest. Amongst writers and poets too, there was a tendency to view the park as site of recurring retreat, much like they viewed the older parks and entertainment districts (*sakariba*) of Tokyo. Asakusa Park, for example, and its adjoining Sixth District (*Rokku*), were by the 1920s well established in the minds of writers and urban ethnographers as other-worldly locales where "people from all classes and ethnicities were mashed together in one giant flow"; where proletarian and bourgeois were treated equally; and where "the line between stage and audience disappeared, everyone melting into a single entity."[46] These were places designed not for marking time, but for forgetting its passage amidst the phantasmagoric chaos of commodity exchange and mass spectacle. This may have been the image Miyazawa had in mind when he visited a local shrine festival in 1926 and, upon seeing the strings of gas lights, the fruit and sweets vendors, and the tea shops, referred to the scene as a "pastoral Asakusa" (*den'en Asakusa*).

This image of an other-worldly site recurring at the boundaries of the everyday also emerged amongst contemporary ethnographers of rural life, who associated traditional village festival with "semi-public" spaces marked as secluded or liminal. Of particular interest to them was the summer Obon celebration, whose defining feature was the Obon dance (*bon odori*), wherein residents of area hamlets came together for a nighttime parade through the community. In the late 1920s, ethnographers sought to capture the essence of this dance in all its regional variation, partly out of fear that recent efforts to strip the dance of its lewder elements and bring it under the jurisdiction of official village organizations like the *seinenkai* (youth groups) were erasing its "authentic" form. The picture they collectively painted of the dance was one in which villagers both young and old, male and female, gathered at dusk on sacred temple grounds, or on the fringes of the community, and spent a night engaged in revelry and social release under the ethereal light of the moon.[47] A similar portrait of liminal community space was also to be found in contemporary discussions of rural theater (*mura shibai, jikyōgen*). One historian, noting the strict prohibitions to which such performances were once subject, wrote of instances in the early 1880s when communities, in order to evade the police, set up temporary stages in the forests outside their villages and snuck out under cover of night to watch, or sometimes perform in, amateur productions.[48] In linking festival and theater with "public space at-a-remove" (i.e., a space both physically and socially distant from the everyday), these images exhibit considerable structural affinities with *Poran's Square*. One could even suggest that Miyazawa's story predicts the discourse of rural festival as a socially liberating, yet also clandestine activity.

There are consequences, however, should we read his image of the *hiroba* as conforming solely to the cyclically determined spaces of the entertainment district or rural festival. To seek affinities only along this horizon would place it onto a non-dialectical plane of history extending flatly both forward and back, on which it cycles in and out of presence much like a seasonal occurrence. In relation to history conceived as a forward progression of events, it could thus only ever play a passive role, similar to how traditional forms of rural entertainment (*goraku*) were at the time being reimagined by folk ethnographers and social conservatives as essential to preserving village harmony. Yanagita Kunio and Orikuchi Shinobu, for instance, increasingly viewed these older forms—which in the 1920s included the Obon dance, village performances (*mura shibai*), and amateur wrestling (*sumō*)[49]—as "monuments to the past" that could be "imitated" endlessly, consciously enacted and performed in the interest of preserving, or renewing, for Japanese the memory of themselves as a community and, more importantly, as a single communal body.[50] A second consequence of a cyclical reading would be the implication that the "public" formed at Poran's Square lasted only as long as the space itself. An end to the festivities, no matter how subversive of normative practices, would mean a return to prior social relations. Or even a potentially more dangerous kind of mass hallucination in which, as Hannah Arendt warns, "all people suddenly behave as though they were members of one family" and, "deprived of seeing and hearing others," precipitate "the end of the common world."[51]

Looking now to the monumental horizon, we find that public sites susceptible to this particular ideological formulation were those whose high visibility also meant that authorities more strictly enforced legal measures for maintaining public order. Such measures, inscribed most explicitly in the Peace Police Law (Chian Keisatsu Hō) of 1900, gave authorities power to suppress any kind of discourse or assembly that might potentially disrupt the peace, or harm the decency, of places where the public gathered. Though the law's obvious targets were oppositional political organizations, labor strikes, and rural tenancy disputes, the law also made it illegal for women and minors to participate in political events (e.g., rallies or speeches) and required that police be notified of any large, outdoor public gathering at least twelve hours in advance.[52] The Peace Preservation Law (Chian Iji Hō) of 1925 was less specific in its restrictions on gathering, but effectively suppressed any activity that sought to reform the national body or repudiate the established system of private ownership.[53] Such regulations paradoxically facilitated the openness of parks and *hiroba* to the monumental horizon. For one, visibility made them the perfect stage to engage with historical memory and collective identity. Moreover, the laws meant to impose order on these spaces, and keep them free of unintended or unsanctioned uses, insured that any activity deemed unacceptable would, if carried out there, take on the air of an extraordinary occurrence.[54]

In this respect, the placement of Poran's Square in the far-off fields clearly diminishes its monumental potential, at least at the level of material form. Yet if we maintain that those gathered there are not merely disparate revelers but representatives of larger social groups (e.g., poor peasant and greedy capitalist), then we still have reason to read the space as monumental in its ideological intent. To do so implies an image of public space naturally more abstract in its symbolic structure, as it reduces the complexities of relations between social groups in space to a single site where all come together in the form of caricatured spokespeople. But if Miyazawa wanted his audiences to believe that real physical locales could be infused with political promise, then it was this kind of utopian representational mode—where actions taken in public are imbued with a socially instrumental purpose—

that was needed. Such a mode could also help convey to students the radical potential of performing and imagining public roles overtly transgressive of conventional behavior rather than merely imitative of it.

Community Takes the Stage: Theater as Public Space

Whether or not we imbue the temporal horizon of *Poran's Square* with such potential depends not only on how we read its narrative content in relation to other figurations of public space at the time, but also on how we situate the context of its original production within contemporary attitudes toward the stage. Although Miyazawa never stated explicitly his ideas about theater as a form of social praxis, he was working at a time when the stage was being redefined by Japanese educators and intellectuals as an ideal medium for social integration and class leveling, and thus as a new kind of public forum. For some, it was a forum envisioned from on high as a mechanism of moral and cultural edification. For others, it became a means to democratize the production and reception of art. In both cases, the assumption was that theater could bring a community together in ways that other forms of art could not. Knowing the lengths to which Miyazawa went in order to see his vision of renewed community come to life on stage—to the point of paying for costumes and props from his own pocket—it is certain that he too was convinced of theater's transformative power. How he sought to translate that conviction into a meaningful *network* of actors and objects is what we must now try to understand.

The idea of theater as an instrument of social reform gained ground in the early years of Taishō when the discovery of *minshū* (the people) as a new object of political ideology was carried into the field of aesthetics through debates on "people's art" (*minshū geijutsu*).[55] At a time when mass-produced entertainment (silent film, popular fiction, serialized storytelling) captured ever more of the public's attention, and when the sanctity of "authentic culture" seemed threatened by the alienating effects of consumerism and urban life, some intellectuals sought to maintain their relevancy by leveling the artistic playing field and by positioning themselves as authorities on what an art *for* the people should look like.[56] One of the first to propose a definition was critic Honma Hisao (1886–1981), who in 1916 set the tone by declaring theater to be the truest form of "people's art." Borrowing from Swedish educational reformer and feminist Ellen Key, who in turn was inspired by French dramatist Romain Rolland, Honma argued that theater, when con-

ducted properly, was the purest kind of "recreation" available to the laboring masses.[57] The following year, Rolland's *Le Théâtre du peuple* (1903)—in
Ōsugi Sakae's translation, *Minshū geijutsu ron* (Treatise on People's Art)—
helped to cement the association of theater with "people's art" so that the
two became virtually synonymous in the minds of some, which Rolland
himself had never intended. His treatise emphasized the specificity of the
theater space as a site of social gathering, and encouraged playwrights to
capitalize on the force latent within this site by writing plays that "opened
the stage to mass and heroic action."[58] Nevertheless, the misreading structured much of the early debate on *minshū geijutsu* and it became a common
conceit to treat theater as an art capable of synthesizing all other art forms,
and thus uniquely accessible to each and every citizen.[59]

The early advocates of *minshū geijutsu* like Honma and Ōsugi had difficulty in translating their visions of a popular theater into tangible results,
however, in large part because their focus was on making the content of
theater both intelligible and morally edifying to the masses rather than on
finding ways to involve the people themselves in production and performance. This emphasis shifted in the years to follow as dramatists engaged
with increased seriousness the idea of theater as an art of the people. Hirasawa Keishichi (1889–1923), a key figure in the early proletarian drama
movement, placed the urban working class at the heart of his definition
of "the people" and established a small acting troupe called Rōdō Gekidan
(Workers Company) in 1920. His troupe signaled a rare instance in which
productions were not only aimed at the sensibilities of workers, but performed by worker actors for predominantly worker audiences.[60] At the more
conservative end of the political spectrum was Tsubouchi Shōyō, who took
cues from civic theater movements in England and America and promoted
an outdoor "pageant theater" to be performed both *for* and *by* the people.
This "public theater" (*kōkyō gekijō*), as he once referred to it, would combine
song, dance, verse, and other forms of folk performance into a single display, much like a local religious festival, but with the aim of fostering a sense
of common culture and "democratic spirit."[61] By this he meant a spirit that
arose naturally from the kinds of collaboration and shared sense of purpose
necessary for realizing such a large-scale, community-wide event.[62]

For Tsubouchi, the success of pageant theater as a mechanism of social
cohesion was predicated on its being performed both outdoors and free of
charge.[63] The nature of the venue, in other words, as much as the content,
was essential to creating the hoped for leveling effect. One finds a similar

concern with theatrical space by others at the time, including the renowned Osanai Kaoru (1881–1928), whose Little Tsukiji Theater, which opened in June 1924, and became a crucible for *shingeki* (new realist theater), proletarian, and avant-garde plays, was ostensibly founded with "the people" in mind. Osanai declared that the site would provide a theater to make the people "happy, give them strength, and instill them with life," and with its raised and open seating, his ideal of providing equal access to all was uniquely inscribed into the structure of the theater hall itself.[64] For those interested in developing a theater *by* the people, however, nothing surpassed the outdoor stage. Honma, for instance, cited as a potential model the passion plays performed in the public squares of medieval Europe. Similarly, the American dramatists who were so influential to Tsubouchi's work hailed the public park as an ideal site of performance. One of them even asserted that the civic function of parks could only be fulfilled through the binding force that cooperative artistic ventures like theater provided.[65] Miyazawa did not have to look as far as Europe, America, or even Tokyo, however, to encounter this bias towards public, outdoor sites. In 1923, an essay in the local paper insisted that outdoor performances were the most ideally suited for children's theater. Not only did they promote a sense of freedom and imaginative possibility, they were inherently "of the people" (*minshūteki*) in that they offered a space where audience members could literally sit on equal ground.[66]

Poran's Square may not have been performed outside in its original incarnation, but the re-creation on stage of a public outdoor festival in which all could ostensibly participate suggests more than a passing familiarity with the ways theater was being framed as a populist art. By the early 1920s, these ways had become increasingly diversified as intellectuals did away with *minshū* in order to concentrate on ever narrower segments of the population. Two of the strands that developed, and with which Miyazawa engaged most directly, were "school theater" (*gakkō geki*), which focused on children and students, and "farmers' theater" (*nōmin geki*), which focused on the rural laborer. The former, as previously mentioned, had a substantial following amongst progressive educators by the time Miyazawa began writing plays for his students. Its most vocal proponents, Obara Kuniyoshi (1887–1977) and Tsubouchi Shōyō, touted it as a means of nourishing the spirit, inculcating morality, and nurturing the child's innate ability to imitate life. While both stressed the development of the individual over any benefits that child acting might have for civil society, they also proceeded on the assumption that theater was well suited for cultivating "true humans" since it gave children the chance to perform the required roles of an enlightened citizenry. Obara, for his part, argued in his 1923 treatise on school theater that by engaging students in every aspect of production, from set design to actual performance, one could nurture within them spontaneity, self-awareness, and freedom.[67] Tsubouchi, who issued his own treatise on theater and education the same year, believed that performance would help guide the imaginative instincts of children while "lovingly nurturing and cultivating their inner nature in manifold ways, both naturally and in a well-rounded fashion."[68] He drew inspiration this time from an American, Alice Minnie Herts, who a decade earlier had established a children's educational theater in New York. Theater was for her a panacea that could not only integrate communities divided along class and ethnic lines, thus easing the tensions exacerbated by a rising immigrant population, but also nurture the character of youth so as to make them self-reliant and law-abiding citizens.[69]

What must be emphasized here is not that practitioners of school theater sought to mold the morality of children in ways that served the interests, and allayed the fears, of an enlightened social elite. Rather, it is their conviction that by merely acting out and imitating a set of proper roles, children would come to adopt those same roles as adults. The strength of this conviction is most apparent in anxieties over the potential harm to children were they made to play less savory or even villainous characters. Tsubouchi, for instance, felt that only by eliminating all morally or socially inappropriate roles could children's innate capacity for goodness grow unimpeded. Obara's emphasis on freedom and spontaneity, in contrast, suggests a more flexible conception of the child subject as stable enough to avoid merging completely with the roles he or she is made to play. And yet he had to deal constantly with criticism from parents who objected to their children having to play morally inferior characters (*akuyaku*).[70] In conservative rural communities, traditional associations of popular theater with lasciviousness and depravity had some parents balking at the thought of sending their children to school to become, of all things, "actors" (*yakusha*).[71] When guidelines for school theater were finally set down at the national conference on arts education in 1924, progressive educators thus hedged their bets and declared that all elements that might contribute to vanity (*kyoeishin*) or decadence (*kabi*) in students be removed.[72] In the minds of some, the stage was apparently so like the world that mere imitation of socially reprehensible behavior posed a threat to the social order itself.

Miyazawa took the opposite tack, of course, looking to the transformative power of theater as a force for social improvement. Not just for moral edification, but also, as can be inferred from the utopian trajectory of *Poran's Square*, for creating opportunities for his students to imagine alternative realities and alternative future selves. He was clearly mindful that his plays were to be performed in an educational context *and* a social one, and that most of his student actors came from poor rural families. The Hanamaki School of Agriculture, a second-tier vocational school offering two years of study in practical farming, was the only option for sons of middling farmers who could not afford elite middle schools or higher-level agricultural schools. Nearly eighty percent of its students came from owner-cultivator or owner-tenant families and many returned after graduating to farm the family land.[73] Miyazawa's desire to extend school theater in ways that made it more relevant to the lives of these students can be seen as early as 1924, when he marketed his productions as "country plays" (*den'en geki*). But it seems to have truly crystallized the following year when he wrote to a friend of wanting to start his own farmers' acting troupe (*nōmin gekidan*).[74] In expressing such a sentiment, Miyazawa was quietly joining the ranks of a fledgling theater movement that aimed to make the stage less a moral training ground than a gathering place for rural laborers in need of being awakened to the enriching power of art and to their own class position.

The most vocal advocates of the movement were novelist Nakamura Seiko (1884–1974) and dramatist Iizuka Tomoichirō (1894–1983), who began writing on the subject as early as 1925. Nakamura was convinced that a non-written-based art like theater was best suited to the intellectual capacities of present-day farmers, but he also felt that provincial youth could no longer be satisfied with the muddled old kabuki plays and the simplistic contemporary restylings (*zangiri mono*) that had entertained an earlier generation while squeezing from them what precious little pocket money they had. He argued in a series of essays that a new kind of farmers' theater (*nōmin gekijō*) was needed, one that adopted the same amateur-run, noncommercial quality of school theater and that employed the classroom, schoolyard, and even the local shrine as stage. He also urged that performances be "held out-of-doors in the style of a pageant." Predicting that village youth and intellectuals interested in the plight of farmers would assume initial leadership for such productions, Nakamura hoped that all community members would eventually take part and thus acquire techniques for expressing themselves with greater vivacity, directness, and courage.[75] Iizuka, who believed theater to be inherently social, called for a village theater (*nōson gekijō*) equivalent in spirit to what earlier advocates of "people's art" proposed, but also liberated from the bourgeoisie and the suffocating grip of commercialism. He felt that such a theater, once passed from the hands of a concerned intellectual elite into the hands of the farmers themselves, would encourage a love of the soil, of one's neighbors, and of society as a whole.[76]

Yet even as Nakamura and Iizuka extolled the virtues of farmers' theater from their privileged positions in the center, some in the provinces were already looking to nontraditional and nonprofessional theater as an antidote to the cultural malaise rural youth were said to be suffering from. In fact, the more Nakamura wrote on the topic, the more letters he received from individuals either looking for advice on how to start their own amateur troupes or who saw in him a chance to tout their achievements. A letter from Hiroshima, for example, spoke of a group called Nōmin-za (Farmers' Theater) that was performing its own plays with the help of local elementary school teachers and clerks from the village office. The sender expressed interest in having Nakamura deliver some summer lectures on farmers' theater. In another letter, a Nagoya youth interested in starting a troupe of his own asked if there were any scripts or reference books that Nakamura could recommend. Nakamura typically responded to these inquiries by directing people to the Wakaba Kai (Young Leaves Association), a troupe based in a small village in northern Kyūshū whose members had contacted him as soon as they read his first essay on *nōmin gekijō*. Led by a local doctor named Yasumoto Tomoyuki, these young farmers had been doing amateur theater since 1923. All the while, Yasumoto had kept a detailed record—which he shared with Nakamura—of plays performed (many adapted from modern realist works by Tokyo and Western playwrights), financial costs incurred, and actions taken to transform the group from a casual gathering of friends that performed for each other indoors to a regionally active troupe with its own outdoor, hilltop amphitheater.[77] Holding high this valuable record of what a farmers' theater could hope to achieve, Nakamura took advantage of his position in the nation's larger media ecology to act as spokesperson for those in the field who, like Miyazawa, were trying to bring into being what he himself had only written about in the abstract.

Regardless of the different methods and aims of proponents of amateur theater in the early 1920s, all of them shared a conviction in the stage as a mechanism of social unification. If this generally meant unification in the interest of a morally enlightened and politically benign community, it is still significant that they saw the stage as a place where disparate individuals could assemble in public without regard to socially prescribed roles or hierarchies, nurture their creative instincts, and practice ostensibly egalitarian forms of community. *Poran's Square* took this conceit further by literalizing a desire for unity through the figure of a magical clothing attendant. Though his presence is minimized on stage, we learn in the first prose version that he greets visitors by not only taking their jackets, but by offering to dress them up in whatever clothes they might imagine. Thus while patrons appear to be aristocrats of the highest rank, a fact of great concern to "sixteenth-ranked," and poorly dressed, civil servant Kyuste, the reality is that all outward marks of class status have been rendered indeterminate. Simply by dreaming up a suitably elegant outfit, a visitor enters on the same material footing as everyone else. Fashion, being one of the primary media through which class and social standing are performed in public, is here rendered unintelligible as a semiotic system linking appearance to the essence of the individual. Ragged and shoeless Fazero ends up in gold-striped red pants, shiny new boots, and three-starred epaulets, looking as if he might be mistaken for a distinguished soldier (*heitai*).[78] Kyuste opts for a black velvet suit, long leather boots, and pure-white gloves.

The leveling effect of this clothing change—itself a literal representation of the "dressing up" to which Miyazawa's students, the sons of farm families, would have been temporarily privileged—is precisely what generates the opportunity for Fazero to wage his contest of authority with Dr. Wildcat and win back the *hiroba* from the hands of a controlling minority. Visual markers of class distinction that before seemed "readable" and transparent have no relevance here, producing a public space no longer tethered, at least momentarily, to the hierarchies born of socioeconomic reality and the roles that such hierarchies prescribed. In an era when one of the first attainable steps toward a representative politics was seen to be the extension of suffrage to all adult males, irrespective of how much land they owned or how much they paid in taxes, Miyazawa may have been keen to demonstrate, through its very performance on stage, the idea that young farmers were able to represent the moral and political interests of the community at large.[79] They had a right to be judged in public not for their apparent station in life, but for their potential to act out roles denied them by conventional social hierarchies.

What Miyazawa fails to elaborate on in both the play and the first prose version of *Poran's Square*, however, is the ultimate purpose of such acting out. What, in other words, is the lasting significance of Fazero's victory? Was it his intention to reinstate some prior, ideal vision of rural community? Or did he instead seek to redefine the rationale for which a community could legitimately come together in public? Neither version resolves this ambigu-

ity, for we do not know if the victory is restorative, and thus an attempt to
escape from history (cyclical), or if it is progressive, and thus a push toward
the image of a public body perpetually unfinished (monumental). The first
prose version speaks only of a second, failed search for the site carried out
too late in the summer, and thus leaves us in the dark about the exact linkages Miyazawa hoped to make with the various *networks* traced above.

Poran's Square *Revisited*

After founding the Rasu Farmers Association in 1927, Miyazawa was in a
better position to articulate concretely how rural social space might be recon-
stituted in the interests of the farming class. He was no longer orchestrating
a simple school play, but a real-time social experiment intent on repurposing
private land (the family cottage) for cooperative use and on disseminating
practical knowledge outside of institutional constraints. Soon after beginning
this experiment, in fact, he returned to the prose version of *Poran's Square* to
offer a more conclusive ending. In this revision, the lines of class conflict are
drawn much more starkly: Fazero is a seventeen-year-old youth who works as
a kind of indentured laborer for an overbearing landowner, while Dr. Wildcat
is a powerful prefectural assemblyman named Destupaago to whom Fazero's
sister has been pledged in marriage. The *hiroba* too, here renamed Poraan,
traces a clearer narrative arc and historical progression. Beginning in the
minds of Fazero and Kyuste as a local legend and mythical symbol of communal harmony and abundance, its rumored reincarnation on the outskirts
of town is soon revealed to be a sham. Destupaago, to win votes in an upcoming election, has merely appropriated the legend as a way to promote an
open-air establishment where free alcohol is served.[80] Upon entering the site,
Kyuste and Fazero quickly realize that the site is anything but public. "Everyone stopped what they were doing at once and looked at us with a suspicious
eye. Then they looked to Destupaago" (87).[81] When he reluctantly offers the
uninvited guests some bootleg liquor, they ask for water instead, setting up
the climactic duel and Fazero's eventual victory. This time, however, there is
no return to dancing, nor any call for mutual understanding. Instead, the
"old" Poraan's Hiroba is abandoned by Fazero and his friends for a small factory (*kōjō*) that lay farther out—the very site where Destupaago had been
cooking up his illicit brew and falsely labeling it as medicinal acetone. There
they establish a cooperative whose members, men both young and old, utilize
their technical skills and practical knowledge to produce a range of goods—

leather products, ham, oatmeal, chestnuts—for sale in regional markets. Significantly, these men imagine themselves to be creating the "true Poraan's Square of old" with their very own hands. "Not a dirty, despicable Poraan's Square meant to deceive, but one where we can go at night and sing—a wonderful place where you feel energized just from taking the wind into your lungs, where you feel ready to work the next day through full of vigor" (118).

What emerges in this version, then, is the image of a public space to be built in the here-and-now through a dialectical process. That is, it arises in direct response to previous iterations of Poran's Square within the narrative, ultimately tending toward the monumental horizon by refusing the cyclical closure that might otherwise reduce it to mere temporary festival or seasonal occurrence. Instead, it seeks a role in civil society as an autonomous site administered in the interests of all its members—a kind of Kropotkinian updating of the traditional village "common land" where the land is now the shared agricultural and manufacturing resource base for the community and where the claims of older families for exclusive rights of access are no longer recognized. It has also shifted from a site of passive consumption to one of active production and labor where participants no longer succumb to the deceitful and hidden agendas of men like Destupaago, but rather act with a shared sense of purpose. Yet ironically, the more it gains in monumentality, the less outwardly public this space becomes both within the text and *as* text. On the one hand, the space itself has been transformed from a nondescript open area where anyone can gather into a formally organized site defined by a select group of men with technical training and a shared desire for economic independence. Though ostensibly still open to all, entry is in reality now limited to those who align themselves with the ideological mission of the group. Captured in this transformation is the unavoidable fracturing of the public sphere under democratic rule. To grant everyone the right to speak is to open the door to manifold competing interests, much like the awarding of male suffrage in 1925 prompted a flowering of diverse political parties in Japan, each claiming the right to realize its own future vision for society. Fazero too, once given the opportunity to speak for the community, must choose a political path along which he and his followers can proceed even at the risk of foreclosing on other possibilities.

The accessibility of Poraan's Square is also diminished by added spatial and temporal layers placed between Kyuste and the events of the narrative. In this second version, seven years have passed since he first stumbled upon the magical square, and he writes from the hectic environs of urban "Tokiio" where he has no friends and is confined to a small room in a massive stone building, assailed by the violent sounds of a printing press next door. From within this cavernous vault he thinks back fondly to the events of that summer, now no more definite than an "old-fashioned, blue-green lantern slide (*gentō*)." In a place where opportunities for public encounter should be plentiful, Kyuste, appearing closer in image to the cloistered Taishō intellectual, envisions his ideal public forum by looking away from the city to a distant rural locale.[82] The distance is amplified by Miyazawa's strategic labeling of himself as the translator of Kyuste's story, and not as the original author. One likely reason for this added distance is the increasing suppression to which "socialist" organizations were subject in the late 1920s. Authorities, in accordance with new restrictions set down in the Peace Preservation Law, more forcefully clamped down on organizations that appeared in any way to be socialist or antigovernment. Of particular concern were intellectual "outsiders," as Andrew Barshay calls them, who were only loosely affiliated with official institutions or who failed to express allegiance to orthodox visions of community.[83] Miyazawa experienced the impact of this increased authoritarianism, significantly, on a deeply personal level. In his support of the local arm of the Labor-Farmer Party (Rōdō Nōmin Tō), for instance, he felt it prudent to make his donations of money and supplies covertly so as to avoid any unwanted public scrutiny.[84] And soon after the local newspaper publicized his role in founding the Rasu Association, he came under police suspicion and temporarily suspended the group's meetings. It is perhaps not surprising that his most definitive image of public space as it potentially related to the transformation of civil society—the image he was attempting to act out in real time—saw *him* standing furthest back from the limelight.

So far back that he thought it necessary after 1927 to excise a four-page section in which Kyuste, upon hearing the men talk about the future of the cooperative and a lack of educational opportunities, jumps to his feet and, criticizing the education system for its narrow focus and emphasis on physical training, offers to help by giving practical instruction in farming. Together, he predicts, they can create a Poraan's Hiroba "even greater than the [one in the] old fairy tale," a place where "a thousand geniuses will soon gather" to work in mutual respect. Upon expressing his desire to join the group, however, he quickly reconsiders.

> No, I must still continue to study. . . . I will not join you. I can't join you. [My body] is no longer able to do whatever it pleases. I was born the child of a poor teacher and grew up only reading books. I wasn't raised like all of

you, battered by the rain and blown by the wind. My thoughts are exactly the same as yours, but my body won't follow suit. But of course I'll do whatever job I can do. I've been thinking for a while now about how to triple the bounty of the fields.[85]

Despite this backpedaling, that Kyuste does not shy away from voicing his commitment to the group distinguishes him from common figurations of the interwar intellectual as one who "subordinated public to private considerations" while insisting "upon the isolation and self-centeredness of the aesthetic man."[86] Although his reflections on public engagement and the possibility of social transformation are written behind closed doors (and under the hazy glow of distant memory), this isolated stance stems more from feelings of inadequacy—and an implicit fear of exposure—than from a wish to privilege a private culture of *being* over a public culture of *doing*. In fact, we see here a rejection of this wish, which has proved a powerful narrative device for explaining the failings of conscience of the prewar intellectual, in favor of a belief in private intellectual work (e.g., thinking about how to improve soil fertility) as publicly and politically meaningful. Yet, curiously, even as this belief speaks to Miyazawa's own efforts to restructure rural social space, he went so far as to take the excised passage above and bundle it separately from the manuscript, almost as if to insure its future invisibility within the archive. Firm as he may have been in his convictions, there were limits to what he was willing to share.

Hiroba *in Hiding*

Having surveyed the multilayered history of *Poran's Square* as a piece of theater and a work of prose fiction, we see that Miyazawa, in his struggle to bring a renewed vision of the village square to the public eye, was adroit at activating, and in some cases reconfiguring, the linkages that upheld certain popular and progressive conceptions of public space and amateur theater. At the same time, it is clear that as innovative as he was in engaging these *networks*, the social and historical imprint left by *Poran's Square* remained shallow. By all accounts, the staging in 1924 was the last public performance to be held during Miyazawa's lifetime. And yet even in this one instance when the play did command an audience, we know little of how it was received. It may have been interpreted as nothing more than a routine scene of summer festival interrupted by an unwelcome bully, even if the event itself had allowed the local public to come together in new patterns of association. New for audience members because they were watching students step into social roles slightly transgressive and distinctly different from any of the stereotypical roles common to traditional rural theater; new for students because they were being asked to fulfill those roles before elders while projecting an image of public space where power relations between the haves and have-nots were open to negotiation. As it turned out, any potential for sustaining such an image of monumental space (i.e., one with political purpose) was cut short just a month after the curtain fell, when criticism by the minister of education prompted school administrators across the country to institute an unofficial national ban on all school plays.[87]

There were obvious practical issues, then, that kept Miyazawa from rendering more durable his idea that the nexus of theater and public space could be socially transformative. His school could no longer be a *mediator* in the *networks* he was trying to extend, a fact made all the more final in late 1925 when the head principal, a man who had looked leniently upon Miyazawa's unorthodox teaching methods, was transferred elsewhere and replaced by a less open-minded administrator.[88] This did not deter Miyazawa from exploring alternative venues, as is clear from the newspaper report cited at the beginning of this chapter. But here too it is uncertain what became of the six-act version of *Poran's Square* that Miyazawa and Rasu Association members were preparing for in 1927. We do know from the second prose version that he was still wrestling with the work's core ideas and with the question of how public and open his imagined *hiroba* should be. Yet in the end, *Poran's Square* spoke most forcefully to the monumental potential of public space, and the possibility of political engagement by intellectuals, in its least public of manifestations, both *as* text and *in* the text.

This paradox returns us to the question posed earlier about how to assess the "failure" of intellectuals in a time of rural crisis to extend their ideas for reform in durable and lasting ways. More specifically, how are we as historians to evaluate the significance of those ideas, texts, and events that remained largely unseen and unheard despite a clear intent to address the import and meaning of public space and public action? Such hidden ideas and events maintain a different relation to the archive than more public ones, their historical relevance acknowledged after the fact and always with the benefit of hindsight. Yet the very fact that they initially failed to attract attention can also make them a valuable record, in the form of a negative imprint, of established social structures and the possibilities for speaking and acting publicly within those structures. In other words, we learn something of these structures through the ideas and events they disrupted and disallowed, whether in the name of public order and moral authority or for reasons of sheer impracticality (e.g., a lack of money, a failure to arouse interest, an inability to bridge social divisions). The former reasons point to the workings of political and ideological control; the latter to issues of practical viability within the social and economic constraints that circumscribe activity in any community. To the extent that any of these factors render invisible or irrelevant alternative forms of public space and praxis, however, we must treat them as part of the total structure delimiting the physical and representational character of public life at any one moment.

In the case of *Poran's Square*, the alternative form denied was a kind of counter public space defined discretely and negatively against a corrupt social order. This form, while showing an awareness of its more visible contemporary brethren (e.g., the park, the small open space, the stage) ultimately gestured, especially in the final prose version, toward a semi-public space set off from the rest of the community and from the influence of politicians and landlords. Here, a subset of the rural population could assemble under the banner of self-sufficiency and economic independence to reorganize agrarian life, with some technical help from intellectuals like Kyuste, in ways more humane and more conducive to their own class interests. As we have seen, though, the time and place were not fit for publicly sustaining such an imagined space in either a staged or textual form, at least not for very long. And however much Miyazawa wanted to believe in its possibility, it is telling that he situated this space so comically far from the interdiegetic reality of the narrative. Not only did he bury it behind the façade of translation and political ploy, he also placed it at a temporal remove from the narrator and at the end of a long trail of tiny numbered flowers. This may be an indication of how challenging and painstaking even he knew it would be, given the established structures of rural public life, to actualize such a space in the here-and-now. That he proceeded to try anyway through the Rasu Association, armed with a philosophy of art and life oriented toward the unique hardships of agrarian labor, offers continued opportunity in the next chapter to explore what about the time and place of 1920s Iwate allowed him to extend his ideas as far as he did, but also no further.

CHAPTER SEVEN

Farmers' Art in an Age of Cosmopolitan Agrarianism

Around the time Miyazawa began to think about resigning his teaching post, he also began thinking seriously about how to extend established connections between rural labor and art into a localized cultural praxis. In doing so, he joined an expanding network of intellectuals, both in Japan and elsewhere, who were trying to extend this dyad in similar directions. By 1926, the year he delivered a series of lectures on "farmers' art" (*nōmin geijutsu*) before officially stepping down, this term had already found its way—alongside competing terms like *kyōdo geijutsu* (local/native art), *kyōdo bungei* (local/native literature), *tsuchi no geijutsu* (art of the soil), *nōmin bungei* (farmers' literature), and *nōmin bijutsu* (peasant art)—into a wide range of literary journals, general interest magazines, newspapers, and scholarly volumes. Like Miyazawa, contributors to this emergent discourse were, in their own ways, attempting to reconceive the ontological and cultural divide that generations before them had placed between those who worked the land and those who did not. The divide was so vast that a decade earlier Natsume Sōseki saw nothing wrong in describing the pitiful lives of peasants (*hyakushō*) as akin to that of maggots while regretting that "humans living in such a way reside not only in our own times (*dōjidai*), but in the countryside not too far from the imperial capital."[1]

As Partha Chatterjee has observed, "the relationship between the modern state and a peasantry is ambiguous and shot through with tension," a natural consequence of the fact that institutionalizing power in the state has typically coincided or followed the extinction of the peasant class.[2] In states like Japan, where the late-nineteenth and early-twentieth centuries saw a steady shift away from rural settlement and communal agricultural production toward industrial production and urban habitation, this tension often manifested itself in the ways the "peasant" (increasingly defined as anyone who worked the land as a primary means of subsistence) was represented vis-à-vis historical consciousness. In such places, the peasant made for a convenient, and contested, reference point by which to measure change and progress. This contention, Chatterjee asserts, typically amounted to a disagreement between the "modernizers who thought of peasants as embodying all that was backward and premodern" and the "modern critics of modernity, especially romantics, who saw in a peasantry the rapidly vanishing virtues of simplicity, naturalness, and cultural authenticity."[3] In Japan too, one finds ample evidence of such a split. On one side was the rhetoric espoused by upper- and middle-class urbanites and ideologues who, like Sōseki, felt peasants were outdated in their customs, misguided in their beliefs, or lacking in the qualities necessary for membership in the civilized world. On the other was a rhetoric popular with both bureaucrats and romantics alike who, in their own ways, sought to preserve the agricultural way of life as essence of the nation and/or lamented the spiritual and moral cost of its forever imminent disappearance.[4] Both rhetorics, however, similarly objectified the peasant class as existing in *negative* relation to a present naturalized as the foremost edge of historical progress. When not seen as always already several steps behind the modern moment, they and their livelihood were figured as historical remnants that either had to be preserved or shielded from change.

Positioning the rural laborer in this way may seem reasonable in an age when so many of us live beyond what Eric Hobsbawm calls "the death of the peasantry," a change so dramatic and far-reaching that it "cuts us off forever from the world of the past."[5] But whether modernizer or romanticist, those who defined social or national progress through the figure of the peasant did so at a time when the fate of the rural laborer, at least in Japan, had yet to be decided. Granted, the signs of a momentous shift were already apparent by the 1920s. Increased opportunities for nonagricultural employment had driven rural emigration to never before seen levels even as greater price disparity between agricultural produce and manufactured commodities, especially fertilizer, were making it difficult for small-scale owner-cultivators to stay afloat. Class tensions swelled accordingly, especially in southwestern Japan where the integration of agriculture into the money economy had proceeded at a relatively fast pace. Yet even as these dramatic transformations took place, few thought that agricultural work itself was going to soon disappear. The dire conditions merely demanded more effective measures of protection or reform. And as long as the fate of agriculture remained uncertain, there was still room to imagine a "peasant" who could play an integral role in future society rather than be shoved to the margins as a historical relic.

This, at least, was the premise under which Miyazawa and fellow advocates of *nōmin geijutsu* worked as they set out to reposition the farmer as both agricultural *and* cultural producer. Their predecessors, in contrast, had tried to reclaim agrarian labor for the present by rediscovering in it the spiritually and morally ennobling charms of physical toil carried out in an idyllic rural setting.[6] But they rejected this bourgeois ethos and instead refigured the "peasant" as part of a class of laborers suffering from underrepresentation in both art and politics. They believed that Japan's *hyakushō*, whom they marked with the less pejorative term *nōmin* (farmers or rural laborers), deserved a place in modernity radically different from that which they had heretofore been assigned. Their rhetoric leaned at times in the direction of nativist ideology and nationalist particularism, as was conventional in more conservative strains of interwar agrarian thought, but they also consciously flaunted, like their fellow modernists, the cosmopolitan and transnational contours of their ideas. This was a fight not just for the farmer next door, or in the next village over, but for farming as a universal way of being. What they shared in this fight, and the reason I use *nōmin geijutsu* as a provisional catch-all for their activities, was the desire to create a space where the country's struggling rural laborers could make themselves heard through new forms of art and in turn transform their present condition. The unfolding of this desire serves as a final means by which to interrogate the possibilities and limits of local cultural production in a highly centralized field.

Can the Farmer Write? The Trouble with Authenticity in Nōmin Geijutsu *Discourse*

As interest in *nōmin geijutsu* grew during the 1920s, proponents had constantly to address two enduring questions: what exactly constituted an authentic farmers' art and what was the role of intellectuals and established artists in helping farmers to create this art? Leading the way was painter and woodblock artist Yamamoto Kanae (1882–1946), who in 1919 set forth a plan for a peasant art movement (*nōmin bijutsu undō*) in his native Nagano village.[7] He was inspired by a visit two years before to the Moscow Kustar' Museum, which since 1885 had been exhibiting the most exemplary and ornate products of the various *kustar'* trades (e.g., woodcarving, toy-making, lace-making, embroidery, and weaving).[8] In a pamphlet he created to recruit local youth for a three-month training workshop, Yamamoto declared that "peasant art" is "distinguished by its ethnic or provincial design, its plain workmanship, and its sturdy quality," and that it "exists in every country." It had long since flourished in Japan too, he wrote, but mechanized production and a lack of promotional prowess had recently led its value as art to decrease to the point that nothing worthy of the name "peasant art in Japan" could be said to exist.[9] Yamamoto saw himself as an intermediary who could restore this value and make peasant art a pleasurable form of creative labor (*sōzōteki rōdō*) that enhanced farmers' quality of life even as it became a source of supplementary income during the unproductive winter months.[10] During the winter of 1920, he guided sixteen local youth, male and female, in making simple handicrafts to be exhibited at the Mitsukoshi department store in Tokyo, thus replicating the circuit by which *kustar'* handicrafts had traveled from the hands of rural laborers to some of Western Europe's most elite sites of commodity consumption.[11] The response from the public was so positive that intellectuals and government bureaucrats came out in strong support of the project, allowing Yamamoto to establish the Japan Peasant Art Institute in 1923. After 1925, additional funding from the government made it possible to expand the institute's operations, such that "prefectural governments throughout the country were calling upon Yamamoto and his research center for advice and aid in organizing production of their own farmers' art."[12]

Despite its success in official circles, *nōmin bijutsu* was not without its critics. The literary elder statesman Uchida Roan (1868–1929), for instance, had earlier expressed his concern that encouraging farmers to produce handicrafts en masse would strip the objects of their original simplicity. Painter Yamashita Shintarō (1881–1966) was even more adamant about the impossibility of a true peasant art existing in modern, civilized nations, and dismissed the whole idea as sheer historical anachronism.[13] Yamamoto's response shows him to harbor a very different image of the farmer's place in the here-and-now.

If one decides that artistic value is greater the further one goes back in history, then our artistic sensibility has no choice but to live upon the path of nostalgia. If one decides that only *nōmin bijutsu* of earlier times has value as *nōmin bijutsu*, then individuality (*kosei*) and creativity (*dokusōryoku*) become useless things. I am surely the first one to express a fondness for old, honest handicrafts constructed from simple tools and materials. That said, I also believe the following:

　. . . For the same reason that art was born amongst farmers of old, one expects that art can be born amongst the farmers of today. It is no different than the fact that love and poetry existed in previous ages and yet are today not in decline, but are being expressed with increasing vitality even while their form has changed.[14]

For Yamamoto, the farmer was not a figure who stood outside the present or one whose art needed to be shielded, as Roan had suggested, from commodity capitalism. After all, what was there to protect if farmers today had their own individual creativity to draw upon? It made more sense to recognize the value of this creativity in the present and direct it to the proper consumer channels.

The notion that farmers could claim an artistic sensibility uniquely their own formed the ideological bedrock of Yamamoto's entire project. It also raised the difficult question of what his role, as cosmopolitan intellectual, was to be in the creative process. Why was it necessary for him to instruct farmers in something that was supposed to be instinctual? It is telling that his first group of trainees either did not believe they could produce the kind of "art" Yamamoto wanted them to, or else found that their initial attempts to do so—by fashioning clay models of opera singers and classical feminine nudes—only earned his disapproval.[15] Neither party was aware yet of what the other wanted from the whole exchange. Yamamoto's response was to argue that even though it was undesirable, and even though a true *nōmin bijutsu* had to proceed from the farmers' own patterns and designs, it was necessary to first correct their bad habits (*aku shumi*) by allowing them the chance to engage in free creation (*jiyū seisaku*). Despite this need for intervention, he still imagined his role to be nothing more than "following his own ideas to provide farmers with good patterns and designs so as to invite them into an artistic mood."[16] This notion that one could guide the production of authentic otherness without exercising any artistic control or judgment points to a deeper ideological impasse at the heart of *nōmin geijutsu* discourse.

In 1922, a second branch of this discourse arose from some of the writers and critics who, as discussed in Chapter Two, were to converge after the Kantō Earthquake around the notion of a quintessentially nonurban literature born of the everyday realities of rural labor and livelihood. Triggering this emergence was a symposium held in December to honor French novelist Charles-Louis Philippe (1874–1909), known for his intimate portrayals of the urban and rural poor. The idea for the event had come from Komaki Ōmi (1894–1978), a leading figure in Japan's proletarian literature movement, who two months earlier had used the pages of the *Tōkyō Asahi shinbun* to call out to those who, like the rural-born Philippe, could rise up to represent the farmer and create an "art born of the land."[17] Attendees, while few and almost exclusively male, included the novelist Nakamura Seiko, future chronicler of the movement Inuta Shigeru (1891–1957), and even the poet Paul Claudel (1868–1955), who had just taken up his post as French ambassador to Japan.[18] It was Yoshie Takamatsu (1880–1940), a professor of French literature at Waseda University and the son of a farm family, who set the tone for the evening by declaring Philippe's work to be an honest and authentic voice for those farmers (*nōjin*) who had toiled in silence for centuries. How, he asked, could Japanese society possibly move ahead without hearing similar voices?

> A majority of our brethren confront the ancient earth of Japan and pass their days in silence. Lacking even the consciousness for suitable self-expression, their dark lives continue from one age to the next. I cannot but yearn for the day when many of them will—having risen from the black earth and shaken off their long slumber, showing now their black faces and black smiles—make clear the history of those humans who have lived with the soil of Japan and the vitality (*seiki*) it harbors. It is within the power of these spokespeople that a new Japanese culture (*bunmei*), a new Japanese art, indeed a truly creative mode of Japanese expression, lies yet to be awakened.[19]

Earlier in the year, Yoshie had written on the glaring absence of literary works depicting the livelihood of Japan's farmers, a situation that seemed preposterous given that the majority of the nation's population still subsisted by farming. If there was to be a true "people's art" he argued, it had to be first and foremost an art "for and by the farmers."[20] The rhetoric of underrepresentation was to be a common refrain for Yoshie and other advocates of *nōmin geijutsu*. Some, including Miyazawa, went so far as to cite government population statistics in order to suggest that that the quantity and content of artistic production in a society, if it was to be truly of the people, must be made to correspond proportionally to actual ratios of social occupation.[21] In what amounted to a crude politics of numbers, writers emphasized again and again the gross disparity between the number of farmers in Japan and their representation in literature and other arts.

Yoshie's remarks at the symposium also underscored two issues that would frame much of the debate in the years ahead: the orientation of this art toward generating radically new aesthetic forms, and the problem of finding authentic, truly representative voices. On the one hand, advocates were keen to defend farmers' art, especially in its literary manifestations, as the antithesis of the bourgeois pastoralism and rural nostalgia felt to be integral to earlier naturalist depictions of the countryside and the farming class. This art was not meant to represent a retreat into the rural, but a forward-looking and socially engaged search for untapped artistic energy and inspiration. Critic Chiba Kameo captured this sentiment well in 1923 when he called for revenge against the privileged urban elite who were destroying village culture, and yet simultaneously retaining their power over it, by enshrouding it in their own biased views of what counted for "traditional" and "natural."[22] The question that still remained, of course, was who was going to exact this revenge. Was it to be the farmers themselves? The intellectuals who sympathized with their plight? Or perhaps some combination of both? One thing of which all were certain was that the literature of the day was woefully inadequate to the task. Kurata Ushio put it bluntly when he remarked that any tenant farmer was likely to vomit if made to read a story like Shiga Naoya's *An'ya kōro* (A Dark Night's Passing, 1921–1937). He called for a literature that not only represented the farmers' plight and their revolutionary spirit, but one created with their own forms and techniques, their own eyes and hands.[23]

The search for this new literature, and for this new art (distinctions between genres were often blurred), intensified in the years after the quake, led primarily by attendees at the Philippe symposium. In 1924, several of them formed the Nōmin Bungei Kenkyū Kai (Farmers' Literature Research Group), an informal study group whose participants included Yoshie, Inuta, Nakamura, the socialist thinker Ishikawa Sanshirō, the anarchist Shiina Sonoji, the poet Shirotori Seigo, the agrarian novelist Katō Takeo, a scholar of William Morris named Ōtsuki Kenji, and several aspiring writers recently graduated from Waseda University.[24] They dedicated much of their time to investigating foreign sources and models and took turns lecturing at Shiina's house in northeast Tokyo on such topics as village theater, rural life in France, William Morris, French peasant literature, the Irish tenant movement, and Norwegian rural fiction.[25] Though the group failed to attract much attention early on and continued to have internal disagreements over what to name their new art, its prominence rose in 1926 when the debate over *nōmin geijutsu* as a legitimate category of literary and artistic activity reached a kind of critical mass.[26] In June, for instance, Katō Takeo (1888–1956) leveraged his position as editor at the publishing house Shinchōsha to help assemble a volume of "peasant fiction" (*nōmin shōsetsu*) original in both content and rationale. Pulling together twenty stories with contemporary agrarian life as their theme, the collection was intended—at least as stated in the preface—as a vehicle to fund the creation of a school in Niigata for the displaced children of protesting tenant farmers.[27] In August, a special issue of *Waseda bungaku* was dedicated to "The Art of the Soil," with some key members of the study group contributing essays on the current state of *nōmin* literature.[28] The year also witnessed the publication of a large number of short fictional works, and several poetry volumes, designated as worthy candidates for the growing canon of *nōmin* literature.[29] Before the year was up, two sizable scholarly works appeared attempting to situate the farmers' literature movement in its national and international contexts. One of these, *Nōmin bungei jūrokkō* (Sixteen Lectures on Farmers' Literature), was the study group's attempt to offer a definitive statement on the state of the genre in Japan and to align it with parallel trends in France, Germany, England, Russia, Poland, Norway, and Ireland.[30] The conviction that this was a genre of global importance was surely strengthened by the fact that two of the past six Nobel laureates had been awarded the prize for novels that dealt specifically with agrarian themes.[31]

With increased visibility naturally came increased criticism. Some, particularly hard-line Marxists, expressed their doubts in a language of ideological critique.[32] Others resorted to a more basic line of questioning. In April 1926, critic Nakamura Murao had this to say:

> There is a small group of people now advocating this thing called farmers' art (*nōmin geijutsu*). But I do not really understand what it is they are advocating. Is farmers' art an art born of the suffering of agrarian life, a kind of appeal to that suffering? Or is it an art to be appreciated by farmers, an art that will comfort them and make their lives enjoyable? Or perhaps it is something less than that, just a name for literary works that take agrarian life as their theme?[33]

Inuta was quick to respond and used this as an opportunity to clarify the study group's position. The impetus for *nōmin geijutsu* lay not in suffering, he proclaimed, but in something much more profound. This was an art meant to challenge and reform the organization of contemporary society by rediscovering and utilizing the forgotten power of the soil. Nakamura was also wrong in thinking that *nōmin geijutsu* might be an art created solely for the farmer. Rather, it expressed a "consciousness of the soil" (*tsuchi no ishiki*) that could potentially improve the lives of *all* humankind and generate a "future social ideology" rooted in this very consciousness.[34] With this, Inuta rejected the critique of particularism. Yet he was also careful, both here and in his other writings, to assert the fundamental importance of knowing the real conditions under which the present-day farmer labored. The art of the soil had to be universal in its aims, but also relevant to that vast majority who, in the minds of Inuta and his compatriots, lived closest to the earth.

Inuta's professed commitment to keeping *nōmin geijutsu* relevant reflects his awareness of the general atmosphere of urgency and optimism surrounding the status of agrarian labor at this time. Urgent because the lines dividing the urban and rural economies had become increasingly stark. Outmigration of youth, falling rice prices, expanding debt, and a rising tide of tenant protest: all were omens of an impending rural crisis that had yet to generate a concerted response from urban intelligentsia or the central government. Yet their also remained a sense of optimism and hope that led many rural youth to seek out independent solutions to the social and structural problems facing their villages.[35] On the political front, for instance, the awarding of manhood suffrage in 1925 saw the creation of local branches of new political parties seeking to represent the interests of struggling tenant farmers. That a discourse promoting self-expression for the farming class should reach its zenith just as these parties were gearing up for the first post-suffrage general elections in 1928 seems hardly coincidental. It is also telling that the Farmers' Literature Research Group initially forged close ties with an organization like the Nōmin Jichi Kai (Farmers' Autonomous Society), which sought solutions to the socioeconomic crisis of the village in the principle of cooperation and the idea of political autonomy for the farming class. Made up as it was of "Tokyo intellectuals"—as they were referred to within the group—and "actual farmer" activists from Nagano and Saitama, the Jichi Kai was itself emblematic of the new linkages being formed, if only tenuously, between farmers' art and politics during these years.[36] Miyazawa too, as noted in the preceding chapter, showed a similar inclination to forge such connections. Though more silent benefactor than vocal participant, he gave generously to the Hanamaki branch of the Labor-Farmer Party just as he was transforming his own vision of *nōmin geijutsu* into praxis.

If Inuta and others were convinced of the timeliness of *nōmin geijutsu*, they found it harder to articulate the farmer's own stake, either as producer or consumer, in this new cultural movement. Having himself grown up in a sharecropper family before working his way into the editing offices of Hakubunkan, Inuta was oddly insistent that a literature of the soil need not necessarily come from the pens of farmers. On the contrary, where or by what means one lived was less significant for him than whether one possessed a "consciousness of the soil"—a kind of critical, and yet devoutly focused, insight into agrarian life.[37] And this, according to Inuta, was not something the poor tenant farmer, uneducated and oppressed as he was, was likely to have. To instill in farmers such consciousness, and thus allow for their active participation in the revolutionary new art being proposed, the farmer's soul would have first to be "awakened to the soil." What this art demanded was a "new farmer" (*shin nōjin*) with a "new soul"—one plucked from the "pure sprouts of youth" and thus unsullied by the stagnant feudal mentality and customs of previous generations and of the "old peasant" (*furui hyakushō*).[38] Farmers had, in other words, to be rescued not only from the blinding oppressiveness of their condition, but also from their own muddied past.

In contrast to Inuta, writer Nakamura Seiko, also the self-declared son of a poor farmer, insisted that the most authentic form of *nōmin geijutsu* had to come from the farmers themselves. This did not include those who sympathized with agrarian life, nor those who willfully moved to villages to take up the plow. Not even members of the landowning class would do.[39] This insistence on a strict homology of occupation and subjective expression, however, presented a problem: Nakamura was well aware that overwork, a lack of time and money, and insufficient intellectual and technical training all combined to make it difficult for the tenant farmer to appreciate, let alone produce, a genuine literature, poetry, or theater. True, the expanding education system offered tenant farmers an opportunity for social advancement, and some in recent years had even achieved success as professional artists. But such artists, prone as they were in the course of their social ascendancy to grow distant from, and even disdainful of, the soil, no longer counted as *nōmin* in Nakamura's eyes. Apparently, one could not be both intellectual and farmer at the same time. Backed into a corner, Nakamura retreated through a logic of class awakening—structurally similar to

Inuta's—wherein the farmer's consciousness of a new, liberated age would become a source for an autonomous new art. Since present conditions prevented farmers from waking on their own, however, there was little choice but for those who could speak in their place (i.e., the intellectual class) to lead the charge.

> To those who were once farmers, or to those who intend to be in the future . . . , to those who carry the knowledge and skills for expression, I ask you to rise up for the ordinary farmer of today who lacks time, words, color, and music. Rise up and be their companion! Be their spokesperson! Their painter! Their musician! Their psychologist! Even if that day when the farmer will create literature by himself is still far off, the path for literature created by sympathetic supporters must depart from here.[40]

Here we find Nakamura, like Inuta and others in the movement, venturing in the direction of what Benjamin called an "impossible place"—that place where intellectuals, "struggling to find [a] place *beside* the proletariat," inevitably position themselves as benefactors and patrons of a process for which they are an integral, but in the end disposable, part.[41] What he and others had trouble imagining was their own transition from being *integral* to being *disposable*. In lieu of any clear resolution, they simply held on tighter to the reins of aesthetic authority.

The impossibility of finding a place *beside* the farmer is perhaps best illustrated by the publication, also in 1926, of a poetry collection titled *Nora ni sakebu* (Shout to the Fields). The collection belonged to Shibuya Teisuke (1905–1989), one of the core farmer activists in the fledgling Nōmin Jichi Kai. Shibuya, a poor tenant farmer who, with little more than a primary school education, had become a local labor organizer, was encouraged to publish some of his poems by the philosopher and critic Tsuchida Kyōson. He described them at the time as "his record of wandering around the problem of a farmers' movement (*nōmin undō*) at once both art and practical social movement."[42] Their unambiguous and unornamented language, with titles such as "Living Hell," "I'm Alive," and "Manifesto of a Child Raised under Scorn and Persecution," were hardly subtle in conveying the physical toil, mental anguish, and public disdain that came with life as a radicalized tenant farmer. As such, they were quickly proclaimed by intellectuals in the Jichi Kai to embody the authentic voice of the oppressed farmer proletariat.

If it looked to some like the farmer subaltern had finally spoken, prefatory comments to the work indicate that no one, not even Shibuya, was quite sure how to evaluate the status of his language as poetry or as art. Proletarian writer Nakanishi Inosuke, for instance, suggested that he was not really a poet at all, at least not in any conventional sense. "He is not one of those polished 'proletarian farm poets' or 'poets of the soil' who sigh for-lornly at the lives of the impoverished farmer. He is rather a blood-stained warrior of peasant liberation, his poems little more than hasty scribbles in the margins of his battlefield diary."[43] Tsuchida, in contrast, claimed that Shibuya's work counted as poetry proper, but only after he invoked Trotsky to explain how simplistic and clumsy the sprouts of proletarian poetry must inevitably appear when set against the long-established roots of bourgeois letters. In his view, this was only because they signaled "an entirely new direction for poetry" in which form and content were finally to be uni-fied through experience.[44] Shibuya himself asked his readers to avert their eyes from his admittedly infantile language and focus instead on "the tragic aspect of contemporary farming life lurking in the depths of the words."[45] What need, he wrote, was there to focus on lyricism or style when he had "completely ignored the forms and techniques of existing poetry."

At first Shibuya is not a poet, at least not a conventional one. Then he is one, but part of a radically newer, and thus less polished breed. And finally he is a poet of the everyday who has no need for the art and technique of poetry. All this confusion points back to the hazy, shifting line drawn by Inuta, Nakamura, and others as they tried to demarcate and patrol the di-vide that separated them intellectually and professionally from those whom they wished to incite to speak. Too much poetic artifice or too much adher-ence to form would imply an impostor—an educated poet merely posing as soil-hardened rural laborer. Too little would render the farmer's voice meaningless as an aesthetic object, reducing it to mere political slogan or, worse, crude ramblings, thus excluding it from the field of poetry proper. Shibuya had, to borrow from Gayatri Spivak's language, stepped into the shadow cast by metropolitan intellectuals in their search for an agrarian Other only to find that there was not yet a place for him to stand as both farmer *and* poet.[46] This may explain why his exit from the literary scene was as sudden as his entrance. The Jichi Kai too suffered a quick demise. It fell apart in 1928 after the intellectuals and farmer-activists failed to agree on what constituted meaningful political engagement.[47] As eager as *nōmin geijutsu* advocates were to give farmers the opportunity to speak for them-selves, it was not so easy to concede the authority that assured them of their role as arbiters of value and as those capable of harnessing the universal forces of which they spoke. The result was that few were able to extend their ideas much beyond their own narrow personal networks.

Where they did succeed was in changing the *subject* of the modern pastoral. Not only did they reconceptualize rural labor as a universal mode of being impacted by new global economic pressures, they also treated the farmer as a historical agent who rightfully had a say in the social transformations by which his fate was being decided. This farmer was not to be cast aside in the wake of capitalist-driven industrialization, nor preserved as vanishing folkloric remnant or silent literary prop. Instead, farming was itself to be a vehicle for new forms of cultural production and for patterns of social organization different from those predicted by dominant teleological narratives of progress. Compared with how rural labor had been imagined in the arts and letters of a generation earlier, this was truly a radical vision. Yet as long as these self-declared "sons of farmers" deferred the participation of still practicing farmers until some later moment of awakening, the latter would remain potential contributors to the field of cultural production only in the abstract.

Miyazawa's Lectures on Nōmin Geijutsu

Implicit in the arguments of early proponents of *nōmin geijutsu* was the assumption that when farmers finally awoke to their plight and rose up to represent themselves, they would do so in locales where farming was already an integral part of daily life. Agrarian labor may have been a universal mode of being in their minds, but it was not imminently mobile nor extractable from the specific suffering of Japan's rural communities. When carried through to its logical end point, then, *nōmin geijutsu* potentially opened paths to new forms of local imagining and local praxis. Considered in this light, Miyazawa's own interventions into this discourse stand out for their locus of articulation. For he delivered his thoughts on *nōmin geijutsu* not to an audience of like-minded intellectuals, nor through the medium of print, but directly to rural youth in whom so many in the farmers' art movement placed their hope. The thirty or so young men who attended his lectures were area farmers participating in a three-month educational program known as the Iwate People's Higher Level School. It seems, however, that the size and makeup of his audience in no way restricted the breadth of Miyazawa's vision. Indeed, as we will see, his ideas were forged from the same global circuits of inter-textual and material exchange utilized by his urban contemporaries. What will also become apparent is that Miyazawa's psychological and physical proximity to his audience forced him to confront the issues of authenticity and aesthetic evaluation in ways his metropolitan counterparts had never imagined.

In December 1925 a county newspaper announced that, with the start of the new year, a People's Higher Level School (Kokumin Kōtō Gakkō) would be opening on the grounds of the Hanamaki School of Agriculture.

> This school, which takes the Danish version as its model, will be the first of its kind in the prefecture. As it elevates the culture of the common people (*ippan minshū*), it will on the one hand help to accomplish the aims of adult education and on the other be a facility for creating the foundation of a sturdy regional autonomy. Those interested in being nominated should apply to the county head of the Iwate Education Association.[48]

Supporting organizations also included the Iwate Agricultural Association and the Iwate Allied Association of Youth Groups. Young men over eighteen, as long as they were graduates of upper-level primary school and interested in working for regional autonomy (*chihō jichi*), were encouraged to apply.[49] The planned curriculum was to comprise courses in ethics, civics, history, and literature, but would also include instruction in agricultural administration, industrial associations, modern scientific advancements, and the problems of contemporary rural society. Organizers asked Miyazawa to contribute to this lineup with a course on farmers' art.

The idea of the People's Higher Level School—where rural youth could devote the off-season to technical instruction in farming, continuing general education, and spiritual guidance—traces its roots to nineteenth-century Denmark and, in Japan, to the early Taishō period.[50] In the 1830s, Danish minister, theologian, and educator N. F. S. Grundtvig (1783–1872) proposed the folk high school (*folkehøjskole*) as a first step to creating an educational system open to citizens of every social standing, including farmers. Designed to instill in students a newfound pride in Danish culture and a love of learning rooted in Christian faith, the schools gained acceptance in the late 1860s after Denmark's defeat in war with Prussia, at which time forty-four new folk high schools were in operation.[51] By the early 1900s, they had become a respected model of rural education and were being written about by foreign educators and diplomats who visited from Germany, England, and America. These writings would arrive in Japan after 1913, whence the folk high school became a panacea to those in search of a pedagogy responsive to the needs of rural society and able to cultivate moral sensibility in the population at large.[52]

Although the history of modern agrarian ideology in Japan is often portrayed as one of increasing nativism, there is ample indication that this ideology participated in, and in some cases grew out of, the same practices of transnational cultural borrowing that characterized the spirit of Taishō internationalism. As the agricultural sector suffered continued decline in the 1920s, some began to look abroad for solutions and rural Denmark became for many a ray of light in an increasingly dark tunnel. Researchers and educators were sent to uncover the secrets of its seeming prosperity and they left behind a trail of official reports and personal accounts.[53] These accounts invariably extolled the folk high school, describing it as both an internationally recognized institution and a key reason for the social and cultural vitality of Denmark's villages. The schools were seen not only to nurture morally upright and patriotic citizens, but also to offer an egalitarian and autonomous learning environment that encouraged participating youth to stay in the countryside and pursue agricultural careers.[54]

As with any cultural borrowing, advocates for the folk high school saw in it what they wanted. Some emphasized its potential to cultivate national character (*kokuminsei*) and ethnic spirit (*minzoku seishin*), substituting for Christian-based spiritualism a faith in the sanctity of the imperial lineage and an invented assemblage of archaic Japanese values. One sees evidence of this emphasis in the Iwate program as well, where the day started with a Shintō-inspired cleansing followed by calisthenics meant to discipline the *yamato* spirit. The classes in history and literature also utilized premodern material in ways that clearly assumed the existence of a transcendent national essence.[55] Other accounts of the folk high school, however, highlighted its democratic qualities, noting that the school was meant to serve all members of the farming class and that the classroom structure and teaching methods deemphasized hierarchy while promoting a relatively free, hands-on learning environment. Sugiyama Motojirō, for instance, who established his own "Farmers' Higher School" in rural Fukushima Prefecture, linked the concept to the spirit of the people's movement (*minshū undō*). He praised the schools for their ability to promote a populist (*kokuminteki*) sentiment that, in contrast to a purely restrictive nationalism (*henkyō na kokkashugi*), saw improving national character as just the initial step to achieving a true cosmopolitanism.[56] Other commentators stressed the importance of the schools for rural Danish society as a whole, claiming that they were instrumental in supporting high levels of cultural and artistic activity at the village level.[57] This more progressive emphasis shows itself in the opening ceremony of the Iwate program, where speakers talked of how critical the school was for nurturing in youth a vested interest in the region and for enhancing the quality of village art and provincial culture. In the interest of such goals, instructors organized evening sessions dedicated to informal lectures, the free exchange of ideas, and musical performances.

It was within such a hybrid institutional framework that Miyazawa delivered his lectures, which today survive as notes taken by student Itō Seiichi and as three manuscripts edited posthumously: "A Survey of Farmers' Art" (*Nōmin geijutsu gairon*), "An Outline Survey of Farmers' Art" (*Nōmin geijutsu gairon kōyō*), and "The Rise of Farmers' Art" (*Nōmin geijutsu no kōryū*). Together, these documents offer a collage of pithy abstractions and citations that resist easy summary.[58] Even his students later admitted to understanding little of what Miyazawa was trying to convey to them.[59] Several persistent themes do emerge, however, and from them it is possible to piece together an image of *nōmin geijutsu* as both a radically new art form and a radically inclusive one. I will first map out the boundaries of this inclusivity before addressing the ways Miyazawa's image deviates from and contests others circulating at the time.

With his very opening salvo, Miyazawa made clear to his audience that *nōmin geijutsu* was an art born of the present moment. It was so new, in fact, that almost every aspect of it had still to be clarified.

> Why must our art arise at this moment? . . . What will be made the core of our art? . . . How will it be categorized? . . . What claims will be possible within these categories? . . . How will we begin and how will we move forward? . . . What does the word "artist" mean for us? . . . How will we evaluate and judge this art correctly?[60]

What Miyazawa also demonstrated through this line of questioning was that, in contrast to some of his contemporaries, he did not stand apart from those he was addressing. His use of the first person plural ostensibly erases any ontological gap between himself as advocate of *nōmin geijutsu* and those for, and by, whom this art was to be produced. This was not "your art," or "the art you will eventually make your own," but first and foremost "our art." Instead of reinforcing a categorical split between critic (the intellectual) and producer (the farmer), he effectively bridged the gap by sublating his own identity into the sign of the latter.

And yet Miyazawa, as those in the lecture hall well knew, was not a farmer by stock and, though he aspired to join their ranks, was hardly one by trade. While his disingenuousness in this case may simply have been for rhetorical effect, his consistent use of "we" does beg the question of whom he meant to include under the label of *nōmin*. The lectures are not very forthcoming with specifics, opting to focus most of their attention on the degraded state of agrarian labor. "Today, all we [farmers] have is labor (*rōdō*) and existence (*seizon*). Farmers work in order to eat, and it is because we work that we must eat. Our lives are nothing but this endless cycle of repetition." Labor, Miyazawa declared, has become "busy and toilsome" (or "ashen-colored," as he often referred to it), abstracted entirely from the inherent creativity of the individual so as to leave only joyless existence.[61] In making such claims, he was borrowing primarily from the socialist tracts of William Morris, who along with fellow Victorians like John Ruskin (1819–1900), Thomas Carlyle, and Friedrich Engels, argued that a shift to mechanization and factory-style manufacturing had forced a split between craftsmanship and labor, and between creative design and production.[62] The result was the alienation of the laborer from his work, robbing the act itself of any and all pleasure.[63] Although Miyazawa hews closer to Ruskin than to Morris in his focus on agrarian as opposed to industrial labor, he saw little need to make strict distinctions between them.[64] In fact, his adherence to a transhistorical conception of labor allows him to cite Morris's own proposals for restoring pleasure to industrial work and to consider their application to farming.[65] These proposals are included in the lecture notes along with parenthetical comments indicating the relative ease with which each might be accomplished:

> Return mechanical labor to creative labor (historical investigation); give labor a new, purposeful objective (already established); have a thorough period of rest (somewhat difficult); insure there is production and that it is abundant (easy); labor time that is not too long and variation in the work (difficult); the ability to develop various skills without limit; a pleasurable environment that lacks anxiety (easy); companions whom you like and enjoy (halfway done).[66]

A willingness to merge industrial and agrarian labor is further evident in a reference made to Peter Kropotkin (1842–1921), whose work is used to illustrate the need for a society in which industry and agriculture are more efficiently combined, and in which rural workers pilfer elements of urban industry so as to produce essential necessities on their own.[67]

Taken together, the above statements suggest the image of an ideal *nōmin* as one who floats somewhere between independent cultivator, small-scale craftsman, and creative artist. Miyazawa clearly did not want to set too many limits on who could and could not belong to this social category, a fact further hinted at in a remark made at the very start of his lectures: "Instead of farmer (*nōmin*), I want to say 'person of the earth' (*chijin*). Instead of art (*geijutsu*), I want to say 'creativity' (*sōzō*)."[68] The latter term, which reflects a move toward inclusivity by reducing the formal category of "art" to the generic actions of making and inventing, will be taken up in a moment. The term *chijin* provides for an analogous kind of leveling, though its meaning is not immediately obvious. Miyazawa likely appropriated the word from Ishikawa Sanshirō (1876–1956), who had in turn adopted it from the work of French geographer and social anarchist Elisée Reclus (1830–1905). What attracted Ishikawa to Reclus's work was the idea that humans, in their ideal state, are intimately and inevitably bound up with their surrounding natural environments, and that they must adapt and harmonize with these complex environments through endless creative engagement.[69] He went on to integrate this idea into his own articulation of the human ideal, variously referred to in essays at the time as *chi no ko* (earth child) and *tomin* (people of the land). The first was a person who "loved heaven and earth like father and mother" and who tilled the soil conscious of his or her affinity with all living things. The second was derived from the Greek *demos* and captured the idea of a person living inseparably from the perpetual cycles of the soil and the natural movements of the solar system.[70] Although Miyazawa's lectures made no reference to either of these terms, their overall content suggests that, like Ishikawa, he aimed to disassociate agrarian labor from any one socioeconomic class or status. *Chijin*, in other words, was a means to open up the practice of *nōmin geijutsu* to any and all who worked the earth with a particular consciousness of their place within it. This included well-to-do intellectuals like himself and the urbanites (*tojin*) whom he at one point encouraged to "come and join us."[71] Miyazawa was, to invoke Benjamin again, placing himself "beside the proletariat" not as distant benefactor but rather as a fellow worshipper and custodian of the soil.

The ideological implications of this strategy will have to be addressed, but it is useful to first consider how the lectures redefined *geijutsu* so as to similarly open art to a broader range of participants. Here, the flood gates were opened in the opposite direction, for while *chijin* allowed urbanites and intellectuals to imagine themselves as farmers, the redefinition of *geijutsu* allowed those who worked the land to rise up and stake a claim on an activity presently dominated—and poorly at that—by urban intellectuals.

> Those who call themselves artists and religious practitioners today seem to carry on just for the sake of eating. . . .
>
> Art today is separated from us, much of it bleak and morally depraved (*daraku shita*). Tolstoy tells us that most art is for but a fraction of the people; it is art that does not well up from the depths of one's chest but is instead overly academic.
>
> It is said that today's Art is impotence and falsehood, merely the plaything of urban intellectuals. It is an Art done for the purposes of wit, fame, and money. . . .
>
> Today's religious practitioners and artists monopolize truth, goodness, and beauty so as to sell it; all those who harbor other intentions merely perish. (194–95)[72]

Given such a state of affairs, Miyazawa asserted that now was the time "to alight upon our own new path and create our own beauty (*bi*). Let us take up art so as to ignite ashen-colored labor!" (195). His greatest intellectual debt here seems to be to Tolstoy's *What Is Art?* (1898), a text that had influenced earlier debates on *minshū geijutsu* (people's art) owing to its claims that art was monopolized by the upper classes, that it had been thoroughly corrupted by commercialism and professionalization, and that a universal art was possible only to the extent it drew on the sincere and unperverted "feelings" of laboring individuals.[73] Such claims likely reinforced for Miyazawa the logic of cultural production that had been implicit in these debates—a logic which stated that the "people" (and here he inserted *chijin*) have been unjustly excluded from the world of art. And if this was a world anyway dominated by professionals whose motives were less than genuine, or so the logic went, then it was a perfect chance for the so-called amateurs to use their peripheral, uncorrupt positions to create an original and authentic art that had relevance for them in the here-and-now. All that remained for Miyazawa (and "we" *chijin*) to do was determine the precise shape this art should take.

Over the course of the lectures there are three central posts around which Miyazawa erects a methodological framework for this task: subjectivity, syncretism, and evaluation. The first pertains to the individual consciousness of the artist as he or she engages in the act of creation. This was of critical concern for Miyazawa because, as he explained in the introductory lecture, the world had entered a new age in which self-consciousness was being superseded by group, social, and even universal consciousness. With society evolving into "a single consciousness, a single living thing (*seibutsu*)," what, he wondered aloud, was to be the fate of individual consciousness (193)? Would it have to be sacrificed in a world where universal forces seemed increasingly to pervade, in unseen and unknowable ways, all aspects of existence? Such questions were motivated by his own struggle to articulate a notion of subjectivity that explained the creative method behind his poems. These "mental-image sketches" (*shinshō sukecchi*), as he called them, experimented with an anti-Cartesian, anti-positivist representation of the mind as fully embedded within the world—a mind that was at once a uniquely particularized, but also momentary, instantiation of the interplay between myriad social forces, natural processes, and sensory experiences. It was this idea of a subject formed at the nexus of both individuating and associational tendencies—"a unity that is multiple and a multiplicity that is one," to borrow from Henri Bergson—that lodged itself at the heart of Miyazawa's vision for *nōmin geijutsu*.[74]

> Farmers' art is the concrete expression of the cosmic spirit (*uchū seishin*) as it passes through the individuality (*kosei*) of a person of the earth (*chijin*). It is an artistic act of both unconscious and conscious creativity whose material is drawn internally from intuition (*chokkan*) and feeling (*jōsho*). It is forever an affirmation of actual life and it seeks to both deepen and elevate that life. . . . It makes possible the communication of people's spirits and the socialization of emotion, and carries all of this to the most supreme level. (196–97)

Here Miyazawa tries to describe a creative process in which the unique contribution of the individual would be recognized even as individuality itself was submerged under greater, impersonal forces. The act of artistic creation is seen as both a locus of individual experience *and* as the conduit for a universal pulse. A precarious balance is thus struck between the subjective input of the artist and a cosmic will meant to be the source of individual expression as well as the medium of its social exchange. The lectures, however, provide little insight into how Miyazawa imagined these two forces pulling and pushing against one another. Nevertheless, by striking this precarious balance he was able to propose an art that is inherently particular even as it responds to impulses emanating outside the borders of the community, the nation, and the world. An art, in other words, that avoids an inward-looking provincialism without necessarily downgrading the value of the particular, localized in this case at the level of the perceptually aware body.

The second post Miyazawa uses to build his methodological framework, and thereby enlarge the tent of *nōmin geijutsu*, is that of syncretism. In his view, this was to be an art inclusive of all types of creative expression, which could themselves be reduced to the constituent elements of human experience.

> When voice is given tone and rhythm, choral music is born. When the same is done for sound there is orchestral music. . . .
> When language is given true expression there is prose; when given rhythm, poetry.
> When movement is given true expression there is silent theater; when given rhythm, it becomes dance. . . .
> Optical images are formed from shape, color, and the absence or presence of light. When [these images are] depicted by the hand there is painting; when depicted through material, then sculpture. . . .
> When given expression through a photographic device, one makes artistic photographs of movement and stillness. . . .
> By way of synthesis [of all these elements], one creates theater, opera, and moving pictures with sound. (197)

Miyazawa also added smell, sound, and the essential element of "purpose" (*junshi*) to this list. For him, it was the last that helped to generate the more complex arts of speech, debate, essay, architecture, clothing design, gardening, cooking, athletics, agriculture, and all varieties of industrial arts. By this logic, there was really no end to the categories of art that could count as appropriate to the goals of *nōmin geijutsu*. And significantly, the lectures do not privilege any one of these creative activities over others, preferring to emphasize their shared origins in bodily experience, itself the primary filter for the cosmic forces motivating creative energy. Miyazawa urged students to study all forms of art and all methods of expression, noting elsewhere that the possibilities for expression were delimited only by the character of the individual, not by any one set of aesthetic principles (e.g., realism, romanticism, formalism, or programmism).[75] What mattered was the mindset behind the form, not the form itself. Miyazawa was determined, it seems, to avoid putting up any unnecessary barriers to the practice of farmers' art.

This determination is apparent too in Miyazawa's comments on aesthetic evaluation. Tied to this third methodological post was a desire to shake loose the ingrained hierarchies of critical judgment that other proponents of *nōmin geijutsu* found so difficult to let go of. As he saw it, his task was simply to set the creative process in motion and offer guidelines for its continued renewal. In the lectures, he insisted that "criticism (*hihyō*) must happen above the level of social consciousness (*shakai ishiki*). Erroneous criticism occurs when one employs one's own inner art to judge the external art of others" (199). If the former is merely a temporary mental expression of the creative process, the latter is what results when this expression is translated into a concrete, external form. What the lectures suggest is that criticism should only be based on these externally realized objects and not on the inward manifestations of creative energy that are specific to each individual and thus prone to subjective bias. It's not clear what was to operate in place of inner art as a means for assigning relative value to these objects, but Miyazawa tried to clarify later by stating:

> Criticism relies on three foundational modes: destructive (*hakai teki*), creative (*sōzō teki*), and contemplative (*kanshō teki*).
>
> Destructive criticism summons the producer to action. Creative criticism offers suggestions and guidance. The creative critic requires qualifications *above* those of the producer. Contemplative criticism is directed at an art that is complete.
>
> The producer should respond to all criticism in a way that goes beyond the level of social consciousness. (199, emphasis mine)

Vague as these guidelines were, that Miyazawa substituted "above" with "equal to" in the written version of the lectures hints at a continuing concern with the possible ill-effects of social hierarchy on the evaluation of *nōmin geijutsu*. He may not have been willing to let go of the notion that some sort of "qualification" was needed to offer artistic guidance, implying that some creations were not as complete (i.e., valuable) as others. But he was also loath to suggest that there was a privileged position to which only he, as intellectual, had access and from which he could adjudicate what did and did not count for farmers' art. What mattered most was that practitioners drew on the "hope" and "anguish" brought on by their daily toil and that they constantly directed their creative energy toward "a true and bright future" (198–99).

On the whole, Miyazawa's attempts to open up the practice of *nōmin geijutsu* through an expansion of its borders on three fronts—subjectivity, form, and evaluation—have the effect of outwardly minimizing his intrusion in the creative process. The gap between intellectual and farmer, between patron and producer, appears less severe than in the writings of Yamamoto, Inuta, Nakamura, and others. Yet the lectures by no means circumvent the impossible problem of defining an art through which cultural subalterns could authentically speak their name. In his brief comments on aesthetic evaluation, for instance, we find Miyazawa having to set the artistic process in motion with categories of feeling (e.g., hope, anguish) so abstract that they could be made to serve almost any ideological imperative. His use of the term *chijin* invites a similar criticism. It was certainly useful for broadening the concept of agricultural labor in ways that disassociated authentic artistic expression from a static, preformed notion of a single economic class or social status, thereby shifting the ground of authenticity to a higher and more universally accessible plane. But his attempts to capture the impressive breadth of this plane with terms like "cosmic spirit" and "cosmic will" (*uchū ishi*)—described in the lectures as a diffuse yet powerful energy extending across the limitless expanses of the Milky Way—tended toward the same level of abstraction that leaves words like hope and anguish endlessly open to co-optation by arbiters of artistic value. Miyazawa's audience may have been inspired by the thought that "to live truly and strongly, one must be conscious of the Milky Way Galaxy within themselves," but how were they to know if they were doing this properly?[76] Was he merely using this language metaphorically to get them to think beyond their immediate environs, or did he truly expect them to confront the material reality of their place in the galactic order?

As a point of comparison, it is useful to return to Ishikawa's work and what appear to be similar appeals to a "cosmic consciousness" (*uchūteki ishiki*). In 1925, borrowing from the poet Edward Carpenter, he wrote:

> Our lives are but one part of the life of the cosmos. It follows that our art must be one small part of a cosmic art (*uchū geijutsu*). The tiny violet that blooms at the edge of a field, the constellations of stars that shimmer high in the sky, each are one small part of this cosmic art. . . . To make just one patch of violets bloom requires that the light and heat of the sun, the nutrients and water in the earth, and all the various functions of the cosmos work together. Similarly, the flowering of our own selves requires us to fully and deeply accept the collaboration of the universe. Above the limits of time, above the limits of space, we must absorb fully and deeply all the nutrients that will nurture and raise us.[77]

Here again we see significant overlap with Miyazawa in this idea that creative expression should be nurtured by a consciousness of one's place in an interconnected field of earthly and cosmic forces. Miyazawa likewise insisted that creators of *nōmin geijutsu* take energy from the wind and clouds (i.e., from nature) even as they harnessed the power of the "Milky Way

Galaxy within."[78] And unlike some of their immediate contemporaries, specifically Inuta and Nakamura, both men significantly avoided reifying the soil as the singular mark of authenticity.[79] For Miyazawa's part, an extensive background in soil science and geology likely suppressed the kind of ideological abstraction that reduced the complex and variegated composition of the earth into a unified essence. This proclivity for viewing the phenomenal world through the objective lens of scientific knowledge must also be taken into account in his references to the cosmos and the Milky Way. At a time when astronomers were only just beginning to verify that the Milky Way did not represent the whole of the universe, Miyazawa invoked the name less as a vague allusion to a supramundane universal, as with Ishikawa's use of "cosmos," than as a concrete reference to the universe as scientifically known.[80] This divergence is not readily apparent in the lectures, where a failure to explain terms like "cosmic spirit" left them to float wistfully into the rhetorical ether. But in the written version of the lectures, there is far less ambiguity as to what "cosmos" stood for: "while we feel [the world] differently and live separate, distinct lives, this place [we are at] is a field in the land of Rikuchū, in Japan, in the solar system, in the space of the Milky Way Galaxy."[81]

If we grant that certain universals to which Miyazawa appealed were more concrete and localized than those of other contributors to *nōmin geijutsu* discourse, we have still to consider how his project of opening up farmer's art through increasing levels of abstraction might have been received by its intended audience. What did attendees at the Iwate People's Higher School have to latch onto so as to make the content of the lectures relevant to their daily lives and to the task of rural revitalization? Although they were being invited into a future that promised a new kind of cultural and social autonomy, it was not a future they themselves had dreamed up nor to which they could immediately relate. Which is not to discredit the power of their imagination. It is only to suggest that in broadening the definition of, for instance, agrarian labor, Miyazawa was also whitewashing differences that would have been critical to any attempt at restructuring the social space of the village: differences between landowning farmers and the tenants who worked that land, between men's and women's work, and between the haves and the have-nots. To ignore the first was to neglect one of the most volatile sites of rural conflict in the 1920s, but also to paint over the very real economic disparities that were fracturing villages from within. To ignore the gendered division of labor, certainly one of the core structuring elements of rural society, was to effectively vote in favor of the status quo and what business as usual meant to household members responsible for far more than tilling the soil. To ignore variation in income was to presume, among other things, that all would have equal access to those tools and technologies most certain to alleviate the pain and unpredictability of farming. Moreover, to link the authenticity of *nōmin geijutsu* to concepts as vague as hope, suffering, and cosmic spirit—no matter how much emphasis was given to their basis in ontological reality—was to enshroud it in a veil of subjective anonymity. That is, to paraphrase Adorno, in casting out a word (or words) that said nothing of what the thing was, thus denying the word any subjective determination, the word was effectively left open to determination by the arbitrariness of the subject.[82] Behind the misty veil thus lay, to continue the analogy, a vacant seat of power ready to be occupied by anyone claiming to know, for example, the "truth" of which the cosmic will spoke. This is not to say that the seat had to be occupied, or that it had to be so by anyone other than the young farmers to whom Miyazawa spoke, but that the potential for easy co-optation remained latent in the rhetorical gesture itself.

Here, however, we should remember that Miyazawa did not deliver his lectures in a vacuum nor in a venue he could claim as his own. This is a point often lost in discussions of his agrarian philosophy. In fact, he delivered them over several months alongside lectures on a wide range of academic and technical subjects, many with immediate relevance to agricultural practice in 1920s Iwate. Considered within their curricular context, his contributions to the Iwate People's Higher Level School arguably functioned to supplement mundane material with grand visions upon which the imaginations of his audience might feed. They did so by providing students with a conceptual framework—intellectually cosmopolitan and spiritually cosmic in scope—by which to reorient their daily work and struggle. In essence, *nōmin geijutsu* presented to them the prospect of placing themselves at the center of their own modes of cultural production and self-expression, thus freeing them to create alternatives to the dead-end narratives that left them to either wallow on the margins of modern civilization or else stand motionless in nostalgic renderings of a lost time and place. Miyazawa assured them that, on the contrary, they were active agents in a grand social transformation by which humanity was awakening to a new consciousness of itself in the universe and within history. "The great theater of human life," as he put it, was preparing to "shift the axis of time" so as to make "a ceaseless, fourth-dimensional art (*yoji no geijutsu*)."[83] What this meant, as can be inferred from some of his other writings, is that society was moving to a new stage in which it would recognize that the present moment (now the past) was but one in an agglomerative series of layered moments, each with its own attendant epistemology, its own particular way of seeing the world. Furthermore, this future society was sure to see in the present (i.e., 1920s Iwate) something very different from what "we" see now, a fact that relativizes its truth value and makes it possible for us to imagine a time when the idea of farmers producing an enduring culture and art of their own will seem perfectly normal.[84] Such a remote prospect no doubt left Miyazawa's listeners scratching their heads as to how any of this might relate to their everyday lives. That a figure of intellectual authority had charged *them* with the task of leading such a momentous transformation, however, and this is the critical point, must have seemed revolutionary indeed.

Praxis Makes Imperfect?

Hardly a week after giving his final lecture, Miyazawa left his family home and took up residence at the future site of the Rasu Farmers Association. At the time, the local paper reported that he was resigning from his teaching position to establish a "new farm village" (*atarashiki nōson*) where he hoped to organize lantern shows, record concerts, and a barter system for exchanging crops.[85] With this short move, made in less than an afternoon, he began the arduous process of translating theory into practice. This was a chance to remake himself as a new brand of intellectual whose mode of being, to borrow from Antonio Gramsci, "can no longer consist in eloquence, [that] exterior and momentary mover of feelings and passions, but in active participation in practical life, as constructor, organizer, 'permanent persuader' and not just simple orator."[86] Although he would struggle to connect his distinctive brand of "agrarianism without tradition" to the hard socioeconomic realities of rural Hanamaki, this chapter concludes by looking at some of the tangible actions he took and what their limited reach tells us about both the impossibility of certain kinds of rural reform in the 1920s, and also alternative agrarian futures cut short before their time.[87]

Miyazawa's "return to farming" (*kinō*), which is how such acts have typically been categorized in Japanese historiography, cannot help but evoke the many varieties of rural return that preceded it and that, according to Iwasaki Masaya, constitute a social phenomenon peculiar to the 1910s and 1920s.[88] Tokutomi Roka set an important precedent with his well-documented retreat to the Tokyo suburbs in 1907, itself a kind of referential reenactment of Tolstoy's pastoral life at Yasnaya Polyana. Like Roka, many returnees in the late Meiji and early Taishō periods were in the mold of the gentleman farmer, motivated by a desire to reinvigorate their life and writing through the simple act of tilling the land (often referred to as *hannō seikatsu*, or "semi-farming life"). Katō Kazuo, for instance, also an avid worshipper of Tolstoy, rented land in the Tokyo suburb of Mejiro in 1916 to try his luck at just such a lifestyle, but the endeavor ended quickly owing to money trouble and the realization—shared by many of his fellow returnees—that trying to manage even a plot of land left little time for creative activity.[89] In 1927, Ishikawa Sanshirō moved to the same Tama village that Roka had twenty years earlier and began a "semi-farming life" that he hoped would evolve into a full-fledged center for cultural activity, cooperative learning, and communal labor. It never did, but his move was celebrated in the media much like Miyazawa's, with a reporter from the *Yomiuri shinbun* sent to check up on his new living situation soon after his arrival.[90]

Others "returned" to the land with visions of renewed rural community already at the center of their ideological agendas. Tachibana Kōzaburō (1893–1974), for example, established his Fraternal Village (Kyōdai Mura) in 1915 in Ibaraki Prefecture and, admitting his intellectual debt to Tolstoy and Robert Owen, aspired to create there a utopia based on the integration of "soil and sincerity" (*tsuchi to magokoro*). The village grew to be popular with local politicians and students by the mid-1920s, and was to be the stepping stone to the short-lived Community Loving Society (Aikyōkai), a producers' cooperative established in 1929 that aimed to be both a practical economic movement and an impetus to the radical reconstruction of Japanese society along agrarian lines.[91] Perhaps the most recognized communal experiment of the interwar period was Mushanokōji Saneatsu's New Village (Atarashiki Mura), established in Kyūshū in 1918. From the start, however, it had the flavor of a social movement concerned primarily with building a utopia disentangled from the modern condition, not in reviving the spiritual and cultural health of Japan's agricultural communities.[92]

Historians have found it easy to look back upon all of these "returns," regardless of their different motivations and aims, as failures of both ideology and implementation. Some returnees have been accused of acting out of guilty conscience, and of believing naively that they might be able to redeem themselves of their privileged class and economic backgrounds even as those backgrounds provided the necessary funding and material support for their ventures. Others are said to have lacked a genuine understanding of village structure and the origins of rural crisis, thus preventing them from devising truly practical solutions with local import.[93] Still others have been criticized for their turn to proto-fascist visions of society or for their slide into right-wing idolatry. Valid as these critiques may be, we miss something if we filter our reading of these "returns" solely through the retrospective awareness that they were short-lived and destined to fail. For this tells us nothing of what it was to stand at the precipice of a perceived crisis and try to radically reinvent social life in both thought *and* action, all the while knowing that one's objectives might be impossible to achieve.[94] Faced with such a situation, what steps could a person like Miyazawa take to extract himself from life-as-usual? More to the point, if these steps obviously extended beyond what was practically realizable for his place and time, is this not an opportunity to learn something, as was suggested in Chapter Six, of a particular social reality through that which it did not allow for, or else left room enough only to imagine?[95]

One of the first steps Miyazawa took was to "divert" the family's second home and former place of convalescence into a site better suited to his purposes.[96] This meant digging a new well so as to have ready access to water, building an outdoor stove for cooking, and clearing the overgrown fields below the house to ready them for planting. Not much had to be done to the house itself, however, and by May he was already using it for weekly gatherings with area farmers. Personal accounts from early participants indicate that he used these meetings to share records from his classical music collection, but also to hold rehearsals for an amateur orchestral ensemble. On first violin was Itō Katsumi, a sixteen-year-old who worked for his father in the family-owned dye shop. Joining him on second violin was the twenty-year-old self-employed farmer Itō Sei and Takahashi Keigo, a twenty-one-year-old who worked in town for the Consumers Cooperative and who was soon to become an active member in the local branch of the Labor-Farm Party. Eighteen-year-old Itō Chūichi, also a self-employed farmer, played the flute while Miyazawa provided accompaniment on organ and cello.[97] If this first foray into "farmers' art" seems to smack of cultural elitism, it is important to remember that the choice of Western classical music and instruments would have signified rather differently in a context where exposure to such things was rare and where traditional music instruction relied on a lineage model in which students were expected to imitate their mentors. In contrast, here was an opportunity to create something both collaboratively and relatively spontaneously, but also far outside the prescriptive reach of classical music's legitimating actors and institutions.

As the year wore on and as Miyazawa began to settle in, friends and former students routinely stopped by to take stock of his new living arrangements, graciously accepting the ripe tomatoes he offered from his garden and speaking to him of his plans for the official opening of the Rasu Farmers Association. The inaugural meeting finally occurred in December, and participants recall engaging in both a lively exchange of used goods and a brainstorming session on the kinds of handicrafts (e.g., worker's clothes, hats, furniture) and food products the group would try to produce over the upcoming winter months. It was just a month later that the local media announced the official founding of the group to the public, including its plans to set up an exchange system for agricultural produce, to engage in theater and music, and to institute a "comfort day" (*iyasu dee*) two or three times a month.[98] As strange as all of these activities may have sounded to Iwate readers, the newspaper clearly felt no hesitation in reporting them, even if it had to couch things, as we saw in the last chapter, in the politically safe language of antiurban sentiment and rural revitalization. Editors must have believed that a good number of their readers would take Miyazawa's efforts seriously.

The article was selective in its description, however, focusing mostly on certain cultural activities at the expense of some of the direct interventions Miyazawa was making into the economic and political quality of life of farmers. In addition to lecturing on farmers' art (*chijin geijutsu*), farmers' poetry (*rōnō shi*), and Esperanto, he was also instructing members in subjects like agricultural chemistry, soil science, plant growth, and fertilizer application. Making use of his personal mimeograph (*gariban*), he created elaborate handouts to help members learn the basic scientific principles behind the improvement of crop yields and the enhancement of soil quality. In fact, from the summer of 1927 until his collapse from physical exhaustion a year later, more and more of his pedagogical energy was spent outside the group as he tried to help area farmers maintain their yields under near-drought conditions. He conducted research into weather patterns and crop enhancement, visited schools in the region to lecture on agricultural techniques, and set up free fertilizer consultations in surrounding towns. It was in activities such as these that Miyazawa ultimately proved most valuable to the distressed farmers he was so eager to help, earning praise in the official bulletin of the Iwate Agricultural Association and becoming known by many locals as the "God of Fertilizer."[99] Even if the poorest of farmers could not afford the fertilizer he was recommending, at least they could see the link between higher yields and a higher standard of living. In terms of helping farmers gain political representation for their plight, here too Miyazawa was most valuable in work done outside the Rasu Association, in particular, as was discussed earlier, through his generous offer of financial and material support to a local branch of the leftist Labor-Farm Party.

While it was these sorts of activities that proved the most durable and extendable as forms of praxis, they were ultimately not sustainable. The former because of the toll they took on Miyazawa's body (he simply could not keep up with demand for his expertise nor with the fickleness of mother nature), the latter because of increasing political repression. Fear of the authorities was so great, in fact, that upon seeing the January article from the *Nippō*, Miyazawa felt it necessary to suspend the group's meetings as he did not want the Rasu Association to be mistaken for a place of socialist learning.[100] The moratorium was brief, and a member of the group even stepped forward to allay any concerns by claiming in a letter to the *Nippō* that poor farmers too busy to receive a proper education had found in Miyazawa a new leader and a true sympathizer.[101] That such a misunderstanding was possible at all, however, hints at the delicate balancing act he had to perform even in trying to narrow the cultural divide keeping farmers from acquiring their own rich forms of self-expression.

If the activities he devised to compensate for the rural laborer's perceived lack of cultural opportunities were still the easiest to share with the public, they also turned out to be more ephemeral than his other endeavors. This is in part because rather than merely preserving or enhancing patterns of social and spatial organization already in place, with these activities he was trying to weave together entirely new and unfamiliar patterns. How much easier must it have been to play the role of a consultant with scientific expertise, or of a covert political donor, than to introduce and sustain the idea of a cultural center where farmers could learn the seemingly impractical skills of acting, playing music, and speaking Esperanto. That the Rasu Association lasted as long as it did can cynically be attributed to the social standing and financial security guaranteed by Miyazawa's family and its prominent place in the local community. Yet to make this the final word on the matter is to forget David Harvey's sober reminder that "everyone who moves to establish difference in the contemporary world has to do so through social practices that necessarily engage with the mediating power of money. . . .

Possession of sufficient money power is a necessary condition for exploring difference through place construction."[102] Economic privilege is, for our purposes here, less interesting than what it meant for Miyazawa and others of his generation to be exploring different possible futures for agrarian-based living outside the limitations of rational economic choice.

Harry Harootunian, in his impressive study of interwar intellectual thought, writes of the "moderns against modernity" who "sought in historical representations a refuge against the alienating effects of everyday modern life and thus attributed to art and culture, in the broadest sense, absolute value that remained immune from the changing valuations of the market and the political world." These spokesmen of modernism sought to flee the present even as they appealed to "older historical representations of the authentic cultural object as a way to replace abstraction and fragmentation with concreteness and wholeness."[103] If this broad assessment of metropolitan thinkers such as Yanagita Kunio, Watsuji Tetsurō, and Orikuchi Shinobu appeals to our understanding of their respective confrontations with the unevenness of modernity, it should also strike chords with conventional wisdom about interwar agrarian ideology and the many rural returns it fostered. With the advantage of historical hindsight, these returns tend to be similarly construed (i.e., as the romanticization of rural labor and village life for the purpose of safeguarding against capitalist modernity, moral decay, and social division). While this may ring true for the likes of Katō Kanji or Mushanokōji Saneatsu, and while it is certainly applicable to the state-sponsored and imperial fascist forms of agrarianism that emerged in the 1930s, I think it important to resist characterizing *nōmin geijutsu* discourse in a similar fashion.[104] As we have seen in its various instantiations, particularly as praxis, its aims were not simply regressive, myopically nativist, or neutered of political intent. To varying degrees, it even signaled an attempt to shuffle the overdetermined categories of rural and urban, provincial and modern, and to chart an alternative course for Japan's farming communities in the face of real economic and social crisis. This was not a fleeing from history, but a direct confrontation with it and with those who insisted on narrating the fate of the farmer as either hopelessly outmoded or in need of sealing under a waxy sheen of nostalgia. It was an attempt, in short, to change "the subject" of history so that the rural laborer might have a greater say in charting its future course. As it turned out for Miyazawa, the community of Hanamaki was neither ready for nor interested in such a change, at least not in the manner he had envisioned it.

How bewildered Miyazawa would surely have been had he lived just a few years longer. In 1939, his *Poran's Square* was revived in its original one-act version by a popular children's theater troupe and staged at Tokyo's renowned Little Tsukiji Theater. The revival was partly a response to a surge of public interest in Miyazawa from the preceding year when a production called *Shout to the Soil* (*Tsuchi ni sakebu*) ran for a month to packed houses at the Yūraku-za Theater.[105] The play was an autobiographical account of Matsuda Shinjirō (1909–1943), one of the young men whom Miyazawa encouraged to "do farmers' theater" back in 1927. He had gone on to establish a cooperative and study center in his native Yamagata village in the early 1930s where, in addition to leading his own amateur theater troupe, he emphasized practical instruction in farming and various craft industries as a path to communal self-sufficiency. *Shout to the Soil* was a record of this activity, and Miyazawa's *nōmin geijutsu* lectures and the Rasu Association figured large as inspirational sources in both the theatrical version and in the best-selling book from which it was adapted.[106] That the performance was attended even by Minister of Agriculture Arima Yoriyasu is indication of how well suited it was to the kinds of narratives that had proliferated since the start of a massive state-led rural revitalization campaign in 1932. These were narratives of a rural Japan made "economically secure and culturally vibrant through careful planning, sound leadership, and a willingness to work together," and they flourished at a time when the plight of the farmer and farm village were more closely tied to the imperial cause and to the gaze of mass consumer culture.[107]

One of the more popular narratives from the era, Kagawa Toyohiko's novel *The Land of Milk and Honey* (1935), told the story of a poor farmer's son who overcomes opposition and bullying by local elites (e.g., a landlord's son and a Diet politician) and, relying on "the expertise and passions of each member of the community," helps to purchase land for cooperative farming. He even introduces goats and bees as a way to help diversify the local economy. The obvious overlap with the second, prose version of *Poran's Square*, first published in 1935, points to a changed ideological milieu where such visions of rural restructuring were in greater demand. The seriousness of the agricultural crisis, soon to be exacerbated by the Depression, surely led the public, but also the state, to more actively accept and promote the imagining of creative solutions. A sense of their renewed relevancy may even have been what prompted Miyazawa's brother and Kusano Shinpei to make the *nōmin geijutsu* lectures one of the first texts they published after Miyazawa's death.[108] Yet the more that discussion of rural reform took place in the open and through official channels, the more it had to stay on-message, which for the state meant, as Kerry Smith notes, a vision of the village in which class and tenancy, or any sort of political conflict, were largely irrelevant; where self-indulgence and luxury were to be sacrificed at any cost; and where mutual cooperation was a rule, not a choice.[109] Miyazawa's ideas could certainly be made to fit such a message, and indeed they were, but one senses that this eviscerated something of their original intent. If farmers now had more say in their future, and were more actively involved in the production of culture, it was only to the extent that they stuck to the publicly accepted, and now nationally mandated, script. This was hardly the place for the kind of autonomous local art of which Miyazawa had dreamed.

Epilogue
Trading Places

Nearly a decade had passed since the publication of *The Restaurant of Many Orders* when Mori Sōichi, the young student who watched helplessly as copies of the book gathered dust in a Morioka bookstore, had to stare down another stack of unsold books with Miyazawa's name on the cover. This time it was the first edition of the author's collected works, issued in three austere volumes between 1934 and 1935. Much about the situation was different, of course, besides the fact that Miyazawa was now gone and that Mori had himself become an aspiring poet and writer in the local literary circuit. He was now not in the position of wanting to purchase the books before him, but to sell as many copies as he could. As he remembered it,

> the *zenshū* had a print-run of 800 sets, 200 of which were to be sold in Hanamaki and 300 of which were to be sold in Morioka. Kikuchi Jirō and I set off to round up as many buyers as we could. A professor from the medical college looked at us and said, "Miyazawa Kenji? That guy's a mental case." He flatly declined. Then there was the distinguished instructor from one of the higher schools who told us, "I've got so many other books I want to buy." And from the relative of a famous judge: "I'm in the process of buying Shakespeare's collected works at the moment." It was like this wherever we went and so it was not an easy thing to sell 300 sets.[1]

At two-and-a-half yen per volume—roughly the price of five movie tickets or twenty-five bowls of *soba* noodles—it makes sense that Mori looked first to the resident intellectual and social elite. They, however, had their eyes on other segments of the literary market and had no room on their shelves, nor in their pocketbooks, for three volumes from a local, no-name author. In this respect, not much seems to have changed since that cold December day back in 1924.

Or had it? That an edition of his collected works had been published at all, no matter how poorly it might have sold, indicates that there were at least some convinced of the author's value for posterity, if not his value in the current literary marketplace. By 1934, as discussed in the Prologue, there were in fact a growing number of people willing to vouch for Miyazawa's worth, including local poets like Mori, members of the Iwate cultural diaspora in Tokyo, and an assortment of established literary figures. Kusano Shinpei, as a member of the last, once again was instrumental in generating momentum for the *zenshū*. After years of proselytizing for the poet's innovative verse in his own poetry magazine, *Dora*, and having worked to circulate both Miyazawa's poetry and *dōwa* volumes to an expanding circle of associates, Kusano now called on these personal networks to deliver the texts that would finally expose readers to the "genius" that some were already proclaiming. By the time Miyazawa's memorial volume was released in January 1934, the highly acclaimed poet Takamura Kōtarō had already agreed, together with novelist Yokomitsu Riichi and long-time friend Fujiwara Katōji, to help Kusano and Miyazawa's brother Seiroku with the editing and publishing. Takamura initially presented the idea of a Miyazawa *zenshū* to Iwanami Shoten, one of the foremost publishers in Tokyo, but it showed no interest. A month later, Kusano and Yokomitsu tried negotiating with Tenbōsha, a much smaller press, but the results were the same. It was only in August that a willing publisher was finally found—a nearly bankrupt used-book store by the name of Bunpodō—and it only agreed to publish the *zenshū* as long as half of the initial 800 sets were contracted to be sold in Iwate.[2] Though far from what Kusano or any of the others had hoped for, it was the best they were able to get owing to Miyazawa's no-name status. Markets tend to reward rarity, as with truffles or high-grade tuna, but only when it is coupled with preestablished demand. What promoters of the *zenshū* quickly ran up against, and what Bunpodō seems already to have known, was the reality that rarity has little value as long as it remains a locally acquired taste.

Demand for Miyazawa's work did finally materialize, but this early epi-sode in his posthumous reception is worth highlighting because it signals a transitional moment in the way that he and his works have historically circulated in the market for cultural objects. The *zenshū* was but the first in a long line of publications that served to transform the no-name author into a national literary icon and eventually into a symbol for marking and making place. As more and more readers were exposed to his writing, what once had been anonymous and "provincializing" acts of cultural produc-tion *in* the periphery became essential fuel for acts of cultural production *of* the periphery. While most of the focus in *On Uneven Ground* has been on the former—and in particular the ways spatial unevenness structured the possibilities and limits for cultural expressions of provincial locality in the interwar period—I want to end by returning attention to the latter and the question of why Miyazawa remains integral to the production of locality even as the conditions of this production have changed radically.

In the decades since his death, the disembedding that made locality such a key point of contestation and confrontation in his day has only accelerated with the expansion of all kinds of markets under global capitalism.[3] On one hand, the continued compression of social and geographical distance has left the value of local cultural difference to feel far less substantial, and less ideo-logically significant, than in times past. One reason is that, as Sharon Zukin has argued, "abstract market forces that detach people from social institu-tions have overpowered specific forces of attachment identified with place."[4] If these forces have been overpowered, however, it does not mean that the value of local difference as a marker of identity has faded away. On the contrary, as Terry Eagleton has observed, "the more predatory the [global market] forces which lay siege to . . . local identities, the more pathological these identities [have] become."[5] Indeed, we have already seen how local dif-ference has become vitally important in other ways in Japan, namely in the market that trades in *place* as a symbol of desirable values and experiences. This market has generated such commercial phenomena as the Iwate Ginga Plaza and the extension of trademark law to locally branded products, but also efforts to remake place in ways that provide a buffer against rampant de-velopment or else establish new forces of local connection and attachment.

What interests me here is not simply the evolution we see between inter-war assertions of local identity and the market-driven "pathological" forms of today, but rather that Miyazawa and his writings have managed to thrive across this period of transition. To what can we attribute their seeming durability as an adhesive connecting discourse to social space? Do we attribute it to something essential in Miyazawa's work, which would also be to imply that the small-time, provincializing strategies he employed were a precursor to present-day modes of marketing that see every difference as an opportunity?[6] Or should we look to external historical forces that have repositioned him and his writing in the dominant markets for literary exchange and the critical networks through which acts of place making are carried out? Assuming that the most productive response will take into account some combination of the two, it then becomes a matter of asking why his narratives have been imminently adaptable to these historical forces. While it is impossible to give a comprehensive answer to this question, three key episodes in Miyazawa's posthumous reception—beginning with the publication of the first *zenshū*—can help us trace a genealogy of the fundamental ways his value in the market for cultural artifacts has intersected with his value in the market for places.

Once the Bunpodō edition of Miyazawa's collected works were finally published in September 1934, the burden of making him more palatable fell to the networks of minor actors most closely connected to those who might have reason to take interest in this relatively unknown local author. In the suburbs of Tokyo, a Friends of Miyazawa Kenji Society (Miyazawa Kenji Tomo no Kai) was patched together from the remnants of a decade-old Takuboku Society—the same one Miyazawa had been involved with during his brief stay in Tokyo in 1921—and from an assorted cast of Iwate-born artists and poets who had assembled in a suburban enclave affectionately dubbed "Iwate Village." Members of this organization, each of whom was connected in his or her own way to different branches of the cultural field (fiction, poetry, children's literature, music, and painting), but also to media outlets and the lengthening cultural arm of government bureaucracy, helped spread the word about Miyazawa in the months after the *zenshū* publication.[7] Back in Morioka, Mori Sōichi became the central figure in promoting the work, aided by his position as chief editor of the literary pages at the *Iwate nippō*. Beginning in February 1934 and extending early into the following year, he managed to place nearly twenty-five articles relating to the publication or sale of the *zenshū* into the paper. Most of these were accompanied by testimonials to Miyazawa's greatness, which variously described him as "comparable to Mallarmé and Rimbaud," as "Japan's Andersen," as "the kind of poet who is born but once in a hundred years," and as "a poet who will represent the Japanese folk in this century of poets." Some expressed shock at rumors that the *zenshū* was not selling well, berating those who would think of buying anything else first. Mori himself, with all the zealousness of a used-car salesman, urged every Iwate resident with an interest in literature to take this once-in-a-lifetime opportunity and order an advance copy.[8] He also gave extensive publicity to his own Kenji Society (Kenji no Kai), a study group created for local residents who, having purchased their copy of the *zenshū*, could then be guided through an exploration of Miyazawa's enigmatic poetic genius.

It is hard to know how successful was this initial push to promote the value of Miyazawa and his work. Bunpodō issued a reprint just nine months after the original publication, a seeming indication of demand, but when one juxtaposes the rapidity of this reprinting with the memory of uninterested buyers, or with knowledge of Bunpodō's decision to forgo all manner of advertising, it stands to reason that this demand was largely an artificial by-product of promotion. At the very least, however, the foundation for a broader reception had been laid. And this was due in large part to the place-based social networks that tried to raise the value of his work by equating it with universal signifiers of literary value (e.g., French poets, Hans Christian Andersen) and then by capitalizing on the local pride certain to arise with the awareness that one's native place had produced such greatness. Here at last, to recall Latour's discussion of *networks*, was a force to "seize upon" Miyazawa's ideas and make them portable—to translate his artistry into dominant hierarchies of aesthetic value and conventional patterns of provincial imagining. Thus transformed, his relation to the field of production, as well as the culture market, began its radical reversal.

In 1936, for instance, a group of former friends and students raised funds for the erection of a poetry stone at the former site of the Rasu Farmers Association. Into the massive block of slate was etched the last half of "Ame nimo makezu" (Neither Yielding to Rain, 1932), a poem selected by Kusano, Takamura, and philosopher Tanikawa Tetsuzō from amongst the hundreds in Miyazawa's oeuvre. This ode to a kind of selfless devotion to community carried out in total austerity and anonymity would become Miyazawa's cultural calling card in the ensuing years, as it was readily amenable to the needs of wartime ideology.[9] By 1939, a second *zenshū* had entered production, this time a six-volume set from a more reputable publisher.[10] Also released that year was Matsuda Shinjirō's edited selection of "great works," a slim volume that went through eleven printings in three years and that did more than any other publication to help popularize Miyazawa in the prewar period.[11] Equally influential was the 1940 adaptation to film of "Kaze no

Matasaburō," and the launching of a short-lived research journal by Mori's Kenji Society. The latter, under the title *Iihatōvo*, was instrumental not only in solidifying Miyazawa's hagiographical image, but also in linking together the various Kenji Society branches that had sprouted up since 1935, extending as far north as Hokkaidō and as far south as Osaka.[12]

Although the Pacific War years witnessed a continuing succession of Miyazawa related publications, things really began to take off in the late 1940s. His name had now found a place in the nationally standardized elementary-school language primers and he was the subject of well over a dozen publications every year through the 1950s.[13] It was also during this time that our second episode in his posthumous reception, the Kenji Festival (Kenji-sai), came to prominence. The event had officially been inaugurated in 1940 to memorialize Miyazawa at the anniversary of his death and it was held each year at the site of the "Ame nimo makezu" poetry stone. Within a decade, it attained the status of a public celebration attended by relatives and friends, local residents, and Kenji fans from across the country. Some of these fans published firsthand accounts of the festival in the journal *Yojigen* (Fourth Dimension), a direct successor to *Iihatōvo*, and their comments help to shed light on Miyazawa's changing relation to the culture market. They also indicate how his increasingly mythologized image was becoming ever more entangled in the machinery of contemporary place making.

In 1953, at the twentieth anniversary of Miyazawa's death, nearly 150 people gathered for the annual festival and there took part in ceremonial offerings, poetry readings, eloquent tributes to the author, and an open forum for sharing personal memories. Two different observers noted the diverse social and geographical makeup of the crowd, some of whom had traveled great distances to visit this "Mecca Hanamaki." Both wondered if there was any other poetry stone in Japan that could lay claim to such an assembly.[14] A message to festival-goers from Takamura Kōtarō expressed similar astonishment at the dramatic changes of the past two decades, both in terms of what "we Japanese" have experienced, but also in the conversion of "backwater Miyazawa" into the "people's Miyazawa" of today. Enough had changed that one of the observers felt compelled to warn against turning the "propagation of Miyazawa's spirit" into a kind of "business." Should anyone start demanding donations or charging an entrance fee for the event, this would certainly "trouble Miyazawa's soul and trouble his family, ultimately distorting Kenji's spirit to the point of crushing it to death." Such commodification, he continued, was exactly the thing that "Kenji lovers" would have to guard against

as the author "finally permeated the general populace."[15] What is most striking about all these comments is that they assume the ready transportability
and accessibility of Miyazawa as text and as psychobiographical signified.
There no longer seems to be any problem in conveying his message out
beyond the local limits of the "backwater" market within which it originated. Having apparently transcended the always uneven ground of cultural
production, however, there arose a new problem: how to keep the value
of his image from being diluted or maligned by the fact of its increased
circulation. How, in other words, to preserve an awareness of Miyazawa in
his "authentic" form (i.e., as unconnected to the marketplace) at the same
time his image was being de-localized and propelled into ever more diffuse
streams of cultural production and consumption. As the festival grew in the
years ahead, so too did the intractableness of this problem.

In 1954, attendance rose to a thousand as the event began to incorporate
performances such as children's theater and a local variation on the area's
traditional deer dance (*shika odori*). An observer reconfirmed the notion
of Hanamaki as a Mecca, predicting that people would soon gather from
across the globe to share in the spirit of a figure whose existence could not
be confined to Hanamaki, or Iwate, or even Japan.[16] Visitors in 1959 and
1960 expressed a similar sense of participating in something much larger
than themselves, the space of the event having become for them like "a
scene in one of Kenji's *dōwa*," like "Iihatōvo under the Milky Way," and
like a *hiroba* where "ancient and modern, tradition and creativity, coexist
in harmony."[17] Alongside these appeals to the spiritually unifying character
of Miyazawa's life and work, we once again find warnings against turning
the festival into a "touristic show." The presence of newer technologies like
tape recorders, flash bulbs, and television cameras surely exacerbated such
anxieties, as each was capable of mobilizing Miyazawa's image for new and
ever larger segments of the culture and tourism markets.

The growing rift between an "authentic Miyazawa" and an "overly commodified" one is best encapsulated in the account of a self-proclaimed devotee who recalls a visit to the area in 1952. Arriving at the Hanamaki train
station after a long night's journey from Tokyo, he found himself welcomed
by a light drizzle and by the soothing rhythms of the Tōhoku dialect, or
what to his ears sounded like "the language of Iihatōvo."

> I'm certain that here, within the landscape of Iihatōvo, I'm hearing now
> for the first time the fresh voice of Kenji. The light rain falling now is the
> same that fell upon him. Sunlight pierces the clouds, drenching the roofs

and smokestacks—I'm sure that all of it was depicted somewhere in one of Kenji's mental sketches. . . . On the street outside the station I find tire ruts and black soil—the same soil that Kenji must have tread upon each time he left for Tokyo and each time he returned home. What a thrilling sensation. I'm so glad I came.[18]

When the station attendant handed him a sightseeing map and inquired if the man was a "Kenji fan," however, the thrill quickly dissipated. A great number of these "fans" must come through the station every day, he mused, looking down grimly at the map with its illustration of the famous poetry stone off to the side. "Not one step out of the station and my Iihatōvo landscape has been challenged by a landscape both touristic and all too real."[19] Here is further evidence of a growing divide between a personal and thus more authentic relation to Miyazawa—one that sees through to his essence—and a relation mediated by his commodified image and thus somehow untrue to his spirit. What also becomes clear is how much his relation to his native place had changed. The more his image circulated outside Iwate, the more it was woven into the fabric by which the local presented itself to the outside world. In ways he never intended, he was finally having an impact on how Iwate imagined itself as place and as destination.

Had the above devotee visited four decades later, how much greater would have been his disenchantment. By the mid-1990s, Hanamaki was in the throes of a Kenji boom, the ground for which had been laid in prior decades by an ever increasing flow of publications and scholarship, but also an expanding infrastructure of cultural appreciation. A critical piece of this infrastructure came in 1982 in the form of the Kenji Memorial Museum, the result of a largely grassroots effort by fans and school groups and assorted other community organizations to build a place of retreat and quiet communion in a forested setting much beloved by Miyazawa.[20] But the museum was unprepared for the busloads of tourists and students that began to arrive as soon as the doors opened.[21] Its success in drawing visitors from around the country likely had a hand in the city of Hanamaki's decision in 1993 to create a local research center with its portion of a local tax allocation grant awarded by the central government to dozens of municipalities as part of a "native-place making" initiative.[22] This "Iihatov Center" was intended to provide a base of operations for Kenji scholars, but also to facilitate, and provide some financial support for, the activities of regional study groups that might later become a wellspring of future visitors. The center joined a wave of museums and memorial archives that swelled in the 1990s as localities across Japan sought to profit from literary heritage and its potential for attracting tourist traffic.[23]

Cultural and capital investment in Miyazawa reached a high point in 1996, at the hundredth anniversary of his birth. Publishers predictably took advantage of this important milestone and helped to generate a sharp rise in Miyazawa-related book publications, from an average of 20 to 30 per year in the early 1990s, and from a total of 64 in 1995, to an astounding 65 by July alone. Two major film studios, Tōei and Shōchiku, produced feature-length films depicting his life and work while the national broadcast company NHK put together two separate documentaries for August release. Corporations also jumped on the bandwagon, most notably East Japan Railways, which employed the author's image liberally for its summer campaign promoting travel to the Tōhoku region.[24] Given such publicity, it was only natural that Miyazawa scholars, local Kenji fans, and the Hanamaki city government would seek to make the most of the occasion. Yet not everyone could agree on how best to do so. Whereas scholars proposed holding an international conference coupled with various community-based educational events, and whereas the devoted supporters of the ongoing Kenji Festival sought to build upon their own tradition, members of city hall brought forth a rather different vision of how to maximize Miyazawa's potential for raising the value of local difference.[25]

Their driving concern was with how Miyazawa's image might best be utilized for "local revitalization" (*chiiki kasseika*) and "town planning" (*machi-zukuri*) initiatives. Nearly a third of the twenty-two projects for which revitalization funds were allocated in 1996 had a connection to the now celebrated native son.[26] These included projects intended to support fans of Miyazawa as they sought to connect their personal visions of his life and work with the physical environment (e.g., the landscaping and preservation of sites linked to his poems and stories, posting of signage to help with navigating "Iihatov Hanamaki," and construction of a Kenji Plaza near the Miyazawa family home). The most ambitious project, however, was the Fairy Tale Village (Dōwa Mura), proposed as a kind of centerpiece for the centenary celebration and as a central stage for all related festivities. It comprised, among other things, a Kenji Dome, which made use of high-tech digital imagery so as to convey to visitors the messages of "love, hope, and bravery" embodied in his stories; a series of educational pavilions sponsored by the likes of Coca-Cola, Pioneer, and Mitsubishi Motors; and a botanical garden filled with many of the plants mentioned in Miyazawa's texts. Members of the festival committee were hopeful that the Village would contribute to their overall goals of "raising the cultural consciousness of Hanamaki citizens" and of "introducing locals and outsiders alike to the spirit of this magnificent poet."[27] What it most certainly did do, despite the best of intentions, is veer toward the quality of a theme park, described by theater historian Dennis Kennedy as that "most logical model of how to present a culture of pastness in a global economy . . . an accessible and diverting thoroughfare to an imagined history or mythical world."[28] Ironically, Miyazawa was now the very filter by which locals were asked to reimagine their place in the world (and in cultural history), having gradually been transformed from an instigator of such creative work to its raison d'être.

It is amidst this concerted reorganization of place in the name of Miyazawa that we find a third episode illustrative of some of the new dynamics in play. Early in 1996, a resident amateur historian named Satō Takashi made what would seem an innocuous discovery. As a member of the Hanamaki Beech Preservation Society, he discovered in the course of working for the group, and with the aid of a Meiji-era topographical survey, that a small peak located deep in the city's western hills, and whose name had long been forgotten, might in fact be the mountain once called "Nametoko."[29] News that a nondescript, 860-meter hill—one barely visible from the nearest county road and sheared decades before of the native beech trees that grow thick in the surrounding area—went by such-and-such a name would, under other circumstances, likely pass without notice. But this was not just any hill. It was the very one that Miyazawa had referenced in the posthumously published "The Bears of Mt. Nametoko" (Nametoko yama no kuma). The story, which depicts the life of an aging bear hunter, opens as follows:

> They're interesting, those bears of Mt. Nametoko. The mountain itself is large, and from within flows the Fuchizawa River. On most days of the year it breathes in and out cold mists and clouds. All the peaks around it, too, look like blackish green sea slugs or bald-headed sea goblins. About half-way up Nametoko you'll find a big opening in the rock. The Fuchizawa comes rushing out from there, falling some 300 feet through thick stands of cypress and maple before reaching bottom. . . . It's the Ōzora waterfall of Mt. Nametoko. And I hear that in days gone by the whole area was just crawling with bears. To tell you the truth, though, I've never actually seen any of it, Nametoko nor the bear livers, with my own eyes. They're all just things I've heard about from people or thought up on my own. So there may be some inaccuracy in what I tell you, but I for one believe it to be true.[30]

Until Satō's discovery, no one else had been able to verify the existence of Mt. Nametoko either. Readers simply took the narrator at his word that it was situated out somewhere near the Ōzora falls, just as the narrator had himself taken others at their word. Satō's findings, which he later verified with two late-Edo maps in municipal archives, changed all that. Supported by the Beech Preservation Society and other Kenji fans, he convinced Hanamaki's mayor and the local Forestry Department to petition the National Ordnance Survey Office, which in turn, aware of the impending centenary celebrations, rushed to put, as it were, Mt. Nametoko on the map.[31] An interpretive signboard was later erected near the site, photographs of the mountain were displayed at city hall, and the "real" Mt. Nametoko entered the popular consciousness only because of its prominent place in Miyazawa's story. In the most circuitous of fashions, this story had become what John Dorst calls the "legitimizing antecedent" of a geographical feature that Miyazawa himself may never have actually laid eyes upon.[32] Now it was visible to anyone who knew where to look.

It is episodes like this last one where we see that the socio-spatial dialectic set in motion by Miyazawa's representational strategies has come full circle. Texts that once aspired to rewrite the local landscape in a provincializing idiom now potentially shape and reorganize it, elevating spaces within it into higher-order cultural economies. One such economy is the tourist economy, which thrives on the market in distinctive places and which, at least in the decade that followed Miyazawa's centennial celebration, saw Hanamaki city officials take every opportunity to use him to attract more visitors and to establish the value of the area as a unique place.[33] This trend has subsided somewhat as declining attendance at museum-style facilities and amusement sites has forced local governments to recalibrate their level of investment in Miyazawa. But one can still find examples of Miyazawa's cachet being appropriated for acts of creative place making, whether of a cultural or commercial sort.[34] It is telling, for instance, that while no roads have yet been paved to Mt. Nametoko, as some feared might happen, a recently finished highway through the area was affectionately dubbed the "Milky-Way Nametoko Line." Another economy that Miyazawa's image and texts have had the power to influence is one intimately related to the first, though its aims are at times directly antithetical. This is the economy of cultural and natural heritage preservation, which values places for their historical or ecological significance and, as in the case of Mt. Nametoko, potentially removes them from economies of resource extraction and development so as to enlist their value in the pursuit of other causes (e.g., protecting endangered beech-forest habitat).[35] Although it remains to be seen how powerful or enduring an impact Miyazawa will have on this preservationist economy, one place where his influence has been felt is within local environmental educational projects. School teachers and nature guides have found it easy to meld his proto-ecological message and extensive references to regional flora, fauna, and geological features with their attempts to bring youth into more intimate contact with the nature surrounding them.[36] Further indication of the influence he might yet wield in this arena comes from the fact that Japan's Agency for Cultural Affairs has singled out natural and historic sites written about by Miyazawa as ideally suited to its recently revised guidelines for preserving and managing the nation's "cultural landscapes" (*bunkateki keikan*).[37]

Despite their divergent ends, both the tourist and preservationist economies ultimately help to augment the value of a place—and thereby maintain its viability—even as the shifting tides of social and economic restructuring lead to its devaluation on other levels. One economy insures a steady stream of visitors and thus of potential income for locals tied to the tourist trade; the other helps to preserve those things that make the place valuable as a destination. One facilitates the transformation of place into a site of leisure like any other; the other offers a bulwark to this sort of homogenization by encouraging the reevaluation of local resources and local knowledge in ways that do not blindly submit to external market forces or demands. That Miyazawa's image and texts have been valuable to both economies speaks to the resourcefulness of contemporary acts of place making, but it also leaves us to wonder why they have proved so useful compared with those of other canonical literary figures. The broad-based nature of his popularity, which spans generational and social divides, is surely a large part of why he has been so attractive to Iwate residents and outsiders alike as a vehicle for local imagining. But this explanation overlooks a critical aspect of his reception. At each step of the way in his posthumous rise, we have seen individuals attracted to him for reasons that have everything to do both with his status as a writer who stayed in the provinces and with the locally oriented strategies he adopted in response to his marginal position. Kusano Shinpei, for instance, along with many of Miyazawa's early promoters, found his poetry to be just as inspiring as his perceived willingness to lay down his pen and muddy his hands for the sake of area farmers and the local community. Later on, Kenji fans came looking for an image of Iihatov that could only have been nurtured by his sustained narrative focus on the particular land-scapes and lifeways, both real and reimagined, of a specific place. Even the recent commercial ventures that utilize Miyazawa as a marketing tool bor-row from the provincializing logic inherent in the idea of Iihatov, which aimed to open up the place of Iwate to new meanings and to instill in it an atmosphere of wonder and discovery. This book too, of course, belongs to this same arc in the history of Miyazawa's reception, one which finds his life and work to be good for thinking about locality.

One side effect of this arc, however, is that as Miyazawa's presence on bookshelves and in the cultural imaginary has continued to expand, it has made it hard to see in parts of Iwate anything *but* his image. And the more this image has circulated in popular media and scholarly channels, the more it has become subject to orthodox and expert interpretations, or even to a corporate kind of mentality in which those who have the greatest financial stake in his image strive to protect the pristine value of their brand.[38] This inevitably opens the door to what Chris Wilson calls "historical amnesia," or the process by which a romanticized or official version of history effectively paints over relations of production and conflict that previously existed in a place, thus interfering "with public understanding of the origins of con-temporary social, economic, and political structures."[39] Overemphasis of a romanticized history can also, Wilson warns, "deprive people of an image of themselves as active agents for contemporary social change."[40] And, we should add, as active agents in the processes by which the value of places are made and thought anew. To the extent that a commodified or overly roman-tic image of Miyazawa serves only as the end point of local imagining, then something of the original impulse underpinning his various provincializing strategies is lost. Also obscured are the socioeconomic shifts that force provin-cial localities like Hanamaki to rely on cultural heritage in the first place just to remain relevant as communities, as other forms of capital move elsewhere.

My hope for *On Uneven Ground* is that it discourages this sort of obfus-cation while also directing attention to the role that individuals can play as agents in the making of place. I think it has this potential precisely because it historicizes Miyazawa's literary and extra-literary strategies in ways that help us understand the conditions that produced them and *by* which their efficacy and durability were inevitably circumscribed. Doing so has meant infusing the archive with both spatial and social dimensionality, first by calling attention to geographical unevenness as a defining factor in local cultural production in the modern period, and then by outlining the kinds of social and material *networks* that helped and hindered the circulation of ideas on locality within and beyond their places of origin. Only in this way, however, was it possible to recover a sense of what it was, on the one hand, to think and act as a producer of culture in a field saturated with voices of differing force and amplitude, and on the other, what it was to try to invest a locality with new ideas and stories that had meaning for the people who lived there, not for those content merely to gaze from afar. If the conditions that once motivated Miyazawa's strategies have changed irrevocably since his death, and so too the immediate relevancy of his responses, the felt need for creative acts of place making has certainly not, nor the inherent unevenness of the structures through which these acts have always to be propagated. To the extent that we can look back and examine the reasons why his strategies failed, and indeed had to "fail" in order to succeed in the ways that they subsequently have, they may serve as lessons on how to confront this uneven ground, and thus as the seeds for newer ideas and newer strategies of local imagining.

Reference Matter

Notes

Prologue

1. Borges, "Borges and I," 324.
2. *Shin kōhon Miyazawa Kenji zenshū*, vol. 16, part 2 (*nenpu hen*): 519.
3. It is ironic, as David Ellis notes, that "at a time when the triumph of 'Theory' in the universities has widened the gap between the academic world and the rest of society, biographies represent one of the few remaining points of interaction. Such is the popularity of the form that bulky and highly detailed lives, composed over a long period, with the Academy principally in mind, can be shorn of their more obviously scholarly appurtenances, published in a 'trade' form, and left to compete with the work of professional writers." See *Literary Lives*, 1.
4. In order to free discourse from the limitations of the author as both ideological and functional principle, Michel Foucault argues that we move away from questions like "Who really spoke?" to questions such as "What are the modes of existence of this discourse? Where has it been used, how can it circulate, and who can appropriate it for himself?" In other words, that we shift from the author as a primary principle for deriving textual meaning to that of discourse. See his "What Is an Author?"
5. Blanchot, *The Infinite Conversation*, 139. For Blanchot, this interest arises because for those who depart before their time, or after a descent into madness, death can bring to their surviving words "an astonishing value and false nocturnal brilliance." It is, he says, as if these words harbor the very secret to the writer's all-too-sudden departure.
6. Latour, *The Pasteurization of France*, 16.
7. The passages cited here are drawn from memorial essays reprinted in *Shin kōhon Miyazawa Kenji zenshū*, vol. 16, part 2 (*hoi · denki shiryō hen*). All were published in the *Iwate nippō*, a regional newspaper based in Iwate's capital city of Morioka. The editor of the paper's literary pages, Mori Sōichi, was a close friend of Miyazawa's and, as discussed in the Epilogue, played a key role in announcing his death and publicizing the events surrounding it. He, as well as fellow Iwate poets Hahaki Hikaru and Umeno Kenzō, were the most vocal in praising Miyazawa early on. See their essays on pp. 375–76, 395–97, and 384–85 respectively. The examples of localized praise can be found on pp. 393–94 and 398.

8. Yoshida's essay, which ran in the evening edition of the *Iwate nippō* on Oct. 26, 1933, is reprinted in ibid., 387–90.

9. The memorial volumes for Kōyō and Sōseki are reprinted in volumes 1 and 5 of *Kindai sakka tsuitōbun shūsei*. Both were published as special issues of the literary magazine *Shin shōsetsu* (New Fiction).

10. One indication of the dominance of "lifestyle" in literary criticism at this time comes from commentary made during the awarding of the first Akutagawa and Naoki literary prizes in 1935. One judge observed that the Akutagawa committee, which knew nothing of its winning recipient, was able to make a selection based solely on literary achievement. Thus he wondered why the Naoki committee still insisted on bringing the writer's *attitude toward life* into their deliberations just because the winner's biography was better known. See Mack, "The Value of Literature, 334.

11. Kusano had been a vocal proponent of Miyazawa's work ever since reading his only published poetry collection as a university student in China. After returning to Japan in 1925, he began to correspond with Miyazawa and convinced him to contribute several verses to a regional poetry magazine, *Dora* (Gong), that he was hand-printing at the time. Kusano never met Miyazawa in person, though he did attempt to visit him in January 1927, in the hope of working at what he knew as the "Miyazawa Farm" (actually the Rasu Farmers Association).

12. See the contributions by Nagase Kiyoko, Komori Sei, Ono Tōzaburō, and Ozaki Kihachi. The entirety of the memorial volume has been reprinted in *Miyazawa Kenji kenkyū shiryō shūsei*, vol. 1: 67–141.

13. See the contributions by Kō Ei and Takamura Kōtarō, each of whom had met Miyazawa only once.

14. It is worth noting that not a single copy of the memorial volume was actually sold. Kusano was able to print 100 copies of the work out of a friend's apartment, largely owing to the generosity of Miyazawa's family. He even tried to publicize it by placing notices in several metropolitan poetry magazines and by hosting an informal reception at a beer hall in the city's Shinjuku district, hailing Miyazawa as "one of a rare breed, a great ray of light on the line of poetic history that stretches from Japan's primitive age through to the future." No one took the bait, however, and Kusano wound up mailing unsolicited copies to acquaintances. The above quote appeared in *Nihon shidan* 1.7 (Dec. 1, 1933): 80–81. On the publication of the *tsuitō*, see Saiki, *Saiki Ikurō to shōwa jūnen-dai no shijin-tachi*, 15–16.

15. After being turned down by two larger publishers, a nearly bankrupt used-book store by the name of Bunpodō eventually agreed to publish the *zenshū*. It did so only on the condition that the proposed nine volumes be cut back to three and that half of the 800 sets be contracted for sale in Iwate. I will discuss this in more detail in the Epilogue.

16. The short piece ran on October 26, 1934. Yokomitsu observed that when critics had to write a recommendation or preface for the work of a friend, they tended to focus less on the work and more on capturing a sense of that person in daily life. This inevitably led to exaggeration as they tried to respond to inflated images of

their friend's abilities. Having never once met Miyazawa, however, he felt in this case that there was *no need to exaggerate*. A lack of familiarity with a writer's life was thus paradoxically a way to elevate the authenticity and sincerity of statements about that life.

17. Tanikawa's essay appeared in February 1935 and is reprinted in Tsuzukihashi, *Miyazawa Kenji kenkyū shiryō shūsei*, 168–73. He notes that his discovery of Miyazawa was due mainly to the excitement shown by Kusano, Takamura, and Yokomitsu, and also to what he read in the memorial volume.

18. Foucault, "What Is an Author?" 160.

19. Chartier, *The Order of Books*, 28.

20. Ibid., 58.

21. Burke, *The Death and Return of the Author*, 202 (Burke's emphasis).

22. Ibid., 203.

23. For example, in Seiji Lippit's *Topographies of Japanese Modernism*, writer Akutagawa Ryūnosuke comes to epitomize a general anxiety about the status of literature as representational form in the 1920s, with works from his oeuvre selected for their relevance to a larger narrative of crisis within modernist literary practice. Similarly, in Gregory Golley's recent book on literary modernism, Miyazawa Kenji is positioned alongside Tanizaki Jun'ichirō and Yokomitsu Riichi as the quintessential spokesperson for a revolutionary new scientific realism—a mode of perception which sought to push beyond the sensory immediacy of reality to the vast social webs of interconnections that lay beyond. He writes in regards to Miyazawa's fiction that, "no body of work could tell us more about the oppositional grammar of the *realist* disposition I have identified in this study as the defining feature of Japanese literary modernism" (*When Our Eyes No Longer See*, 164).

24. Moretti, *Graphs, Maps, Trees*, 4.

25. On his mother's side was grandfather Miyazawa Zenji (1854–1939), an ambitious man who took over the stationery and paint store opened by his grandfather and developed it into a successful retail business selling assorted dry goods and monopoly-controlled commodities like tobacco, salt, sugar, and gasoline. Business was so good, in fact, that Zenji eventually assumed the role of a regional magnate, investing time and money into the establishment of a town bank, a hot-springs resort, and a railroad line connecting Hanamaki with the industrial port of Kamaishi. On the opposite side of the family was father Miyazawa Seijirō (1874–1957), the second-generation owner of a pawnshop and used-clothing store who had built a thriving business around the pecuniary needs of Hanamaki's poorer residents and area farmers. A man who prided himself on his shrewd business sense, he also did well for the family by investing in the stock market during the boom years of the First World War. In a 1926 publication about economic conditions in the northeast region, both Zenji and Seijirō are recognized as two of the most socially prominent citizens in the county. See *Tōkeijō yori mitaru Tōhoku sangyō keizai taikan*, 476 and 586. The genealogies of both his mother and father, when traced back several generations, reunite in a single line of Miyazawa patriarchs, the first of whom settled in the Hanamaki area in the 1690s.

26. He spent four years at the school teaching algebra, composition, chemistry, English, fertilizer use, soil science, and meteorology to seventh- and eighth-year students. This time was arguably the most productive for him in terms of his literary output.

27. Arjun Appadurai writes productively of this struggle when he asks, "What can locality mean in a world where spatial localization, quotidian interaction, and social scale are not always isomorphic?" That is, in a world where people live in geographically specific locales (what he calls "neighborhoods") that are altered and transformed by social processes operating on much vaster scales. See his *Modernity at Large*, 178–99.

28. Leitch, *Cultural Criticism, Literary Theory, Poststructuralism*, 38.

Chapter One

1. On the store's opening, see Nakata, "Shop Brings Famed Goods of Chilly Iwate to Tokyo."

2. According to a Tokyo travel site—http://season.enjoytokyo.jp/antenashop/ (accessed June 25, 2009)—there are currently forty-nine such outlets in the city. Hokkaidō and Okinawa are each represented by five stores, and three shops are advertised as being national in scope. The prefectures not represented are located adjacent to Tokyo (Saitama, Chiba, Ibaragi), in the Kansai area (Mie, Aichi, Osaka, Hyōgo, Nara, Okayama), or on the southern island of Kyūshū (Saga, Fukuoka, and Nagasaki). These shops are typically funded by prefectural chambers of commerce.

3. The story, which was reconstructed from at least four variant drafts, attained its now canonical form in the 1973 edition of Miyazawa's collected works. See *Kōhon Miyazawa Kenji zenshū*, vol. 10. Today it exists in numerous illustrated editions, translations, and adaptations to both *manga* and *anime* formats.

4. For a list of these memorials, see *Miyazawa Kenji no hi*.

5. In the late 1990s, the Miyazawa Kenji Ki'nenkan had an average yearly attendance of nearly 320,000. Only the Lafcadio Hearn Museum came close to approaching these numbers with around 280,000 visitors per year. See *Bungakukan wandārando*. To date, over five million people have passed through its doors.

6. One example of such a guidebook, the result of collaboration between a scholarly association and a local citizens group, is *Kenji no Iihatōbu Hanamaki*.

7. The structure was former home to the Mizusawa International Latitude Observatory. Fans lobbied the city mayor to preserve the building and pushed through a plan for its restoration. Their success was bolstered by the promise of monetary support from a national network of Miyazawa fans. See "*Ginga tetsudō* kansokujo nokotta," *Asahi shinbun*, Dec. 15, 2005.

8. The "Ginga Iwate Festival" was held in September 2003 at a small park near the retail outlet. Visitors were handed brochures welcoming them to "Miyazawa Kenji's native place, Iihatov." The brochure, which praised Iwate's bountiful nature, its varied climate, and the humble character of its people as a kind of guarantor for the quality of its products, also came with a map of "Kenji Street" and a list of all that was to be on display. "Your guide [to the festival]," it noted, "is the silhouette

of Miyazawa Kenji, children's author and pride of Iwate. Any place you find this symbol will be brimming with Iwate's bounty." This silhouette, not surprisingly, is a registered trademark.

9. For current debates on the application of trademark law to local products, see Kamikuri, "Chiiki burando omowanu kabe"; and Suzuki and Turner, "Japanese Patent Office Swamped by Local Lines." It has become popular not only to preserve existing monopolies on local difference, but to produce new ones too. Consider, for instance, the appearance of consulting-style manuals that offer strategies for enhancing a place's "local brand" within the expanding market for local goods. See *Chiiki burando: Nihon o sukū chiiki burando ron* (Tokyo: Kōbundō, 2006) and *Chiiki burando manejimento* (Tokyo: Yuhikaku, 2009).

10. Eagleton, *The Idea of Culture*, 73.

11. The rise of this new discourse of place making—as much in evidence in the urban wards of Tokyo as in the remotest rural districts—is attested to by a burgeoning literature on the subject. It consists of popular guides and handbooks, government-issued surveys and reports, and several academic studies. Local governments have been particularly active in documenting their most successful initiatives. For a general sense of the popular discourse as it stands presently, and for examples of the kinds of community projects being undertaken, see the special issue of *Ningen kaigi* (Human Conference) published June 2004. On the emergence of place-making efforts in the 1980s as a response to regional economic decline, see Hiramatsu, *Chihō kara no hassō*. As governor of Oita Prefecture, Hiramatsu initiated the "One Village, One Product" (*isson ippin*) movement, which became an important model for how to develop local brands. On the *furusato* as an organizing ideological concept in contemporary acts of place making, see Robertson, "It Takes a Village," 110–29. While the importance of *furusato* cannot be overstated, it is also essential to recognize that the market for place is not driven by a single idea of *furusato* competing with the metropolis, but by competition between each as they try to distinguish the unique value of their respective locales.

12. On the rise of the local as an effect of the rise of global capital, see Harvey, *The Condition of Postmodernity*.

13. As Harvey notes, the tension between fixity and mobility under capitalism leads to generalized crises wherein "old places have to be devalued, destroyed and redeveloped while new places are created. The cathedral city becomes a heritage centre; the mining community a ghost town; the old industrial centre is deindustrialized; speculative boom towns or gentrified neighbourhoods arise on the frontiers of capitalist development or out of the ashes of deindustrialized communities." See "From Space to Place and Back Again," 7.

14. Coca-colonization as part of a "global homogenization paradigm" is discussed by David Howes in *Cross-Cultural Consumption*, 3. Howes argues convincingly that this paradigm often covers over the multiple ways that "global" products are consumed and recontextualized at the local level.

15. Wigen, "Culture, Power, and Place," 1188. A clear sign that symbols of local distinctiveness are functioning more like corporate logos is the recent move by Jap-

anese cities and regions to adopt "local mascots" (*jimoto kyara*). On acts of place making in China, see Oakes, "China's Provincial Identities."

16. A useful guide to the many different kinds of place-making projects that have been attempted in Japan can be found in Tamura, *Machizukuri no jissen*. Tamura also provides an exhaustive list of the natural and cultural elements that might potentially contribute to the value of a place.

17. Harvey, *The Condition of Postmodernity*, 271–73.

18. The following studies have been the most helpful in thinking about modern place making in comparative context: Applegate, *A Nation of Provincials*; Jenkins, *Provincial Modernity*; Gerson, *The Pride of Place*; and Dorman, *Revolt of the Provinces*.

19. "Subarashii keiki no Tōhoku bussan chinretsukai," *Iwate nippō*, Sept. 8, 1921: 3.

20. See Yoshimasa, "Tōhoku Shinkō Kai no keika ippan," 10.

21. Ibid., 22. For an assessment of the 1917 exhibition and an evaluation of the products displayed, see the statements published by Mitsukoshi's head purchaser, Ikutabi Hisashi. They appear in Ikutabi, "Tōhoku bussan no chōtan."

22. Giddens, *The Consequences of Modernity*, 21.

23. On the weakening of ties between culture and place, see Tomlinson, *Globalization and Culture*. He adopts what others have referred to as the "global homogenization" paradigm, which downplays the agency of local actors and posits a vanishing "local world" where "everyday meanings" were once anchored firmly in place. Ursula Heise looks at the impact of globalization on the experience of place, or rather the possibility of its experience, in "Local Rock and Global Plastic." Also see Dovey, "The Quest for Authenticity and the Replication of Environmental Meaning."

24. Harvey, "From Space to Place and Back Again," 14.

25. Ibid., 4. On the rhetoric of regionalism as a repetition of nationalist discourse, see Dainotto, *Place in Literature*, 5–7.

26. See the introduction to *Global/Local*, 5.

27. Harvey, "From Space to Place and Back Again," 8. On the notion of producing local culture as a "museum item," see Howes, *Cross-Cultural Consumption*, 12.

28. Massey, "Power-Geometry and a Progressive Sense of Place," 64.

29. Lefebvre, *The Production of Space*, 86 (his emphasis). Lefebvre defines "social space," a term I use throughout the book, as the combined symbolic and material product of, among other things, property relations, forces of production, and distinct social relationships.

30. Foucault, "Two Lectures," 82. The examples he gives of such local, disqualified knowledges are "that of the psychiatric patient, of the ill person, of the nurse, of the doctor—parallel as they are to the knowledge of medicine."

31. Ibid., 83.

32. Rafael, "Regionalism, Area Studies, and the Accidents of Agency," 1208–9.

33. *Global/Local*, 6. Similar arguments are made by Arif Dirlik in his contribution to the same volume, "The Global in the Local," 21–45. Bhikhu Parekh and Jan Nederveen Pieterse suggest that a modernist binary is also at work in decolonization narratives, where it promotes a particularistic nativism (as against Western uni-

versalism and colonial power) that leaves no room for imagining interstitial spaces of mixture and hybridity. See their "Shifting Imaginaries," 14–15.

34. *Global/Local*, 8.

35. Massey, "Power-Geometry and a Progressive Sense of Place," 66. My only addition to her list of constitutive forces would be that of physical environment, in both its natural and built forms, for it provides the relatively fixed ground to which each node must attach itself and feel out its relation to the others.

36. On the relationship of story and narrative to social perceptions and under-standings of place, see Ryden, *Mapping the Invisible Landscape*; Basso, *Wisdom Sits in Places*; Marmon-Silko, "Landscape, History, and the Pueblo Imagination"; Tuan, *Topophilia* and *Space and Place*; Johnstone, *Stories, Community, and Place*; and Buell, *The Environmental Imagination*, chap. 8.

37. *Imagined Communities*, 25. Many have since contested Anderson's formula-tion as he articulated it, or have at least proposed alternative models, but few have denied the critical link he draws between narrative and a sense of nationhood.

38. As historian Harry Harootunian notes, he appealed "to the trope of a nonlin-ear history of custom by employing the vivid imagery of a stalactitic formation that grows unobserved into the shape of a large icicle." See his *Overcome by Modernity*, 31.

39. Ibid., 345.

40. Larsen, *Modernism and Hegemony*, xliii.

41. Latour, *We Have Never Been Modern*, 75–76 (Latour's emphasis). For him, "temporality" is defined as a particular way of interpreting the passage of time (68).

42. Jenkins, *Provincial Modernity*, 148–50.

43. Rafael, "Regionalism, Area Studies, and the Accidents of Agency," 1209.

44. Applegate, "A Europe of Regions."

45. Chakrabarty, *Provincializing Europe*, 46.

46. Harootunian, "Some Thoughts on Comparability and the Space-Time Prob-lem," 35. This warning is actually given as a response to Chakrabarty's work, though the latter never calls for the kind of exclusivist paradigm that Harootunian is criti-cizing.

47. Negri, *Time for Revolution*, 40.

48. Harootunian, "Some Thoughts on Comparability and the Space-Time Prob-lem," 46.

49. Fabian, *Time and the Other*, 154.

Chapter Two

1. "Morioka no honya wa minna aoiki-toiki," *Iwate nippō*, Sept. 14, 1923: 3.

2. Edward Mack offers the most thorough account in English of the damage done to the publishing industry by the Great Kantō Earthquake. My own analysis is greatly indebted to the groundwork he has laid on this subject. See chap. 2 in "The Value of Literature."

3. On centrality as both social and conceptual form, see Lefebvre, *Production of Space*, 331–33 and 399.

4. "Honshi o Tōkyō ni," *Hokkai taimusu*, Sept. 9, 1923: 2.

5. Mack, "The Value of Literature," 131–33. The two subsidiaries were the *Tōkyō Nichinichi* and the *Tōkyō Asahi*, respectively. Both fared better than any of the other newspapers in the immediate aftermath of the quake. They did so well that by the mid-1930s they came to dominate the national market.

6. "Gakujutsu no ken'i wa Kyōto ni utsuran: shuppankai wa Osaka e?" *Tōkyō Nichinichi shinbun*, Sept. 8, 1923: 1. The same article ran on September 9 in the *Fukuoka Nichinichi shinbun* and on September 10 in the *Hokkai taimusu*.

7. A professor at Kyoto University, Katayama Koson, similarly predicted that the publishing world would move either to Osaka or Kyoto. See his "Shinsai to waga bungei." In the same issue of this weekly magazine, however, another critic offered a slightly more balanced assessment of the situation. He remarked that Osaka printers could hardly be expected to take on the needs of literary publishing when they were already busy with orders from banks, corporations, and the central government. See p. 21.

8. As late as November, a reporter in the northern city of Sendai still felt compelled to insist that local publishers rise up to claim their share of the market. See "Chihō no shuppankai: Kyōto to Sendai," *Kahoku shinpō*, Nov. 3 1923, late ed.: 2.

9. This discussion of "the center" as a structuring element and of the conceptual possibilities opened by its absence builds on Jacques Derrida's "Structure, Sign, and Play in the Discourse of the Human Sciences," 278–94.

10. See Takahashi Masami, "Shuppan ryūtsū kikō no hensen: 1603–1945," 192–93. Despite Edo's ascendancy in the late Tokugawa, there remained a degree of balance with markets in Kyoto and Osaka. In addition, provincial publishers could be found in roughly fifty other castle towns, ten of which boasted ten or more bookseller-publishers. These smaller operations enjoyed substantial growth from the 1780s and were able to sustain the activities of local intellectuals, writers, and scholars by utilizing distributors in the three principal nodes to gain access to national markets. On provincial publishing in the early-modern period, see Kornicki, "Provincial Publishing in the Tokugawa Period," 188–97. In Japanese, see Asakura Haruhiko and Ōwa Hiroyuki, *Kinsei chihō shuppan no kenkyū*.

11. Oda Mitsuo makes this argument in *Shuppansha to shoten wa ika nishite kieteiku ka*, 93–102. See also *Shoten no kindai*, chap. 6. Plenty of smaller presses were active in publishing literary or intellectual material, but few had the capital to weather financial instability, the capacity to produce larger print runs, or easy access to a guaranteed sales network.

12. Hashimoto, *Nihon shuppan hanbai-shi*, 87–88. At the back of one Hakubunkan magazine, Hashimoto found a list of nearly two hundred bookstores where company products could be purchased. For an early history of the company, see Tsuboya, *Hakubunkan gojūnen-shi*. Also see Richter, "Marketing the Word," 205–23.

13. The Ōji Paper Company, founded in 1873 by industrialist Shibusawa Eiichi, was the first manufacturer of Western-style paper in Japan. Headquartered in Tokyo, it grew quickly to dominate the paper-making business.

14. By 1894, the largest company, Tōkyōdō, had nearly 1,800 agents situated

NOTES TO CHAPTER TWO 217

throughout Japan. Richter, "Marketing the Word," 215–16. It was owned by Ōhashi's brother-in-law.

15. For a brief account of how the early distribution companies got started, see Hashimoto, *Nihon shuppan hanbai-shi*, 90–98. Also see Takahashi, "Shuppan ryūtsū kikō no hensen," 196–208.

16. Nagamine, *"Dokusho kokumin" no tanjō*, 30–31.

17. Nagamine, *Modan toshi no dokusho kūkan*, 4. Nagamine draws his statistics from the annual reports of the Home Ministry. For all but the last few years of Taishō, the reports list the number of books published in each prefecture under the regulations of the Publication Law.

18. Nagamine, *"Dokusho kokumin" no tanjō*, 12. The list of nineteen authors is drawn from a column called "Chihō no dokusho kai" (The World of the Provincial Reader), which ran in the journal *Bunko* between 1898 and 1900. Contributors to the column acknowledged the popularity of the *shōsetsu* genre and named some of its most widely read authors. Nagamine's list includes Iwaya Sazanami, Ozaki Kōyō, Kōda Rohan, and Izumi Kyōka, among others.

19. See Edward Mack's dissertation on the various social and cultural mechanisms by which centralization continued during the Taishō and early Shōwa periods. Mack focuses on the evolution of the literary establishment (*bundan*) and discusses how the literary marketplace in Tokyo came to be coterminous with the nation itself after the First World War, noting that, "while modern Japanese literature began to be consumed by the citizenry of the Japanese nation . . . it remained, in terms of production and consumption, limited in terms of geography and class" ("The Value of Literature," 91).

20. Ibid., 88. Original reference is from *Chūō kōron* (July 1918), 164. Kikuchi's narrator was at the time in Kyoto.

21. Richard Torrance has written extensively about the Osaka publishing industry in his "Literacy and Literature in Osaka, 1890–1940." He argues that many of the genres developed in Osaka, which were intent on appealing to mass audiences, influenced the form of mass media in the rest of the country.

22. Torrance has provided ample evidence of such activity in the Izumo region. See his "Literacy and Modern Literature in the Izumo Region, 1880–1930." To give some idea of the overall amount of literary output, Torrance provides the following statistics: "In 1900, there were nine magazines and newspapers in Izumo publishing 2,338,000 issues annually. In 1927, the number of issues published was 10 times the 1900 figure, and by 1935, there were 74 periodicals being published in the region" (337). In Japanese, there is a considerable amount of scholarship on regional literary activity in the modern period. A key source is the 55-volume *Furusato bungakukan*. The set, arranged by prefecture, operates upon a very broad definition of what counts for regional literature. It can be literature written by prefectural natives for local audiences, literature written by natives who have moved elsewhere, or literature that employs the prefecture as setting, regardless of the author's origins. For specific regional studies, see Kihara, *Hokkaidō bungaku-shi*; *Kobayashi Tenmin to Kansai bundan no keisei*; and Shutō, *Kindai bungaku to Kumamoto*.

23. One such short-lived outlet, the literary magazine *Sakufū*, even published a commemorative issue in October 1915 outlining the history and future course of the Iwate *bundan*. The journal was only a year old at this point. For an overview of Iwate's modern literary history, see Urata Keizō's *Shiryō—Iwate no kindai bungaku* and *Takuboku · Bimyō sono hoka: Iwate no kindai bungaku*.

24. Nagamine, *Modan toshi no dokushō kūkan*, 5.

25. Kihara, *Hokkaidō bungaku-shi*, 7.

26. In December 1925, in an apparent show of support for these groups, the journal produced a "Dictionary of Common Publishing Terms for Amateur Publishers."

27. Torrance, "Literacy and Modern Literature in the Izumo Region, 1880–1930," 354–56.

28. Ibid., 362.

29. Torrance is well aware of this fact when he describes the literary activity of four Izumo men who tried to make careers out of writing narrative prose. All four affiliated themselves with Tokyo writers or publications at some point in their career. Ibid., 344–46.

30. On the formation of a national readership, see both Richter's and Nagamine's work. See especially Nagamine's *"Dokusho kokumin" no tanjō*. The statistics on the number of bookstores comes from Hashimoto, *Nihon shuppan hanbai-shi*, 220.

31. It is striking, though, to see how many places now claim native-born writers as their own, even if these writers had to flee their homes in order to make a name for themselves.

32. Moretti, *Atlas of the European Novel, 1800–1900*, 3.

33. "Bundan: chikagoro no koto," *Sandee mainichi* 44 (Oct. 7, 1923): 16.

34. Tsubouchi, "Kongo no geijutsukai."

35. Yamada, "Bundan no kongo."

36. Kojima, "Kyōdo bungaku no tame ni."

37. Kanō, "Kongo no bundan to sono chihōka." The ideas in this essay originally appeared in the November 1923 issue of *Zuihitsu* (Literary Jottings) under the title "Shinpen zakki" (Notes on Personal Matters). On Kanō's post-quake movements and the largely autobiographical material he wrote while in Ishikawa, see Sakamoto, *Kanō Sakujirō no hito to bungaku*, 201–18.

38. The novel *Kisei* (Returning Home, 1890), by Miyazaki Koshoshi (1859–1919), marks a starting point for modern literary appropriations of the rural and the native-place as aestheticized objects of anti-urban retreat. It tells the story of a youth who, having spent six years in Tokyo for his studies, returns home to commemorate the first anniversary of his father's death. While there, he awakens to the futility of city life as compared to the beautiful simplicity of the rural home. As Stephen Dodd notes, the work was so popular that it went through 25 editions by the end of the Meiji period and was remembered by Yanagita Kunio for its "unparalleled ability to capture the feelings of young people at the time." See his *Writing Home*, 18.

39. Shirotori, "Tokai bungei no hōkai to den'en bungei no fukkō," 235. The essay was originally published in the literary journal *Shinchō* in November 1923. That the

majority of people who perished in the disaster were residents of Tokyo's poorest neighborhoods was a fact apparently lost on Shirotori.

40. Ibid., 237.

41. Yasuoka, "Nōson geijutsu ni tsuite."

42. Kanō, "Kongo no bundan to sono chihōka."

43. Watanabe, "Shinkō bungei no teishō."

44. Nakazawa, "Kyōdo geijutsu no kitai." Nakazawa had been residing in Tokyo since 1902, after moving there from Gunma Prefecture at the age of seventeen.

45. Kawanishi, *Kindai Nihon no chiiki shisō*, 257.

46. Fukushi, "Kyōdo bungaku shuchō no kiso," Feb. 9, 1924: 5. Originally dated January 21, the essay was published again in August in pamphlet form by the Regional Culture Society. It is reproduced in *Fukushi Kōjirō chosakushū*, vol. 2: 65–69.

47. Fukushi, "Kyōdo bungaku shuchō no kiso," 5. In the pamphlet version of the essay, the phrase "limited to a particular kind of person (*ningen*)" was altered to read "limited to a particular kind of environment (*kankyō*)."

48. Fukushi, "Kyōdo bungaku shuchō no kiso," Feb. 13, 1924: 5.

49. Ibid., Feb. 14, 1924: 5.

50. Ibid., Feb. 15, 1924: 5.

51. Kawanishi, *Kindai Nihon no chiiki shisō*, 256–57. "Traditionalism" (*dentōshugi*) was a set of ideas imported from the French novelist and regionalist thinker Maurice Barres (1862–1923). It was an anti-intellectual and antiurban movement that sought to organize the nation not around a centralized state, nor around the laboring masses, but around a select group of middle-class citizens who would help to guide and develop the "traditions" that lived on in the common people. The intellectual class could not be trusted with this mission, for their thinking had been irreversibly "Westernized." Nor could the people alone, for they were not capable of acting in their own best interest. Thus it was up to men like Fukushi to preserve and nurture those unique "traditions" of Japan (e.g., loyalty, piety, duty, and feeling) that would help the nation to reconstitute itself in the face of social fragmentation. On Barres and the regionalist philosophy of France's New Right, see Wright, *The Regionalist Movement in France, 1890–1914*.

52. On debates in 1924 between Fukushi and several progressive intellectuals over the proper meaning of a regionalist movement, see Kawanishi, *Kindai Nihon no chiiki shisō*, 259–62. Amongst the latter were socialist activist Ozawa Kyūmei (1901–1985) and the local literary figure Awaya Yūzō (1897–1995). Awaya had from the early 1920s been advocating his own vision for a "native-place art"—what he saw as a "protest against the art born of the present civilization, the present social system, and present economic conditions"—in a regional culture magazine, *Reimei* (Dawn), that he himself had founded in 1919 as a gathering place for "all those left behind" in the provinces. See Long, "Finding 'Place' in the World: The Currency of Local Culture in Interwar Japan."

53. Casanova, *The World Republic of Letters*, 196.

54. Moretti, "Conjectures on World Literature," 64–66.

55. Kawabata, "Kyōdo geijutsu mondai no gaikan." Despite this dismal outlook,

Kawabata did seem to believe that provincial writers would one day produce distinctive works in the same way that regions produced their own unique local goods (*meibutsu*).

56. Williams, *Marxism and Literature*, 185.

Chapter Three

1. Mori, "*Chūmon no ōi ryōriten*," 9–10. The essay was originally published in 1954. Mori, an early fan of Miyazawa's *dōwa* and poetry, later became a prominent local poet and writer. He was an active member of the Iwate Shijin Kyōkai (Association of Iwate Poets) in the mid-1920s and went on to win the Naoki Prize in 1943.

2. Toryō Shuppanbu had used this sales method before with several of its pamphlets and books. It sent complimentary copies to agricultural schools across the country and would then solicit orders. While this had been successful in the past, it did not work for Miyazawa's book. Payment was eventually received for five hundred copies, but only over a period of many years. See Horio, "*Chūmon no ōi ryōriten* kankō goro makki" (1967), 70.

3. Cohen, *The Sentimental Education of the Novel*, 21–23.

4. Moretti employs the "great unread" in a much broader sense, using the concept to "come up with a new sense of the literary field as a whole" and to promote the "distant reading" of entire genres and systems of texts over the close reading of a few canonical ones. See "Slaughterhouse of Literature."

5. On the inseparability of these two categories, see Bourdieu, "The Field of Cultural Production, or: The Economic World Reversed," in *The Field of Cultural Production*, 30.

6. I add the term, of course, to the well-recognized forms of capital that Bourdieu elucidates in his sociological theory: economic capital (one's access to economic resources), social capital (one's associations and relationships), cultural capital (one's investment in legitimate forms of knowledge or valued material objects), and symbolic capital (one's social prestige and recognition).

7. Nagamine makes this point when discussing the bifurcation between the central media (as producer) and the provincial reader (as consumer) that took place over the course of the Meiji period. See *"Dokusho kokumin" no tanjō*, 44. The comment recalls Octavio Paz's description of the relation of Latin American writers to the West in *The Labyrinth of Solitude*. "As people of the fringes . . . we Latin Americans are uninvited guests who have sneaked in through the West's back door, intruders who have arrived at the feast of modernity as the lights are about to be put out. We arrive late everywhere, we were born when it was already late in history, we have no past or, if we have one, we spit on its remains." Cited in Casanova, *The World Republic of Letters*, 82.

8. These statistics were compiled through a search of the most complete catalogue of children's literature in Japan (*Jidōsho sōgō mokuroku*), which draws from several collections around the country, including the International Children's Library in Osaka and the National Diet Library in Tokyo. Included in the 495 total volumes are several collections of children's plays and a handful of scholarly criticism.

9. The two graduated from the school in 1919, just one year behind Miyazawa. They went their separate ways after graduation, but found themselves back in Morioka in 1923. Oikawa was at the time managing a failing dairy and Chikamori was employed as a research assistant at their alma mater. See Mori, "*Chūmon no ōi ryōriten*," 22.

10. This was a fact Chikamori remembered vividly even decades later. See Suzuki, "Dōwa-shū *Chūmon no ōi ryōriten* hakkan o megutte," 112.

11. So little is known about the details of Oikawa and Yoshida's contract that it is impossible to determine what Yoshida was actually held responsible for in terms of distribution. Tōkyō Kōgensha is listed at the back of the volume as the place to which one can send orders for the book, but we do not know how many copies Yoshida kept on hand after the initial printing. It is likely that a majority were sent back to Oikawa in Morioka. Incidentally, Oikawa continued to use Tōkyō Kōgensha as a printer at least through 1925.

12. The monthly trade journal put out by the union contained a list of new members in every issue. Yoshida's company does not appear until 1926. See *Tosho geppō* 24.4 (April 1926): 86. Each issue of the journal also contained an extensive list of publications released the previous month.

13. The main thrust behind the policy, and the general effort to strengthen the union at this time, were the result of a desire to institute a fixed-price (*teika*) system. World War I had driven up the price of paper and other materials such that publishers needed to find a way to maintain the cost of books at a certain level and prevent them from being sold at a discount. Although it was only within the Tokyo union that such policies were instituted, the exclusionary rules led to the quick formation of prefectural unions, most of which adopted similar constitutions since the Tokyo organization had assigned itself the task of approving all other constitutions. A national union was formed in May 1920. For a detailed account of these developments, see Hashimoto, *Nihon shuppan hanbai-shi*, 253–65. The constitution of the Tokyo union as it appeared in late 1924 can be found in *Tosho geppō* 23.2 (Feb. 1925). It should be noted that members of the Tokyo union were not restricted from doing business with non-Tokyo companies as long as those companies were members of their own regional unions. And it is almost certain that Oikawa's company was, since the name Kōgensha is one of ninety-nine that appear on a list of members published by the Iwate union (Iwate-ken Shoseki Zasshi Shō Kumiai). The document carries no date, but prefectural statistics provided by the national union (reprinted in Hashimoto, *Nihon shuppan hanbai-shi*, 530) state that there were 87 members in 1923 and 110 in 1925, thus leading us to assume that the list appeared around 1924. Even if Kōgensha's membership was certain, however, this did not guarantee privileged access to the Tokyo market.

14. Casanova, *The World Republic of Letters*, 39.

15. In the 1970s, Maeda Ai laid the groundwork for these discussions with his insightful readings of urban space as it was variously encoded and reinterpreted in texts from the modern literary canon. Karatani Kōjin would later read the "landscapes" of modern literature as the product of an epistemological configuration

both historically unique and constructed—one which distanced the world "out there" from the singular subjectivity of the observer.

16. Morris, "Metamorphoses at Sydney Tower," 10.

17. Shift the terms around, and one could ask the same questions of the national writer on the world stage or the colonial writer on an imperial one. And there are obvious parallels between the problematic described here and the one through which national literatures have recently been reconceived in relation to a "world republic of letters." But it is important to be attentive to the fact that the case of a marginalized literature in a global framework involves a different set of linguistic, economic, and geo-political relationships than one in a national framework. Those differences are part of what this project seeks to elucidate.

18. Examples of these narratives include that of nostalgia for a lost provincial home, discovery of an exteriorized rural landscape, and fascination with urban so-cial forms. Significantly, although Tokyo writers could ignore provincial literary production without consequence, the way power relations were inscribed in the geography of the field meant that non-Tokyo writers who wanted to make a name for themselves had always to take Tokyo trends seriously.

19. Take Arishima Takeo, for instance, whom Paul Anderer has described as a writer "who throws off the chains of local fact and sensual experience (which Maruyama Masao has said 'cling like leeches' to the Japanese writer), only to im-prison himself in fantasy and abstraction." See *Other Worlds*, 30.

20. The great satirist Santō Kyōden (1761–1816) is credited with first using the term as an equivalent for "folk-tale" (*mukashibanashi*) in his *Dōwa-kō* (Thoughts on *Dōwa*, 1790). By late Meiji, it had come to be equated with morally instructive folk tales aimed at children. See *Nihon jidō bungaku daijiten*.

21. This label had itself been reintroduced to the literary lexicon just two decades earlier by writer Iwaya Sazanami (1870–1933). He too had tried to stake out a space for an "original" and homegrown children's literature. For Iwaya, however, this meant adapting native folk-tales, legends, biographies, and historical chronicles for a stylistic idiom and moral vision attuned to the nationalistic education policies of the Meiji state. On his role in redefining juvenile literature in the 1890s, see *Nihon jidō bungaku-shi*, 79–83. Also see Maeda, *Toshi kūkan no naka no bungaku*, 280–86. Both discuss the dominance of biographies and histories during a period of rising nationalist sentiment. It was these genres that were deemed most capable of instill-ing in children an awareness of their role as the succeeding generation of a young Meiji state. What this meant, as Maeda notes, was "that content with the kind of literary and emotional substance that developed children's sensibilities and imagina-tion was likely to be ignored" (281). History and biography remained the dominant forms of "acceptable" children's literature into the last decade of Meiji, at which point they had to contend with the rising popularity of entertainment-oriented narratives (e.g., swashbuckling adventures) on the one hand, and the efforts of *bun-dan* writers to make juvenile literature properly literary on the other. By 1909, even Iwaya felt a need for more poetic and lyrical tales. See *Nihon jidō bungaku gairon*, 33.

22. *Nihon jidō bungaku gairon*, 53–54.

23. "Dragon's gate" was the popular term for *Chūō kōron* (Central Review), a magazine that by 1918 served as a physical manifestation of the *bundan* itself. To have a story published in *Chūō kōron* was to pass through the "dragon's gate" and to virtually insure one's success as a writer.

24. *Akai tori* 1 (July 1918): 78.

25. At the back of every issue, Suzuki and Kitahara provided a list of submissions deemed most outstanding along with commentary and critique. Suzuki also notified readers how many entries he had received that month, thus providing a rough measure for how quickly *Akai tori* grew in popularity.

26. See *Shin kōhon Miyazawa Kenji zenshū*, vol. 16, part 2 (*nenpu hen*): 161. The two stories Seiroku recalls hearing were "Futago no hoshi" (The Twin Stars) and "Kumo to namekuji to tanuki" (The Spider, the Slug, and the Raccoon). He also remembers the great hope that Miyazawa seemed to harbor for the future. What Seiroku does not tell us, however, is how these two stories compared with later versions. The surviving manuscripts date back only to 1921, and thus the specific form and quality of Miyazawa's first attempts at fiction are uncertain. We do know that he was experimenting with other prose styles as late as 1921, the results of which are compiled as "Shoki tanpen tsuzuri" (Early Short Writings).

27. The creation of a space for nonprofessional authors to contribute original work was certainly not a new phenomenon. Open-submissions magazines (*tōsho zasshi*) had provided nonprofessional poets and writers with the opportunity to form broad-based and "mediated" literary coteries since the 1890s, when the nationalization of the postal infrastructure made such forms of social organization possible. See Richter, "Marketing the Word." Newspapers were also part of the open-submission phenomenon, organizing periodic contests as early as 1893. Kōno Kensuke provides an analysis of these contests in his *Tōki toshite no bungaku: katsuji, kenshō, media*.

28. Ogawa, "Watashi ga 'dōwa' o kaku toki no kokoromochi," 21.

29. For Saitō, the recent reforms in children's reading material, while praiseworthy, had gone too far. Efforts to make stories more artistic were actually making them too difficult for children and incapable of offering adequate moral guidance. See *Kin no fune* 1.1 (Nov. 1919): 80. The endorsement of Tōson and Ikuma lasted until June 1922, when a dispute with the printing and distribution company forced a change in name of the magazine to *Kin no hoshi* (Golden Star). See Saitō's own *Saitō Sajirō: jidō bungaku-shi*, 154–61.

30. By one estimate, the height of the boom saw nearly sixty publishers trying to repeat the success of *Akai tori* with their own children's magazines. *Nihon jidō bungaku-shi*, 151.

31. For a description of the links between *dōwa* and late-Taishō educational reform movements, see Kan, *Nihon no jidō bungaku*, 114–20. Miyazawa too was a part of these movements during his tenure at the Hienuki School of Agriculture between 1921 and 1926. Infamous for deviating from the prescribed curriculum, he read his own *dōwa* aloud in class and actively promoted school theater, as will be discussed in Chapter Six.

32. For a discussion of the romantic notions of childhood espoused by writers in the *dōwa* movement, as well as the connection to changing middle-class values in the 1920s, see Jones, "Children as Treasures," chap. 8. Jones argues that "the literary celebration of the childlike child became an important way to distinguish the leading edge from the mass of the middle class, a group regularly depicted as singularly concerned with the child's future success and unable to appreciate the child's childlike qualities" (295).

33. Hamada Hirosuke (1893–1973) and Niimi Nankichi (1913–1943) are the best examples of writers who began their careers in this way. Hamada, a native of northern Yamagata Prefecture, was enrolled in the English Department at Waseda University when he was awarded a hefty sum of fifty yen by the *Ōsaka Asahi shinbun* for his *Kongon no inetaba* (The Golden Bundle of Rice, 1917). As a result of winning this contest, he soon found himself writing *dōwa* for the magazine *Ryōyū* (Good Friend), a precursor of *Akai tori*. Nankichi's career began in 1931, years after the initial boom. But his story is similar in that he was "discovered" via a submission contest, in this case through *Akai tori*.

34. Kōno, *Tōki toshite no bungaku*, 61.

35. Suzuki Miekichi, *Akai tori* 1.6 (Dec. 1918): 79. Incidentally, Suzuki had no qualms about editing winning entries as he saw fit.

36. *Kin no fune* 2.1 (Jan. 1920): 78. Outside of the magazines, a few established authors wrote at great length about their own criteria for what made an ideal *dōwa*. An essay by Hamada Hirosuke represents well the party line, emphasizing as it does the need for *dōwa* to be easily comprehensible to the child even when the author is attempting to communicate complex thoughts. *Dōwa*, he argued, should offer children "a beautiful, pure (*junshin*) world" not far from their feelings, thoughts, and desires. Moreover, they should be written in a simple language that expresses as realistically as possible the words and movements of children. The essay was included in Noguchi Ujō's *Dōyō tsukurikata mondō*, 94–119.

37. Suzuki was no exception to this. His first collection of *dōwa*, *Kosui no onna* (Lady of the Lake, 1916), consisted only of translated Western fairy tales. Much of his later work also relied on retold or translated material.

38. Casanova, *The World Republic of Letters*, 43.

39. Dodd, *Writing Home*, 42. The degree to which "local color" was read and appreciated in late Meiji through the lens of an author's native place is discussed by Mukubō Tetsuya in "Kyōdo geijutsu · den'en · chihōshoku." It should be pointed out that some argued for the equal applicability of the term to the complex social landscapes of urban environments. See the brief note on "local color" by Shimamura Hōgetsu, from 1910, in *Hōgetsu zenshū*, vol. 2 (1920): 276–77. The term was first employed, in fact, by critics commenting on Higuchi Ichiyō's depiction of the licensed quarters in *Takekurabe* (Growing Up, 1895–1896). Mukubō, "Kyōdo geijutsu · den'en · chihōshoku," 184.

40. An example of editorial praise for local color can be found in *Dōwa* 4.4 (April 1923): 96. For an example of critique, see Suzuki's comments on a win-

ning submission in *Akai tori* 2.6 (June 1919): 79. He felt the author had not done enough to capture the atmosphere of the Taiwanese village where the story was set.

41. The irony is well illustrated by a comment made by Tayama Katai in 1909. In *Shōsetsu sakuhō*, after writing at length on the importance of knowing intimately the dialect, customs, and practices of the locality one writes about, he noted that contributors to magazines (i.e., nonestablished writers) often lack the skills to depict local color because they have never traveled outside their native place (117). It seems that the writers most capable of deploying local color were those privileged enough to be *from* somewhere and to have traveled *everywhere*.

42. Katai's account appeared in *Dōwa* 1.11 (Nov. 1920): 16–19. It is significant that a few months before, editor Chiba Shōzō promised readers that Katai would be writing about rare natural scenery and the lives of people in distant locales in a way that would make readers "feel close to people who they had never even thought about before." See *Dōwa* 1.6 (June 1920): 94.

43. The first advertisement for the volume appeared in the December 1920 issue of *Akai tori*. It seems that Tōson's decision to write *Furusato* stemmed from the success of an earlier volume, titled *Osanakimono ni* (To the Young Ones, 1917), in which he had collected vignettes from his time in France as a kind of gift for his children.

44. Tōson, *Furusato*, 14–15.

45. We see this again in Kitamura Hisao's "Inaka monogatari" (Tale of the Countryside), from the January 1923 issue of *Dōwa*. He opens the piece by telling readers that he was born in Tokyo, but spent a part of his childhood in the countryside, and that he would like to record for readers as precisely as possible his fond memories of that time. Here too, the countryside is made more interesting by virtue of its being filtered through personal recollection and a temporal gap. The notion that childhood memory remained somehow pure and untouched in the adult mind was common in *dōwa* circles, and we see it too in Hamada's previously cited essay. There he writes that "all the feelings and concepts we experienced as children remain with us, undiminished. And not just those remarkable impressions that are unforgettable. All of the innumerable impressions that sink below the realm of consciousness with the passing of time remain as in the shape of a 'sleeping tower'" (Noguchi, *Dōyō tsukurikata mondō*, 109). Ogawa Mimei wrote in 1921 that "just as everyone has a village into which they were born, and just as everyone never forgets the scenery of that village, so too have all humans experienced childhood. The things of that time—feelings of love, pain, sadness, and surprise . . . can never be forgotten" (Ogawa, "Watashi ga 'dōwa' o kaku toki no kokoromochi," 21).

46. Suzuki's two key commentaries on dialect use in student compositions can be found in *Akai tori* 4.9 (Sept. 1921): 93–94, and 7.9 (Sept. 1924): 148–49. *Dōwa* was also supportive of dialect use in reader submissions, encouraging children to use "the words of their region" whether they hailed from Tokyo or the countryside. See *Dōwa* 2.6 (June 1921): 97. In fact, editor Chiba Shōzō reportedly took hints from these submissions in crafting his popular "Tora-chan no nikki" (Little Tora's Diary, 1925), a kind of autobiographical sketch of village life as seen through the

eyes of a sixth-grade child. Dialect is used extensively to represent both the speech of the narrator and the other children in the story. See *Nihon jidō bungaku-shi*, 140. For more on this story and on Chiba's editorial stance regarding dialect, see Tsuzukihashi, *Taishō jidō bungaku no sekai*, 216–34.

47. *Akai tori* 1.4 (Dec. 1918): 78.

48. Oddly, the first "legend" selected told of events that had taken place just ten years earlier. When a group of children took a Buddhist statue swimming with them one day, they were reprimanded by an elderly woman for desecrating the sacred object. Not long after, the woman fell gravely ill and it was believed that the spirit of the statue was haunting her for having denied it a chance to play. Ever since, villagers made it a practice to take the statue out each year and allow it to play in the river with the children. Although hardly a decade old, the brand of folk wisdom displayed in this local legend must have given it the requisite scent of the distant past. See *Akai tori* 2.9 (Sept. 1919): 74–75.

49. See *Akai tori* 2.10 (Oct. 1919): 80. In this issue, the submissions page contained a heading that called for *densetsu* in much the same way as before, except now submitters were told to label their material "*chihō dōwa*." In the following month, selected entries were published under this same label.

50. *Dōwa* 2.6 (June 1921): 97.

51. *Kin no hoshi* 5.8 (Aug. 1923): 101. Due to the Kantō earthquake, winning entries were not published until January 1924.

52. The kinds of folk material selected by editors varied somewhat with each magazine. Ogawa Mimei's *Otogi no sekai* tended toward conventional *mukashi banashi* (folk tales), while *Kin no hoshi* concentrated on lesser-known oral narratives. See *Nihon jidō bungaku-shi*, 131. As Joan Ericson has pointed out, the early embrace of folktales as children's literature was "both emblematic of cultural identity and fundamental for the construction, through children, of national citizens." Obvious parallels can be drawn with the development of children's literature in other European nations, particularly Germany. See her Introduction to *A Rainbow in the Desert*, viii–x.

53. The six-volume series, titled *Hyōjun Nihon otogi bunko* (Standard Collection of Japanese Tales), was co-edited with Mori Ōgai and published between 1920 and 1921. The set included variants of traditional folk tales such as "Momotarō" and "Kachi-kachi yama," but also well-known *densetsu* and myths (*shinwa*). The cited passage comes from an early advertisement for the series in *Akai tori* 3.7 (July 1920).

54. The best examples of his regionalist work can be found in the collection *Kumano mairi* (Pilgrimage to Kumano, 1919), published in Tokyo. A few of the stories in the collection are based on childhood reminiscences, but most are retellings of regional folklore. Okino originally moved to Tokyo to attend seminary school in 1904 before moving there permanently in 1917.

55. de Certeau, *Heterologies*, 132.

56. The notion of "anachronistic space" comes from Anne McClintock's *Imperial Leather*, which draws it from Johannes Fabian. Anachronistic space is engendered by a view of history that spatializes time and renders peripheral regions as prehis-

toric, static, irrational, atavistic, and inherently out of place in the historical time of modernity (40–41). Here, I use it to refer to the process by which a nation's less developed areas are presented as spaces of tradition and as the site of an ethnic or cultural essence. The best study of how this process was carried out by ethnographers in Japan, particularly Yanagita Kunio, is still Marilyn Ivy's *Discourses of the Vanishing*.

57. Moretti, "Conjectures on World Literature," 64.

58. Like other women's magazines of the time, *Aikoku fujin* devoted the bulk of its pages to topics like child rearing and education, supplementing this with original *dōwa*. Manuscripts were solicited with the promise of up to five yen in payment. The magazine served as the monthly bulletin of the Women's Patriotic Association (Aikoku Fujin Kai), a conservative organization whose primary objectives consisted of providing care packages to departing troops and raising money for families of soldiers. Its monthly bulletin, which began publication in 1903, helped to support such activities and also became a mouthpiece for promoting conservative ideals amongst the middle- and upper-class women who were the organization's most prominent members. At its peak, it had nearly 3.5 million members. See *Aikoku fujin kai yonjūnen-shi*. Significantly, Miyazawa's mother and aunt were active members of the association's Iwate branch, a fact that may have influenced his decision to submit the story to this particular journal. He received four yen for the manuscript.

59. Although translation cannot do justice to the onomatopoetic qualities of the verse, in English it might look something like this: "Crunchy snow crunching, icy snow icing." The phrase both describes the hardness of the snow and uses alliteration to evoke the sound of walking upon that snow. I have chosen to retain the Japanese when referring to this refrain and its variations within the story. The original text for the opening verse is in *Kōhon Miyazawa Kenji zenshū*, vol. 11: 101. All quotations come from the story as originally published in *Aikoku fujin*.

60. See *Shokoku dōyō taizen*, 625. The full verse as it is listed here translates to, "*Katayuki kanko, shimiyuki shinko*, the peddler's kid wants a bride." As indication of how much folk and children's culture came to overlap in late Taishō, it is interesting to note that the volume was reprinted as *Nihon minyō taizen* (Collection of Japanese Folksongs) in 1926.

61. For further discussion of "improvisation" in the context of Miyazawa's fiction, see Andō Kyōko's chapter on "Kashiwabayashi no yoru" (Night of the Oak Forest) in *Miyazawa Kenji: "chikara" no kōzō*, 150–72. *Kaeuta* refers to the popular practice of altering the lyrics of a tune while retaining its original melody.

62. Incidentally, Miyazawa's initial foray into the world of *dōyō* was nothing if not conventional. He began writing them while in Tokyo and published his first in the September 1921 issue of *Aikoku fujin*. Titled "Ama no gawa" (Milky Way), it read, "Oh Milky Way / You can see the pebbles on its banks! / You can see the sand in its depths! / But no matter how long you look / The one thing you can't see is the water."

63. Their activities led to a veritable *dōyō* boom in which many of their fellow

poets participated. The movement became so popular that the Ministry of Education, which had until then steadfastly relied on moralistic *shōka* (songs) composed in the 1880s and popularized through official songbooks, relented to the trend and began including *dōyō* in its textbooks. See *Nihon jidō bungaku-shi*, 150–51.

64. See Hatanaka, *Dōyōron no keifu*, 41. Kitahara is cited as saying in 1923 that *shōgaku shōka* entirely ignore both the landscape and tradition of Japan. While most *shōka* were in fact created under the influence of foreign sources, Kitahara must have been aware that by the 1920s they had been so internalized by several generations of youth that they were as representative of Japanese popular culture as any song that could claim earlier origins.

65. Hatanaka observes that the style of Noguchi's *dōyō* relied on nostalgia-laden appropriations of the native place as a site of sadness and longing. It also tended toward the superficial, emphasizing "things" readily visible as opposed to the social relations that hovered beneath the surface. Ibid., 38.

66. Noguchi, *Dōyō tsukurikata mondō*, 148. One of his clearest statements on *kyōdo dōyō* can be found in *Kin no hoshi* 4.9 (Sept. 1922): 107–8.

67. Hatanaka, *Dōyōron no keifu*, 111.

68. The magazine, titled *Otento-san*, remained in publication just over a year. See Hatanaka, "Taishō-Shōwa ki ni okeru chihō no dōyō undō," 4–5. Awa is a region on the southwest shores of the Bōsō peninsula, in present-day Chiba Prefecture.

69. Miyazawa originally ran away to Tokyo in January with little notion of embarking on a literary career. In April, however, after a reconciliatory visit from his father, he began experimenting with free-verse poetry and urban literary sketches. Miyazawa's motivations for leaving centered around both family troubles and a newly found religious zeal for Tanaka Chigaku's Kokuchūkai, a new religion organized around devotion to Nichiren and the Lotus Sutra. He had joined the organization just two months before fleeing home. See Onda, "Miyazawa Kenji ni okeru Taishō jūnen no shukkyō to kitaku."

70. *Kōhon Miyazawa Kenji zenshū*, vol. 13: 214–15. The two books he refers to here are Tokuda Shūsei's *Shōsetsu no tsukurikata* (Tokyo: Shinchōsha, 1918) and Yatsunami Norikichi's *Sōsaku he no michi* (Tokyo: Kōdōkan, 1921). The story of Shimada Seijirō (1899–1930) is fascinating. Having dropped out of professional school and suffered through a number of odd jobs in his native Ishikawa Prefecture, he serialized a novel in a Kyoto Buddhist newspaper, which eventually led to an introduction to writer Ikuta Chōkō (1882–1936) in Tokyo. On Ikuta's recommendation, Shinchōsha agreed to publish Shimada's massive, four-part novel *Chijō* (On this Earth) in 1919. It sold far beyond expectations and at the age of twenty Shimada was hailed as a literary genius and the *bundan*'s new superstar. The four parts, published between 1919 and 1922, sold roughly 500,000 copies all together, providing him enough in royalties to set off on a trip around the world. In what signaled a new age for the business of literary production, publisher Kaizōsha responded in 1920 with *Shisen o koete* (Transcending the Line of Death) by Kagawa Toyohiko (1888–1960). Also by an as yet unknown author, it was the top-selling novel of the Taishō period.

71. *Kōhon Miyazawa Kenji zenshū*, vol. 13: 218. Beriberi is a medical condition, arising from a lack of vitamin B1 (thiamine), characterized by weight loss, emotional disturbances, weakness and swelling of the limbs, and periods of irregular heartbeat. It is common in those whose diets consist mainly of polished white rice.

72. The motives for the group's founding, along with the names of at least fifty supporters, were reported back home in the *Iwate Mainichi shinbun* (June 18, 1921): 3. Takuboku, whose stature as Iwate's premier poet had been well established by this time, was a key figure around which the place-based networking activities of Iwate natives were organized in the Taishō and early Shōwa periods.

73. The story was published in the April 1922 issue of *Fujin kōron*, a popular women's magazine.

74. de Certeau, *Heterologies*, 218.

75. What Fabian means by a "denial of coevalness" is "a persistent and systematic tendency to place the referent(s) of anthropology in a Time other than the present of the producer of anthropological discourse" (*Time and the Other*, 31). The tendency, in other words, to isolate and fence off different societies within a taxonomic and ultimately hierarchical frame. And because the taxonomist generally takes "a position on a temporal slope [that is] uphill, or upstream, from the object of his scientific desire," what results is "a concept of culture devoid of a theory of creativity or production," at least for those cultures in the unenviable position of being classified (ibid., 151, 62).

76. Miyazawa wrote two other stories in which foxes play central roles, "Tokkobe Torako" and "Tsuchigami to kitsune" (The Earth God and the Fox). Both invoke the idea of the fox as lying trickster, but in ways that complicate its conventional manifestation in folklore. The first looks at how the idea circulates as both truth and fiction in real historical time. The second presents a fox who lies to others in order to present himself as highly refined and cultured, and yet who carries the burden of knowing that his lies are both wrong and part of an inner compulsion he cannot resist.

Chapter Four

1. Miyazawa did not approach Tōkyōsha directly, but asked his younger brother to inquire for him. A brief account of Seiroku's visit can be found in *Shin kōhon Miyazawa Kenji zenshū*, vol. 16, part 2 (*nenpu hen*): 251–52. The company, established in 1907, began publication of its signature children's magazine, *Kodomo no kuni* (Child's Land), in January 1922. Directed at a fairly young audience, it was best known for the highly artistic children's paintings (*dōga*) that graced its cover. Ogawa Mimei and Hamada Hirosuke were occasional contributors. A member of the editorial staff at the company, a minor *dōwa* author by the name of Ono Hiroshi, was the one who agreed to meet with Miyazawa's brother before rejecting the manuscripts. Ono Hiroshi later worked as an editor and contributor for *Akai tori*.

2. Kuwahara, *"Akai tori" no jidai*, 360–61. Legend has it that Suzuki, upon seeing the manuscript sent to him by Miyazawa, said something to the effect of "it might be suitable for Russia, but not my magazine."

3. A thorough discussion of when and where "Iihatov" appears in Miyazawa's texts can be found in Yonechi Fumio's "Miyazawa Kenji no sōsaku chimei 'Iihatov' no yurai to henka ni kansuru chirigakuteki kōsatāsu."

4. The precise day of Chikamori's visit is uncertain, but it is believed to have fallen soon after December 10, the date of publication for his *Hae to ka to nomi* (Flies, Mosquitoes, and Fleas). He was likely in Hanamaki to promote this new textbook on pest control.

5. The advertisement for *Yama otoko*, inserted into editions of *Hae to ka to nomi*, contained both an excerpt from one of the stories and the projected publication date. See *Kōhon Miyazawa Kenji zenshū*, vol. 11: 387. While all this was occurring, Miyazawa was simultaneously pursuing the publishing option open to anyone with enough available funds: self-funded publication. Working with a local printer who convinced a Tokyo bookstore to sign on as publisher, he borrowed money on his own—and from family—to produce a thousand copies of the poetry volume *Spring and Asura* in April 1924. Most of the money came from a *nattō* (fermented soybean) producer. Despite its humble origins, the volume was more successful than the *dōwa* collection because of its greater access to Tokyo distribution and media channels. Three months after its publication, it garnered a positive review in the *Yomiuri shinbun* from Dadaist critic Tsuji Jun (1884–1944), reprinted in *Kōhon Miyazawa Kenji zenshū*, vol. 14: 1077–81.

6. *Kōhon Miyazawa Kenji zenshū*, vol. 11: 390. The advertisement appeared in a textbook on the cultivation of pest-resistant chrysanthemums, a project that Oikawa took on, in part, as a means to fund the publication of Miyazawa's book. See Mori, "*Chūmon no ōi ryōriten*," 40–41.

7. Oikawa's contract with Yoshida required that 800 yen be paid at least twenty days before the publication date, a truly overwhelming figure for a small-time outfit like his. Scrambling to put the funds together, he sent off what few textbooks were in the company's catalogue to agricultural schools across Japan. As the money trickled in (books in its catalogue ranged in price from sixty sen to slightly under two yen), Oikawa transferred the needed amount over a two-month period. Just as things looked to be in the clear, however, Yoshida asked for another 300 yen, forcing Oikawa to ask a former teacher for a loan. See Oikawa, "*Chūmon no ōi ryōriten shiki*," 74–77. There he recalls that the loan amount was equal to what it would cost to build a new house. In order to pay back the loan, Miyazawa later purchased 200 volumes of the book with money borrowed from his father.

8. After this, Oikawa seems to have given up on all marketing. Of the three books that his company published in 1925, only one contained a list of its other publications. Instead of an entry for the *dōwa* collection, however, there is a listing for Miyazawa's *Spring and Asura*, a project with which Oikawa had never been involved. See the back matter of *Kachikubyō to sono taisaku* (Measures against Livestock Illness), published in June 1925. It is possible, of course, that Oikawa inserted advertisement postcards and flyers into these publications.

9. Mori, "*Chūmon no ōi ryōriten*," 40. Marks left by the printer on the one extant copy indicate that printing costs came to just over thirty yen. It is unknown

how exactly they were distributed, but one was found in a copy of another Tōryō Shuppanbu publication. (Personal conversation with Sugiura Shizuka.) In addition to this pamphlet, Oikawa also produced a postcard and an abbreviated version of the pamphlet. Four of Morioka's most prominent bookstores were listed on this shorter version, suggesting that it was aimed at local buyers.

10. *Kōhon Miyazawa Kenji zenshū*, vol. 11: 388.

11. Ibid., 388–89. I return to address the concept of "mental-image sketch" in Chapter Seven. Here, it is enough to note that Miyazawa saw it as an objective in-scription of external phenomena as they appear in the mind at a specific temporal and spatial instant. See Sugiura, *Miyazawa Kenji: meimetsu suru haru to shura*, 24–26.

12. It was common for Miyazawa to affix to a particular work the date corre-sponding to its moment of inception. Such dates are particularly prominent in his poetry. Even when a poem was edited to the point that it hardly resembled earlier versions, the date attached often remained unchanged, indicating how important for him was the link between the idea for a sketch and its original moment of inscription. As for the tales included in the *dōwa* volume, a lack of extant manu-scripts prevents us from knowing the extent to which Miyazawa edited them before including them in the volume. Given that he wrote the preface so soon after his visit with Chikamori, however, we can assume the stories were fairly complete by late 1923.

13. The exact date of his return is yet to be resolved. Onda Itsuo concludes that he was back in Hanamaki by August, though much of the analysis is based on a biographical reading of other fictional works. He does, however, report that when he put the question to Miyazawa's younger sister Shige in 1961, she said that her brother had returned in August. But Shige also informed Mori Sōichi that Toshiko, after coming down with a fever in August, began coughing blood in early Septem-ber. Fearing the worst, it was *then* that Miyazawa was called back home. See Mori, *Miyazawa Kenji no shōzō*, 226.

14. Derrida, *On the Name*, xiv.

15. Jameson, *The Prison-House of Language*, 30.

16. *Den'en* was by the 1920s dispersed over a wide nexus of discourses. Not only popular with the naturalist writers of Taishō, who were inclined to represent *den'en* as a site of retreat from the urban way of life, the word was also woven into dis-courses of urban planning from late Meiji onward (e.g., *den'en-toshi*, or the gar-den city). An obvious exception to its positive evocation by writers is Sato Haruo's *Den'en no yūutsu* (Rural Melancholy, 1919). Even here, however, the negative assess-ment of rural living comes only after the narrator's initial hope of finding an ideal urban retreat has faded.

17. Williams, *The Country and the City*. As for the affinity of *den'en* and *toshi* at the time Miyazawa was writing, consider titles like *Toshi oyobi den'en no kyōiku* (Ed-ucation in the City and Country, 1913), *Toshi yori den'en e* (From City to Country, 1915), Noguchi Ujō's *Tokai to den'en* (City and Country, 1919), a special July issue of *Chūō kōron* titled *Toshi to den'en* (1921), Chikamatsu Shūkō's *Tokai to den'en* (City and Country, 1923), and *Toshi ka den'en ka* (City or Country? 1924).

18. *Alice's Adventures in Wonderland* had by 1923 appeared in nearly eight separate translations according to *Jidō bungaku honyaku sakuhin sōran*, vol. 1. Andersen's tales were translated extensively from the 1890s, the first Japanese rendition of "Lille Claus og Store Claus" appearing in 1891 as Ozaki Kōyō's "Futari Mukusuke" (The Two Mukusukes). Tolstoy's "Ivan the Fool" was first translated by Uchida Roan in 1906. Tagore's work appeared in numerous translations from 1915 onward, two years after his selection for the Nobel Prize in literature and a year before his four-month sojourn in Japan. *The Crescent Moon* was translated as a collection of children's poems in 1915 by Mashino Saburō and published as *Shintsuki*.

19. The duality of "Iihatov" as a space both separate from reality and grounded in a specific region has also been pointed out by Sugiura in *Miyazawa Kenji*, 146–56.

20. One of the more popular theories put forth by scholars argues that the word is a combination of three elements: the older kana spelling of Iwate (the *iha* of *Ihate*), an Esperanto-like variation of the syllable *te* (changes into *to*), and a German suffix indicating place (*vo*)—thus Iha-to-vo. Making the task of deducing its origins even more complicated is the fact that Miyazawa altered the notation of the word through his career. I have chosen to stick with "Iihatov" here as it most closely approximates the notation used in the title of the *dōwa* collection.

21. Kären Wigen writes on the cultural history of the Shinano highlands in "Discovering the Japanese Alps." Walter Weston coined the term in his landmark *Mountaineering and Exploration in the Japanese Alps* from 1896, but it was geographer Shiga Shigetaka (1863–1927) and amateur climber Kojima Usui (1874–1948) who helped to cement its place in the cultural imaginary. Shiga is also responsible for first referring to the Kiso River as the Rhine of Japan. This eagerness to reenvision native landscapes through foreign names and images is humorously parodied by Natsume Sōseki in his 1906 novel *Botchan*. The narrator, a Tokyo-born gentleman teaching in the provinces, finds ridiculous the attempts of some locals to see in a small, rocky, pine-covered island the elements of a painting by English Romantic painter Joseph Turner. Even more laughable and annoying is their suggestion to rename the barren pile of rock "Turner Island."

22. Foucault, *The Archaeology of Knowledge and the Discourse on Language*, 99.

23. Following the work of Rogers Brubaker and Frederick Cooper, I use "identification" to highlight the processual and contextual nature of the act, to foreground the agency of the social actors involved, and to avoid the essentialist traps created by a term such as "identity." See their "Beyond 'identity.'"

24. Bakhtin, "Discourse in the Novel," 276.

25. On the terms *problematic* and *thematic*, see chap. 2 in *Nationalist Thought and the Colonial World: A Derivative Discourse?* published in 1986 and later compiled in the *Partha Chatterjee Omnibus*.

26. Chatterjee, *Nationalist Thought and the Colonial World*, 42.

27. In earlier years, the prefecture went by the name of Morioka, the domainal capital once occupied by the ruling Nanbu clan. Convinced that this name would not allow the prefecture to break free from the Nanbu clan's legacy, however, government officials replaced it with the name of the county in which Morioka was

located. The use of Iwate itself as a place name dates to the late tenth century. See *Kadokawa Nihon chimei daijiten*, vol. 3: 118 and 121.

28. Kawanishi Hidemichi charts the history of "Tōhoku" as a toponym in his *Tōhoku: tsukurareta ikyō*, x. He writes that by the 1880s and 1890s, Ōu and Tōhoku were used interchangeably even as some ambiguity remained as to what geopolitical entities were included under the name. Niigata was often included and also the southern part of Hokkaidō.

29. Ibid., 11–12. Such stereotypes were prevalent from well before the Restoration.

30. Ibid., 19–20. The Meiji emperor embarked on his first tour of the northeast in 1876, signaling government interest in developing the region. That same year, Chief of Internal Affairs Ōkubo Toshimichi sent the Ministry of Finance a list of measures for supporting development in the region. Ōkubo was assassinated, however, before he could help to see any of the measures through.

31. Kawanishi cites numerous articles from the 1880s and 1890s from area newspapers and journals. Perhaps the best example of such regionalist rhetoric comes from Hangai Seiju, a Fukushima native and textile industrialist who believed that the region's development must come *before* that of Hokkaidō, Taiwan, or Korea. See *Shōrai no Tōhoku*, 5–9. This important work is discussed further by Kawanishi in ibid., 114–18.

32. Ibid., 51–55. For example, in an 1889 editorial in Aomori's *Tōōu nippō*, the gentlemen of Tōhoku are compared to those of Japan's southwestern regions and deemed better capable of leading the nation under the emperor, and of thus transforming Tōhoku into the new center of Japan. Another example of a call for a second Restoration can be found in Kayahara Rentarō's "Tōhoku taiseiron" (The Current Situation in Tōhoku, 1895). In the essay, which was first serialized in several Tōhoku newspapers and journals, he urges the six prefectures to unite under their common qualities and begin a second Restoration (*dai ni ishin*) (ibid., 107–10).

33. On the importance of regional histories for telling a more "bifurcated history" of the nation and national identity, see Duara, *Rescuing History from the Nation*, 177–204.

34. Plans for rail lines that would have bolstered development also had to be scrapped. See *Iwate-ken no rekishi*, 284–86.

35. Yamashita, *Shōwa tōhoku daikyōsaku*, 34.

36. This was the city of Sendai. Incidentally, Hokkaidō could lay claim to three. See Kawanishi, *Tōhoku: tsukurareta ikyō*, 190.

37. The case of the regional press forces a reconsideration of the causal link drawn by Benedict Anderson between print capitalism (newspaper consumption) and the rise of an "imagined community" inherently *national* in character. See *Imagined Communities*, 22–36. Anderson focuses on the novel and newspaper as forms of print that "provided the technical means for 're-presenting' the *kind* of imagined community that is the nation" (25, his emphasis). I agree on this point, but his tendency to go directly to the level of the nation hides from view other possible layers of spatial identification. For a comparative study of the regional press as a determinant of subnational identity, see Moores, "The French Press and Regional Identity."

38. Praiseworthy objects included everything from locally bred horses, silk cocoons, and Nanbu ironware, to famous places like Hiraizumi, Mt. Iwate, and the newly branded Tōhoku Alps. Although rarer, one can also find statements praising the admirable qualities of Iwate's citizens. For example, the director of the Japan Society of Industry was impressed by the desire for knowledge displayed by Iwate folk at an exhibition in Morioka. See "Chishikiyoku ni moyuru tanomoshii Iwate kenmin," *Iwate nippō*, June 23, 1921: 5.

39. In November 1921, the assassination of Hara, arguably Iwate's most famous native-born politician, led to an outpouring of regionally inflected responses in the pages of the *Iwate nippō*. Headlines from the 6th included, "The death of this great man is a loss to our nation; not one inhabitant of his native Iwate is without limitless sorrow," and "News of Prime Minister Hara's tragedy shocks every resident of Iwate." A few days later, Hara was lauded by a local notable as the greatest hero of Tōhoku since the nation's founding, his death decried as a loss to Japan and the world. See *Iwate nippō*, Nov. 6: 1921: 2 and 14; also "Hara-shi wa makoto ni Tōhoku daihyō ijin," *Iwate nippō*, Nov. 10, 1921: 3.

40. The Hokkaidō Exposition, held to celebrate the fiftieth anniversary of the island's official colonization, prompted several articles on the need for Tōhoku and Iwate to take advantage of the celebration. One article pitted the Tōhoku region against the Hokuriku region, viewing the exposition as a chance to reclaim ground in the competition for commercial influence over Hokkaidō. See "Ōu ka, Hokuriku ka," *Iwate nippō*, Feb. 24, 1918: 3. A series of editorials also urged the citizens of Iwate to utilize the event as a way to publicize the prefecture and introduce it to other Japanese. In the first of these, the author—fearing that the winds of Taishō might pass over "our Iwate" and head to nearby prefectures—called upon residents to plan for the oncoming surge of visitors to the exposition, both for the sake of Iwate's cultural growth and its industrial development. "Hokkaihaku no riyō," *Iwate nippō*, Feb. 26, 1918: 1.

41. The decision to make the *Iwate nippō* my primary archival source in this chapter follows in the footsteps of recent historical scholarship that utilizes provincial sources not simply to add to the historical record, but to rethink "Japanese modernity" from a position other than that of the nation-state. See, for instance, Hanes, *The City as Subject*; Tamanoi, *Under the Shadow of Nationalism*; and Wigen, *The Making of a Japanese Periphery*.

42. The first regional papers appeared in 1870, two years after the *Yokohama Mainichi shinbun* began publication. In Tōhoku, they appeared as early as 1873 but remained, as elsewhere, virtual mouthpieces for the prefectural government. They were also constrained by limited circulation, infrequent print runs, and financial instability. With the rise of the People's Rights movement in the early 1880s, however, regional newspapers found a new sense of purpose and became a key launching pad for debates on the future of the national government. On the early Tōhoku press, see Toyoda, *Tōhoku no rekishi*, vol. 3: 243–54.

43. Huffman, *Creating a Public*, chap. 8. Newspapers in Tokyo and Osaka were naturally the first to move in this direction, but as Huffman notes, "even in the

provinces, in fact, news and readability were becoming the journalistic norm in these years, although most readers and publishers there would remain too poor, or too restricted by political connections, to allow for thoroughgoing commercialism until the Shōwa era" (246).

44. This was a period of intense competition and rapid expansion of regional media, as noted by Nagamine in *"Dokusho kokumin" no tanjō*, 29. Small commercial newspapers popped up all over the country, some short-lived and some surviving to become the dominant papers in their region. In Iwate alone, eight newspapers went into publication between 1897 and 1907. See *Iwate nippō hyakujūnen-shi*, 140. A list of the major regional papers started in this decade is in Ono, *Nihon shinbun hattatsu-shi*, 281–83.

45. The *Nippō* also had to keep up with its foremost local rival, the *Iwate Mainichi shinbun*. Established by prefectural assemblyman Takahashi Kitarō in 1899, and with the financial and political backing of future prime minister Hara Kei, it remained the *Nippō*'s main competitor until the early 1920s.

46. See *Iwate nippō hyakujūnen-shi* and *Chihōbetsu Nihon shinbun-shi*, 21–29. With Iwate's total population hovering around 900,000 in late Taishō, a circulation of 10,000 does not seem like much. Based on a total number of households of roughly 130,000 in 1920 (seventy percent of which were registered as farming households), the *Nippō*'s circulation accounts for just under seven percent. See *Iwate tōkeisho: 1920*. The number 10,000 refers to households, however, not to individual readers, and thus is not an accurate reflection of the total number of people through whose hands the paper passed. Moreover, those reading the paper were likely the ones most capable of influencing the political and economic course of the region. The next two largest newspapers, the *Mainichi* and the *Iwate Nichinichi shinbun*, had circulations of 7,500 and 3,500 respectively. *Iwate-ken shi*, vol. 10: 673.

47. Huffman, *Creating a Public*, 247.

48. As late as 1922, Ono Hideo characterized the opposition between the central and provincial press as one between a powerfully homogenizing form of media and media struggling to keep regional particularities from vanishing. See Ono, *Nihon shinbun hattatsu-shi*, 472–81.

49. Nitobe Inazō, "Tōhoku hatten no zentei," in *Iwate gakuji gahō* 974 (Oct. 31, 1914): 4.

50. Asano, *Tōhoku oyobi Tōhokujin*, 227–30. The work was endorsed by all six prefectural governors.

51. Oshikawa Masayoshi, "Tōhokujin to kinbenryoku," *Iwate nippō*, July 17, 1912: 1. Oshikawa was originally born in Ehime Prefecture and moved to Sendai in 1886 as a Protestant missionary.

52. See the series of essays "Danketsu no chikara," *Iwate nippō*, May 20–25, 1923, and the editorial "Tōhokujin wa danketsushin ni toboshii," Feb. 3, 1924: 2.

53. That this rhetoric had a prominent place in discourse on Tōhoku is evidenced by the fact that some tried to take it to task in the pages of the *Nippō*. See for example "Tōhoku no kyōsaku to kikō to no kankei wo ronji," *Iwate nippō*, May 11, 1915: 1. Also "Tōhoku shinkōsaku," *Iwate nippō*, Sept. 23, 1915: 1. Both articles try

to show that the rhetoric of an unblessed environment only holds because of the region's reliance on rice agriculture, which is not suited to the climate.

54. "Ken no kaihatsu," *Iwate nippō*, June 14, 1924: 2.

55. Tamari, *Tōhoku shinkōsaku*, 6–7.

56. Hangai, *Shōrai no Tōhoku*, 8–9.

57. Asano, "Saikin ni okeru Tōhoku chihō no keizai jōtai," in *Tōhoku nippon* 4.8 (April 1920): 4. Asano was actually the chief editor of this journal, which he founded in 1916 to provide a forum for ideas on how to promote development in Tōhoku.

58. Satō Shōsuke, "Tōhoku shinkōsaku ni tsuite," in *Tōhoku nippon* 4.8 (April 1920): 1. Satō, born in Hanamaki in 1856, studied at the Sapporo School of Agriculture in the 1870s before going to America and Europe in the 1880s to earn his doctoral degree.

59. For the last two items, see Takano Tohacchō, "Honken shisōkai no ichinen kan," *Iwate nippō*, Jan. 1, 1918: 9, and "Fuguteki bunka shisetsu to keiji atsukai no Tōhoku," *Iwate nippō*, Feb. 18, 1923: 3. In the latter, the author wonders why Hokkaidō is so much further ahead in its development of communications infrastructure despite its harsher environment.

60. The area known as "Ura Nihon" (lit., backside of Japan), which comprised several prefectures that face the Japan Sea (Niigata, Fukui, Ishikawa, Toyama), was also largely defined in the early twentieth century by its state of underdevelopment. Abe Tsunehisa examines the region's place in the popular imagination in *"Ura Nihon" wa ika ni tsukurareta ka*.

61. This strain of commentary is best symbolized by the Local Improvement movement (*chihō kairyō undō*), a policy initiative undertaken by the Home Ministry in 1909, which aimed to bring a diverse body of rural associations into closer ideological alignment with national and local governments. See Pyle, "The Technology of Japanese Nationalism."

62. For more on the history of the group, see Iwamoto, *Tōhoku kaihatsu 120 nen*, 61–66, 73–75; also Yoshiike, *Tōhoku sangyō shinkō kōen-shū*, 1–23. The group is not to be confused with the *Tōhoku shinkō* movement of the 1930s, which was a concerted and more effective set of policies implemented by the national government.

63. This notion of Tōhoku as wedded to the nation-state in a kind of semicolonial relationship goes back almost to the birth of the modern state itself. In 1882, an official in Aomori likened its relation to the central government as that of India to Britain (Kawanishi, *Tōhoku: tsukurareta ikkyō*, 40–42). Later, some would draw comparisons with Scotland, suggesting that the people of the two regions shared a similar spirit, environment, and political relationship to the ruling order. Tōhoku residents were encouraged to emulate the Scots in their cultural accomplishments and in their display of regional pride (ibid., 163). In 1914, a lecture on the personal character of the Scots was given by the director of Tōhoku Imperial University and reproduced in *Iwate gakuji gahō* 965 (June 15): 33–41. The analogy was also favored by American missionaries in an account of the region titled *Tōhoku: The Scotland of Japan* (1918).

64. Tamari, *Tōhoku shinkōsaku*, 9. Hangai Seiju also professed anger at the government's neglect of Tōhoku in contrast with the treatment afforded to Taiwan and Manchuria. See *Shōrai no Tōhoku*, 227–28.

65. "Nosaka gishi no Tōhokukan," *Iwate nippō*, May 31, 1912: 2.

66. Satō Shōsuke, "Tōhoku no shinkō," *Iwate nippō*, Oct. 31, 1915: 2.

67. "Tōhoku no shinkō," *Iwate nippō*, Nov. 6, 1915: 2. This solution was also put forth by Asano Gengo in *Tōhoku oyobi Tōhokujin*, where he proposed that harder-working farmers be moved into the region (226). In 1928, the contributor to a volume on Tōhoku development also made reference to population issues using the language of internal colonization. See Kobayashi, "Shizen to jin'i," 39. In the early days of the Tōhoku Shinkō Kai, members were in fact convinced that the best way forward was to treat the region as an internal colony and promote economic policies accordingly. Iwamoto, *Tōhoku kaihatsu 120 nen*, 63–64.

68. One historian felt that the story of how "our ancestors" assimilated the indigenous Emishi might become a manual for present-day colonization policy: "The Tōhoku of today is now like the Kinki region [Nara, Kyoto] of long ago. And the Tōhoku of old is like the Manmō region [Manchuria and Inner Mongolia] of today." See Tsuji Zennosuke's preface in Takeuchi Unpei's *Tōhoku kaihatsu-shi*.

69. Akita, "Tōhoku bunka no tokuchō ni tsuite," 29.

70. In Japan, as Kären Wigen has pointed out, these alternate regional histories tended to be "weak" and were typically articulated within a nationalist framework. She refers to them as weak in the sense that they were mild, apolitical inflections of a shared national identity and thus never became the basis of a regional autonomy movement. See "Constructing Shinano," 235–36.

71. Iwamoto, *Tōhoku kaihatsu 120 nen*, 59–61. Hangai Seiju was one of the earliest to proclaim that rice agriculture was unsuited to the Tōhoku region. See *Shōrai no Tōhoku*, 96–97.

72. Satō, *Tōhoku no jigyō*.

73. An instructive example of how this vision was deployed by experts can be found in Okada Takematsu, "Tōhoku no fūdo," *Iwate nippō*, Mar. 26, 1924, late ed.: 1. Okada directed the Central Meteorological Observatory in Tokyo and was in Morioka to lecture on the climatic disadvantages faced by the region and on how residents might be able to overcome them. On Seki's scientific accomplishments, see Kamei, "Seki Toyotarō to Miyazawa Kenji."

74. Kuroda, "Tōhoku kankōkyaku yūin saku."

75. See, for example, "Iwate keitetsu no zentsū," Nov. 28, 1915: 1; "Kōtsū kikan no kanbi wa yagate keizaiteki kakumei o," Feb. 5, 1920: 2; and "Tōhoku shinkō no kagi wa kōtsū kikan no kanbi," Sept. 11, 1921: 5.

76. Suzuki Katsujirō, "Toshokan ni hairu no kotoba," *Iwate nippō*, Feb. 18, 1923: 3.

77. Soja, *Postmodern Geographies*, 57. For Soja, the workings of this dialectic are particularly evident in the way that class relations are determined by and also determine (or even radically alter) the continual division of physical space into dominant centers and subordinate peripheries under capitalism. Social and spatial relations are thus not only homologous in his mind, but also dialectically inseparable (78).

78. Lefebvre, *The Production of Space*, 53.

79. The absence of "Tōhoku" in the text of the advertisement, and its minimal presence in Miyazawa's total oeuvre, is striking given its overall significance in popular discourse, especially considering that it was a place name he surely encountered often as an agricultural school student in Morioka, as a local teacher, as an official geological surveyor, and as member of a politically active family.

80. As was his habit, Miyazawa affixed dates to most of the drafts in this volume. Roughly half were given a date from 1924. Sugiura Shizuka notes, however, that many of the poems in the volume were edited and re-edited between the time of their "original" inscription in 1924 and the author's death in 1933 (*Miyazawa Kenji*, 108, 131–32).

81. *Nassen* refers to a style of dyeing, popular since Edo, in which colors are painted onto stenciled cloth in multiple layers. The poems mentioned here have been given the following titles in the collected works: "25—Sōshun dokuhaku—senkugata A" (25—Monologue in Early Spring—Draft A), "75—Kitakami sanchi no haru—senkugata" (75—Spring in the Kitakami Highlands—Draft), "93—Futari onnaji soiu kitaina funsō de—senkugata" (93—The Two Wore the Same Strange Costume—Draft), and "155—Atatakaku fukunda minami no kaze ga—senkugata" (155—A Warm South Wind—Draft).

82. Hokkaidō was a popular choice for these school excursions in the Tōhoku region. Miyazawa himself went several times while a student in Morioka.

83. Miyazawa, "Shūgaku ryokō fukumeisho" (Report on the School Trip), *Shin kōhon Miyazawa Kenji zenshū*, vol. 14: 64. Miyazawa too expressed an acute awareness of this need to improve and industrialize outmoded forms of labor. Earlier the same day, after visiting the Sapporo bottling plant, he could not help but wonder why farming had not made similar gains in reducing the physical hardship and long hours of agricultural labor. "After all, is there anything humans can't accomplish when they put their mind to it? . . . Couldn't we build a rectangular, high-density planting machine, or equipment for concentrating and storing the rays of the sun? . . . Even as we preserve what's good about the old customs and train people to work diligently, we cannot let ourselves be satisfied with farming's older modes" (64).

84. Ibid., 65. It goes without saying that Miyazawa's uncritical praise for the diorama willfully ignores Hokkaidō's previous inhabitants, in what amounts to an ahistorical vision conforming to the worst conceits of colonialist discourse. It is a vision all the more striking in light of several of his contemporary stories that exhibit an acute awareness of the colonized Other (both human and nonhuman) as a speaking subject with the legitimate right to react violently against outside oppression. The contradiction is perhaps indicative of how powerful was the rhetoric of internal colonization, and of feeling left behind, that we see in other local media of the time.

85. Ibid., 66. Michinoku was another name for the Tokugawa-era province of Oku, which made up the eastern half of what is today Tōhoku. Its use here deliberately reinforces the sense of an antiquated past. "Skimmed milk" appears in English

in the original text. Editors believe it was a mistaken spelling of "skim milk." It may well refer, however, to a milk whose cream has been skimmed from the top.

86. See Lefebvre, *The Production of Space*; Soja, *Postmodern Geographies*; Harvey, *The Condition of Postmodernity* and "From Space to Place and Back Again"; Massey, *Space, Place, and Gender* and *For Space*.

87. Indeed, ideology, which relies heavily on narrative, is considered by Lefebvre to "achieve consistency" and take root *only* by intervening directly, and often violently, in social space and its production. Lefebvre, *The Production of Space*, 44. He goes on to say that "ideology *per se* might well be said to consist primarily in a discourse upon social space."

88. Edward Kamens has written extensively on the function of poetic place names in premodern Japan. See *Utamakura, Allusion, and Intertextuality in Traditional Japanese Poetry*. William Cronon discusses the influence of "the sublime" on American notions of wilderness, and actions taken to preserve this wilderness, in his "The Trouble with Wilderness; or, Getting Back to the Wrong Nature."

89. On the powerful effect Hardy's "partly-real, partly dream-country" had on the English cultural imaginary, see Pite, *Hardy's Geography*, 1.

90. Harvey, *The Condition of Postmodernity*, 271–73.

91. Kikuchi had a friend who worked for the magazine and who hailed from the same town in Iwate. He apparently sent off a copy of the book to Suzuki along with his own design for the advertisement, but did not mention how he might pay for it. Suzuki did not look kindly on this but decided to run the ad anyway. It was likely Kikuchi's friend who had the final say in placing the ad. See Horio, "*Chūmon no ōi ryōriten* kankō goro makki," 68–73.

92. A survey of *Akai tori* and other popular *dōwa* magazines through the year 1925 suggests that this was the only instance of "Tōhoku" to appear in any advertisement. Drawing on the exotic appeal of a seemingly foreign place, however, was not uncommon. One can find instances in advertisements for Tōson's *dōwa* collection *Furusato*, in the title of Okino's *Kumano mairi*, and in advertisements for various collections of Russian tales.

93. Interestingly, an ad from December 1924, printed in the regional education journal *Iwate kyōiku*, contains some of the same language as the *Akai tori* ad, including "splendid yacht." Tōhoku, however, is nowhere to be found. Instead, we find the phrase "Iihatov is Japan's Iwate Prefecture as a dreamland." If this was Kikuchi's original design for the ad, then it seems likely that the definition of "Iihatov" was intentionally cut by editors at *Akai tori*.

Chapter Five

1. *Oxford English Dictionary*, 2nd ed., 1989.

2. The manuscript can be dated with such accuracy because it exists as a handwritten copy made by one of Miyazawa's students at the time. Miyazawa routinely paid students to recopy his manuscripts as a pretext for offering them sorely needed financial assistance. As is the case with many of his extant manuscripts, it is par-

tially incomplete. Its first appearance in print was in a 1940 edition of his collected works. See Tsuzukihashi, "'Kaze no Matasaburō' shōron," 47.

3. This second version, assembled posthumously from several incomplete manuscripts, tells the story of a group of rural schoolchildren whose lives are temporarily disrupted by the appearance of a peculiar transfer student named Takada Saburō. The children embark on a series of fantastic adventures with Takada—who reacts strangely whenever the wind blows—through the Iwate countryside and experience a number of inexplicable, weather-related events. The cinematic adaptation, directed by Shima Kōji and produced by Nikkatsu at their Tama Studio, was shown in major cities across Japan as well as the larger empire. For a discussion of the film within the context of wartime ideology and the generous backing given to it by the Ministry of Education, see Yonemura, *Miyazawa Kenji o tsukutta otokotachi*, chap. 3.

4. *Kōhon Miyazawa Kenji zenshū*, vol. 8: 6–7.

5. Even before entering the classroom, however, we see the instruments of disciplinary training at work. In a routine that would have been common, if lengthier and more intense, at schools of the time, we find the teacher employing the methods of *signalization* (the whistle blow) and *partitioning* (the lining-up into rows). The first refers to a relation between the master and the student in which the latter is trained to respond automatically to a prearranged system of signals and codes. The second refers to the creation of a serialized, or hierarchical, space by assigning individuals to specific positions (the students are lined up by grade, in this case), thus allowing for easier supervision of each individual. These terms are taken from Michel Foucault's *Discipline and Punish*, 166, 147. A more complete analysis of the classroom space is provided by Yahata Yō in *Miyazawa Kenji no kyōikuron*, 201–10.

6. The context makes it clear that Matasaburō was doing something to attract the students' attention, but a gap in the manuscript at this point makes it impossible to know exactly what.

7. According to Hara Shirō, "Kaze no Saburō" was common in Niigata as both the name for a local wind spirit and as that by which residents referred to the wind that blew on the ominous 210th Day (see the following note). Along with its appearance in local folklore, there are also examples of its use in children's songs native to Niigata and neighboring Yamagata Prefecture. Both lie to the immediate southwest of Iwate. See his *Shin Miyazawa Kenji goi jiten*, 140. Hara suggests that the addition of the ideograph *mata* to the name—signifying the idea of again, also, or another—served a rhythmical effect while also imparting a sense of difference from the Saburō of local legend (i.e., another "Kaze no Saburō").

8. The 210th Day (*nihyakutōka*), which was counted from the start of the lunar spring and fell roughly on September 1, marked an auspicious period in the traditional calendar (of which it was an official part from the late 1600s). Late-blooming rice generally flowered at this time and was thus susceptible to powerful winds and typhoons that would blow the tiny flowers from their stalks and devastate the harvest. To ward off such calamity, "wind festivals" were held on this day in some parts of Japan. The 220th Day (*nihyakuhatsuka*), also part of the official calendar, was considered auspicious for the same reasons. The fact that Matasaburō arrives on

the 210th Day, and also tells of his intended departure on the 220th Day, is thus a direct reference to this anxiety-filled period in the agricultural cycle.

9. The song they sing is an altered version of the following folk song, said to be unique to Iwate: "Come on wind, come blowing down; Come on wind, blow the seeds on down; Come on wind, blow from the ocean's edge." Miyazawa includes part of this song verbatim, but also substitutes "Matasaburō" for "wind" and inserts several improvised verses of his own.

10. *Kama'itachi* refers to a tiny whirlwind that creates a small laceration in the skin wherever it comes into contact with the body. In parts of central Japan where these winds occur with great frequency in the winter months, locals once believed the cut to be the mischievous work of a sickle-wielding, weasel-like goblin. By the modern era, however, a more scientific explanation had developed. It was reasoned that the vacuum at the center of the whirlwind, upon touching the body, eliminated all external air pressure and thus allowed blood at the surface to rise up quickly and break the skin. This, in fact, is the explanation given by Matasaburō when he discusses *kama'itachi* with the children. At present, it is believed that the cut occurs due to a quick change in skin temperature induced by the wind.

11. The Beaufort Wind Scale was devised by British admiral Sir Francis Beaufort in 1805 as a means to estimate wind speed based solely on visual cues (e.g., the shape of the waves, the motion of tree branches). The scale runs from 0 to 12, with "calm" being the lowest and "hurricane" the highest. Rather than refer to the scale directly, Miyazawa embeds terminology associated with it into the dialogue between the Chinese meteorologist and his assistant. Every time Matasaburō passes, the assistant tries with little success to rate his strength, thinking it first to be a "Hurricane Wind" (*gufū*), or a level twelve on the scale, and then a "Violent Storm Wind" (*bōfū*), or a level eleven.

12. George Hidy offers an overview of the various theories of general circulation in *The Winds*, 82–88. Also see Grotjahn, *Global Atmospheric Circulations*, 6–14.

13. The primer, titled *Shōgaku rika* (Elementary School Science), is reprinted in *Nihon kyōkasho taikei*, vol. 23 (1966). The cited passage can be found on pp. 420–21.

14. See Kusano and Nakamura, *Kikō kyōkasho*, 22–39. We know that this text was assigned to Miyazawa's students because it is listed in the schedule and roster printed by the school in 1923. See *Iwate-ken Hanamaki nōgakkō ichiranhyō*.

15. Fukuzawa's text was an attempt to introduce popular audiences to the basic principles of Western science by explaining natural phenomena in ways appealing to native sensibilities. Notably, he devoted a section to the wind in which he explained the fundamental laws of wind movement (e.g., between cooler and warmer bodies of air, between land and sea) and suggested several experiments designed for the Japanese home. See *Nihon kyōkasho taikei*, vol. 21: 36–38. For a critical study of the work, see Sakurai, *Fukuzawa Yukichi no "kagaku no susume."*

16. Ishii, *Rika jūnikagetsu, dai kyū getsu.*

17. The experiment, significantly, is the same as that suggested by Fukuzawa in his *Kyūri-zukai*. It involves three candles being placed, each at a different height, alongside the door frame where a large and small tatami room adjoin one another.

With the sliding doors closed, the smaller room is then heated. Once sufficiently warm, a single door panel is slid back and, if all has been done correctly, the flames of the top and bottom candles will begin to blow in opposite directions and create a miniature model of general air flow.

18. "Stories of Nature" (*Shizen no hanashi*) refers to a nine-volume series published by Meguro Shoten in 1923. It included such titles as *Taiyō, tsuki, hoshi* (Sun, Moon, Stars), *Kūki, mizu, hi* (Air, Water, and Fire), and *Yama, kawa, umi* (Mountains, Rivers, and Ocean). Most of these volumes were into their seventh printing by July of the following year. "Science Fairy Tales" (*Rika dōwa*) refers to a six-volume series published by Jirūsha in 1924. Oriented more toward the biological sciences, it included volumes on birds, insects, animals, and forests. The final title, *Kodomo no kikitagaru omoshiroi kagaku no hanashi*, belongs to a single edition of science stories published in 1922 by Seibundō. Its primary author, Harada Mitsuo, was responsible for a previous multivolume series of "Stories That Children Want to Hear" dealing with astronomy, electricity, chemical engineering, and other advanced subjects.

19. Yoshizawa, *Kumo, ame, kaze*, 214–64. Like most of the volumes in the "Stories of Nature" series, this volume too was in its seventh printing by 1924.

20. Ishii, *Rika jūnikagetsu, dai kyū getsu*, 1 (emphasis added).

21. Ibid., 5.

22. Kusano and Nakamura, *Kikō kyōkasho*, 33–38.

23. Yoshizawa, *Kumo, ame, kaze*, 240–41.

24. The heavy reliance on Tokyo-based examples was largely a result of the textbook being written by professors and former students of Tokyo Imperial University. While an obvious shortcoming, the authors did at least make the fact known to readers. In the preface to the teacher's edition for the fifth-year textbook, it is stated that the plants and animals included in the volume "are common to the Tokyo area" and that teachers in other regions should adapt or supplement the material accordingly. See article 3 of this preface, reprinted in Itakura, *Nihon rika kyōiku-shi*, 245.

25. Teachers were also instructed to explain to students how specific plants and animals related to certain social aspects of human life, including agriculture, industry, and diet. These principles of science instruction borrowed primarily from the philosophies of German scientists Freidrich Junge and W. Beyer. For more on the importance of "observation" in Meiji and Taishō period science instruction, see Kaigo, "Rika kyōkasho sōkaisetsu," 131 and 138. Also see Wigen, "Teaching about Home," 554. A survey of Iwate's premier education journal, *Iwate kyōiku*, shows that here too, at least through the teens and early twenties, outdoor learning and local observation remained the cornerstones of science education.

26. The statement is cited in Itakura, *Nihon rika kyōiku-shi*, 266.

27. For a full overview of the textbook debate, see ibid., 254–59. Also see his edited series, *Rika kyōiku-shi shiryō*, vol. 1: 221–26, and vol. 3: 287–96. Evidence for the involvement of Iwate educators comes again from *Iwate kyōiku*. See especially "Kyōzai kenkyū ni tsuki" (On the Study of Teaching Materials) (May 24, 1914); "Chirika kyōiku no chihōka no hitsuyō" (The Need for Localizing Geography and

Science Education) (Sept. 10, 1915); "Rika kyōju fushin no gen'in to sono kyūsai hōan" (The Cause of Stagnation in Science Instruction and Methods for Its Recovery) (Sept. 20, 1917); and "Rika kyōju no kakudai" (Expanding Science Instruction) (July 15, 1919). On similar local educational reform movements in Germany at the time, see Jenkins, *Provincial Modernity*, 149–62.

28. Hori Shichizō, "Shōgaku rikasho no katsuyō ni tsukite," *Iwate kyōiku*, May 15, 1919: 14.

29. In the 1918 and 1921 editions of the textbook, the passage on the wind reads: "When a single part of air is heated up, the air rises and the surrounding air that has not been warmed up moves to fill its place. The natural blowing of wind is a result of this air that has been warmed by the heat of the sun." See *Nihon kyōkasho taikei*, vol. 23: 546.

30. Sakai, *Hyōden Miyazawa Kenji*, 234. Also see Hatayama, *Kyōshi Miyazawa Kenji no shigoto*.

31. Miyazawa struggled elsewhere with the problem of how to represent a narrator both universal and linguistically neutral. How, in other words, does one tell a story attuned to the specificities of local dialect yet which does not, by subsuming all under the "standard" tongue of the narrator, reproduce the same linguistic hierarchies that one is trying to overturn? In "Shika odori no hajimari" (The First Deer Dance, 1924), Miyazawa attempts to resolve the issue by displacing the source of the narrative to the nonhuman realm. Here, it is the wind that carries the story to the ears of a man who then reproduces it as a "Japanese" text. Thus we do not know what dialect or language it was originally conveyed in, only that it comes already in a mediated form. If such a technique does not resolve the problem, it does force an awareness of the structures inherent to that problem and the impossibility of its resolution.

32. *Kōhon Miyazawa Kenji zenshū*, vol. 8: 36–37. Matasaburō's remark is interesting in light of another figure from the time who amazed children with his ability to fly. Named Tobitarō (lit., flying Tarō), the character was created in 1918 for a series called "Otogi ryokō" (Tales of Travel). In addition to being able to fly, he could also make any object appear with the clap of his hands and turn himself into any object he wished (e.g., whale, sparrow, pigeon, wind, rain, rock, or sand). Essentially a glorified tourist from Tokyo, he set out across Japan to survey famous landmarks and talk with famous sites (*meisho*) and famous goods (*meibutsu*) at a lightning fast pace. As if this were not enough, the boy was everywhere greeted by hundreds of cheering fans. Two volumes of Tobitarō stories were produced by Fujikawa Tansui, one focused on the Chūbu region and one on the Kinki region. Published in Tokyo by Keibunkan, the former was in its fifteenth printing by 1924 and the latter its tenth printing by 1921.

33. Harvey, *The Condition of Postmodernity*, 273.

34. *Kōhon Miyazawa Kenji zenshū*, vol. 8: 179. I have not provided the idiomatic translations for *uzu no shuge* and *okinagusa* for reasons that will become clear.

35. See *Nihon shokubutsu hōgen shūsei*, 111–14.

36. Bakhtin, "Discourse in the Novel," 358. The doubly voiced quality of the

passage has also been highlighted by Komori Yōichi in *Saishin Miyazawa Kenji kōgi*, 193–97.

37. On Ueda's attempts to define and implement a standard language, see Yasuda, *"Kokugo" to "hōgen" no aida*, 90–94, and Twine, "Standardizing Written Japanese." Ueda was fully aware that a standard had to be created, and not simply found, but his recent travels in Europe convinced him that success as a modern nation was dependent on being able to carry out this painstaking process.

38. On the importance of Taiwan in the development of a national language curriculum, see Komori, *Nihongo no kindai*, 178. The subject of *kokugo* was incorporated into the Taiwanese educational system in 1898, a full two years before it was incorporated into the domestic curriculum.

39. Contrast this with attitudes toward dialect in the early-modern period. Under the Tokugawa polity, while it is true that certain styles of speech were designated as more refined than others (e.g., upper-class Kyoto dialect) or more suitable to communication in the commercial sphere (e.g., Kamigata and Edo dialects), none was held up as a standard to be adopted by all. Even the dialect of Edo, which by the mid-Tokugawa period was conceptualized as a kind of common language (*kyōtsūgo*), never served as more than an entryway to the vibrant style of speech heard in that city and necessarily spoken by those who traveled between it and the outlying feudal domains. On the growing recognition of *Edogo* as a common language, see Yasuda, *"Kokugo" to "hōgen" no aida*, 39–41. Also see Twine, "Standardizing Written Japanese," 436–38.

40. The publication of such collections, referred to as *hōgenshū*, reached a peak in the last decade of Meiji. According to Yasuda, nearly sixty-four were published between 1900 and 1912, as compared with just eleven in the 1880s and 1890s. Of these, seventeen were published in Tōhoku, far more than any other region. See Yasuda, *"Kokugo" to "hōgen" no aida*, 114–17. Miyazawa, it should be noted, attended primary and middle school during this same period.

41. Ibid., 95.

42. On the creation of a written vernacular and a model image of *hyōjungo* based on the Tokyo dialect, see Komori, *Nihongo no kindai*, chaps. 4 and 6. He notes the particularly influential role played by the era's most popular novelists, Ozaki Kōyō and Tokutomi Roka. Their writing, as well as domestic fiction (*katei shōsetsu*) generally, helped to cement a kind of standard for the Tokyo dialect and to popularize it as a mark of social success. Komori also argues that because much of the audience for this fiction was made up of mothers, these women would have strongly encouraged their children to learn the Tokyo dialect, thus aiding in the diffusion of a standardized speech (205–6).

43. Ibid., 200–201.

44. The contrast between standard- and nonstandard-dialect speakers in these two novels is made even starker by the fact that the main protagonists, who hail from the regions depicted and whom one would expect to converse in dialect with other locals, only use *hyōjungo*.

45. Elsewhere in Japan, writers responded to the situation by resisting Tokyo-

based vernacular styles well into late-Taishō. Richard Torrance shows how in the Izumo area, pseudo-classical Japanese and classical Chinese styles of writing remained the preferred medium for some time. Very few local writers succeeded in adopting the narrative prose styles of Tokyo writers. See "Literacy and Modern Literature in the Izumo Region, 1880–1930."

46. As Yasuda notes, the idea of regional dialect words as historical artifacts goes back almost to the beginning of the language reform movement (*"Kokugo" to "hōgen" no aida*, 80). It would reach its clearest articulation, however, in the writing of Yanagita Kunio, who in 1927 put forth his theory that dialects represented the older layers of a once unified national language that had over time radiated out from a central dynamic core (ibid., 147–51).

47. I provide literal translations of names only to hint at the possible visual associations they might conjure up, as these are what "Okinagusa" is itself trying to problematize. Incidentally, the correct Linnaean spelling is *anemone cernua*, which was the name given to the plant by Karl Thunberg in his *Flora Japonica* of 1784.

48. According to the *Nihon shokubutsu hōgen shūsei*, *chigo-gusa* is a name common to several areas throughout Japan. *U'naiko* hails from the Kyoto and Fukui regions, while *neko-gusa* is popular in Fukuoka. The fourth name, *kawara-ichigo*, is found in Ibaragi, Aomori, and Gunma prefectures.

49. In Siebold's entry for the flower in *Flora Japonica*, which would have appeared a few years after Kawahara's text, the colloquial names for *anemone cernua* are listed as *shaguma-saiko*, *kawara-saiko*, and *okina-gusa*, in that order.

50. On the confluence of plant and dialect collecting in the Edo period, see Yasuda, *"Kokugo" to "hōgen" no aida*, 40.

51. Western classificatory systems were applied to Japanese flora as early as the 1770s, when Thunberg, a student of Linnaeus, traveled to Japan to collect and classify native plants. He was followed in the 1820s by Siebold, who began publishing his well-known *Flora Japonica* in 1835. It was Siebold, in fact, who handed a copy of Thunberg's own *Flora Japonica* to the young Itō Keisuke (1803–1901), who produced the first translation of Linnaeus' famous system in Japanese as part of his two-volume *Taisei honzō meiso* (1828). Keisuke later went on to take a position at Tokyo Imperial University. On the introduction of the Linnaean system into *hakubutsu-gaku* discourse, see Fukuoka, "Between Knowing and Seeing."

52. These guides included the eleven-volume *Shinsen Nihon shokubutsu zusetsu* (The Newly Revised Illustrated Guide to Japanese Plants) (Tokyo: Keigyōsha, 1899–1903), the four-volume *Dai-Nihon shokubutsu-shi* (The Flora of Japan) (Tokyo: Tokyo Imperial University, 1900–1901), and the *Nihon kōzan shokubutsu zufu* (Illustrated Guide to Japanese Alpine Plants) (Tokyo: Seibidō, 1907–1909). The journal Makino helped start, *Shokubutsu-gaku zasshi* (The Botanical Magazine), began in 1887 as the mouthpiece of the Tokyo Botanical Society. It included highly technical articles from Japan's leading botanists as well as detailed accounts of the many expeditions taken by members to domestic locales and other parts of East Asia, including Taiwan and southern Manchuria. The accounts document the objectifying and colonialist practices by which the flora of these regions were "discovered,"

catalogued, named, and brought back to the metropole. As of 1907, Makino himself had participated in trips to Shikoku, Taiwan, Tōhoku, Iwate, Hokkaidō, and Kyūshū.

53. See Kayaba and Sakaba, *Shinpen shokubutsu zusetsu*, 33–34. The 1917 edition was published by Kōbundō Shoten.

54. Makino's volume, published by Hokuryūkan, was to become one of Japan's canonical botanical reference guides and was in its eighth edition by 1950.

55. Liu, "The Question of Meaning-Value in the Political Economy of the Sign," 24.

56. In the original manuscript of the story, Miyazawa wrote the phrase *uzu no hige* in two separate places only to later erase it. I suspect that using *hige*, the common word for "beard," would have been to spoil the rhetorical effect he sought. See *Kōhon Miyazawa Kenji zenshū*, vol. 8: 480–81. It is unclear what *uzu* might refer to, although some scholars have suggested that it is a variation on *onzu*, a dialect equivalent for "old man." See Hara, *Shin Miyazawa Kenji goi jiten*, 105.

57. This is Claudette Sartiliot's paraphrase of Derrida's argument from the essay "Glas." See *Herbarium/Verbarium*, 17.

58. Ibid., 28.

59. Merleau-Ponty, *Phenomenology of Perception*, vix.

60. Koiwai Farm, established in 1891, was one of Japan's first Western-style commercial farms. It occupied 3,000 hectares at the southern base of Mt. Iwate and was a critical entry point for Western methods of crop production, dairy farming, and livestock operations. Miyazawa was fond of the area near the farm and often wandered its fields and forests in search of poetic inspiration.

61. Foucault, *The Order of Things*, 137.

Chapter Six

1. The house was built in 1912 by Miyazawa's grandfather and had been a place of convalescence for family members.

2. *Iwate nippō*, Jan. 31, 1927, late ed.: 3. Reproduced in *Shin kōhon Miyazawa Kenji zenshū*, vol. 16, part 2 (*hoi · denki shiryō hen*): 358.

3. He wrote this in a letter dated June 25 to his friend Hosaka Ka'nai. The other letters are dated April 13 and June 27. See *Kōhon Miyazawa Kenji zenshū*, vol. 13: 224–26.

4. Andō Tamaji, *"Kenji seishin" no jissen*, 11–12. The two men, who learned of Miyazawa from the newspaper, were taking a farm practicum course at the Morioka Higher School of Agriculture.

5. The downturn in crop prices wiped out many of the gains that had been made during the boom years of World War I, which included higher wages for tenant farmers. Rice prices, which had risen or remained constant in seven of the years between 1910 and 1920, fell in eight of the next ten and in every year from 1925 to 1931. For farmers, this meant having to produce higher yields on the same amount of land and having to sell so much of the crop that little was left for self-consumption. Additionally, costs of fertilizers and other inputs outpaced crop prices in ten of fif-

teen years between 1920 and 1934. The government, fearing a repeat of the rice riots of the late teens, kept rice prices low by promoting the importation of rice from the colonies. See Smith, *A Time of Crisis*, 47–48.

6. Rapid expansion of light and heavy industry during World War I, much of it centered in urban areas on the Kantō plain or near Osaka, was the driving force behind rural emigration. As Smith notes, "In 1920, one in eight Japanese lived in a city of a hundred thousand or more; by 1935, one in four did. More than 80 percent of the population growth in that fifteen-year period was absorbed by urban centers, so that whereas in 1920 there had been only sixteen communities with populations of a hundred thousand or more, by 1935 there were thirty-four such cities" (ibid., 43). Between 1911 and 1930, the number of people engaged in agriculture or forestry-related jobs fell from 16.1 million to 13.5 million, a nearly 16 percent drop. Tokyo alone saw a 70 percent increase in its male population between 1920 and 1935, compared with just a 24 percent increase for the mainland as a whole. Most of these men were between the ages of 15 and 30. See Ōkado, *Kindai Nihon to nōson shakai*, 71–73, and Iwasaki, *Nōhon shisō no shakai-shi*, 125.

7. Regional and national newspapers of the time confirm how serious a threat emigration was perceived to be. In countless articles and editorials, ideologues and officials expressed concern over the fate of the farm village in the wake of an urban fever (*tokai netsu*) that seemed endemic among the younger generation; they urged that preventive measures be taken immediately, backing up their proposals with repeated warnings to youth about the dangers to body and mind that lay waiting for them in the city. For examples, see Ōkado, *Kindai Nihon to nōson shakai*, 72–73, and also his "Nōson kara toshi e," 175. In the *Iwate nippō*, the discourse of "urban fever" persisted from the teens well into the 1920s. A public service announcement that appeared repeatedly told of a youth whose life had been ruined in the city by too much smoking, too much coffee, and too little sleep.

8. I use "political" broadly here to mean the redistribution of power through a restructuring of established social or material relations. I thus diverge from the tendency in historiography of the period to characterize these activities, as does Harry Harootunian, as "bizarre experiments in utopianism" that merely substituted the practice of politics for a "conception of society as a distinct and self-subsistent entity" ("Introduction: A Sense of An Ending and the Problem of Taishō," 22). Such a narrow definition of the political obscures their inherently public and performative dimension.

9. Latour, *The Pasteurization of France*, 93.

10. In order to distinguish Latour's notion of *network* from the other ways I have used the word in this volume (i.e., as simple descriptor of connections between like entities, as metaphor for describing a system of linkages), I will hereafter put the word in italics when it is necessary to make clear that I am using it in the Latourian sense.

11. Latour traces the new *networks* of actors and objects that allowed Pasteur and his followers to push out those of earlier hygienists in *The Pasteurization of France*. In his later work, he offers clarification for his approach to social analysis by defining more rigorously many of the terms I employ here. See *Reassembling the Social*,

esp. 37–42, 106–8, and 128–33. His point is not that there is no reality beyond these networks, but that what we recognize as reality in any social or disciplinary context requires, like theater, an elaborate and active assemblage of accessories in order to appear as such.

12. A letter to a friend indicates that Miyazawa had an interest in promoting theater from the very moment he took up his teaching position. See *Shin kōhon Miyazawa Kenji zenshū*, vol. 16, part 2 (*nenpu hen*): 243. Students performed *Kiga jin'ei* (Starvation Camp), a comedic operetta, as early as September 1922.

13. Attendance figures were reported in "Hanamaki nōkō no den'en geki," *Iwate nippō*, Aug. 13, 1924, late ed.: 1. The play was part of festivities to celebrate the completion of a new school building, and nearly thirty students (out of seventy total) participated. *Shin kōhon Miyazawa Kenji zenshū*, vol. 16, part 2 (*nenpu hen*): 278–79.

14. *Kōhon Miyazawa Kenji zenshū*, vol. 11: 341–42.

15. Benjamin, "Program for a Proletarian Children's Theater," 205.

16. Following Prasenjit Duara, I understand civil society to represent "a domain of private and collective activity that is autonomous from the state. It includes economic activities as well as associational life and the institutions of sociability, but excludes political parties and institutionalized politics in general." See *Rescuing History from the Nation*, 148. An important institution of sociability is public space, in the strict sense of a material site where members of a community can come together in relative freedom (or at least in the perception that all in the community are welcome). Such sites are utilized for expressing public opinion or for defending certain ideas of civil society (i.e., as the locus of articulation for a particular kind of "public sphere"), but must not be conflated with civil society itself. Jürgen Habermas has argued that they may even be detrimental to the latter in that they reduce authentic public debate to ritual and spectacle, encouraging as they do the performance of what he calls "representational publicness." For a synopsis and critique of this argument, see Hurd, "Class, Masculinity, Manners, and Mores," 80–83.

17. The conference, held in Tokyo, is described by Kido Wakao in "Gakkō geki kinshi kunrei no zengo."

18. Miya Teiji, "Gekiteki honnō no keibai," *Iwate nippō*, May 26, 1924: 4.

19. The first prose version, likely drafted before the play, exists only as the transcription of a nonextant original and contains some minor edits by Miyazawa. It was produced between February 1924 and March 1926. The second version, which he began in 1927, was edited at least twice before his death and then pieced together by editors in different variants at different times due to uncertainty about the order of the manuscript pages.

20. Lefebvre defines "horizon of meaning" as "a specific or indefinite multiplicity of meanings, a shifting hierarchy in which now one, now another meaning comes momentarily to the fore, by means of—and for the sake of—a particular action." He uses the phrase to link physical sites and social action, forcing us to read the "texture" of spaces—the continual back and forth between what the space is and what happens there—rather than space as text. *The Production of Space*, 222.

21. The announcement stated that the play was to depict a nighttime summer festival in Italy. "Hanamaki no shiröto den'en geki," *Iwate nippō*, Aug. 5, 1924: 3.

22. Early examples appear in deliberations over plans for restructuring Tokyo's core municipal wards (*shiku kaisei*) in 1884. See Fujimori, *Meiji no Tōkyō keikaku*, 178–88. In later decades, the equivalence between *hiroba* and "square" underwent further linguistic sedimentation. Frank Brinkley's *Unabridged Japanese-English Dictionary* (1896) is one of the earliest examples I have found, but later dictionaries tended to follow suit, as in Tobari Chikufū's German-Japanese dictionary (*Shinshiki dokuwa daijiten*, 1912). It defines *hiroba* as equivalent to "platz."

23. Nagai Kafū wrote about the plaza in *Amerika monogatari* (American Stories, 1908). See the chapter titled "The Inebriated Beauty," in which the narrator gazes upon the plaza in awe as dusk approaches.

24. The aforementioned Brinkley's dictionary lists this definition alongside "square."

25. This is the definition given in the *Nippo-jisho* (Japanese-Portuguese Dictionary, 1603). The word was also said to describe a person comfortable with crowds. See *Jidai betsu kokugo daijiten*.

26. Throughout the Meiji period, the word was used in the *Yomiuri shinbun* to designate areas in front of official or administrative buildings, school courtyards, open spaces near bridges, and in some cases the grounds at the main entrance of the Imperial Palace. Futabatei Shimei also used the word to translate "field" in his 1888 translation of Turgenev's "The Tryst" (Aibiki).

27. Most of these thoughts, however, were not realized until the era of reconstruction following the Great Kantō Earthquake. On the station *hiroba*, see Worrall, "Railway Urbanism." On post-quake reconstruction, see Koshizawa, *Tōkyō toshi keikaku monogatari*. According to Koshizawa, only a few of the *hiroba* and mini pocket-parks planned after the quake were actually built, typically at strategic intersections, the ends of bridges, and in front of train stations (58). Jinnai Hidenobu writes on the post-quake history of the *hiroba* in *Tōkyō no kūkan jinruigaku*, 265–72.

28. Koshizawa, *Manshūkoku no shuto keikaku*, 69–75.

29. Sorensen, *The Making of Urban Japan*, 43. Though city and state officials had by the late teens reached agreement on the need for parks and open spaces to boost the quality of life of urban citizens, other sectors of the government, mainly the Finance Ministry, remained convinced that such projects should be left to local residents. Officials were thus unable to tap what they hoped would be a key source of funding (110–11).

30. Miyazawa's brother Seiroku describes their visits to the area in the 1910s in *Ani no toranku*, 39–51. He notes that the atmosphere of the festival likely influenced a story called "Matsuri no ban" (Night of the Festival, 1924), in which a "mountain man" comes to enjoy the festivities but is tormented by locals for not being familiar with the concept of money.

31. These last three sites are discussed as *hiroba*-like in Fukuta, "Nihon no buraku kūkan to hiroba." The final two sites divide geographically, with the former more common in western Japan, where homes were built densely together, and the latter more common in eastern Japan, where the opposite was the case.

32. This was Japan's first Western-style park. Its treatment as a space for personal use is also attested to by the ubiquitous presence of police and the many signs in the park prohibiting carts, carriages, rickshaws, entertainers, peddlers, and the improperly attired. See Aoki, *Meiji Tōkyō shomin no tanoshimi*, 226–27.

33. Sennett, *The Fall of Public Man*, 27.

34. He also dreams of being served by a young woman in Western clothing whose face is veiled and who stays forever silent. See the autobiographical "Sōretsu" (Funeral Procession), which appeared in the literary journal *Meisei* in December 1906. Reprinted in *Ishikawa Takuboku sakuhin-shū*, vol. 2. Significantly, Takuboku expresses some anxiety over making these thoughts public to the people of Morioka.

35. Hagiwara, "Sabishii jinkaku" (A Lonely Personality), in *Hagiwara Sakutarō shishū*, 43.

36. Terada Torahiko, "Zakki ichi," *Chūō kōron* (Sept. 1922).

37. They variously imagined the park as an oasis of rejuvenation for high density urban deserts, a symbolic city lung for improving air quality and hygiene through exposure to light and wind, a recreational space for physical exercise, a site for leisurely walks and nature appreciation, and a place for emergency refuge. See Takei, "Toshi no kōen keikaku"; Tamura, *Gendai toshi no kōen keikaku*, 1–7; Orishimo, "Kōen keikaku"; Uehara, *Toshi keikaku to kōen*, 1–10; and essays by Hongō Takanori and Inoshita Kiyoshi in *Toshi to kōen*.

38. A few even went so far as to differentiate the *hiroba* and the small park as uniquely localized forms of public space to be administered and used by community members to facilitate social integration and exchange. See Takei, "Toshi no kōen keikaku," and Inoshita Kiyoshi, "Shōkōen ni tsuite," in *Toshi to kōen*. The latter was at the time head of the Tokyo City Parks Department.

39. Gordon, *Labor and Imperial Democracy in Prewar Japan*, 46, his emphasis.

40. For a timeline of major demonstrations, and the parks in which they were held, see Maruyama, *Kindai Nihon kōen-shi no kenkyū*, 93–101.

41. *Kōhon Miyazawa Kenji zenshū*, vol. 9: 169.

42. Ibid., 177. Specifically, Wildcat mentions the "Han-Ye-Ping affair" to another gentleman, a reference to a Chinese iron manufacturer heavily supported by Japanese interests and made a joint concern of the two nations under the Twenty-One Demands, a set of demands forced upon China's Republican Government in 1915. In the 1920s, it was beset by low productivity and labor disputes. Also noteworthy is Wildcat's frock coat, a kind of formal wear popular since the 1890s that was often employed by Miyazawa as dress for characters who put on airs in an attempt to secure their social status. See Hara, *Shin Miyazawa Kenji goi jiten*, 630.

43. Chakrabarty, "*Adda*, Calcutta," 152.

44. *Kōhon Miyazawa Kenji zenshū*, vol. 9: 178–79.

45. I borrow here from Ken Hirschkop's work on conceptions of the public square in Bakhtin's writing on Goethe and Rabelais. See *Mikhail Bakhtin: An Aesthetic for Democracy*, 259.

46. Cited in Yoshimi, *Toshi no doramatōrugii*, 204–12. The quotes are from Soeda

Azenbō's *Asakusa teiryūki* (A Record of Asakusa's Underworld, 1930), Ishizumi Harunosuke's *Asakusa urabanashi* (The Untold Story of Asakusa, 1927), and again from Soeda. Yoshimi posits that shared economic and social backgrounds (many visitors to the area were but one generation removed from the countryside) contributed to the sense of solidarity and unity felt by Sixth District crowds (209).

47. This image was collated from articles appearing in the journal *Minzoku geijutsu* (Folk Art) between 1928 and 1930. Most are ethnographic accounts detailing the practices specific to a local district or county. See especially the issue from July 1928, which was dedicated entirely to accounts of the Obon dance. Also see Mitsuyoshi Natsuya, "Gaijin no mita bon-odori," parts 1 and 2, 1.7 (July 1928): 83–86; 1.8 (Aug. 1928): 27–40, which brings together excerpts from Meiji period accounts of the Obon dance by foreign observers, including Basil H. Chamberlain, C. F. Brinkley, and Lafcadio Hearn. Hearn's description is interesting as it combines many of the signature elements listed above (nightfall, moonlight, temple grounds) and narrates them as a kind of dreamlike, mystical experience.

48. See the study published by folklorist Hayakawa Kōtarō as "Jikyōgen zakki" (Notes on Rural Theater), *Minzoku geijutsu* 1.1 (Jan. 1928): 87–94. Of course, as historian Ann Waswo notes, overtly political gatherings were subject to even greater secrecy. "Until roughly 1917–18 . . . if tenant farmers met with one another at all, they did so furtively, late on moonless nights in the hamlet forest or some other secluded place. To be seen together was considered illicit, an offense against their community as well as against their landlords" ("The Transformation of Rural Society, 1900–1950," 576).

49. National surveys and studies of popular entertainment from the early 1930s consistently list these three activities as the most cherished forms of leisure in rural areas. See, for example, Gonda Yasunosuke's *Minshū goraku ron*, 145–46.

50. Harootunian, *Overcome by Modernity*, 293–306. Yanagita and Orikuchi embraced the image of a "repetitive, collective history" that called for "constancy" and that sought to hold back the destabilizing forces of an external capitalism so as to expand the "imminence" of native, and as yet uncorrupted, cultural practices (303).

51. Arendt, *The Human Condition*, 58. Arendt's conception of public life is founded on the idea that being seen and heard by others derives its significance from the fact that everyone sees and hears from different positions. Under conditions of mass society or mass hysteria, however, people are "imprisoned in the subjectivity of their own singular experience, which does not cease to be singular if the same experience is multiplied innumerable times" (58).

52. This precluded, however, student recreational activities or activities occurring on temple and shrine grounds (e.g., festivals, funerals, sermons). Okudaira Yasuhiro notes, however, that authorities tended to disrupt public gatherings whenever and however they saw fit (*Chian iji hō shōshi*, 23–24). In 1922, women were given the freedom to participate in political events when Article 5 was repealed through the efforts of feminist activist Hiratsuka Raichō. In 1926, labor activists were also successful in repealing Article 17, which had severely restricted their ability to strike.

53. Ibid., 59–62.

54. On the longer history of municipal restrictions that pushed street performers and vendors off of roadsides and open spaces and into areas where they could
be better monitored and taxed, see Ishizuka, "Meiji Tōkyō no sakariba · dōro o
meguru kisei."

55. Beginning in 1916, nearly ninety essays were written by more than fifty individuals seeking to integrate the concept of *minshū* into the realms of art and artistic
creation. The discussion ranged to forms of art as diverse as novels and *haiku*. See
Nihon kindai bungaku daijiten, vol. 4: 494.

56. This positioning finds a historical parallel in calls by urban elites for the reform of everyday life (*seikatsu kaizen*). Fears over the ill-effects of mass consumerism prompted reformers to try to direct behavior with appropriate models of consumption. See Sand, *House and Home in Modern Japan*, chap. 5.

57. Honma, "Minshū geijutsu no igi oyobi kachi," 10–11.

58. Fisher, "Romain Rolland and the French People's Theatre," 87. Soda Hide-
hiko describes in further detail the misreading of Rolland by both Honma and
Ōsugi in *Minshū gekijō*, 84. They had been misled by Ellen Key's application of
Rolland's thesis to all forms of art.

59. Outside Japan, the promise of inclusiveness had become so diffused by the
1920s that it was subject to parodic send-up in Kafka's *Amerika* (1927). There, a
young German immigrant who spends months trying, and failing, to find his place
in America, is eventually welcomed by the "Oklahoma Theater" despite his lack of
identification papers, lack of a proper education, and his nickname from a prior
post: "Negro." See pp. 234–54.

60. Brian Powell discusses Hirasawa and the proletarian drama movement in
Japan's Modern Theatre, 66–76.

61. See Tsubouchi, *Waga pējento geki*, 44–59. His first proposal for a pageant theater
appeared in the August 1919 issue of *Kaizō* under the title "Shakai kaizō to engeki"
(Social Reconstruction and Theater). The idea for a modern pageant is said to have
begun with Englishman Louis Parker in 1905. This hybrid, largely amateur theatrical
genre came to be defined as a partly processional open-air show celebrating the history or legends of a particular place. See *The Concise Oxford Companion to the Theatre*.

62. In stating these principles, Tsubouchi borrowed heavily from Louise Burleigh's *The Community Theatre* (1917).

63. Tsubouchi, "Pējento to togaigeki," in *Atami pējento*, 73–84.

64. Powell, *Japan's Modern Theatre*, 61–65.

65. Burleigh, *The Community Theatre*, 109.

66. Kudō Shijaku, "Yagai geki toshite no dōwa geki," *Iwate nippō*, Mar. 6, 1923: 4.

67. See Obara, *Gakkō geki ron*, 55–68. The ideas and practical instruction in this
treatise represent the culmination of an educational experiment that began in 1918
in Hiroshima and that was seen to fruition during Obara's long tenure at the privately run Seijō Elementary School in Tokyo. The school became a center for the
movement during the 1920s, and a bastion for progressive and art-oriented education at a time when officials were becoming less inclined to tolerate unorthodox
teaching methods.

68. Tsubouchi, *Jidō kyōiku to engeki*, 138. Tomita Hiroyuki notes that Tsubouchi had been interested in the social potential of children's plays at least since 1900. He did not become active, however, until 1921, when he began lecturing on the topic and writing plays of his own. He even formed his own children's theater troupe, leading it on tours of southwestern Japan in 1923 and 1924 while giving lectures to help promote the movement. See *Nihon jidō engeki-shi*, 138–47.

69. Alice Minnie Herts wrote about the experience of starting a community children's theater in *The Children's Educational Theatre* (1911). It was never translated into Japanese, but her second book, *The Kingdom of the Child* (1918) contained very similar content and appeared as *Jidō no ōkoku* (Tokyo: Shūseisha) in 1924.

70. See Obara's interview with Ochiai Sōzaburō in "Obara Kuniyoshi sensei ni Nihon no gakkō geki no oitachi o kiku," 27.

71. Terai Iichirō's attempt to introduce school theatre in Akita Prefecture in 1921 sparked a debate with the governor and with parents in the pages of the local newspaper. Terai eventually moved to join Obara at Seijō Elementary when opposition proved overwhelming. See Kido, "Gakkō geki kinshi kunrei no zengo," 22.

72. Ibid., 22. Contemporary debate on the merits of school theater can be found in the March 1923 issue of *Jyosei* and the May 1923 issue of *Shakai to kyōka*.

73. See *Iwate-ken Hanamaki nōgakkō ichiranhyō*, which provides information on students for the years 1921 and 1922. About 10 percent of students came from landlord families. Only one was from the poorest class of tenant farmers (*kosaku*).

74. See the previously cited letter by Miyazawa from April 13, 1925.

75. Nakamura, *Nōmin gekijō nyūmon*, 38–40, 77.

76. Iizuka Tomoichirō, *Nōson gekijō*, 7, 33. He went on to write *Nōson to engeki* (Village and Theater) in 1946, a history of farmers' theater in which Miyazawa was given a pivotal role.

77. Nakamura, *Nōmin gekijō nyūmon*, 96–111. A history of the Wakaba Kai can be found in Inoue, "Yasumoto Tomoyuki no bōken," 185–221. Another figure mentioned by Nakamura is Itō Matsuo, who started a *kyōdo gekidan* (native-place troupe) in 1926 in Nagano Prefecture and later became an influential figure in the movement in the 1930s.

78. *Kōhon Miyazawa Kenji zenshū*, vol. 9: 175. Fazero's choice of a military-style uniform should be read within the historical moment of late Taishō. This was a time when conscription often represented for rural youth a path out of abject poverty and into an institution where former land-based class divisions dissolved under merit-based systems of evaluating rank and establishing hierarchy.

79. An overview of the suffrage movement can be found in Matsuo, *Futsū senkyo seido seiritsu-shi no kenkyū*, and Ōkado, *Kindai Nihon to nōson shakai*, 182–93. Debate over suffrage was especially vociferous in the late teens and early 1920s, when many activists attempted to link the right to vote to class struggle. Slow response from the government, however, stifled much of this early energy. Bureaucrats and other elites feared what might happen if the vote was given to those who had not the proper cultivation or knowledge to use it. They tried to disconnect the issue from class interests and framed it instead as a movement to encourage middle-level

citizens to take responsibility and feel pride in local governance. For them, as long as radical or minority parties were kept from gaining a representational majority, the community and the political process would benefit. Thus when suffrage was granted in 1925, it came with limits on how far an individual's vote extended as well as a new police law and strengthened educational reforms.

80. *Kōhon Miyazawa Kenji zenshū*, vol. 10: 93.

81. When the two explain how they found the *hiroba* by counting tiny flowers, they are heartily laughed at and told, "I'm sorry to tell you this, but Poraan's Hiroba belongs to Sir Destupaago."

82. This image typically finds the Taishō intellectual privileging a private culture of *being* over a public culture of *doing*. See the essays on Abe Jirō and Kurata Hyakuzō by Stephen Kohl and Thomas Rimer, respectively, in *Culture and Identity*; and Elaine Gerbert's analysis of Taishō writers and the private spaces (attics, hidden rooms, closets) where their imaginations found freedom in "Space and Aesthetic Imagination in Some Taishō Writings."

83. Barshay, *State and Intellectual in Imperial Japan*, 15.

84. The Labor-Farmer Party was originally established in March 1926 after its predecessor, the Farmer-Labor Party (Nōmin Rōdō Tō), had been outlawed at its inception four months earlier. The group, which explicitly excluded left-wing activists, was initially headed by Sugiyama Motojirō (1885–1964), a Christian pastor based in Fukushima Prefecture. Leftists demanded that they be allowed to join the party, however, and began to organize their own local branches. Later that year they assumed full control after centrists in the group broke away to form the Japan Labor-Farmer Party (Nihon Rōnō Tō). In October 1926, a local branch opened in Hanamaki to which Miyazawa gave aid in many forms. In addition to repeated financial donations, which he paid for by selling books from his personal library, he also arranged for a family storehouse to be used as headquarters, donated desks and chairs, and gave the group a mimeograph (*gariban*) for printing campaign posters. According to members, most of whom were closely watched by authorities, Miyazawa maintained a low profile in all these transactions. On his involvement with the Labor-Farmer Party, see *Shin kōhon Miyazawa Kenji zenshū*, vol. 16, part 2 (*nenpu hen*): 322; Nasukawa, "Kindai-shi to Miyazawa Kenji no katsudō"; and Itō, *Iihatōbu no shokubutsugaku*, 101–7.

85. *Kōhon Miyazawa Kenji zenshū*, vol. 10: 370.

86. Harootunian, "Introduction," 15–17.

87. Kido, "Gakkō geki kinshi kunrei no zengo," 26–27. The minister saw no benefit in dressing children up to perform for the public and feared the classroom was being misused for mere entertainment.

88. *Shin kōhon Miyazawa Kenji zenshū*, vol. 16, part 2 (*nenpu hen*): 300.

Chapter Seven

1. Ironically, Sōseki made these comments in his preface to Nagatsuka Takashi's *Tsuchi* (The Soil), later hailed by those in the farmers' literature movement as the first truly sustained and sympathetic account of Japanese farming life in fictional

form. See *Tsuchi*, 10. This would have been the only edition available to readers until 1926. Nagatsuka's story was set in a village roughly forty-five miles northeast of Tokyo.

2. Chatterjee, *The Nation and Its Fragments*, 158.

3. Ibid., 158. For examples culled from European fiction, see Blum, "Fiction and the European Peasantry."

4. Examples of this duplicitous discourse can be found in Gluck, *Japan's Modern Myths*, 178–204, and Havens, *Farm and Nation in Modern Japan*.

5. Hobsbawm, *The Age of Extremes*, 287–95.

6. Tokutomi Roka, who left Tokyo in 1907 to farm a plot of land on the city's southwestern fringes, is perhaps the best example of this. He was part of a cultural movement that extolled the virtues of simple living as embodied in the image of the gentleman farmer. Then, as now, the image was easily appropriated and commodified by suburban developers and fashioned as a kind of ethical return to the land. Sand, *House and Home in Modern Japan*, 148–50.

7. I use "peasant" here as a translation for *nōmin* because this is how Yamamoto translates it in his own texts.

8. *Kustar'* designated small-scale domestic manufacturing in contrast to factory-style production. These cottage industries had been revived in the late 1800s by government officials and educated elites who, influenced by William Morris (1834–1896) and the rediscovery of folk art elsewhere in Europe, established schools where professional artists taught peasants to make intricate handmade goods. As a prominent advocate described it, the schools were part of a larger project to "capture the still-living art of the people and give it the opportunity to develop." See Siegelbaum, "Exhibiting *Kustar'* Industry," 42. Yamamoto describes his visit to the museum in "Nōmin bijutsu to watashi," in *Bijutsuka no akubi*, 139–40. Ironically, by the time of his visit many artists and critics in Russia's avant-garde had already come to disdain *kustar'* crafts because of their overcommercialization. Siegelbaum, "Exhibiting *Kustar'* Industry," 56.

9. Yamamoto, "Nōmin bijutsu kengyō no shui oyobi sono keika," 35. "Peasant Art in Japan" is printed in English both here and in the original pamphlet.

10. Ibid., 36. The perception that farmers could be making more productive use of the off-season was common in *nōmin geijutsu* discourse. Yamamoto even went so far as to compute the number of labor hours that went unused during the winter months in his "Nōson fukugyō no shinseimen," 12.

11. The Moscow Kustar' Museum supplied goods to Paris's Bon Marché and Samaritaine department stores, as well as Liberty's of London (Siegelbaum, "Exhibiting *Kustar'* Industry," 48). Details on the Mitsukoshi exhibition can be found in *Bijutsu no akubi*, 151–58. The items on display apparently sold out in the first two days of the three-day event. Yamamoto attributed this less to the quality of the products than to the good graces of Mitsukoshi and the interest shown by intellectuals.

12. Brandt, *Kingdom of Beauty*, 93. Bureaucrats in the Ministry of Agriculture were especially keen on the increased possibilities for supplemental labor (*fukugyō*). As Brandt notes, Yamamoto's movement fizzled out in the 1930s, just as Yanagi

Sōetsu's folk-craft movement (*mingei undō*) gained momentum. In 1935, Yanagi criticized *nōmin bijutsu* for lacking authenticity, declaring that it reflected none of the regional, functional character of "purely Japanese," "purely agrarian" objects "born" rather than "made" in the countryside (93–94). His comments hint at an ultra-nationalist, ultra-romantic turn in the appreciation of "local" art.

13. Yamamoto, "Nōmin bijutsu to watashi," 161.

14. Ibid., 162.

15. Ibid., 147–48.

16. Yamamoto, "Nōmin bijutsu kengyō no shui oyobi sono keika," 38.

17. Komaki was apparently inspired by a trip to the provinces the previous summer, where he was amazed by "the fluttering of a red something filling the chests of provincial youth." See Yamada, *Kindai Nihon nōmin bungaku-shi*, 23.

18. For an account of the symposium, see Inuta, *Nihon nōmin bungaku-shi*, 10–20. In the lecture Claudel gave at the event, he noted the impact of Philippe's work on himself and told the audience that, "Philippe's works give us pause for thought. With what attitude should artists approach the act of creation? Rather than for the sake of our own ideas, we must create for the sake of the people (*minshū*). That doesn't mean creating works that speak at the people, but which speak for them." Cited in Yamada, *Kindai Nihon nōmin bungaku-shi*, 31.

19. Inuta, *Nihon nōmin bungaku-shi*, 16. These excerpts come from a transcription of Yoshie's speech published in the literary magazine *Shinchō*.

20. Yoshie, "Nōmin seikatsu to gendai bungei." Also cited in Nagumo, *Gendai bungaku no teiryū*, 38–39.

21. Yoshie provided estimates of the farming population in a 1925 essay. Citing statistics from a 1921 survey by the Ministry of Agriculture and Commerce, he put the total number of tenant and landed farmers at 30 million, claiming this to be more than half of the total mainland population (which the 1920 census gives as 56 million). See "Nōjin to bungei," 211. Miyazawa, in his notes on "The Rise of Farmers' Art," estimated 30 million *nōmin* out of a total population of 55 million. See *Kōhon Miyazawa Kenji zenshū*, vol. 12, part 1: 19.

22. Chiba, "Nōson bunka undō no kishi," 241.

23. Kurata, "Nōmin bungaku no teishō," 37. Shiga's magnum opus was still being serialized at this point, the first half having appeared in *Kaizō* in 1921. Falling into the genre of *shishōsetsu* (I-novel), the work has been easily caricaturized by its detractors as self-centered, narcissistic, emotionally claustrophobic, and elitist.

24. Women were noticeably absent from the group and do not figure large in histories of the movement. That said, Sumii Sue (1902–1997), Inuta's wife from 1919, showed an interest in the genre as early as 1921 and was known by the mid-1930s as the leading female writer of *nōmin* literature.

25. Inuta, *Nihon nōmin bungaku-shi*, 23–24.

26. Ibid., 24–25. Inuta and Nakamura were at the center of this continued disagreement. Nakamura tried to unite the various genre names (e.g., *tsuchi no geijutsu, kyōdo geijutsu, nōson bungaku, chihōshugi bungaku*) under the title of *daichi-shugi* (earthism), reflecting his vision of the soil as both transcendent universal and

place-specific. Inuta, however, was critical of this. He felt *daichishugi* was too philosophical and potentially obscured the immediate social and political imperatives of the movement.

27. Escalating tenant protests in the Niigata village of Kisaki had recently led to the expulsion from local schools of all children of tenant families. In response, the leadership of the Japan Farmers' Union (Nihon Nōmin Kumiai), which included Sugiyama Motojirō and activist writer Kagawa Toyohiko, appealed to members of the *bundan* to help establish a separate school for these children. Katō's volume, titled *Nōmin shōsetsu shū* (Collection of Peasant Fiction), was their response. It included works by such prominent figures as Akutagawa, Satō Haruo, Kikuchi Kan, Ogawa Mimei, Akita Ujaku, and Nakamura Seiko, as well as pieces by Inuta Shigeru, Katō himself, and a number of up-and-coming writers. Few of the works, however, were originally written for the volume. See Nagumo, *Gendai bungaku no teiryū*, 14–22.

28. The head editor of this special issue was Honma Hisao, who, as discussed in the preceding chapter, had been one of the torchbearers of the "people's art" movement before it was pulled apart by competing notions of who constituted "the people."

29. For a comprehensive list of this material, see Inuta, *Nihon nōmin bungaku-shi*, 254–59.

30. The volume was published in October by Shunyōdō. The other scholarly volume, *Nōmin no bungaku* (Farmers' Literature), was the work of Kimura Ki, who was a member of Japan's Fabian Society and a vocal supporter of the tenancy movement. The book was part of a twelve-volume series on the "rural village problem" headed up by the leadership of the Japan Farmers' Union and Waseda professor Abe Isao.

31. The two recipients were Norwegian Knut Hamsun in 1920 for his *Growth of the Soil* and the Polish novelist Władysław Reymont in 1924 for his *The Peasants*. Both works could be found in Japanese translation by this time.

32. They criticized the movement for straying too far from the real economic conditions of the tenant farmer and for lumping together the urban and rural proletariat. Although appearing a bit later, an example of this line of critique can be found in Nakano Shigeharu's "Nōmin bungaku no mondai," originally published in the July 1931 issue of *Kaizō*.

33. Nakamura, an entrenched member of the *bundan* at this time, was a strict humanist who opposed any kind of art limited to a single class or group of people. The comment originally appeared in the literary magazine *Bungei kōdō*. Cited in Inuta, *Nihon nōmin bungaku-shi*, 31.

34. Ibid., 32–33. The response to Nakamura was printed in the *Miyako shinbun* in May.

35. On the new ways rural youth came to think of themselves as social actors and individuals with greater control over the paths their lives might take, see Ōkado, *Kindai Nihon to nōson shakai*, chap. 5. In addition to having more formal schooling than their parents, their experiences in the classroom, as well as the barracks, had taught them that ability was not measured simply by the amount of land one

owned. Some fled to the cities in order to capitalize on this newfound sense of self-advancement, while others channeled their energy into homegrown efforts to reconstruct (*kaizō*) the village from the inside out. On these latter efforts, which took the form of direct political action (i.e., tenant protests) or new strands of popular agrarianism, see Waswo, "The Transformation of Rural Society, 1900–1950."

36. The group identified with the short-lived Nonpartisan League, a progressive political party established in 1915 by farmers in North Dakota seeking to eliminate the powerful influence of urban corporate interests on their livelihoods. A brief description of the organization, which began publication of its own journal, *Nōmin jichi*, in April 1926, can be found in Inuta, *Nihon nōmin bungaku-shi*, 30–31. See also Hayashi, "Nōmin jichi kai ron," 31–44, and Iwasaki, *Nōhon shisō shakai-shi*, 131–33. Though it began as a study group in much the same vein as the Nōmin Bungei Kenkyū Kai, by late 1925 members had turned their attention to more immediate social and economic concerns. The intellectual faction included Ishikawa Sanshirō, labor activist and author Nakanishi Inosuke, and Shimonaka Yasaburō, the president of the publishing house Heibonsha and a vocal proponent of agrarian and educational reform. The activist farmers included Shibuya Teisuke and Takeuchi Aikoku. National membership reached as high as 12,000 members, most of them in Saitama and Nagano prefectures.

37. Inuta is rarely forthcoming about what he means by a "consciousness of the soil." The idea that it is a kind of privileged perception into agrarian life is expressed in an essay from 1925, cited in his *Nihon nōmin bungaku-shi*, 26.

38. Inuta, "Shoka no nōmin bungei ron o hyōsu," 53. Inuta may well be speaking of his own father, whom he left at the age of twenty-five on bitter terms. Also see his comments in *Nōmin bungei jūrokkō*, 52–54, where he again relies on metaphors tied to biological cycles of growth and decay.

39. He was willing to grant, however, that Japan's only "peasant novel" had been written by the son of a landlord (i.e., Nagatsuka Takashi). This summary of Nakamura's views is based on a May 1925 essay published in the *Hōchi shinbun*. Reprinted as "Nōmin bungei no shuppatsuten" in his essay collection *Nōmin gekijō nyūmon* (1927).

40. Ibid., 33–34. The patronizing tone reflected here was not unique to Nakamura. Yoshie evinces the same tone in his "Nōjin to bungei" (1925). There he admits to having received about a dozen works in recent years from provincial farmers, all of which were aesthetically insufficient. He did believe that a true "art of the soil" could emerge, but would require a kind of "mutation" in farmers by which they gained cognizance of a life force (*seimeiryoku*) that shattered the archaic structures of the everyday environment and broke through to a new frontier (213).

41. Benjamin, "The Author as Producer," 228 (Benjamin's emphasis).

42. Shibuya, *Teihon nora ni sakebu*, 246. On Shibuya and the significance of his poetry volume to the *nōmin* literature movement, see Yamada, *Kindai Nihon nōmin bungaku-shi*, 397–401, and Inoue, *Nōmin bungaku ron*, 67–75.

43. See Nakanishi Inosuke's prologue to the collection in *Teihon nora ni sakebu*, 239–40.

44. Ibid., 241–45.

45. Ibid., 247.

46. I borrow here from Spivak's *A Critique of Postcolonial Reason*, in which one of her central concerns is "the possibility that the intellectual is complicit in the persistent constitution of the Other as the Self's shadow" (266).

47. The group's main literary organ, *Nōmin jichi* (Farmers' Autonomy), initially contained few contributions from the intellectual contingent. By 1927, some of the farmer-activists leading the group demanded that the intellectuals be purged altogether in order to steer the organization toward direct participation in the labor movement. When the ideological thrust of the group swung back the other way in 1928 as a result of renewed involvement by Inuta and other members of the Nōmin Bungei Kai, actual farmers like Shibuya withdrew and left the remaining members to disband within the year. Iwasaki, *Nōhon shisō shakai-shi*, 133–34.

48. The announcement, which appeared on December 27 in the *Waga shinbun*, is reprinted in its entirety in *Shin kōhon Miyazawa Kenji zenshū*, vol. 16, part 2 (*nenpu hen*): 302–3. The paper was printed in Kitakami, a town just south of Hanamaki.

49. At a cost of around 45 yen—roughly equal to the starting monthly salary of a primary school instructor—tuition would have been quite high for the average tenant or middling farmer. The starting monthly salary for a teacher ranged from 40 to 55 yen in 1920, rising only slightly over the next decade (*Zoku nedan no Meiji Taishō Shōwa fūzoku-shi*, 19).

50. The idea is invariably associated with right-wing agrarianist Katō Kanji (1884–1965), who founded the Japan People's Higher Level School (Nihon Kokumin Kōtō Gakkō) in 1926. His school, however, opened a full five months after the Iwate program, a fact that points to the movement's origins outside his own personal emphasis on a "farm-spirit" ethnically nationalist and rooted in the practices of an imperial Shintōism. For a history of his movement, see Havens, "Katō Kanji (1884–1965) and the Spirit of Agriculture in Modern Japan." On his colonialist aspirations and the school's connection to imperialist expansion in the 1930s, see Young, *Japan's Total Empire*, 318.

51. Grundtvig's followers were responsible for much of this growth in the years before his death. For a recent account of the movement, see Borish, *The Land of the Living*.

52. For a list of works translated, see Ōhashi, "Nihon ni okeru nōhonshugi kyōikuron no kenkyū (III)." It includes A. H. Hollmann's *Die dänische Volkschochschule und ihre Bedeutung für die Entwicklung einer Völkischen Kultur in Dänemark* (Berlin, 1909), H. R. Haggard's *Rural Denmark and Its Lessons* (London, 1912), and H. W. Foght's *Rural Denmark and Its Schools* (New York, 1915). It was Hollmann's book that was translated in 1913 by Nasu Hiroshi, an acquaintance of Katō Kanji, as *Kokumin kōtō gakkō to nōmin bunmei*.

53. Utsunomiya Sentarō, for instance, who headed the Hokkaidō Cattle Research Group, saw in Denmark the solutions for revitalizing Hokkaidō's stagnant rural economy and sent a number of researchers to the country in 1921 to carry out multiyear surveys. The following year, the acting commissioner of Hokkaidō dispatched

his own group of agricultural technicians in the hope of transforming the island into "Japan's Denmark." See Ōhashi, "Nihon ni okeru nōhonshugi kyōikuron no kenkyū (III)," 565–66. This moniker was soon to be claimed by Hekikai County in Aichi Prefecture, an area recognized in state textbooks as a model of community solidarity and innovative agrarian education. See Okada, *Taishō demokurashii shita no "chiiki shinkō,"* 33.

54. See the collection of essays published as *Denmāku no nōgyō*, 208–30; Yamada Katsutomo, *Yo ga mitaru Denmāku nōson*, 43–48; and Uchiyama Kazuo, *Denmāku nōson seikatsu*, 9–20.

55. For a schedule of the daily routine and a list of courses, see *Shin kōhon Miyazawa Kenji zenshū*, vol. 16, part 2 (*nenpu hen*): 308–9. We have a good idea of what was taught in the literature course because one of the students, Itō Seiichi, took copious lecture notes. See vol. 16, part 1 (*hoi · shiryō hen*): 165–203.

56. Sugiyama, "Minshū undō toshite no nōmin gakkō." His own school, which he established at his home and church in 1913, operated until 1920. No more than ten local students were enrolled at any one time.

57. See the previously cited book-length accounts. On the broad range of responses to the folk high school movement, see Uno, *Kokumin kōtō gakkō undō no kenkyū*, 137–52.

58. The three texts were composed at roughly the same time as the lectures. For a comparative analysis of how they relate to Itō's notes, see Kikuchi Chūji, "Shiryō 'Nōmin geijutsu gairon no hikkiroku' ni tsuite," in *Miyazawa Kenji ronshū*. Also see Fromm, *Miyazawa Kenji no risō*.

59. *Shin kōhon Miyazawa Kenji zenshū*, vol. 16, part 2 (*nenpu hen*): 331.

60. Ibid., part 1 (*hoi · shiryō hen*): 192. These questions, recorded by Itō in his notes, appear almost verbatim in "A Survey of Farmers' Art." Unless otherwise noted, all references are taken from these notes.

61. Ibid., 193–94. This is an oblique reference to an essay by Oscar Wilde and the common vitalist critique of social and labor relations under capitalism as injurious to the "true personality of man." The essay, published in *The Soul of Man under Socialism, The Socialist Ideal-Art and the Coming Solidarity* (1891), was translated by Honma Hisao as "Shakaishugi to ningen no reikon" and included in the fifth volume of *Wairudo zenshū* (Tokyo: Tenyūsha, 1920). See pp. 10–11 in the original English. For an introduction to the competing discourses of vitalism in the Taishō period, see *Taishō seimeishugi to gendai*, 2–15. Vitalism, defined broadly, was rooted in the belief that life could not be explained in purely physical or chemical terms, and that it drew its essence from a universal life force.

62. First introduced to Japan as a literary figure in 1891, Morris later became known for his writing on guild socialism and his foundational role in the Arts and Crafts movement. By 1927, at least 139 books and articles related to Morris had been published, compared with 102 on John Ruskin. On the reception of these figures in Japan, see Kikuchi, *Japanese Modernisation and Mingei Theory*, 24–26. Also see *Aatsu ando kurafutsu to Nihon*. A complete bibliography of Morris-related publications appeared in *Morisu kinen ronshū* (1934), 185–238, and it indicates that

the period between 1920 and 1927 saw the greatest number of Morris-related publications (202). Miyazawa himself was especially taken by Morris's notion that "real art is the expression by man of his pleasure in labour," which is quoted in both the lecture notes and in "The Rise of Farmers' Art."

63. James A. Schmiechen has argued that for all the vehemence with which Morris and others lamented the decline of the craftsman ideal, early nineteenth-century technological advancements and changes in consumer demand actually increased the opportunities for art-labor employment and led to a new interest in art training for working people. See "Reconsidering the Factory, Art-Labor, and the Schools of Design in Nineteenth-Century Britain."

64. Ruskin made agricultural work a crucial element of his own utopian experimental project, the Guild of St. George. See Kikuchi, *Japanese Modernisation and Mingei Theory*, 27–28. Established in the 1870s, some of its grand schemes included "the acquisition and cultivation of land, industrial enterprises, the education of labourers, the establishment of museums and schools, the preservation of rural crafts, and programmes of communal manual labour by the gentry."

65. Moishe Postone, in *Time, Labor, and Social Domination*, distinguishes between a concept of labor understood as historically specific to capitalism and a transhistorical conception as "a goal-oriented social activity that mediates between humans and nature, creating specific products in order to satisfy determinate human needs" (4–5). He argues that any critique of labor dependent on the latter concept will ultimately fail as a critique of capitalist society.

66. Itō's notes, 195. These proposals were made by Morris in a lecture titled "Useful Work *versus* Useless Toil: The Socialist Platform," originally delivered to the No. 2 Socialist League Office in 1885. See Morris, *The Collected Works of William Morris*, vol. 23: 98–120. Honma Hisao translated it as "Yūyō no shigoto to muyō no shigoto" (Useful Work and Useless Work) and included it in the volume *Warera ikani ikubekika* (1925).

67. Itō's notes, 196. Kropotkin was best known in Japan for his *Fields, Factories, and Workshops* (1898), translated by Nakayama Kei in 1925 as *Den'en, kōjō, shigotoba* (Tokyo: Shinchōsha). Proponents of *nōmin geijutsu* were attracted to his vision of "a society where each individual is a producer of both manual and intellectual work . . . and where each worker works both in the field and the industrial workshop; where every aggregation of individuals . . . produces and itself consumes most of its own agricultural and manufactured produce" (*Fields, Factories, and Workshops*, 23).

68. Itō's notes, 192. Despite the declared substitution, Miyazawa continued to use both *nōmin* and *geijutsu* throughout the lectures.

69. Ishikawa drew specifically from Reclus's *L'Homme et la Terre* (Humanity and the Earth, 1875–1894). Translating a portion of the work as *Chijinron* (Treatise on People of the Earth), he amalgamated the two nouns of the original French title into a two-character compound. The translation was published in his 1925 essay collection *Hi-shinkaron to jinsei*. Miyazawa is known to have had the volume in his personal library and may well have been reading it at the time. On the influence of this collection on his thought, see Sakai, "Ishikawa Sanshirō to Miyazawa Kenji."

70. Sakai, "Ishikawa Sanshirō to Miyazawa Kenji," 131. Ishikawa explains his derivation of *tomin* in the essay "Tomin seikatsu" (The Life of the People of the Land, 1921), which was included in *Hi-shinkaron to jinsei*. The idea apparently came out of a conversation with English poet Edward Carpenter (1844–1929), during which Carpenter explained that the "demo" of democracy came from *demos*, which connoted "the people of a particular land."

71. This call appears in "An Outline Survey of Farmers' Art." *Kōhon Miyazawa Kenji zenshū*, vol. 12, part 1: 10.

72. This narrative of decline is borrowed in bits and pieces from essays by Leo Tolstoy, Oswald Spengler (1880–1936), Ralph Waldo Emerson (1803–1882), and Romain Rolland. See "The Rise of Farmer's Art," *Kōhon Miyazawa Kenji zenshū*, vol. 12, part 1: 18. Spengler, in his infamous *Decline of the West* (Der Untergang des Abendlandes, 1918), claimed that Western civilization was in the midst of an inevitable cyclic decline and that art had been made impotent and false by academic schools and nepotistic circles of fashionable urban artists. In his mind, music after Wagner and painting after Manet and Cézanne had slipped from an organic and elemental art to something purely artificial. See *Decline of the West*, 155–56. Spengler's work was popularized in Japan in the early 1920s by journalist and philosopher Murobuse Kōshin (1892–1970). Murobuse's *Bunmei no botsuraku* (The Decline of Civilization, 1923), a Manichean rant against "modern civilization" and urban capitalism, is known to have influenced Miyazawa around this time.

73. See chaps. 8, 10, and 12 in *What Is Art?*. In chapter 8 he criticizes contemporary art thus: "For the great majority of working-people, our art, besides being inaccessible on account of its costliness, is strange in its very nature, transmitting as it does the feelings of people far removed from those conditions of laborious life which are natural to the great body of humanity" (70). The work was translated into Japanese as *Geijutsuron* in 1906, a copy of which Miyazawa owned. Katō Kazuo (1887–1951) helped link the work to the people's art movement in the late teens.

74. Bergson, *Creative Evolution*, 258. Bergson is not cited directly in the lectures, but his ideas were a prominent element of the intellectual ether during Miyazawa's formative years as a young poet. On the possible influence of Bergson's thought, see Kurihara, "Shinshō sukecchi no shisō," 35–38. The prefatory poem to *Spring and Asura* presents Miyazawa's clearest vision of the self as a unity and multiplicity forever in process.

75. *Kōhon Miyazawa Kenji zenshū*, vol. 12, part 1: 12. "Programmism" (*hyōdaishugi*) is a reference to the genre of Programme music, which sought to convey through music the impression of a definite series of objects, scenes, or events.

76. *Kōhon Miyazawa Kenji zenshū*, vol. 12, part 1: 9.

77. Cited in Sakai, "Ishikawa Sanshirō to Miyazawa Kenji," 141–42. Interestingly, Carpenter's idea of cosmic consciousness was inspired by spiritual dialogues with Tagore.

78. *Kōhon Miyazawa Kenji zenshū*, vol. 12, part 1: 13.

79. The soil could easily fulfill this role because it was both inherently universal

(where in the world does one not find soil?) and innately particular (living things can be nurtured only by the soil beneath their feet). For examples of such rhetoric, see Inuta's introductory chapters in *Nōmin bungei jūrokkō*, and Nakamura, *Nōmin gekijō nyūmon*, 20. A similar idealization of the soil appears in the writings of agrarian nationalist Tachibana Kōzaburō. See Havens, *Farm and Nation in Modern Japan*, 249.

80. Edwin Hubble's careful observations in the 1920s finally proved the existence of "island universes," or nebulae, outside the Milky Way. Miyazawa occasionally alluded to a "different space" (*ikūkan*) outside the Milky Way, but never recognized the "island universe theory." The fullest expression of his conception of the Milky Way, as both scientific and spiritual object, is found in *Night of the Milky Way Railroad*, which he started in 1924. See Golley, *When Our Eyes No Longer See*, 174–182, on the ontological imperative, which is implicit in the story's opening scene, to orient oneself to distant phenomena.

81. *Kōhon Miyazawa Kenji zenshū*, vol. 12, part 1: 15.

82. Adorno, *The Jargon of Authenticity*, 102–3.

83. This reference is from the written manuscripts. See *Kōhon Miyazawa Kenji zenshū*, vol. 12, part 1: 15. Fourth-dimensional art is also mentioned early on in the lectures: "Why don't we put our true energies together and create from all our shared country settings (*den'en*) and all our shared livelihoods (*seikatsu*) one gigantic, fourth-dimensional art?" (193).

84. In the prefatory poem to *Spring and Asura*, Miyazawa writes, "It's likely that two thousand years from now / a geology appropriate to the time will be in fashion, / and evidence to support it will appear from the past in quick succession. / Everyone will think that two thousand years prior / colorless peacocks filled the blue skies. / Up-and-coming scholars will / excavate splendid fossils / somewhere from the glittering frozen nitrogen / of the uppermost layers of the atmosphere. / Or perhaps they will discover / the gigantic footprints of an invisible mankind / in a stratified plane of Cretaceous sandstone." Captured here is a conception of history as a diachronic series of epochal moments stacked one upon the other, stretching upwards to the atmospheric ether. These moments exist relative to their own historical time and, rather than filtering through from previous ages with their original meanings intact, are defined anew according to whatever epistemological framework is in vogue at the time of their discovery. See *Shin kōhon Miyazawa Kenji zenshū*, vol. 2: 7–10. Also see the passage on human perceptions of time in an early draft of *Night of the Milky Way Railroad*, in *Kōhon Miyazawa Kenji zenshū*, vol. 9: 141–42. For an analysis of the concept of "fourth dimension" and its intellectual origins, see Ōtsuka, *Miyazawa Kenji*, 120–36.

85. The article appeared on April 1, 1926, and is cited in full in *Shin kōhon Miyazawa Kenji zenshū*, vol. 16, part 2 (*nenpu hen*): 311–12.

86. Gramsci, "The Formation of the Intellectuals," 1141.

87. I borrow this phrase from Stephen Vlastos's excellent account of radical agrarianism in the prewar period ("Agrarianism without Tradition," 79–94).

88. Iwasaki, *Nōhon shisō no shakai-shi*, 20–21.

89. Katō made a second "return" to farming in the late 1920s, although this time

to a village in Kanagawa Prefecture. At this point, his thinking witnessed a shift to an agrarian communalism rooted in emperor worship and imperial Shintōism. He explained this new ideology in a volume of essays titled *Nōmin geijutsu ron* (Treatise on Farmers' Art) (Tokyo: Shunjū Bunko, 1931). See Nakao, *Taishō bunjin to den'en shugi*, 147–54. Other figures who "returned" to the land in the tens and twenties and who found it similarly difficult to manage both art and farming include Kinoshita Naoe (1869–1937), Eto Tekirei (1880–1944), Mizuno Yōshū (1883–1947), and Kimura Sōta (1889–1950). All four are discussed by Nakao.

90. Nakao, *Taishō bunjin to den'en shugi*, 138–46.

91. Havens, *Farm and Nation in Modern Japan*, 234–38. The cooperative established upwards of thirty branches in Ibaraki but was ultimately not successful. Its activities ceased after the May 15 Incident of 1932, in which Tachibana and members of the cooperative's educational wing, the Aikyōjuku, helped to assassinate Prime Minister Inukai Tsuyoshi as part of an attempted coup.

92. For a summary consideration of the New Village and its precarious relation to agricultural concerns, see Mochida, *Kindai Nihon no chishikijin to nōmin*, 61–76. Mushanokōji's experiment was also Tolstoy inspired, as were many like it in other parts of the world, including the "New Villages" of Gandhi and Tagore in India. In addition to Tachibana and Mushanokōji, other figures who experimented with communally oriented "return" include Nakazato Kaizan (1885–1944), who established a succession of rural academies in the late 1920s, and Okamoto Rikichi (1885–1963), who created a school for rural youth in Shizuoka Prefecture in 1927. The latter's vision of an autonomous and rural-based society is described in Iwasaki, *Nōhon shisō no shakai-shi*, 157–69.

93. See, for instance, Mochida, *Kindai Nihon no chishikijin to nōmin*, 133.

94. This, as Paul Ricoeur reminds us, is after all the true function of utopia. Not to re-create or mimic social life, which amounts to nothing more than ideology, but rather to rethink its very structure. See *Lectures on Ideology and Utopia*, 16.

95. Frederic Jameson, citing Louis Marin, writes eloquently on what utopia tells us through its very failure. "Historically then, this is the sense in which the vocation of Utopia lies in failure; in which its epistemological value lies in the walls it allows us to feel around our minds, the invisible limits it gives us to detect by sheerest induction, the miring of our imaginations in the mode of production itself, the mud of the present age in which the winged Utopian shoes stick, imagining that to be the force of gravity itself. . . . The Utopian text really does hold out for us the vivid lesson of what we cannot imagine" (*The Seeds of Time*, 75).

96. In *The Production of Space*, Lefebvre writes of a practice called "diversion" by which an existing space, having outlived its original purpose, is reappropriated and put to a use different from its initial one. Lefebvre carefully distinguishes between the diversion of space and its creation, the former serving as only a temporary halt to spatial domination. He also notes that one downside to diversionary tactics is that "groups take up residence in spaces whose pre-existing form, having been designed for some other purpose, is inappropriate to the needs of their would-be communal life. One wonders whether this morphological maladaptation might not

play a part in the high incidence of failure among communitarian experiments of this kind" (167–68).

97. These youth were some of the first to become involved with Miyazawa's experiment in rural living and all lived but a short distance from the house. See the biographical sketch in *Shin kōhon Miyazawa Kenji zenshū*, vol. 16, part 1 (*hoi · shiryō hen*), 337. The bulk of information on the activities at the Rasu Cooperative comes from this source.

98. The report originally appeared in the *Iwate nippō*, Jan. 31 1927, late ed.: 3. Reproduced in *Shin kōhon Miyazawa Kenji zenshū*, vol. 16, part 2 (*hoi · denki shiryō hen*): 358.

99. The article praising Miyazawa was published in *Iwate-ken Nōkai hō* 188 (April 1928). In a prophetic statement, the author opened by saying that, "The specialties (*meibutsu*) of Hanamaki are not limited to hot springs, dolls, and *okoshi* sweets. Miyazawa too, with his amicable appearance and priestly composure, should now be counted among them. And I believe that a time will soon come when this Hanamaki *meibutsu* will be a *meibutsu* for the entire prefecture."

100. *Shin kōhon Miyazawa Kenji zenshū*, vol. 16, part 2 (*hoi · denki shiryō hen*): 343.

101. Ibid., 344. The letter appeared in the paper's evening edition on February 17. Author Kikuchi Shinichi, who had been a participant in the Iwate People's Higher Level School, also urged the *Iwate nippō*, in its role as a provincial newspaper, not to miss out on this opportunity to support agrarian culture.

102. Harvey, "From Space to Place and Back Again," 20.

103. Harootunian, *Overcome by Modernity*, xx–xxi.

104. On farmers' literature as an ideological refuge in the 1930s, see Mochida, *Kindai Nihon no chishikijin to nōmin*, 149. For general accounts of the changing importance of the rural in this period and the shift from an agrarianism centered on local autonomy to one centered on state intervention and the imperatives of imperial fascism, see Havens, *Farm and Nation in Modern Japan*, 142; Smith, *A Time of Crisis*, 94–113; Waswo, "The Transformation of Rural Society, 1900–1950," 593; Iwasaki, *Nōhon shisō no shakai-shi*, 352; and Partner, "Taming the Wilderness," 489.

105. Andō Tamaji, *"Kenji seishin" no jissen*, 142–45.

106. The book was released in May 1938 by Hata Shoten, a Tokyo firm founded by national assemblyman Hata Bushirō. A representative of Nagano with a strong interest in the "village problem," Hata arranged for publisher Iwanami Shigeru to both edit and organize the sale of the book, which was promptly endorsed by both the Ministry of Education and the Central Association for Social Affairs (ibid., 142–53). In March of the following year, Matsuda compiled a "greatest works" volume of Miyazawa's fiction (*Miyazawa Kenji meisakusen*), again published by Hata Shoten and again endorsed by the Ministry of Education.

107. Smith, "A Land of Milk and Honey," 131. On the commodification of the rural in the context of mass consumer culture, see Hayashi, "Traveling Film History."

108. On the initial attempts to publish selections of Miyazawa's work, see *Shin kōhon Miyazawa Kenji zenshū*, vol. 16, no. 2 (*hoi · denki shiryō hen*): 436–39.

109. Smith, "A Land of Milk and Honey," 139.

Epilogue

1. Quoted in Saiki, "Shōwa kyūnen zaikyō 'Miyazawa Kenji tomo no kai' to, sono nettowaaku keisei he no katei ni tsuite," 135.

2. How the first *zenshū* came to be published is more fully described in Saiki Kenji, "Kyū-naimushō keihokyoku toshoka Saiki Ikurō to Miyazawa Kenji no shūhen—Shōwa kyūnen 'Tōkyō Miyazawa Kenji tomo no kai,'" 177–79.

3. I use "market" here to refer to any network of points of exchange that bring together objects or ideas in relationships of comparative valuation. As Lefebvre observes in *The Production of Space*, many kinds of markets function to construct social space in all its diversity: "local, regional, national and international markets; the market in commodities, the money or capital market, the labor market . . . the market in works, symbols, and signs; and . . . the market in spaces themselves" (86).

4. Zukin, *Landscapes of Power*, 4.

5. Eagleton, *The Idea of Culture*, 45.

6. Michael Hardt and Antonio Negri discuss the link between postmodernist logic and contemporary marketing in *Empire*, 150–54. They write that "postmodernist thinking—with its emphasis on concepts such as difference and multiplicity, its celebration of fetishism and simulacra, its continual fascination with the new and with fashion—is an excellent description of the ideal capitalist schemes of commodity consumption. . . . Marketing itself is a practice based on differences, and the more differences that are given, the more marketing strategies can develop. Postmodern marketing recognizes the difference of each commodity and each segment of the population, fashioning its strategies accordingly" (152).

7. On the activities of the Tomo no Kai and its members, see Saiki, "Shōwa kyūnen zaikyō 'Miyazawa Kenji tomo no kai' to, sono nettowaaku keisei he no katei ni tsuite," and "Kyū-naimushō keihokyoku toshoka Saiki Ikurō to Miyazawa Kenji no shūhen—Shōwa kyūnen 'Tōkyō Miyazawa Kenji tomo no kai.'" Kusano, Takamura, and other non-Iwate figures were naturally involved with the group, but most of the legwork fell to the natives of the prefecture. These included Saiki Ikurō, a Waseda graduate who had been part of the Nōmin Bungei Kai in the 1920s and who was soon to have a prominent role in the censorship apparatus of the Ministry of the Interior; Kikuchi Takeo, the illustrator for *Restaurant of Many Orders*, who assumed the role of secretary for the group; Terui Eizō, a musician and poet who from 1934 was utilizing the radio to launch a modern "poetry reading" movement; Fujiwara Katōji, a friend of Miyazawa who was also one of the primary editors for the Bunpodō *zenshū*; and Hahaki Hikaru, a poet who had just moved to Tokyo the year before and who, in addition to helping gather biographical material for the *zenshū*, acted as an important go-between for Iwate poets in Tokyo and those back home.

8. These remarks are cited in Yonemura, *Miyazawa Kenji o tsukutta otokotachi*, 160–64. She also came up with the figure of 25 articles (159). Interestingly, Mori was very candid about both the number of *zenshū* that had to be sold in Iwate and their relatively high price.

9. For more on the construction of this memorial stone and on the appropriation of "Ame nimo makezu" for wartime ideology and propaganda, see ibid., 213–27.

10. The *Miyazawa Kenji zenshū* was published by Jūjiya Shoten between 1939 and 1944.

11. As noted in Chapter Seven, the volume was published by Hata Shoten as *Miyazawa Kenji meisakusen.*

12. By 1940 there were eleven branches in all, six in Iwate, two in Yamagata, and one each in Tokyo, Osaka, and Hokkaidō. See Yonemura, *Miyazawa Kenji o tsukutta otokotachi*, 181–83. Many of the articles in the journal were concerned less with the criticism of Miyazawa's work than with the memory of him as a poet, friend, teacher, and reformer. It should be noted that "Iihatōvo" was the orthography used by the journal and was the predominant spelling through the 1950s.

13. The first work to be included in the national language curriculum was "Donguri to yamaneko" (Wildcat and the Acorns), a story from *The Restaurant of Many Orders* collection. It appeared in the 1946 edition of the elementary-school language textbook. A short biography of Miyazawa was attached in the revised 1951 edition. On his connection to the national language curriculum, see Ushiyama, *Kokugo kyōiku ni okeru Miyazawa Kenji.*

14. See "Kyōdo Hanamaki ni okeru Kenji nijūnen-ki no ki," in *Yojigen* 6.1 (Jan. 1954): 11–12. Also see Toyobumi, "'Konna koto wa jitsu ni mare desu': Miyazawa Kenji nijūnen-ki dansō," *Yojigen* 6.2 (Feb. 1954): 7–14; 6.3 (Mar. 1954): 6–12.

15. These observations come from Ogura's article, cited above.

16. "Kenji-sai," *Yojigen* 7.2 (Feb. 1955): 15–16.

17. See Takahashi Seiichi, "Hatsuaki no Kenji-sai," *Yojigen* 12.2 (Feb. 1960): 9–11; and Kikuchi Chūji, "Kenji-sai no ki," *Yojigen* 13.1 (Jan. 1961): 14–16.

18. Chaen Yoshio, "Iihatōbo o omou," *Yojigen* 10.6 (June 1958): 6. Chaen is recalling a trip he made six years earlier.

19. Ibid., 16.

20. See *Miyazawa Kenji kinenkan*, 116–18.

21. Obara Toshio, personal interview, July 19, 2004.

22. The "Native-Place Making Project" (Furusato Sōsei Jigyō), as it was called, was the brainchild of Prime Minister Takeshita Noboru, who in 1988 proposed that local municipalities be given one hundred million yen (approximately $760,000 at the time) in local tax allocation grants (*chihō kōfuzei*) to be used however they saw fit. Some poured the funds into comically absurd monuments (e.g., Japan's largest replica of the Statue of Liberty) while others embarked on more sustainable place-making ventures (e.g., Hiramatsu Morihiko's "One Village, One Product" movement).

23. Based on my own survey of literary museums across the country, I have found that as of 2006, a solid two-thirds were built in the 1990s.

24. "Kenji būmu Iwate koe," *Iwate nippō*, Aug. 9, 1996, late ed.: 1.

25. Obara Toshio, personal interview, July 19, 2004.

26. "Konnendo kasseika chōsei-hi," *Iwate nichinichi* [Ichinoseki], May 30, 1996: 1. Also see "Kenji to chihō jichi o kangaeru," *Iwate nichinichi*, Feb. 23, 1996: 15. The latter article discusses plans for a symposium that was to become a key forum for thinking about Miyazawa's potential future role in *machi-zukuri* efforts. It was

sponsored by the Hanamaki Institute for Research on Local Government and attendees included representatives from city hall, the Miyazawa Kenji Studies Society, and Citizens for the Appreciation of Hanamaki Culture.

27. On the various elements that made up the Dōwa Mura, see "KENJI dōmu gaiyō katamaru," *Asahi shinbun* [Iwate], Feb. 12, 1996: 25; "Go-sha no shutten kimaru," *Iwate nichinichi*, April 25, 1996: 1; and "Hanamaki no dōwa mura ni sanyasō-en o heisetsu," *Iwate nichinichi*, May 16, 1996: 1. On the overall aims of the festival, see "Kyō kara sutāto," *Iwate nichinichi*, July 1, 1996: 1.

28. Kennedy, "Shakespeare and Cultural Tourism," 179–80.

29. The process of discovery is described in "Hanamaki · Shizukuishi sakai ni mitsuketa," *Iwate nippō*, Mar. 16, 1996: 23.

30. *Kōhon Miyazawa Kenji zenshū*, vol. 9: 232. The mention of "bear livers" seems out of place here until we learn that Miyazawa originally intended to title the story "The Livers of the Bears of Mt. Nametoko." It was the liver and its renowned medicinal properties, as the narrator explains later, for which the bears were predominantly hunted. Miyazawa apparently changed the title without accounting for that change in the body of the text. Scholars believe that the original manuscript was written in 1927.

31. "'Nametoko yama' wa jitsuzaishita," *Iwate nichinichi*, July 25, 1996: 1. Satō's own account of the discovery is in *Miyazawa Kenji ni sasowarete*, chap. 1.

32. John Dorst writes of this paradoxical relationship between landscape and cultural object in his *The Written Suburb*, 57.

33. That Miyazawa remained central to discussions of *machi-zukuri* in Hanamaki well after the centennial is evident in the following articles: "'Kenji no machi' dō uru ka?" *Iwate nichinichi*, Jan. 27, 2002: 1; and "Kenji jidai no machi-nami hōzon," *Iwate nichinichi*, Feb. 24, 2002: 1. Obara Toshio, who at the time I interviewed him worked for the municipal government's tourism department, told me that it was hard to speak of *machi-zukuri* in Hanamaki without including Miyazawa in one way or another (personal interview, July 19, 2004).

34. Local governments have become particularly wary of so-called *hakomono* (white elephant) projects that create public facilities without any long-term strategies for attracting visitors. Instead, they now look to support community organizations that can be meaningful for both local residents and outsiders (Saiki Kenji, personal interview, Oct. 13, 2010). In 2009, for example, Saiki was awarded funds by his city to create a walking map of his native village that highlighted sites connected to Miyazawa's life and writing.

35. In a conversation with a leading member of the Beech Preservation Society, I was told that the discovery of Mt. Nametoko lent their arguments for conservation a new rhetorical force. It became far easier to justify what they were doing, and to raise awareness about beech forest ecology, once they could connect the place they were trying to save with Miyazawa's name and story (personal interview, July 21, 2004).

36. One organization that sees Miyazawa as a valuable role model is the Iwate Shizen Gaido Kyōkai Setsuritsu Junbi Kai (Organization to Prepare for the Formation of an Iwate Nature Guide Association), founded in 1990 and dedicated

to getting Iwate youth interested in the local environment so they might one day become nature guides. As one of the group's founding members explained to me, Miyazawa was an inspiration to them because he had explored the very same landscapes as an adolescent, and had done so over and over again (personal interview, July 11, 2004). Such repetition suggests a logic of place consumption very different from that which drives the tourist economy, where one is encouraged to consume as many unique places as one can.

37. *Nōrinsui-sangyō ni kanrensuru bunkateki keikan ni kansuru chōsa kenkyū.* This preliminary report, issued two years before the expansion of Japan's landscape laws (*keikanhō*), sought to define the categories of sites that might count as cultural landscapes worthy of preservation. Within the group of sites related to literature, six separate "Miyazawa-related cultural landscapes" were proposed. Other authors, who received brief mention, were Kawabata Yasunari and Kitahara Hakushū.

38. A local informant commented on the heavy hand with which certain of Miyazawa's descendants now maintain control over the use of his image in marketing, merchandising, or any activity from which profit might potentially be gained (Personal interview, July 19, 2004).

39. Wilson makes this point in his fascinating exploration of the history of place making in Santa Fe (*The Myth of Santa Fe*, 313).

40. Ibid., 313.

Bibliography

Japanese-Language Sources
(Unless otherwise noted, place of publication is Tokyo.)

Aatsu ando kurafutsu to Nihon. Ed. Design History Forum. Kyoto: Shibunkaku Shuppan, 2004.

Abe Tsunehisa. *"Ura Nihon" wa ika ni tsukurareta ka.* Nihon Keizai Hyōronsha, 1997.

Aikoku fujin kai yonjūnen-shi. Aikoku Fujin Kai, 1941.

Akita Ujaku. "Tōhoku bunka no tokuchō ni tsuite." *Waseda bungaku* (July 1921): 29–33.

Andō Kyōko. *Miyazawa Kenji: "chikara" no kōzō.* Chōbunsha, 1996.

Andō Tamaji. *"Kenji seishin" no jissen: Matsuda Shinjirō no kyōdō-sonjuku.* Nōsan Gyoson Bunka Kyōkai, 1992.

Aoki Kōichirō. *Meiji Tōkyō shomin no tanoshimi.* Chūō Kōron Shinsha, 2004.

Asakura Haruhiko and Ōwa Hiroyuki. *Kinsei chihō shuppan no kenkyū.* Tōkyōdō Shuppan, 1993.

Asano Gengo. *Tōhoku oyobi Tōhokujin.* Tōhokusha, 1915.

Bungakukan wandārando. Ed. Riterēru Henshūbu. Metarōgu, 1998.

Chiba Kameo. "Nōson bunka undō no kishi." *Kaizō* (Sept. 1923): 241–43.

Chihōbetsu Nihon shinbun-shi. Ed. Nihon Shinbun Kyōkai. Nihon Shinbun Kyōkai, 1956.

Denmāku no nōgyō. Sapporo: Hokkaidō Chikugyū kenkyū kai, 1925.

Fromm, Mallory Blake. *Miyazawa Kenji no risō.* Trans. Kawabata Yasuo. Shōbunsha, 1984.

Fujimori Terunobu. *Meiji no Tōkyō keikaku.* Iwanami Shoten, 2004.

Fukushi Kōjirō. "Kyōdo bungaku shuchō no kiso." *Miyako shinbun*, Feb. 9–15, 1924.

Fukushi Kōjirō chosakushū. 2 vols. Ed. Osanai Tokio. Hirosaki: Tsugaru Shobō, 1967.

Fukuta Azio. "Nihon no buraku kūkan to hiroba." *Kokuritsu rekishi minzoku hakubutsukan kenkyū hōkoku* 67 (Mar. 1996): 9–24.

Furusato bungakukan. 55 vols. Eds. Kihara Naohiko et al. Gyōsei, 1993–1995.

Gonda Yasunosuke. *Minshū goraku ron.* Ganshōdō Shoten, 1931.

Hagiwara Sakutarō. *Hagiwara Sakutarō shishū.* Shichōsha, 1975.

Hangai Seiju. *Shōrai no Tōhoku.* Maruyama Shasho Sekibu, 1906.

Hara Shirō. *Shin Miyazawa Kenji goi jiten.* Tōkyō Shoseki, 1999.

Hashimoto Motome. *Nihon shuppan hanbai-shi.* Kodansha, 1964.

Hatanaka Keiichi. *Dōyōron no keifu.* Tōkyō Shoseki, 1990.

———. "Taishō-Shōwa ki ni okeru chihō no dōyō undō." *Kokusai kidō bungakukan kiyō* 8 (Mar. 1993): 1–54.

Hatayama Hiroshi. *Kyōshi Miyazawa Kenji no shigoto.* Shogakukan, 1989.

Hayashi Yūichi. "Nōmin jichi kai ron." *Sekai keizai* 64 (Jan. 1978): 31–44.

Hiramatsu Morihiki. *Chihō kara no hassō.* Iwanami Shinsho, 1990.

Hollmann, Anton Heinrich Hans. *Kokumin kōtō gakkō to nōmin bunmei.* Trans. Nasu Hiroshi. Dōshisha, 1913.

Honma Hisao. "Minshū geijutsu no igi oyobi kachi." *Waseda bungaku* (Aug. 1916): 2–13.

———. *Warera ikani ikubekika.* Tōkyōdō, 1925.

Horio Seishi. "*Chūmon no ōi ryōriten* kankō goro makki." "*Chūmon no ōi ryōriten*" *kenkyū.* Vol. 1. Ed. Tsuzukihashi Tatsuo. Gakugei Shorin, 1975.

Iizuka Tomoichirō. *Nōson gekijō.* Daitōkaku, 1927.

Ikutabi Hisashi. "Tōhoku bussan no chōtan." *Kahoku shinpō,* May 10–15, 1917.

Inoue Toshio. *Nōmin bungaku ron.* Gogatsu Shobō, 1975.

Inoue Yoshie. "Yasumoto Tomoyuki no bōken." *Kindai engeki no tobira o akeru.* Shakai Hyōronsha, 1999. 185–221.

Inuta Shigeru. *Nihon nōmin bungaku-shi.* Nōsan Gyoson Bunka Kyōkai, 1977.

———. "Shoka no nōmin bungei ron o hyōsu." *Bungei sensen* 3.8 (Aug. 1926): 51–53.

Ishii Kendō. *Rika jūnikagetsu, dai kyū getsu: Bōfū'u.* Hakubunkan, 1901.

Ishikawa Sanshirō. *Hi-shinkaron to jinsei.* Hakuyōsha, 1925.

Ishikawa Takuboku. *Ishikawa Takuboku sakuhin-shū.* Shōwa Shuppansha, 1970.

Ishizuka Hiromichi. "Meiji Tōkyō no sakariba · dōro o meguru kisei." *Nihon kindai toshiron.* Tōkyō Daigaku Shuppankai, 1991. 149–62.

Itakura Kiyonobu. *Nihon rika kyōiku-shi.* Daiichi Hōki Shuppan, 1968.

Itō Mitsuya. *Iihatōbu no shokubutsugaku.* Yōyōsha, 2001.

Iwamoto Yoshiteru. *Tōhoku kaihatsu 120 nen.* Tōsui Shobō, 1993.

Iwasaki Masaya. *Nōhon shisō no shakai-shi: seikatsu to kokutai no kōsaku.* Kyoto: Kyōto Daigaku Gakujutsu Shuppankai, 1997.

Iwate-ken Hanamaki nōgakkō ichiranhyō. Morioka: Iwate Kappanjo, 1923.

Iwate-ken no rekishi. Eds. Hosoi Kazuyu et al. Yamakawa Shuppansha, 1999.

Iwate-ken shi. 12 vols. Ed. Iwate Prefecture. Morioka: Toryō Insatsu, 1961–1966.

Iwate nippō hyakujūnen-shi. Ed. Iwate Nippō-sha. Morioka: Iwate Nippō-sha, 1988.

Iwate tōkeisho: 1920. Morioka: Iwate Prefecture, 1921.

Jidai betsu kokugo daijiten: Muromachi jidai hen. 5 vols. Sanseidō, 1985–2001.

Jidō bungaku honyaku sakuhin sōran. 8 vols. Ōsorasha, 2005–2006.

Jinnai Hidenobu. *Tōkyō no kūkan jinruigaku*. Chikuma Shobō, 1985.

Kadokawa Nihon chimei daijiten. 47 vols. Kadokawa Shoten, 1978–1990.

Kaigo Tokiomi. "Rika kyōkasho sōkaisetsu." *Nihon kyōkasho taikei*. Vol. 24.

Kamei Shigeru. "Seki Toyotarō to Miyazawa Kenji." *Hiryō kagaku* 15 (1992): 31–56.

Kamikuri Takashi. "Chiiki burando omowanu kabe." *Asahi shinbun*, April 16, 2006.

Kan Tadamichi. *Nihon no jidō bungaku*. Ōtsuki Shoten, 1956.

Kanō Sakujirō. "Kongo no bundan to sono chihōka." *Iwate nippō*, Feb. 4, 1924: 4.

Katayama Koson. "Shinsai to waga bungei." *Sandee mainichi* 40 (Sept. 16, 1923): 11.

Kawabata Yasunari. "Kyōdo geijutsu mondai no gaikan." *Seinen* (Aug. 1924). Reprinted in *Kawabata Yasunari zenshū*. Vol. 16. Shinchōsha, 1973. 186–95.

Kawanishi Hidemichi. *Kindai Nihon no chiiki shisō*. Madosha, 1996.

———. *Tōhoku: tsukurareta ikyō*. Chūō Kōron Shinsha, 2001.

Kayaba Yasurō and Sakaba Seiichirō. *Shinpen shokubutsu zusetsu*. Shōeidō, 1908.

Kenji no Iihatōbu Hanamaki. Eds. Miyazawa Kenji Gakkai and Hanamaki Shimin no Kai. Hanamaki: Iihatōbukan, 1996.

Kido Wakao. "Gakkō geki kinshi kunrei no zengo." *Shōnen engeki* 6 (Summer 1969): 20–29.

Kihara Naohiko. *Hokkaidō bungaku-shi*. Sapporo: Hokkaidō Shinbun-sha, 1976.

Kikuchi Chūji. "Shiryō 'Nōmin geijutsu gairon no hikkiroku' ni tsuite." *Miyazawa Kenji ronshū*. Ed. Miyazawa Kenji Kenkyūkai. Vol. 1. Kongō Shuppan, 1971.

Kimura Ki. *Nōmin no bungaku*. Nōmin Mondai Soshō Kankō Kai, 1926.

Kindai sakka tsuitōbun shūsei. Ed. Inamura Tetsugen. Yumani Shobō, 1987.

Kobayashi Tenmin to Kansai bundan no keisei. Eds. Shindō Masahiko et al. Osaka: Izumi Shoin, 2003.

Kobayashi Ushisaburō. "Shizen to jin'i." *Tōhoku sangyō shinkō kōen-shū*. 23–43.

Kojima Tokuya. "Kyōdo bungaku no tame ni." *Iwate nippō*, Jan. 28, 1924: 4.

Komori Yōichi. *Nihongo no kindai*. Iwanami Shoten, 2000.

———. *Saishin Miyazawa Kenji kōgi*. Asahi Shinbun-sha, 1996.

Kōno Kensuke. *Tōki toshite no bungaku: katsuji, kenshō, media*. Shinyōsha, 2003.

Koshizawa Akira. *Manshūkoku no shuto keikaku*. Chikuma Gakugei Bunko, 2002.

———. *Tōkyō toshi keikaku monogatari*. Chikuma Gakugei Bunko, 2001.

Kurata Ushio. "Nōmin bungaku no teishō." *Shinkō bungaku* (June 1923): 35–37.

Kurihara Atsushi. "Shinshō sukecchi no shisō." *Kindai bungaku ron* 6 (Sept. 1974): 26–38.

Kuroda Tōkai. "Tōhoku kankōkyaku yūin saku." *Tōhoku nippon* 7.3 (Jan. 1922): 7–13.

Kusano Masayuki and Nakamura Haruo. *Kikō kyōkasho: Nōgakkō yō.* Kōbunsha, 1903.

Kuwahara Saburō. *"Akai tori" no jidai: taishō no jidō bungaku.* Keiō Tsūshin, 1975.

Maeda Ai. *Toshi kūkan no naka no bungaku.* Chikuma Shobō, 1982.

Makino Tomitarō. *Nihon shokubutsu zukan.* Hokuryūkan, 1925.

Maruyama Hiroshi. *Kindai Nihon kōen-shi no kenkyū.* Shibunkaku Shuppan, 1994.

Matsuo Takayoshi. *Futsū senkyo seido seiritsu-shi no kenkyū.* Iwanami Shoten, 1989.

Miyazawa Kenji. *Kōhon Miyazawa Kenji zenshū.* 14 vols. Chikuma Shobō, 1973–1977.

———. *Shin kōhon Miyazawa Kenji zenshū.* 16 vols. Chikuma Shobō, 1996–2001.

Miyazawa Kenji kenkyū shiryō shūsei. Ed. Tsuzukihashi Tatsuo. Nihon Tosho Sentā, 1990.

Miyazawa Kenji ki'nenkan. Ed. Sōkyū Shorin. Obira: Sōkyū Shorin, 1983.

Miyazawa Kenji no hi. Ed. Yoshida Seimi. Hanamaki: Hanamaki-shi Bunka Dantai Kyōgi Kai, 2000.

Miyazawa Seiroku. *Ani no toranku.* Chikuma Shobō, 1991.

Mochida Keizō. *Kindai Nihon no chishikijin to nōmin.* Ie no Hikari Kyōkai, 1997.

Mori Sōichi. *"Chūmon no ōi ryōriten."* In *"Chūmon no ōi ryōriten" kenkyū.* Vol. 1. Ed. Tsuzukihashi Tatsuo. Gakugei Shorin, 1975. 9–67.

———. *Miyazawa Kenji no shōzō.* Aomori: Tsugaru Shobō, 1974.

Morisu kinen ronshū. Ed. Morisu Tanjō Hyakunen Kinen Kyōkai. Kawase Nisshindō Shoten, 1934.

Mukubō Tetsuya. "Kyōdo geijutsu · den'en · chihōshoku." *Nihon kindai bungaku* 74 (May 2006): 182–96.

Nagamine Shigetoshi. *"Dokusho kokumin" no tanjō.* Nihon Editor School, 2004.

———. *Modan toshi no dokusho kūkan.* Nihon Editor School, 2001.

Nagatsuka Takashi. *Tsuchi.* Shunyōdō, 1912.

Nagumo Michio. *Gendai bungaku no teiryū.* Origin Shuppan Center, 1983.

Nakamura Masanori. "Keizai kōsei undō to nōson tōgō." In *Fuashizumu ki no kokka to shakai.* Vol. 1. Ed. Tōkyō Daigaku Shakai Kagaku Kenkyūjo. 197–262. Tōkyō Daigaku Shuppankai, 1978. 8 vols. 1978–1980.

Nakamura Seiko. *Nōmin gekijō nyūmon.* Shunyōdō, 1927.

Nakano Shigeharu. "Nōmin bungaku no mondai." *Kaizō* (July 1931). Reprinted in *Nakano Shigeharu zenshū.* Vol. 9. Chikuma Shobō, 1977. 355–63.

Nakao Masaki. *Taishō bunjin to den'en shugi.* Kindai Bungeisha, 1996.

Nakazawa Shizuo. "Kyōdo geijutsu no kitai." *Tōkyō Asahi shinbun*, Mar. 4–6, 1924.

Nasukawa Itsuo. "Kindai-shi to Miyazawa Kenji no katsudō." *Iwate shigaku kenkyū* 80 (1997): 460–508.

Nihon jidō bungaku daijiten. Ed. Ōsaka Kokusai Jidō Bungakukan. Dai Nihon Zusho, 1993.

Nihon jidō bungaku gairon. Ed. Nihon Jidō Bungaku Gakkai. Tōkyō Shoseki, 1976.

Nihon jidō bungaku-shi. Ed. Torigoe Shin. Minerva Shobō, 2001.

Nihon kindai bungaku daijiten. 6 vols. Ed. Odagiri Susumu. Kōdansha, 1977–1978.

Nihon kyōkasho taikei. 27 vols. Eds. Kaigo Tokiomi et al. Kōdansha, 1961–1967.

Nihon shokubutsu hōgen shūsei. Ed. Yasaka Shobō. Yasaka Shobō, 2001.

Noguchi Ujō. *Dōyō tsukurikata mondō: Atarashii dōwa no tsukurikata.* Kōransha, 1921.

Nōmin bungei jūrokkō. Ed. Nōmin Bungei Kenkyū Kai. Shunyōdō, 1926.

Nōrinsui-sangyō ni kanrensuru bunkateki keikan ni kansuru chōsa kenkyū. Japan, Agency for Cultural Affairs, Dept. of Cultural Treasures, 2003.

Nōsei kenkyū: nōson goraku mondai gō 1.5 (Sept. 1922).

Obara Kuniyoshi. *Gakkō geki ron.* Idea Shoin, 1923.

Ochiai Sōzaburō. "Obara Kuniyoshi sensei ni Nihon no gakkō geki no oitachi o kiku." *Shōnen engeki* 2 (Winter 1968): 24–36.

Oda Mitsuo. *Shoten no kindai.* Heibonsha Shinsho, 2003.

———. *Shuppansha to shoten wa ika nishite kieteiku ka.* Paru Shuppan, 1999.

Ogawa Mimei. "Watashi ga 'dōwa' o kaku toki no kokoromochi." *Waseda bungaku* (June 1921): 19–21.

Ōhashi Hiroaki. "Nihon ni okeru nōhonshugi kyōikuron no kenkyū (III)." *Chūkyō daigaku kyōyō ronsō* 15.3 (1974): 561–96.

Oikawa Shirō. "*Chūmon no ōi ryōriten* shiki." "*Chūmon no ōi ryōriten*" *kenkyū.* Vol. 1. Ed. Tsuzukihashi Tatsuo. Gakugei Shorin, 1975. 74–77.

Okada Yōji. *Taishō demokurashii shita no "chiiki shinkō."* Fuji Shuppan, 1999.

Ōkado Masakatsu. *Kindai Nihon to nōson shakai.* Nihon Keizai Hyōronsha, 1994.

———. "Nōson kara toshi e." *Kindai Nihon no kiseki.* Vol. 9. Ed. Narita Ryūichi. Yoshikawa Kōbunkan, 1993. 174–95. 10 vols. 1993–1995.

Okudaira Yasuhiro. *Chian iji hō shōshi.* Chikuma Shobō, 1977.

Onda Itsuo. "Miyazawa Kenji ni okeru Taishō jūnen no shukkyō to kitaku." *Miyazawa Kenji ron.* Vol. 1. Eds. Onda Itsuo et al. 308–59. Tōkyō Shoseki, 1991. 3 vols.

Ono Hideo. *Nihon shinbun hattatsu-shi.* Osaka: Ōsaka Mainichi Shinbun-sha, 1922.

Orishimo Yoshinobu. "Kōen keikaku." In *Toshi keikaku kōshūroku zenshū.* Vol. 2. Ed. Toshi Kenkyū Kai. Toshi Kenkyū Kai, 1922. 1–52.

Ōtsuka Tsuneki. *Miyazawa Kenji: Shinshō no uchūron.* Chōbunsha, 1993.

Rika kyōiku-shi shiryō. 6 vols. Ed. Itakura Kiyonobu. Tōkyō Hōrei Shuppan, 1986.

Saida Takashi. "Saida Takashi sensei ni engeki no omoidebanashi o kiku." *Shōnen engeki* 4 (Summer 1968): 30–43.

Saiki Kenji. "Kyū-naimushō keihokyoku toshoka Saiki Ikurō to Miyazawa Kenji no shūhen—Shōwa kyūnen 'Tōkyō Miyazawa Kenji tomo no kai.'" *Miyazawa Kenji kenkyū annual* 10 (2000): 171–86.

———. *Saiki Ikurō to shōwa jūnen-dai no shijin-tachi.* Morioka: Morioka City Library, 1994.

———. "Shōwa kyūnen zaikyō 'Miyazawa Kenji tomo no kai' to, sono nettowaaku keisei he no katei ni tsuite." *Miyazawa Kenji kenkyū annual* 16 (2006): 124–44.

Saitō Sajirō. *Saitō Sajirō: jidō bungaku-shi.* Kin no Hoshi Sha, 1996.

Sakai Tadaichi. *Hyōden Miyazawa Kenji.* Ōfūsha, 1968.

Sakai Takeshi. "Ishikawa Sanshirō to Miyazawa Kenji." *Miyazawa Kenji kenkyū annual* 14 (2004): 129–47.

Sakamoto Masachika. *Kanō Sakujirō no hito to bungaku.* Kanazawa: Noto Insatsu, 1991.

Sakurai Kunitomo. *Fukuzawa Yukichi no "kagaku no susume."* Shōdensha, 2005.

Satō Takashi. *Miyazawa Kenji ni sasowarete.* Hanamaki: Kaimeisha, 2001.

Satō Yoshinaga. *Tōhoku no jigyō.* Morioka: Bumeidō, 1909.

Shibuya Teisuke. *Teihon nora ni sakebu.* Heibonsha, 1964.

Shimamura Hōgetsu. *Hōgetsu zenshū.* 8 vols. Tenyūsha, 1919–1920.

Shimazaki Tōson. *Furusato.* Jitsugyō no Nihonsha, 1920.

Shirotori Seigo. "Tokai bungei no hōkai to den'en bungei no fukkō." *Tsuchi no geijutsu o kataru.* Shūeikaku, 1925. 233–41.

Shokoku dōyō taizen. Ed. Dōyō Kenkyū Kai. Shunyōdō, 1909.

Shutō Motosumi. *Kindai bungaku to Kumamoto.* Osaka: Izumi Shoin, 2003.

Soda Hidehiko. *Minshū gekijō: mō hitotsu no Taishō demokurashii.* Shōzansha, 1995.

Sugiura Shizuka. *Miyazawa Kenji: meimetsu suru haru to shura.* Sōkyū Shorin, 1993.

Sugiyama Motojirō. "Minshū undō toshite no nōmin gakkō." *Kagaku to geijutsu* 4.4 (April 1918): 8–13.

Suzuki Kenji. "Dōwa-shū *Chūmon no ōi ryōriten* hakkan o megutte." *Gengo bunka* 13 (Mar. 3, 1996): 93–123.

Taishō seimeishugi to gendai. Ed. Suzuki Sadami. Kawade Shobō Shinsha, 1995.

Takahashi Masami. "Shuppan ryūtsū kikō no hensen: 1603–1945." *Shuppan kenkyū* 13 (1982): 188–228.

Takei Takashirō. "Toshi no kōen keikaku." *Toshi kōron* 2.11 (Nov. 1919): 36–42.

Takeuchi Unpei. *Tōhoku kaihatsu-shi.* Gendai no Kagakusha, 1918.

Tamari Kizō. *Tōhoku shinkōsaku.* Zenkoku Nōjikai, 1904.

Tamura Akira. *Machizukuri no jissen.* Iwanami Shinsho, 1999.

Tamura Tsuyoshi. *Gendai toshi no kōen keikaku.* Naimushō Eisei Kyoku, 1921.

Tayama Katai. *Shōsetsu sakuhō*. Hakubunkan, 1909.

Tobari Chikufū. *Shinshiki dokuwa daijiten*. Ōkura Shoten, 1912.

Tōhoku sangyō shinkō kōen-shū. Ed. Asano Gengo. Tōhoku Shinkō Kai, 1928.

Tōkeijō yori mitaru Tōhoku sangyō keizai taikan. Tōhokusha, 1926.

Tomita Hiroyuki. *Nihon jidō engeki-shi*. Tōkyō Shoseki, 1976.

Toshi to kōen. Ed. Teien Kyōkai. Seibidō Shoten, 1924.

Toyoda Takeshi. *Tōhoku no rekishi*. 3 vols. Yoshikawa Kōbunkan, 1979.

Tsubouchi Shōyō. *Atami pējento*. Hakubunkan, 1925.

———. *Jidō kyōiku to engeki*. Waseda Daigaku Shuppanbu, 1923.

———. "Kongo no geijutsukai." *Sandee mainichi* 49 (Nov. 11, 1923): 23.

———. *Waga pējento geki*. Kokuhonsha, 1921.

Tsuboya Zenshirō. *Hakubunkan gojūnen-shi*. Hakubunkan, 1937.

Tsuzukihashi Tatsuo. "'Kaze no Matasaburō' shōron." *Miyazawa Kenji* 5 (1985).

———. *Taishō jidō bungaku no sekai*. Vol. 2. Ōfū, 1999.

Uchiyama Kazuō. *Denmāku nōson seikatsu*. Seibidō Shoten, 1928.

Uehara Keiji. *Toshi keikaku to kōen*. Rinsensha, 1924.

Uno Tsuyoshi. *Kokumin kōtō gakkō undō no kenkyū*. Hiroshima: Keisuisha, 2003.

Urata Keizō. *Shiryō—Iwate no kindai bungaku*. Morioka: Toryō Kōsoku Insatsu
    Shuppanbu, 1981.

———. *Takuboku · Bimyō sono hoka: Iwate no kindai bungaku*. Morioka: Iwate
    Kindai Bungaku Konenkai, 1968.

Ushiyama Megumi. *Kokugo kyōiku ni okeru Miyazawa Kenji*. Kawasaki: Ushiyama
    Megumi, 1988.

Watanabe Minji. "Shinkō bungei no teishō." *Iwate nippō*, Feb. 9, 1924: 4.

Yahata Yō. *Miyazawa Kenji no kyōikuron*. Chōbunsha, 1998.

Yamada Katsutomo. *Yo ga mitaru Denmāku nōson*. Yūseidō Shoten, 1925.

Yamada Seizaburō. "Bundan no kongo." *Fukuoka Nichinichi shinbun*, Oct. 22,
    1923: 5.

———. *Kindai Nihon nōmin bungaku-shi*. Rironsha, 1976.

Yamamoto Kanae. *Bijutsuka no akubi*. Arusu, 1921.

———. "Nōmin bijutsu kengyō no shui oyobi sono keika." *Mizue* 185 (July
    1920): 35–41.

———. "Nōson fukugyō no shinseimen." *Nōmin bijutsu* 1.1 (Sept. 1924): 11–15.

Yamashita Fumio. *Shōwa tōhoku daikyōsaku: musume miuri to kesshoku jidō*. Akita:
    Mumeisha Shuppan, 2001.

Yasuda Toshiaki. *"Kokugo" to "hōgen" no aida: gengo kōchiku no seijigaku*. Kyoto:
    Jinbun Shoin, 1999.

Yasuoka Kuromura. "Nōson geijutsu ni tsuite." *Shinano Mainichi shinbun*, Oct. 3,
    1923: 3.

Yonechi Fumio. "Miyazawa Kenji no sōsaku chimei 'Iihatov' no yurai to henka ni kansuru chirigakuteki kōsatsu." *Iwate daigaku kyōikubu kenkyū nenpō* 55.2 (Feb. 1996): 45–64.

Yonemura Miyuki. *Miyazawa Kenji o tsukutta otokotachi.* Seikyusha, 2003.

Yoshie Takamatsu. "Nōmin seikatsu to gendai bungei." *Kaihō* (Jan. 1922).

———. "Nōjin to bungei." *Kaizō* (Jan. 1925): 208–22.

Yoshiike Yoshimasa. "Tōhoku Shinkō Kai no keika ippan." *Tōhoku sangyō shinkō kōen-shū.* 1–22.

Yoshimi Shunya. *Toshi no doramatōrugii: Tōkyō sakariba no shakai-shi.* Kōbundō, 1987.

Yoshizawa Yoshihisa. *Kumo, ame, kaze.* Meguro Shoten, 1923.

Zoku nedan no Meiji Taishō Shōwa fūzoku-shi. 2 vols. Asahi Shinbun-sha, 1981.

English-Language Sources

Adorno, Theodor. *The Jargon of Authenticity.* Trans. Knut Tarnowski and Frederic Will. London: Routledge, 2003.

Anderer, Paul. *Other Worlds: Arishima Takeo and the Bounds of Modern Japanese Fiction.* New York: Columbia University Press, 1984.

Anderson, Benedict. *Imagined Communities: Reflections on the Origin and Spread of Nationalism.* London: Verso, 1983.

Appadurai, Arjun. *Modernity at Large: Cultural Dimensions of Globalization.* Minneapolis: University of Minnesota Press, 1996.

Applegate, Celia. "A Europe of Regions: Reflections on the Historiography of Sub-National Places in Modern Times." *American Historical Review* 104.4 (1999): 1157–82.

———. *A Nation of Provincials: The German Idea of Heimat.* Berkeley: University of California Press, 1990.

Arendt, Hannah. *The Human Condition.* Chicago: University of Chicago Press, 1958.

Bakhtin, Mikhail. "Discourse in the Novel." *The Dialogic Imagination: Four Essays.* Ed. Michael Holquist. Austin: University of Texas Press, 1981. 259–422.

Barshay, Andrew. *State and Intellectual in Imperial Japan: The Public Man in Crisis.* Berkeley: University of California Press, 1988.

Basso, Keith. *Wisdom Sits in Places: Landscape and Language among the Western Apache.* Albuquerque: University of New Mexico Press, 1996.

Benjamin, Walter. "The Author as Producer." In *Reflections.* Ed. Peter Demetz. New York: Schocken Books, 1978. 220–38.

———. "Program for a Proletarian Children's Theater." In *Walter Benjamin: Selected Writings.* Vol. 2. Cambridge, MA: Belknap, 1999. 201–6.

Bergson, Henri. *Creative Evolution.* Trans. Arthur Mitchell. Mineola, NY: Dover, 1998.

Blanchot, Maurice. *The Infinite Conversation*. Minneapolis: University of Minnesota Press, 1993.

Blum, Jerome. "Fiction and the European Peasantry: The Realist Novel as a Historical Source." *Proceedings of the American Philosophical Society* 126.2 (April 8, 1982): 122–39.

Borges, Jorge Luis. *Jorge Luis Borges: Collected Fictions*. New York: Penguin, 1998.

Borish, Steven M. *The Land of the Living: The Danish Folk High Schools and Denmark's Non-Violent Path To Modernization*. Nevada City, CA: Blue Dolphin, 1991.

Bourdieu, Pierre. *The Field of Cultural Production*. New York: Columbia University Press, 1993.

Brandt, Kim. *Kingdom of Beauty: Mingei and the Politics of Folk Art in Imperial Japan*. Durham, NC: Duke University Press, 2007.

Brinkley, Frank. *An Unabridged Japanese-English Dictionary*. Tokyo: Sanseido, 1896.

Brubaker, Rogers, and Frederick Cooper. "Beyond 'identity.'" *Theory and Society* 29 (2000): 1–47.

Buell, Lawrence. *The Environmental Imagination: Thoreau, Nature Writing, and the Formation of American Culture*. Cambridge, MA: Belknap Press of Harvard University Press, 1995.

Burke, Seán. *The Death and Return of the Author: Criticism and Subjectivity in Barthes, Foucault, and Derrida*. Edinburgh: Edinburgh University Press, 1992.

Burleigh, Louise. *The Community Theatre*. Boston: Little, Brown, 1917.

Casanova, Pascale. *The World Republic of Letters*. Cambridge, MA: Harvard University Press, 2004.

Chakrabarty, Dipesh. "*Adda*, Calcutta: Dwelling in Modernity." In *Alternative Modernities*. Ed. Dilip Parameshwar Gaonkar. Durham, NC: Duke University Press, 2001. 123–64.

———. *Provincializing Europe: Postcolonial Thought and Historical Difference*. Princeton, NJ: Princeton University Press, 2000.

Chartier, Roger. *The Order of Books*. Stanford, CA: Stanford University Press, 1994.

Chatterjee, Partha. *The Nation and Its Fragments: Colonial and Postcolonial Histories*. Princeton, NJ: Princeton University Press, 1993.

———. *Nationalist Thought and the Colonial World: A Derivative Discourse?* In *Partha Chatterjee Omnibus*. New Delhi: Oxford University Press, 1999.

Cohen, Margaret. *The Sentimental Education of the Novel*. Princeton, NJ: Princeton University Press, 1999.

The Concise Oxford Companion to the Theatre. Eds. Phyllis Hartnoll and Peter Found. Oxford: Oxford University Press, 1996.

Cronon, William. "The Trouble with Wilderness; or, Getting Back to the Wrong Nature." In *Uncommon Ground: Rethinking the Human Place in Nature*. Ed. William Cronon. New York: W.W. Norton, 1996. 69–90.

Cross-Cultural Consumption: Global Markets, Local Realities. Ed. David Howes. London: Routledge, 1996.

Culture and Identity: Japanese Intellectuals during the Interwar Years. Ed. Thomas J. Rimer. Princeton, NJ: Princeton University Press, 1990.

Dainotto, Roberto M. *Place in Literature: Regions, Cultures, Communities.* Ithaca, NY: Cornell University Press, 2000.

de Certeau, Michel. *Heterologies: Discourse on the Other.* Minneapolis: University of Minnesota Press, 1986.

Derrida, Jacques. *On the Name.* Ed. Thomas Dutoit. Stanford, CA: Stanford University Press, 1995.

———. "Structure, Sign, and Play in the Discourse of the Human Sciences." In *Writing and Difference.* London: Routledge, 2001. 351–70.

Dodd, Stephen. *Writing Home: Representations of the Native Place in Modern Japanese Literature.* Cambridge, MA: Harvard University Asia Center, 2004.

Dorman, Robert L. *Revolt of the Provinces: The Regionalist Movement in America, 1920–1945.* Chapel Hill: University of North Carolina Press, 1993.

Dorst, John. *The Written Suburb: An American Site, an Ethnographic Dilemma.* Philadelphia: University of Pennsylvania Press, 1989.

Dovey, Kimberley. "The Quest for Authenticity and the Replication of Environmental Meaning." In *Dwelling, Place, and Environment: Towards a Phenomenology of Person and World.* Eds. David Seamon and Robert Mugerauer. New York: Columbia University Press, 1989. 33–49.

Duara, Prasenjit. *Rescuing History from the Nation: Questioning Narratives of Modern China.* Chicago: Chicago University Press, 1995.

Eagleton, Terry. *The Idea of Culture.* Malden, MA: Blackwell, 2000.

Ellis, David. *Literary Lives: Biography and the Search for Understanding.* New York: Routledge, 2002.

Fabian, Johannes. *Time and the Other: How Anthropology Makes Its Object.* New York: Columbia University Press, 2002.

Fisher, David James. "Romain Rolland and the French People's Theatre." *Drama Review* 21.1 (Mar. 1977): 75–90.

Foucault, Michel. *The Archaeology of Knowledge and the Discourse on Language.* Trans. A. M. Sheridan Smith. New York: Pantheon, 1972.

———. *Discipline and Punish: The Birth of the Prison.* Trans. Alan Sheridan. New York: Vintage, 1995.

———. *The Order of Things: An Archaeology of the Human Sciences.* New York: Vintage, 1973.

———. "Two Lectures." In *Power/Knowledge: Selected Interviews and Other Writings 1972–1977.* New York: Pantheon, 1980. 78–108.

———. "What Is an Author?" In *Textual Strategies: Perspectives in Post-Structuralist Criticism.* Ed. Josué V. Harari. Ithaca, NY: Cornell University Press, 1979. 141–60.

Fukuoka, Maki. "Between Knowing and Seeing: Shifting Standards of Accuracy and the Concept of Shashin in Japan, 1832–1872." Ph.D. diss., University of Chicago, 2006.

Gerbert, Elaine. "Space and Aesthetic Imagination in Some Taishō Writings." In *Japan's Competing Modernities*. Ed. Sharon Minichiello. Honolulu: University of Hawai'i Press, 1998. 70–90.

Gerson, Stéphane. *The Pride of Place: Local Memories and Political Culture in Nineteenth-Century France*. Ithaca, NY: Cornell University Press, 2003.

Giddens, Anthony. *The Consequences of Modernity*. Stanford, CA: Stanford University Press, 1990.

Global/Local: Cultural Production and the Transnational Imaginary. Eds. Rob Wilson and Wimal Dissanayake. Durham, NC: Duke University Press, 1996.

Gluck, Carol. *Japan's Modern Myths: Ideology in the Late Meiji Period*. Princeton, NJ: Princeton University Press, 1985.

Golley, Gregory. *When Our Eyes No Longer See: Realism, Science, and Ecology in Japanese Literary Modernism*. Cambridge, MA: Harvard University Asia Center, 2008.

Gordon, Andrew. *Labor and Imperial Democracy in Prewar Japan*. Berkeley: University of California Press, 1991.

Gramsci, Antonio. "The Formation of the Intellectuals." Norton Anthology of Theory and Criticism. Ed. Vincent Leitch. New York: Norton, 2001. 1138–43.

Grotjahn, Richard. *Global Atmospheric Circulations: Observations and Theories*. New York: Oxford University Press, 1993.

Hanes, Jeffrey. *The City as Subject: Seki Hajime and the Reinvention of Modern Osaka*. Berkeley: University of California Press, 2002.

Hardt, Michael, and Antonio Negri. *Empire*. Cambridge, MA: Harvard University Press, 2000.

Harootunian, Harry D. "Introduction: A Sense of An Ending and the Problem of Taishō." In *Japan in Crisis: Essays on Taishō Democracy*. Eds. Bernard Silberman and Harry D. Harootunian. Princeton, NJ: Princeton University Press, 1974. 3–28.

———. *Overcome by Modernity: History, Culture, and Community in Interwar Japan*. Princeton, NJ: Princeton University Press, 2000.

———. "Some Thoughts on Comparability and the Space-Time Problem." *boundary 2* 32.2 (2005): 23–52.

Harvey, David. *The Condition of Postmodernity: An Enquiry into the Origins of Cultural Change*. Cambridge, MA: Basil Blackwell, 1989.

———. "From Space to Place and Back Again: Reflections on the Condition of Postmodernity." In *Mapping the Futures*. Ed. Jon Bird. London: Routledge, 1993. 2–29.

Havens, Thomas R. H. *Farm and Nation in Modern Japan: Agrarian Nationalism, 1870–1940*. Princeton, NJ: Princeton University Press, 1974.

———. "Katō Kanji (1884–1965) and the Spirit of Agriculture in Modern Japan." *Monumenta Nipponica* 25.3 (1970): 249–66.

Hayashi, Sharon. "Traveling Film History: Language and Landscape in the Japanese Cinema, 1931–1945." Ph.D. diss., University of Chicago, 2003.

Heise, Ursula K. "Local Rock and Global Plastic: World Ecology and the Experience of Place." *Comparative Literature Studies* 41.1 (2004): 126–52.

Herts, Alice Minnie. *The Children's Educational Theatre*. New York: Harper & Brothers, 1911.

Hidy, George. *The Winds: The Origins and Behavior of Atmospheric Motion*. Princeton, NJ: VanNostrand, 1967.

Hirschkop, Ken. *Mikhail Bakhtin: An Aesthetic for Democracy*. Oxford: Oxford University Press, 1999.

Hobsbawm, Eric. *The Age of Extremes: A History of the World, 1914–1991*. New York: Vintage, 1994.

Huffman, James L. *Creating a Public: People and Press in Meiji Japan*. Honolulu: University of Hawai'i Press, 1997.

Hurd, Madeleine. "Class, Masculinity, Manners, and Mores: Public Space and Public Sphere in Nineteenth-Century Europe." *Social Science History* 24.1 (2000): 75–110.

Ivy, Marilyn. *Discourses of the Vanishing: Modernity, Phantasm, Japan*. Chicago: University of Chicago Press, 1995.

Jameson, Frederic. *The Prison-House of Language: A Critical Account of Structuralism and Russian Formalism*. Princeton, NJ: Princeton University Press, 1972.

———. *The Seeds of Time*. New York: Columbia University Press, 1994.

Jenkins, Jennifer. *Provincial Modernity: Local Culture and Liberal Politics in Fin-de-Siècle Hamburg*. Ithaca, NY: Cornell University Press, 2003.

Johnstone, Barbara. *Stories, Community, and Place*. Bloomington: Indiana University Press, 1990.

Jones, Mark. "Children as Treasures: Childhood and the Middle Class in Early Twentieth-Century Japan." Ph.D. diss., Columbia University, 2001.

Kafka, Franz. *Amerika*. New York: Vintage, 1999.

Kamens, Edward. *Utamakura, Allusion, and Intertextuality in Traditional Japanese Poetry*. New Haven, CT: Yale University Press, 1997.

Kennedy, Dennis. "Shakespeare and Cultural Tourism." *Theatre Journal* 50.2 (1998): 175–88.

Kikuchi, Yuko. *Japanese Modernisation and Mingei Theory*. London: Routledge-Curzon, 2004.

Kornicki, Peter. "Provincial Publishing in the Tokugawa Period." In *Japanese Studies*. London: British Library, 1990. 188–97.

Kropotkin, Peter. *Fields, Factories, and Workshops: Or, Industry Combined with Agriculture and Brain Work with Manual Work.* London: Thomas Nelson and Sons, 1912.

Larsen, Neil. *Modernism and Hegemony.* Minneapolis: University of Minnesota Press, 1990.

Latour, Bruno. *The Pasteurization of France.* Cambridge, MA: Harvard University Press, 1988.

———. *Reassembling the Social: An Introduction to Actor-Network Theory.* Oxford: Oxford University Press, 2005.

———. *We Have Never Been Modern.* Trans. Catherine Porter. Cambridge, MA: Harvard University Press, 1993.

Lefebvre, Henri. *The Production of Space.* (1974) Trans. Donald Nicholson-Smith. Oxford: Blackwell, 1991.

Leitch, Vincent B. *Cultural Criticism, Literary Theory, Poststructuralism.* New York: Columbia University Press, 1992.

Lippit, Seiji. *Topographies of Japanese Modernism.* New York: Columbia University Press, 2002.

Liu, Lydia. "The Question of Meaning-Value in the Political Economy of the Sign." In *Tokens of Exchange: The Problem of Translation in Global Circulations.* Ed. Lydia Liu. Durham, NC: Duke University Press, 1999. 13–41.

Long, Hoyt. "Finding 'Place' in the World: The Currency of Local Culture in Interwar Japan." Paper presented at the annual meeting of the Association for Asian Studies, Chicago, Mar. 2009.

Mack, Edward. "The Value of Literature: Cultural Authority in Interwar Japan." Ph.D. diss., Harvard University, 2002.

Marmon-Silko, Leslie. "Landscape, History, and the Pueblo Imagination." *Antaeus* 57 (Autumn 1986): 83–94.

Massey, Doreen. *For Space.* London: SAGE Publications, 2005.

———. "Power-Geometry and a Progressive Sense of Place." In *Mapping the Futures.* Ed. Jon Bird. London: Routledge, 1993. 60–70.

———. *Space, Place, and Gender.* Minneapolis: University of Minnesota Press, 1994.

McClintock, Anne. *Imperial Leather: Race, Gender, and Sexuality in the Colonial Conquest.* New York: Routledge, 1995.

Merleau-Ponty, Maurice. *Phenomenology of Perception.* Trans. Colin Smith. London: Routledge & Kegan Paul, 1962.

Moores, Pamela. "The French Press and Regional Identity." In *France: Nation and Regions.* Eds. Michael Kelly and Rosemary Böck. Southampton: University of Southampton, 1993. 146–53.

Moretti, Franco. *Atlas of the European Novel, 1800–1900.* London: Verso, 1998.

———. "Conjectures on World Literature." *New Left Review* 1 (Jan.–Feb. 2000): 54–68.

———. *Graphs, Maps, Trees: Abstract Models for a Literary History.* London: Verso, 2005.

———. "Slaughterhouse of Literature." *Modern Language Quarterly* 61.1 (Mar. 2000): 207–27.

Morris, Meaghan. "Metamorphoses at Sydney Tower." *New Formations* 11 (Summer 1990): 5–18.

Morris, William. *The Collected Works of William Morris.* 24 vols. London: Longmans Green, 1910–1915.

Nakata Hiroko. "Shop Brings Famed Goods of Chilly Iwate to Tokyo." *Japan Times*, Oct. 19, 2002.

Negri, Antonio. *Time for Revolution.* Trans. Matteo Mandarini. New York: Continuum, 2003.

Oakes, Timothy. "China's Provincial Identities: Reviving Regionalism and Reinventing 'Chineseness.'" *Journal of Asian Studies* 59.3 (2000): 667–92.

Oxford English Dictionary. Second edition, 1989.

Parekh, Bhikhu, and Jan Nederveen Pieterse. "Shifting Imaginaries: Decolonization, Internal Decolonization, Postcoloniality." In *The Decolonization of Imagination: Culture, Knowledge, Power.* Eds. Parekh and Pieterse. London: Zed Books, 1995. 1–19.

Partner, Simon. "Taming the Wilderness: The Lifestyle Improvement Movement in Rural Japan, 1925–1965." *Monumenta Nipponica* 56.4 (2001): 487–520.

Pite, Ralph. *Hardy's Geography: Wessex and the Regional Novel.* New York: Palgrave Macmillan, 2002.

Postone, Moishe. *Time, Labor, and Social Domination.* Cambridge, UK: Cambridge University Press, 1993.

Powell, Brian. *Japan's Modern Theatre: A Century of Continuity and Change.* London: Japan Library, 2002.

Pyle, Kenneth. "The Technology of Japanese Nationalism: The Local Improvement Movement, 1900–1918." *Journal of Asian Studies* 33.1 (Nov. 1973): 51–65.

Rafael, Vicente L. "Regionalism, Area Studies, and the Accidents of Agency." *American Historical Review* 104.4 (Oct. 1999): 1208–20.

A Rainbow in the Desert. Ed. Yukie Ohta. Armonk, NY: M.E. Sharpe, 2001.

Richter, Giles. "Marketing the Word: Publishing Entrepreneurs in Meiji Japan, 1870–1912." Ph.D. diss., Columbia University, 1999.

Ricoeur, Paul. *Lectures on Ideology and Utopia.* New York: Columbia University Press, 1986.

Robertson, Jennifer. "It Takes a Village: Internationalization and Nostalgia in Postwar Japan." In *Mirror of Modernity: Invented Traditions of Modern Japan.* Ed. Stephen Vlastos. Berkeley: University of California Press, 1998. 110–29.

Ryden, Kent. *Mapping the Invisible Landscape: Folklore, Writing, and the Sense of Place.* Iowa City: University of Iowa Press, 1993.

Sand, Jordan. *House and Home in Modern Japan.* Cambridge, MA: Harvard University Asia Center, 2003.

Sartiliot, Claudette. *Herbarium/Verbarium: The Discourse of Flowers, Texts, and Contexts.* Lincoln: University of Nebraska Press, 1993.

Schmiechen, James A. "Reconsidering the Factory, Art-Labor, and the Schools of Design in Nineteenth-Century Britain." *Design Issues* 6.2 (Spring 1990): 58–69.

Sennett, Richard. *The Fall of Public Man.* Cambridge, UK: Cambridge University Press, 1974.

Siegelbaum, Lewis H. "Exhibiting *Kustar'* Industry in Late Imperial Russia/Exhibiting Late Imperial Russia in *Kustar'* Industry." In *Transforming Peasants: Society, State and the Peasantry, 1861–1930.* Ed. Judith Pallot. New York: St. Martin's Press, 1998. 37–63.

Smith, Kerry. "A Land of Milk and Honey: Rural Revitalization in the 1930s." In *Public Spheres, Private Lives in Modern Japan, 1600–1950.* Eds. Gail Lee Bernstein, Andrew Gordon, and Kate Nakai. Cambridge, MA: Harvard University Asia Center, 2005. 117–51.

———. *A Time of Crisis: Japan, the Great Depression, and Rural Revitalization.* Cambridge, MA: Harvard University Asia Center, 2001.

Soja, Edward. *Postmodern Geographies: The Reassertion of Space in Critical Social Theory.* London: Verso, 1989.

Sorensen, André. *The Making of Urban Japan: Cities and Planning from Edo to the Twenty-first Century.* London: Routledge, 2002.

Spengler, Oswald. *Decline of the West.* Trans. Charles Francis Atkinson. New York: Knopf, 1962.

Spivak, Gayatri Chakravorty. *A Critique of Postcolonial Reason: Toward a History of the Vanishing Present.* Cambridge, MA: Harvard University Press, 1999.

Suzuki, Kaori, and David Turner. "Japanese Patent Office Swamped by Local Lines." *Financial Times*, Oct. 6, 2006.

Tamanoi, Mariko. *Under the Shadow of Nationalism: Politics and Poetics of Rural Japanese Women.* Honolulu: University of Hawai'i Press, 1998.

Tolstoy, Leo. *What Is Art?* Trans. Almyer Maude. Indianapolis: Bobbs-Merrill, 1960.

Tomlinson, John. *Globalization and Culture.* Cambridge, UK: Polity, 1999.

Torrance, Richard. "Literacy and Literature in Osaka, 1890–1940." *Journal of Japanese Studies* 31.1 (Winter 2005): 27–60.

———. "Literacy and Modern Literature in the Izumo Region, 1880–1930." *Journal of Japanese Studies* 22.2 (1996): 327–62.

Tuan, Yi-fu. *Space and Place: The Perspective of Experience.* Minneapolis: University of Minnesota Press, 1977.

———. *Topophilia: A Study of Environmental Perception, Attitudes, and Values.* Englewood Cliffs, NJ: Prentice-Hall, 1974.

Twine, Nanette. "Standardizing Written Japanese: A Factor in Modernization." *Monumenta Nipponica* 43.4 (Winter 1988): 429–54.

Vlastos, Stephen. "Agrarianism without Tradition: The Radical Critique of Prewar Japanese Modernity." In *Mirror of Modernity: Invented Traditions of Japan.* Ed. Vlastos. Berkeley: University of California Press, 1998. 79–94.

Waswo, Ann. "The Transformation of Rural Society, 1900–1950." In *The Cambridge History of Japan*, vol. 6. Ed. Peter Duus. Cambridge, UK: Cambridge University Press, 1988. 541–605.

Wigen, Kären. "Constructing Shinano: The Invention of a Neo-Traditional Region." In *Mirror of Modernity: Invented Traditions of Modern Japan.* Ed. Stephen Vlastos. Berkeley: University of California Press, 1998. 229–42.

———. "Culture, Power, and Place: The New Landscapes of East Asian Regionalism." *American Historical Review* 104.4 (Oct. 1999): 1183–201.

———. "Discovering the Japanese Alps: Meiji Mountaineering and the Quest for Geographical Enlightenment." *Journal of Japanese Studies* 31.1 (Winter 2005): 1–26.

———. *The Making of a Japanese Periphery, 1750–1920.* Berkeley: University of California Press, 1995.

———. "Teaching about Home: Geography at Work in the Prewar Nagano Classroom." *Journal of Asian Studies* 59.3 (Aug. 2000): 550–74.

Wilde, Oscar. *The Soul of Man under Socialism, The Socialist Ideal-Art and the Coming Solidarity.* New York: Humboldt, 1891.

Williams, Raymond. *The Country and the City.* New York: Oxford University Press, 1973.

———. *Marxism and Literature.* Oxford: Oxford University Press, 1977.

Wilson, Chris. *The Myth of Santa Fe: Creating a Modern Regional Tradition.* Albuquerque: University of New Mexico Press, 1997.

Worrall, Julian. "Railway Urbanism: Commuter Rail and the Production of Public Space in 20th Century Tokyo." Ph.D. diss., University of Tokyo, 2005.

Wright, Julian. *The Regionalist Movement in France, 1890–1914: Jean Charles-Brun and French Political Thought.* Oxford: Oxford University Press, 2003.

Young, Louise. *Japan's Total Empire: Manchuria and the Culture of Wartime Imperialism.* Berkeley: University of California Press, 1998.

Zukin, Sharon. *Landscapes of Power: From Detroit to Disney World.* Berkeley: University of California Press, 1991.

Index